THE NORTHERNERS

THE
NORTHERNERS

A STUDY IN THE REIGN OF
KING JOHN

BY

J. C. HOLT

OXFORD
CLARENDON PRESS

Oxford University Press, Walton Street, Oxford OX2 6DP
Oxford New York Toronto
Delhi Bombay Calcutta Madras Karachi
Petaling Jaya Singapore Hong Kong Tokyo
Nairobi Dar es Salaam Cape Town
Melbourne Auckland
and associated companies in
Berlin Ibadan

Oxford is a trade mark of Oxford University Press

Published in the United States
by Oxford University Press, New York

British Library Cataloguing in Publication Data
Data available

Library of Congress Cataloging in Publication Data
Data available
ISBN 0-19-820309-8 (Pbk)

Printed and bound in
Great Britain by Biddles Ltd,
Guildford and King's Lynn

TO
HERBERT AND EUNICE HOLT

CONTENTS

MAPS

PREFACE TO THE PAPERBACK EDITION

In this edition no change has been made to the pagination, which is that of the first edition. Wherever possible, references to unprinted sources have been converted to the printed editions which have appeared since 1961. Some references have also been changed where recent editions of the sources are preferable and more accessible. A few minor corrections have been made. Otherwise the book is as it was when first published. At that time it was not possible to include a Bibliography. Notes for Further Reading are now included; they are intended to be helpful, not exhaustive or exhausting. An Introduction has also been added. This discusses matters which were touched on briefly or not at all in the first edition.

J.C.H.

Fitzwilliam College, Cambridge, November, 1991

PREFACE

THOSE who work on the reign of King John are unusually
fortunate in the large amount of material, both government
and private record, which is in print. My first debt, therefore, is to those who have done this work: to the officers of the
Public Record Office, and to a long line of scholars represented
today by Sir Frank and Lady Stenton, Sir Charles Clay, Miss
Kathleen Major, and others. This book could scarcely have been
written without, for example, the aid of the great series of pipe
rolls edited by Lady Stenton, or the volumes of Yorkshire charters
which Sir Charles Clay has added to the work of William Farrer.

Throughout my work I have been especially indebted to Professor V. H. Galbraith; to his dynamic inspiration, his kindly
interest, and his great fund of knowledge of the chronicles and
government records of the period. My interest in King John was
first aroused by the inspired teaching of my tutor, J. O. Prestwich.
His insight into the period has informed my own approach to it.
He has also helped me on points of detail and has kindly read the
work in manuscript.

I must thank the Warden and Fellows of Merton College, who,
by electing me to a Harmsworth Senior Scholarship, provided me
with the means to begin this work. Like all Harmsworth Scholars
of my generation, I owe much to the wisdom, wit, and paternal
concern of H. W. Garrod.

The members of the seminar on King John at the University of
Nottingham have helped to crystallize many of my ideas. Among
my colleagues, Professor J. S. Roskell has been a constant source
of suggestion and helpful criticism; he has also read the book in
manuscript. Mr. B. E. Harris has kindly helped me in reading
the proofs.

My wife has given me encouragement and aid throughout.
Some may read this book; she has had to listen to it and has done
so with tolerance and patience.

J. C. H.

Nottingham, July 1960

ABBREVIATIONS

Annales Monastici	*Annales monastici*, ed. H. R. Luard, 5 vols. (Rolls series, 1864–9).
B.L.	British Museum.
Book of Fees	*Liber Feodorum. The book of fees commonly called Testa de Nevill*, 3 vols. (Public Record Office, 1920–31).
Cal. Charter Rolls	*Calendar of the Charter rolls*, 6 vols. (Public Record Office, 1903–27).
Cal. I.P.M.	*Calendar of inquisitions post mortem and other analogous documents*, vol. i (Public Record Office, 1904).
Cal. Inq. Misc.	*Calendar of inquisitions miscellaneous*, vol. i (Public Record Office, 1916).
Chronicles of Stephen, Henry II, and Richard I	*Chronicles of the reigns of Stephen, Henry II, and Richard I*, ed. R. Howlett, 4 vols. (Rolls series, 1884–9).
Chron. Maj.	*Matthaei Parisiensis, monachi sancti Albani, chronica majora*, ed. H. R. Luard, 7 vols. (Rolls series, 1872–83).
Chron. Melrose	*The Chronicle of Melrose*, ed. A. O. and Marjorie O. Anderson (Studies in Economics and Political Science, London, 1936).
Chron. Melsa	*Chronica monasterii de Melsa*, ed. E. A. Bond, 3 vols. (Rolls series, 1866–8).
Coggeshall	*Radulphi de Coggeshall chronicon Anglicanum*, ed. J. Stevenson (Rolls series, 1875).
Coucher Book of Furness	*The coucher book of Furness abbey*, vol. i in 3 pts. ed. J. C. Atkinson (Chetham Society, 1886–7), vol. ii in 3 pts. ed. J. Brownbill (Chetham Society, 1915–19).
Danelaw Documents	*Documents illustrative of the social and economic history of the Danelaw*, ed. F. M. Stenton (British Academy, Records of the social and economic history of England and Wales, 1920).
Dialogus de Scaccario	*Dialogus de Scaccario*, ed. Charles Johnson (London, 1950).

Diplomatic Documents	*Diplomatic Documents*, vol. i; 1101–1272 ed. Pierre Chaplais (H.M.S.O., 1964).
Earliest Lincolnshire Assize Rolls	*The earliest Lincolnshire assize rolls, A.D. 1202–9*, ed. Doris M. Stenton (Lincoln Record Society, 1926).
Early Yorks. Charters	*Early Yorkshire Charters*, vols. i–iii, ed. W. Farrer (Edinburgh, 1914–16), vols. iv–xii, ed. C. T. Clay (Yorkshire Archaeological Society, Record series, extra series, 1935–65).
E.H.R.	*English Historical Review.*
Excerpta e Rot. Fin.	*Excerpta e rotulis finium in turri Londinensi asservatis, A.D. 1216–72*, ed. C. Roberts (Record Commission, 1835–6).
Foedera	*Foedera, conventiones, litterae et cujuscunque generis acta publica*, ed. T. Rymer, new edn., vol. 1, pt. 1, ed. A. Clarke and F. Holbrooke (Record Commission, 1816).
Gerv. Cant.	*The historical works of Gervase of Canterbury*, ed. W. Stubbs, 2 vols. (Rolls series, 1879–80).
Gesta Abbatum	*Gesta abbatum monasterii sancti Albani*, ed. H. T. Riley, 3 vols. (Rolls series, 1867–9).
Gesta Henrici	*Gesta Regis Henrici secundi Benedicti abbatis*, ed. W. Stubbs, 2 vols. (Rolls series, 1867).
Gilbertine Charters	*Transcripts of Charters relating to Gilbertine houses*, ed. F. M. Stenton (Lincoln Record Society, 1922).
Histoire de Guillaume le Maréchal	*Histoire de Guillaume le Maréchal*, ed. P. Meyer, 3 vols. (Société de l'histoire de France, 1891–1901).
Histoire des ducs de Normandie	*Histoire des ducs de Normandie et des rois d'Angleterre*, ed. F. Michel (Société de l'histoire de France, 1840).
H.M.C.	*Reports and Calendars issued by the Royal Commission on historical manuscripts.*
Honors and Knights' Fees	W. Farrer, *Honors and Knights' Fees*, 3 vols. (London, Manchester, 1923–5).
Hoveden	*Chronica Rogeri de Hovedene*, ed. W. Stubbs, 4 vols. (Rolls series, 1868–71).
Kirkby's Inquest	*The survey of the county of York, taken by John de Kirkby*, ed. R. H. Scaife (Surtees Society, 1867).

Guisborough Cartulary	*Cartularium prioratus de Gyseburne*, ed. W. Brown, 2 vols. (Surtees Society, 1889–94).
Lancashire Final Concords	*Final Concords of the county of Lancaster*, pt. 1, ed. W. Farrer (Lancashire and Cheshire Record Society, 1899).
Lincolnshire Final Concords	Vol. 1. W. O. Massingberd, *Lincolnshire Records, abstracts of final concords* (London, 1896). Vol. 2. *Final concords of the county of Lincoln*, ed. C. W. Foster (Lincoln Record Society, 1920).
Memorials of Bury	*Memorials of St. Edmund's abbey*, ed. T. Arnold, 3 vols. (Rolls series, 1890–6).
Monasticon Anglicanum	W. Dugdale, *Monasticon Anglicanum*, ed. J. Caley, H. Ellis, B. Bandinel, 6 vols. (London, 1817–30).
Pedes Finium Ebor. regnante Johanne	*Pedes finium Ebor. regnante Johanne*, ed. W. Brown (Surtees Society, 1897).
Percy Cartulary	*The Percy Chartulary*, ed. Miss M. T. Martin (Surtees Society, 1911).
P.R.O.	Public Record Office.
Records of Kendale	*Records relating to the barony of Kendale*, by W. Farrer, ed. J. F. Curwen, 3 vols. (Cumberland and Westmorland Antiquarian and Archaeological Society, Record series, 1923–6).
Red Book of the Exchequer	*The red book of the exchequer*, ed. Hubert Hall, 3 vols. (Rolls series, 1896).
Register of Wetherhal	*The register of the priory of Wetherhal*, ed. J. E. Prescott (Cumberland and Westmorland Antiquarian and Archaeological Society, Record series, 1897).
Registrum Antiquissimum	*The Registrum antiquissimum of the cathedral church of Lincoln*, vols. 1–3, ed. C. W. Foster, vol. 4, ed. C. W. Foster and Miss Kathleen Major, vols. 5–10, ed. Miss Kathleen Major (Lincoln Record Society, 1931–72).
Rievaulx Cartulary	*Cartularium abbathiae de Rievalle*, ed. J. C. Atkinson (Surtees Society, 1889).
Rolls of the Justices in Eyre for Lincolnshire and Worcestershire	*Rolls of the Justices in Eyre for Lincolnshire, 1218–19, and Worcestershire, 1221*, ed. Doris M. Stenton (Selden Society, 1934).

Rolls of the Justices in Eyre for Yorkshire	*Rolls of the Justices in Eyre for Yorkshire, 1218–19* ed. Doris M. Stenton (Selden Society, 1937).
Rot. Chartarum	*Rotuli chartarum in turri Londinensi asservati*, ed. T. Duffus Hardy, vol. 1 (Record Commission, 1837).
Rot. Curiae Regis	*Rotuli curiae regis*, ed. Sir Francis Palgrave, 2 vols. (Record Commission, 1835).
Rot. de Ob. et Fin.	*Rotuli de oblatis et finibus in turri Londinensi asservati*, ed. T. Duffus Hardy (Record Commission, 1835).
Rot. Lib.	*Rotuli de liberate ac de misis et praestitis*, ed. T. Duffus Hardy (Record Commission, 1844).
Rot. Litt. Claus.	*Rotuli litterarum clausarum in turri Londinensi asservati*, ed. T. Duffus Hardy, 2 vols. (Record Commission, 1833–4).
Rot. Litt. Pat.	*Rotuli litterarum patentium in turri Londinensi asservati*, ed. T. Duffus Hardy, vol. 1 (Record Commission, 1835).
Rot. Norm.	*Rotuli Normanniae in turri Londinensi asservati*, ed. T. Duffus Hardy, vol. 1 (Record Commission, 1835).
Rot. Scacc. Norm.	*Magni rotuli scaccarii Normanniae sub regibus Angliae*, ed. T. Stapleton, 2 vols. (Society of Antiquaries of London, 1840–4).
Rotuli de Dominabus	*Rotuli de dominabus et pueris et puellis*, ed. J. H. Round (Pipe Roll Society, 1913).
Royal Letters of Henry III	*Royal and other historical letters illustrative of the reign of Henry III*, ed. W. W. Shirley, 2 vols. (Rolls series, 1862–8).
Selected Letters of Innocent III	*Selected Letters of Pope Innocent III*, ed. C. R. Cheney and W. H. Semple (London, 1953).
Three Yorkshire Assize Rolls	*Three Yorkshire assize rolls for the reigns of King John and King Henry III*, ed. C. T. Clay (Yorkshire Archaeological Society, Record series, 1911).
T.R.H.S.	*Transactions of the Royal Historical Society.*
V.C.H.	*Victoria County History.*
Walt. Cov.	*Memoriale fratris Walteri de Coventria*, ed. W. Stubbs, 2 vols. (Rolls series, 1872–3).
Whitby Cartulary	*Cartularium abbathiae de Whitby*, ed. J. C. Atkinson, 2 vols. (Surtees Society, 1879–81).
Yorkshire Fines	*Feet of fines for the county of York from 1218–1231*, ed. J. Parker (Yorkshire Archaeological Society, Record series, 1921).

INTRODUCTION TO THE PAPERBACK
EDITION

This study began with a single question: why were some of
the opponents of King John known as 'the Northerners'? In
effect, although not in intent, it was concerned with the first
use in English history of a party-political label. The analogy
with later labels is but rough; there is no evidence, for
example, that the Northerners described themselves as such;
nevertheless, to a wide range of participants in, and observers
of, the great crisis of 1215, 'Northerner' was sufficient to
identify a specific group which headed the rebellion against
the King and, from time to time, struck out on its own with
distinct attitudes and reactions, perhaps even with considered
policies.

The work then benefited in an unexpected way from one
particular documentary source. The lists of those who came
to the peace of Henry III in 1217, the *reversi*, which are
entered on the Close roll, proved comprehensive enough to
allow an examination of loyalties and alignments throughout
the landowning society of the northern counties. The writs of
restoration were usually issued to the sheriffs. They therefore
provide not only the names of rebels, but also the counties in
which they held their lands; it was then not too difficult to
establish the tenancies and feudal dependence of many of
them, certainly down to and including some who held no
more than a fraction of a knight's fee. Where the writs of
restoration were sent to feudal lords as well as, or instead of,
the sheriff, this task was all the easier. Much more could have
been done and could still be done to flesh out this Namier-
like structure of feudal and political association by examining,
for example, the intermarriage of local families or their
combination in the patronage of monastic foundations. But
the scale of the work did not leave much room for this,
certainly not for the systematic treatment which these matters
deserve. So it became a study in politics, a study of the
reaction to royal government which engendered, for a time—
perhaps for only a short time—the political community
which men knew as the Northerners.

The work was neither inspired nor impeded by any theory. As far as I can recall, this is the first appearance of the word 'feudalism' in the whole book. There is some relish, therefore, in finding it adduced in support by all three participants in a recent debate on the origins of 'bastard feudalism'.[1] Far be it from me to indulge in such momentous matters here; even if there were the inclination, this is neither the time nor the place. But the book is about rebellion in a feudal society, that is to say one in which the relationship between ruler and ruled was also one between lord and vassal; and much turned on the king's exploitation of that feudal relationship and on his management of men who held strong assumptions about, and firm expectations of, their feudal dependence on him.

In 1215, of course, there was more to it than this. There were contentious issues concerning war and peace, finance and taxation, government and law, which were distinct or remote from the feudal tie between king and baron; and the book is also about these. It may seem that in 1961 it was easier to write about them in terms of what was then a traditional approach to constitutional history. In some measure that is true; but if there was any motif to the book, it lay in an increasing determination to break away from that traditional pattern. It sought to do away with the anachronisms of Whig history and replace them by realistic terms much more apposite to the England of the twelfth and thirteenth centuries. The attempt was not wholly successful, partly because the determination only took shape slowly as a response to the accumulating evidence; it was never rationalized except in retrospect. For this reason, and also because the evidence has continued to accumulate, there are now many points of detail, perhaps also of emphasis, where adjustments and corrections might be made. There is some guidance to these in the Notes for Further Reading at the end of this edition. But the main arguments and structure of the book still stand; and it is left to the reader, using the Notes, to make the necessary amendments and additions.

There is one point, however, where further comment at this stage may well be useful. Since 1961 much has been written

[1] David Crouch, David Carpenter and P. R. Coss, 'Debate: Bastard Feudalism Revised', *Past and Present*, cxxxi (1991), 170, 188, 202.

on the structure of northern society in the twelfth century, on the Anglo-Scottish border, on the Border baronage, and on borders and marches more generally. It is reasonable to ask how the Northerners fit into this recent work, and what, if anything, further can be said about how a rebellion was planned and organized in the northern counties in 1215.

Since 1961 the study of the Border regions has been transformed. Starting from the work of Maitland, Rachel Reid, and Jolliffe,[2] Professor G. W. S. Barrow in particular has illuminated the characteristic features of the social and administrative structure of the four northern counties of England, which were shared with Lothian and eastern Scotland, and to a lesser degree with Strathclyde. Socially, it was typified by thanes and drengs. Both performed ministerial services. The thane sometimes appears as a substantial landholder of noble status. The dreng usually held a township or smaller holding for which he performed agricultural services and more menial work alongside his ministerial duties. Administratively the unit was the ancient *scir* or shire. But the *scir* could also be the unit of tenure of the greater thanes, and within the *scir* the enforcement of the law and many other administrative tasks fell on thanes and drengs. This was an ancient structure, sharing its features with Wales and the Welsh borders, and perhaps also, as regards tenures, with parts of southern and eastern England.[3] In the North it was overlain, exploited rather than obliterated, by the Norman conquest. Thanes and drengs survived, sometimes by name sometimes under the new title of sergeants. *Scirs* remained, often determining the boundaries of secular and ecclesiastical administrative divisions. Some coincided with the new Norman baronies; the barons themselves owed the service of cornage which was inherited from the older structure.[4] In the course of the twelfth century the North was

[2] See below, pp. 198–201.

[3] G. W. S. Barrow, 'Northern English Society in the early Middle Ages', *Northern History* iv (1969), 1–28, esp. 10–11, 22–3; 'Pre-Feudal Scotland: Shires and Thanes', in G. W. S. Barrow, *The Kingdom of the Scots* (London, 1973), pp. 7–68, esp. 41–2, 56–7, 64–5; 'Frontier and Settlement: Which Influenced Which? England and Scotland, 1100–1300', in *Medieval Frontier Societies*, ed. R. Bartlett and A. MacKay (Oxford, 1989), pp. 3–21, esp. 4–9.

[4] On the extent and importance of cornage see below, pp. 91–2.

divided into shires, each with its sheriff, but there were no hundreds or wapentakes, and much local government remained in the old *scir*, happily preserved in the new barony, sustained throughout by the old ministerial services. This lay under the control of a new aristocracy which served English and Scottish crowns alike and established itself in midland and northern England and lowland Scotland, if not at one and the same time, at least with little more than two generations or so between the English and Scottish settlements.[5]

The hypothetical elements in this, namely the causes which underlay the similarities between the Border, the Welsh Marches, and parts of southern England, need not detain us. The argument is consistent with an older scholarly tradition summed up in Sir Cyril Fox's little masterpiece, *The Personality of Britain*—'in the Lowland [zone] you get *replacement* in the Highland *fusion*.'[6]

The ambience of the Border laird is a different matter. We need to know in what ways and to what extent this determined the emergence of the Northerners in 1215. Outside this book this problem has rarely been discussed.[7] This perhaps stems from the very nature of Border studies; they tend inevitably to distinguish and separate the Border regions from the rest of the countries they divide. The Northerners were living testimony that there was no such isolation.

But, first, the North deserves closer examination, for it was far from uniform. Indeed, 'northern parts'—the *partes boreales* of King John's safe-conduct of 19 February 1215—is a better description.[8] Tweeddale and Northumberland were separated from Cumberland by the Cheviots. Cumberland, the Eden, and the Solway, were enclosed by Stainmore and Shap. Between Northumberland and Yorkshire, there intervened the bishopric of Durham, in the critical years before

---

[5] G. W. S. Barrow, *The Anglo-Norman Era in Scottish History* (Oxford, 1980), pp. 1–29, 61–90.

[6] *The Personality of Britain*, 2nd edn. (Cardiff, 1933), p. 31, and for the zones, which included the Pennines, Wales, and the south-west in the Highland zone, see the map facing p. 26.

[7] An exception is E. Miller, 'The Background of Magna Carta', *Past and Present*, xxiii (1962), pp. 72–83, esp. 75–7.

[8] *Rot. Litt. Pat.*, p. 129.

1215 in the hands of royal custodians. The Pennines were a barrier which was breached only rarely by the family interests of the Normans. Yorkshire barons were more likely to hold other tenements in Northumberland than in Lancashire, Westmorland, or Cumberland. Northumbrians, likewise, were more likely to hold land in Yorkshire than on the west side of the Cheviots. These geographic obstacles could be overcome, and indeed were in 1216 with Alexander of Scotland's march south to Dover.[9] But they divided the North. The Norman settlements of Northumberland and Cumberland were two distinct operations involving mainly different families. Northumberland still marched with Lothian, Cumbria with Strathclyde, the one Danish, English, and Scot, the other Norse and Celtic in its origins and make-up[10]

Nevertheless, the main features of the Border area, *scirs*, thanes, drengs, ministerial services, customary renders such as cornage, were a common feature, and as we move south from the southern borders of Westmorland and Durham these appear to fade. There were thanes in Lancashire south to the land between Ribble and Mersey. Two services in drengage survived in Richmondshire in the thirteenth century, one only in memory for it had been converted to a money rent.[11] The coincidence of *scir* and barony extended to Blackburnshire, the honour of Clitheroe, west of the Pennines, and to the Hallamshire fee to the east, in both of which some of the older pre-Norman services still survived at the end of the twelfth century.[12] But a fading image is not quite the right picture. It was rather that the old structures were overlain and blended with the feudal arrangements of the Normans and the administrative requirements of nobles, bishops, and kings.

This process was still under way in King John's time. When royal custodians surveyed the bishopric of Durham between 1208 and 1210 thanage and drengage tenures still survived,

[9] See below, p. 138.

[10] G. W. S. Barrow, 'The Pattern of Lordship and Feudal Settlement in Cumbria', *Journal of Medieval History*, i (1975), 117–38, esp. 121–4; id. 'Frontier and Settlement', pp. 4–5; W. E. Kapelle, *The Norman Conquest of the North* (London, 1979), pp. 199–200, 209–13. See also below, pp. 199–202.

[11] *Early Yorks. Charters*, iv. 121, 143.

[12] R. Beverley Smith, *Blackburnshire: A Study in Early Lancashire History* (Leicester, 1961); Barrow, 'Pre-Feudal Scotland: Shires and Thanes', pp. 19–21.

but they were now mingled with sergeanties and socage tenures. Castle-work and other occasional services were still noted, especially from the drengs, but it is plain that rent payments were pervasive and often the only service mentioned. Rents had taken hold before 1135, and the rent paying fee-farm or socage became the normal patterns for new grants under Bishop Hugh du Puiset (1153–95) and Philip of Poitiers (1196–1208).[13] Lancashire presents a somewhat different story. Here, in 1212, the old *scir* was still used to describe the new hundred; many ministerial services still survived, mingling with or transformed into new sergeanties. Nevertheless, in some parts of the county the thanes simply paid rent; no other service was recorded against them.[14] Only in Cumberland and Northumberland did the old services survive relatively unimpaired, but here too the new terminology of sergeanties and rents of uncertain antiquity were present.[15] Throughout the North cornage was expressed and paid as a cash render. By 1242/3 all the Northumbrian baronies returned numbers of rent-paying socage tenants.[16] Money was reducing all to a common denominator.

Yet not entirely so. At almost all social and administrative levels there was fusion or adaptation. In 1212 the survey of Northumberland revealed a large number of ministerial tenures, some classed as sergeanties, many of which must have derived from the old tenures of thanes and drengs. Right at the top of such tenures were the two sergeanties of levying distraint and delivering writs for the king, which, it has been argued, were derived from the two high reeveships into which the old earldom of Northumberland was divided along the line of the Coquet.[17] The Normans not only retained but copied these earlier institutions. The sergeanty of West Derby in Lancashire, apparently instituted by King Stephen's son William, Count of Boulogne, looks very like an old ministerial tenure.[18] Across the Pennines, in Bradford

---

[13] *Book of Fees*, pp. 23–31.   [14] Ibid., pp. 208–10, 213, 216–17.
[15] Ibid., pp. 197–205.   [16] Ibid., pp. 1, 122–30.
[17] Ibid., p. 204. See also H. H. E. Craster in *Northumberland County History*, x. 37–41, a reference which I owe to the kindness of Dr Edward Miller, and Kapelle, *Norman Conquest of the North*, pp. 200–1.
[18] *Book of Fees*, p. 210. It may be that the Count did no more than confirm existing arrangements. The name of the grantee was Waltheof.

and neighbouring manors, a survey of 1341 still recorded carrying, riding, and hunting services which linked the old Lacy possessions of Pontefract and Clitheroe.[19] These can scarcely have been imposed before the two baronies were brought together in the hands of Ilbert de Lacy, at the earliest c. 1087–8.[20]

Across this conglomerate structure there lay the Border, defined in 1157, confirmed in 1237, and perambulated in 1249.[21] The Border was not a frontier with Anglo-Norman and Norman-Scot glaring at each other from either side. Social and administrative patterns, family holdings and interests traversed it throughout its length. But it was a sharply defined jurisidictional line; and there lay the rub. On the English side the line was emphasized by the shireing of the North and the exploitation and control of royal demesne through the shire, by the enforcement of the royal forest law, by the invasion of Angevin justice, both criminal and civil in the shire courts and before the king's justices, and finally under John by the personal visitations of the King, who knew the North better, investigated it more closely, and exploited it more systematically and ruthlessly than any king had done before. These were some of the causes of the northern rebellion of 1215.[22]

But the rebellion did not take the form which we might expect from this. The northern barons, with their many castles and compact *castellarie*, with their lands sometimes enfeoffed to knights but always managed by established ministerial tenants, with their widespread jurisdictional privileges—infangthief, return of writ, in some cases the right to hold the pleas of the Crown—could well have concentrated

---

[19] J. Lister, 'Chapter House Records', *The Bradford Antiquary*, ii (1895), 57–65. 'Roger of Manyngham holds one message and two oxgangs of land, by service of going with the lord to Blakeburnesham, with one lance and one dog to take the wild boar, during forty days receiving from the lord 1½ pennies *per diem* . . . And he shall go with the bailiff, or receiver of the manor, to Pontefract castle, for the safe transport of the lord's money, at his own charges, so often as he shall be forewarned' (p. 63).

[20] W. E. Wightman, *The Lacy Family in England and Normandy 1066–1194* (Oxford, 1966), pp. 36–7.

[21] G. W. S. Barrow, 'The Anglo-Scottish Border', in his *Kingdom of the Scots*, pp. 139–61.

[22] As argued below in Chap. xi, pp. 194–216.

their efforts locally. They could have called on the local peculiarities of their northern tenures to justify resistance to the English Crown's intrusion. They could have relied on their isolation from the centres of Angevin power, on the proximity of a friendly Scottish king who was their lord for whatever land they held in Scotland. Some of this happened. Tenure by cornage was used to resist the demand for service in Poitou in 1213–14; the three Border counties were surrendered to Alexander II of Scotland and homage done in 1215. But overseas service was only one point in the baronial campaign; and, whatever the surrender of the Border shires to Alexander entailed, it did not stand in the way of the homage which he gave to Prince Louis of France at Dover in 1216.[23] In fact, the Northerners' rebellion was always more than local. Their landholdings help to account for this, for their leaders had extensive possessions south of the Border shires. But the spread of Angevin government and justice was another powerful influence. In the end they were driven into rebellion by Angevin government. Before that they were sapped and suborned by Angevin justice. Drengs and their services might still survive in Durham in 1208, but one of the first objectives of the knights and free tenants of the bishopric once Bishop Philip was dead was to have their legal actions determined according to the assizes of the realm. This they achieved by a royal charter of 21 August 1208, four months after the bishop's death. In that charter the sheriff of Northumberland, far from being an objectionable manifestation of royal power, is the one who will come to the tenants' rescue to replevy their stock if the bishop distrains and holds it contrary to security and pledge.[24]

So the common law introduced a deep-seated ambivalence of attitude in the northern landlord. Was he to withdraw into a fastness or participate in a wider system of law? The cross-

---

[23] For the claim based on cornage, see below, pp. 90–2, and for the later resistance to scutage, below, pp. 99–102. For the surrender of the Border shires to Alexander, see below, pp. 131–3, where it is suggested somewhat too confidently that he received the counties as fiefs of the English Crown. The terms of his take-over are not known. The only clue, a puzzling one, is that he was invested in Northumberland by the bestowal of a staff at the hand of Eustace de Vesci. For his visit to Dover, see below, p. 138.

[24] *Rot. Chartarum*, p. 182.

currents are nicely illustrated within a single generation from the region where Kendale, Lonsdale, Craven, and Bowland marched with each other on the borders of Yorkshire, Lancashire, and Westmorland. Here in 1203 Baldwin of Béthune, who had been a doughty supporter of King Richard and was husband of Hawise, Countess of Aumale and lady of Skipton, obtained royal licence to afforest his land in western Craven. The area involved was considerable, extending from the valley of the Wharfe at Appletreewick to the Mowbray forest of Lonsdale to the west and the Lacy forests of Bowland and Pendle to the south. The matter is unremarkable were it not that the licences were issued at Valognes in the Cotentin and were directed to Hugh de Neville, chief forester of England, within whose jurisdiction it must have lain.[25] Such was the route, under the Angevin kings, which the establishment of a liberty might have to take. It is also noteworthy that at that distance royal government could recall that Baldwin's forest might impinge on those of Mowbray and Lacy.

Within a year of this another remarkable document emerges. This was an agreement between William de Mowbray, lord of Burton in Lonsdale, and Adam of Staveley, tenant in the Benthams, Ingleton, Sedbergh, and elsewhere. It concerned forest rights, the management of the pasture-farming typical of these upland townships, and rights of jurisdiction. It confirmed William in his possession of the forests of Lonsdale and 'Mewich' (which lay around Ingleton and the Benthams). Adam could take fox and hare in the former, and was to have his estovers and pannage in the latter. It included detailed arrangements for the pasturing of stock and restricted Adam's cow-byres to three in number, one as remote as Whernside, and also his rights of enclosing meadow. Finally it laid down that William de Mowbray alone could hold the hermitage, which was to remain waste, and that Adam should abandon his gallows and ordeal pit at Sedbergh. The impression is of William de Mowbray and Adam of Staveley managing an extensive, relatively remote area almost at will (and apparently

---

[25] The instructions are contained in two letters close, the first dealing with Appletreewick, the second with 'Graven', which must be Craven; both issued at the same time as letters patent for a market at Skipton. See *Rot. Lib.*, p. 68.

managing it very well). The concord recording the agreement does not survive. We know of it only because the parties chose to agree or record it before the King's justices at York during the royal eyre of 1204, where it was duly enrolled.[26] For William and Adam, as for the knights of Durham in 1208, royal justice was a valuable resource.

A third instance takes us into deeper water. On 15 April 1190, Richard I granted to Gilbert fitz Reinfrey quittance on noutgeld (cornage) throughout his land of Kendal and Westmorland in return for the service of one knight, and also freed him from suit of court of shire, wapentake and riding, and from aid of sheriffs and their bailiffs.[27] This was confirmed in April 1199 by King John, who elaborated the concession as a grant of a 'free court' with gallows and ordeal pit and with soke, sake, toll, team, and infangthief, and added the right to hold a weekly market at Warton.[28] In twelfth-century terms the whole operation was a nice piece of tidying up, with the ancient service modernized, hereditary title confirmed, and local jurisdiction recognized. Gilbert invested heavily in it: £100 promised in 1197, the same again and two palfreys in 1200.[29] The Crown benefited, for Gilbert was to give loyal service as a sheriff in Lancashire and Yorkshire until he joined the rebellion in 1215.[30]

There matters might well have rested. The effect would have been to fuse county jurisdiction in the two southern wards of Westmorland, south of Shap, with the court of the barony of Kendal, thus creating the 'free court' of King John's charter. However, John was never a man to overlook a countervailing opportunity if he could find one. Westmorland had been one of the lordships of Hugh de Morville, one of Becket's murderers, and in 1202–3 the King established Hugh's nephew, Robert de Vieuxpont, as lord of Appleby

---

[26] *Pleas before the King or his Justices 1198–1212*, ed. Doris M. Stenton, iii (Selden Society 83, 1966), no. 926.

[27] *Cartae Antiquae Rolls* (Pipe Roll Society, N.S. xvii, 1939), no. 81; W. Farrer, *Lancashire Pipe Rolls and Early Charters*, (Liverpool, 1902), pp. 396–7. Fitz Reinfrey came in through marriage to Helewise, heiress of William of Lancaster (ibid., pp. 395–6).

[28] *Rot. Chartarum*, p. 50.

[29] *Pipe Roll 9 Richard*, p. 14; *Rot. de Ob. et Fin.*, p. 67.

[30] See below, pp. 223–5.

and Brough and hereditary sheriff of Westmorland.[31] From
that point on there was a risk of conflict between the two
potentates of Appleby and Kendal, the one with hereditary
title to exercise county jurisdiction, the other with hereditary
exemption from it. Nothing seems to have happened immediately. It may be that there was some give and take
between two men who were closely involved in the King's
government and worked as sheriffs in other shires. Westmorland began to divide. In 1219 the justices' return of
escheats in the county was headed 'the county of Appleby'.[32]
However, in November 1224, by which time Gilbert fitz
Reinfrey was dead and had been succeeded by his son,
William of Lancaster, the inevitable quarrel broke out. Robert
de Vieuxpont was now required to answer before the royal
justices why he had vexed William of Lancaster and his men
with a demand for suit of shire and hundred. William's
attorney produced the charters of Richard and John in court,
stated that Robert had distrained for the suit, and claimed
damages of £40 for the resulting deterioration of the stock.
Further details hint at a fine old local squabble. Further stock
involving 15 marks of damages had been seized for failure to
keep watch on the road to Robert's fair at Appleby; Robert
had tried to close William's rival fair at Barton (near Penrith);
distrained oxen were still in Appleby castle; a reeve and four
men had been arrested for the inadequacy of their arrangements
for hue and cry and for failing to bring all males of 11 years
and over before the sheriff. If all that is true, Robert had
clearly been pressing his shrieval duties somewhat eagerly,
and the details are unremarkable. However, Robert's defence
is truly astonishing. It was simply that, whatever the charters
said, William of Lancaster and his father Gilbert had never
used their privilege, that Gilbert's men had always performed
suit of court and given sheriff's aid. William's attorney
countered, claiming that Gilbert had always been seised of the
liberties unless prevented by Robert from time to time. The

---

[31] See below, pp. 220–1. John's charter of 1203 granted Robert the bailliwick and
revenues of Westmorland. Knights and free tenants of the county were ordered to
perform homage in letters of 15 Mar. 1205 and the Barons of the Exchequer were
instructed to seek no further accounts for the county revenues on 14 Apr. 1205 (*Rot.
Litt. Pat.*, p. 51b; *Rot. Litt. Claus.*, i. 27b).

[32] *Book of Fees*, p. 265.

judges could not resolve the issue. It went to King and council in February 1225 and they in turn referred it to the counties of Yorkshire, Lancashire, and Cumberland on whose testimony Robert had put himself. It is unfortunate that no result is recorded.[33]

The quarrel was, in effect, one between two 'private' or delegated jurisdictions, and we might well imagine that the local scene was dominated by the antipathy of Appleby and Kendal. Yet as the case was reaching its climax something quite different intervened. On 11 February 1225, King Henry III confirmed and reissued Magna Carta. He then set about collecting the reward which the Charter promised him, a tax of a fifteenth on moveables. As in other counties, the knights of Westmorland were required to answer for the tax before assessors and collectors at Appleby in mid-Lent.[34] At the same time, on 16 February, new forest perambulations were ordered in the hope of settling grievances which had arisen from the application of the Charter of the Forest.[35] Westmorland was not named specifically in the commission to Hugh de Neville and other forest justices, but the enquiry must have gone forward, and that not very satisfactorily, for on 30 June 1225 the King addressed letters recording that he had received complaints from the knights and worthy men of Westmorland that forests and moors which should have been disafforested were being retained as forests contrary to the provision of the Charter of Liberties that magnates should concede to their men what the king conceded to them—all this to the detriment of the knights and worthy men of the neighbourhood.[36] Now the King's letters were directed to *both* Robert de Vieuxpont *and* William of Lancaster. The complaints came, not from the men of the two distinct baronies, but from the shire, indeed, if we read *comitatus* in its narrower sense, from the shire court. They were aimed against lords who held in their hands all jurisdiction apart from pleas of the Crown, and that at a time when the quarrel between those lords was probably exacerbating local rivalries by setting Kendal against Appleby. It is difficult to determine on what occasion the complaint was generated: perhaps when

[33] *Curia Regis Rolls*, xi. no. 2732.
[35] Ibid., pp. 567–71.
[34] *Patent Rolls 1216–1225*, p. 566.
[36] Ibid., pp. 575–6.

the men of the county met for the assessment of the fifteenth, more probably when the perambulations of the forest were held. It is equally difficult to decide how the complaint reached the King, through delegates who bore the petition of the shire, or through the justices of the forest. Whatever the occasion and the machinery, the county of Westmorland had found a common voice.

Local government and local interest were intermingled. It was a rich mixture in which, by 1215, local complaint had already taken root and flourished. There is no evidence of how the 'frequent and many' complaints concerning the sheriffs of Yorkshire and Lincolnshire were formulated and brought to King John's attention in the winter of 1212/13, but the questions which the reforming commissioners were required to investigate can scarcely have been answered except in the shire courts; and the field was cleared for them by replacing the old sheriffs against whom the complaints lay by local knights who were likely to be more responsive to the local community.[37] From the decades either side of 1215 there is plenty of evidence of local communities—barons, knights, and freeholders, sometimes knights and freeholders without the barons—using the county courts as mechanisms of protest: Devon in 1214, against the sheriff; Lincoln in 1219, against interference with judgement in the shire court before the justices in eyre; Yorkshire in 1220, over carucage; Lincolnshire again, in 1226, over the sessions of the county court.[38] Similar common action must have been taken every time a county or other local community purchased forest privileges or a measure of control over the sheriff or his office.[39] This lies hidden but, here and there, it is possible to reconstruct it. One striking instance is provided by Peter de Brus's purchase in 1208 of the wapentake of Langbargh. Behind that there lay a deal between Peter and his tenants. This included a local charter of liberties which imposed

---

[37] See below, p. 86. The matters to be investigated included increases in revenues of hundreds, wapentakes, and ridings, retention of pledges of the Jews, leasing of Jewish properties, and bailiffs holding the pleas of the Crown (*Rot. Litt. Pat.*, p. 97).

[38] J. C. Holt, *Magna Carta*, 2nd edn. (Cambridge, 1992), pp. 66, 168–9, 390–3, 400, and below, p. 211. See also J. R. Maddicott, 'Magna Carta and the Local Community 1215–1259', *Past and Present*, cii (1984), 25–65, esp. 27–30, 33–5.

[39] Holt, *Magna Carta* (1992), pp. 60–4; Maddicott, 'Local Community', pp. 27–8.

limitations on the revenues, restricted the number of sergeants in charge, regulated their accounts, and in some of its jurisdictional provisions foreshadowed Magna Carta. But for the fact that a scribe at Guisborough chose to enter it in the Priory's cartulary, we should know nothing of it.[40]

Two of these instances take us deep into the sessions of the shire court. In September 1220 the sheriff of Yorkshire, Geoffrey de Neville, had to report to the justiciar, Hubert de Burgh, on his failure to collect the carucage. He had summoned earls, barons, and all free tenants to York for 14 September, and he himself had attended in person to expedite the matter. The royal precept for the tax was read out. The magnates were not present in person, but their stewards and bailiffs took counsel. They denied knowledge of the tax and asked for respite until the next shire court so that they might consult their lords meantime. Geoffrey could get no further, unless perhaps the King on his arrival at York convened the magnates and asked them in person.[41] In Lincolnshire in a celebrated case of 1226 which stemmed from the provisions of the Great Charter, the role of the magnates' stewards is once again apparent. In a vain attempt to continue the session of the shire court into a second day, the sheriff invited both stewards and knights (so distinguished) to enter the court house to render judgement. They refused. When he tried to transfer the cases to the court of Kesteven (the ten wapentakes of Ancaster), the knights refused to render judgement on the ground that the cases pertained to the county court. When one of the stewards sided with the sheriff he was brusquely informed by a fellow knight: 'You render judgement now, but we shall soon see your lord and we shall tell him how you have behaved in that county court.'[42] Between them these two cases establish beyond doubt that royal mandates were published (that is, read out) in sessions of the county (in Yorkshire in 1220, a special one), and that the magnates, if absent, exercised a powerful influence through their stewards. They could block action by the sheriff and effectively delay the king's business.

[40] Holt, *Magna Carta* (1992), pp. 67–70.
[41] *Royal Letters of Henry III*, p. 151.
[42] *Curia Regis Rolls*, xii. no. 2142.

There need be no surprise, therefore, that in 1215 the King's opponents appointed their own sheriffs in a bid to seize control of local government. The object was not simply to get rid of the King's agents and sabotage his revenues. It was also to control the county court, the chief instrument whereby the local community could find a structure for its actions, bringing with it all the advantages of regular meetings and ordered administration. In short, the main agencies of Angevin government were converted into revolutionary councils with executive power: self-government with a vengeance, but not at the King's command. By the autumn of 1215 there were at least seven baronial sheriffs in ten counties, all but one of them drawn from the Twenty-Five. Among them, Robert de Ros was sheriff of Northumberland and also for a time of Yorkshire; John de Lacy, of Nottinghamshire and also for a time of Yorkshire; William de Albini of Belvoir, of Lincolnshire.[43] Some of them collected revenues, but there were limits to what they could do, for they were opposed by royal castellans in charge of the royal demesne and of great escheats and wardships.[44] Our only evidence that Robert de Ros was sheriff of Yorkshire is provided by letters from four of the Twenty-Five empowering him to raise the *posse comitatus* against the garrison of Knaresborough.[45] The castellan, Brian de Lisle, and his mercenaries remained unmoved by this amateur army. There were limits to what the county could do.

This was the ultimate stage in the baronial bid for power. Before that we can only reconstruct their organization from fragments of evidence or from the administrative logic of their interchanges with the King. The plot of 1212 was just that, a conspiracy hatched in secret meetings.[46] But the Northerners' challenge of overseas service and the Poitevin expedition and scutage of 1214 was a very different matter. This had to be made in the open, in the case of the scutage probably in open

[43] *Walt. Cov.*, ii. 224; Holt, *Magna Carta* (1992), pp. 357–8.
[44] See below, pp. 200–1.
[45] Holt, *Magna Carta* (1992), pp. 499–500.
[46] See the reference to the 'colloquio proditionis contra nos prolocute' in the letters of 24 Aug. which voiced the King's suspicions of Richard de Unfraville (*Rot. Litt. Claus.* i. 122b, and below, p. 83).

court. Some time in the summer of 1214, probably early in June, sheriffs were instructed to collect the scutage from all tenants-in-chief who did not have the King's quittance; they were to be ready to account at the Exchequer on 9 September. From Northumberland, to which a special mandate was also despatched, the sheriffs accounted for the scutage of some, not of others. Richard de Unfraville, Roger de Merlay, Roger Bertram paid: Eustace de Vesci did not; and by 15 October Eustace and others throughout the North had already incurred the penalty of distraint of stock.[47] It is difficult to see how that could have happened within such a time-scale unless the county court were the vehicle used both to promulgate the summons and express the resistance.

Such a reconstruction has important implications. The two others against whom distraint was deployed were Roger de Montbegon of Hornby and Robert Grelley of Manchester, both of whom were normally summoned in Lancashire. To cast the net a little wider, no payment of scutage was recorded against Peter de Brus or Richard de Percy, and only a minute one against William de Mowbray for a portion of a knight's fee held of the honour of Knaresborough. Now none of these barons held any considerable portion of their lands of any of the others. Their feudal linkages were quite minor. But their influence intermingled in the county courts of the shires in which they held their lands: all of them in Lincolnshire; all of them in Yorkshire; Mowbray, Montbegon, and Grelley in Nottinghamshire; Brus and Vesci in Durham. This network was extended when Robert de Ros, John de Lacy, and the Gant cousins joined the movement, for Lacys lands extended into Yorkshire, Lancashire, Cheshire, Nottinghamshire, and Derbyshire, and the Gant interests stretched from Lincolnshire into Yorkshire, Nottinghamshire, and Derbyshire, while de Ros held baronies or fees in Northumberland, Yorkshire, and Lincolnshire, along with escheats in Cumberland. All this is apart from tenancies which these men held in more southerly shires. Behind this network there was another, comprising the lines of communication from the baron to his stewards in the county courts. But once his

----

[47] See below, pp. 99–100.

stewards had made his attitudes known it is easy enough to see how they might spread from county to county, first perhaps as gossip, then for serious consideration, finally adopted by others as policy. It is very probably by such a process that the resistance to the Poitevin scutage spread in the autumn and winter of 1214, to such effect that in the end it seemed to be a *casus belli.*

That the wind blew from one county to another in some such way is indicated by yet another case. The protest of the Lincolnshire knights which sought a strictly minimal interpretation of the provision of the Great Charter concerning county sessions came before the royal justices in the Hilary term of 1226. But the dispute in the county court which originated it must have occurred months earlier, for the King himself took up the matter in letters of 8 August 1225. Writing to the sheriff of Yorkshire, he laid down that, as King, he was to enjoy all customs and liberties which his father had held except those specifically abandoned in the Charter, and this even though royal liberties were not included in its saving clause; in particular, the sheriff was to pay no attention to the bad example set by Lincolnshire.[48] Similar letters were sent to Cumberland, and these specifically excluded the reference to Lincolnshire. The King, in short, felt that Lincolnshire might enflame Yorkshire but not Cumberland. He was taking precautions against a bush fire where it was most likely to spread.

We have, then, to imagine a network of associations centred in the county, in special meetings, or in the regular sessions of the county court. It must have varied in strength; perhaps for much of the time it was no more than a facility, a web which was spun and extended as required. It was subject to circumstance. The network of a great lord would probably be diminished the more his scattered holdings became mesne tenancies.[49] Conversely, the more the sheriffs, under instruction from the King, collected the names of pledges for the repayment of debts and offerings through the county organization and very probably at sessions of the court, the more he was likely to call into being and strengthen

[48] *Rot. Litt. Claus.* ii. 48b–49.
[49] I leave this part of the problem on one side. It requires further investigation.

associations which boded ill for the Crown. One such arrangement is of special interest. When Peter de Brus proffered £1,000 for the manor of Danby in 1200 he found immediate pledges for 700 marks. William de Stuteville, the sheriff, undertook along with Robert de Ros and Eustace de Vesci, that Peter would find adequate pledges for the rest of the debt at the next session of the county court of York.[50] At times deeper matters were part of the shared experience. In 1208 Peter de Brus's charter for Langbargh was attested by these same two men, Eustace de Vesci and Robert de Ros. That, too, was most probably executed during a session of the county court.[51]

These considerations put the Border laird in his place. He might enjoy jurisdictional provilege within a compact barony which would be the envy of a southerner, he might participate in the customs, tenures, and administrative structures of Border society, but he would not pull real weight unless his interests extended widely into the web of county government. Vesci, Mowbray, Ros, Lacy, Percy, and Montbegon were of the Twenty-Five. Only two of these, Vesci and Ros, were Border lairds, with wives from the royal line of Scotland and Scottish lands to boot; but both were more than that, men of widespread interests, men of affairs and experience who served King John in his earlier campaigns abroad and were familiar at court. The leading Northerners were not backwoodsmen. They got their name because they thrust themselves into the affairs of the whole realm of which they were a part.

One final reflection. Our text-books tell us that the scattered holdings of many of the great Anglo-Norman families reduced their capacity to resist the authority of the Conqueror and his sons. If that was so, matters had changed by 1215; indeed, by then the opposite was true. For the authority of King John was now brought down by the widespread involvement in local government which scattered holdings gave to his opponents.

[50] *Rot. de Ob. et Fin.*, p. 110. On pledging in general, see below, pp. 72–8.

[51] Other witnesses included Roger de Lacy, constable of Chester and sheriff of Yorkshire, Robert Walensis, his deputy, and William of Boynton, treasurer of St. Mary's York, along with tenants of the honour of Richmond and others (Holt, *Magna Carta* (1992), p. 69).

I

INTRODUCTION

ON 1 January 1216 John de Lacy, Constable of Chester and lord of Clitheroe and Pontefract, set out to meet King John, who was travelling on that day from Laxton, in Nottinghamshire, to Doncaster. The Constable, an erstwhile rebel and one of the Twenty-Five barons of Magna Carta, was seeking peace with his king. King John was at the head of an army which he was to lead as far north as Berwick in an attempt to crush the rebellion of the northern lords. The surrender of de Lacy was an important victory for the King's cause.

The terms King John imposed were strict. Among them John de Lacy gave this guarantee: 'If I have sworn an oath to the King's enemies, then I will not hold to it, nor will I adhere in any way to the charter of liberties which the lord king has granted in common to the barons of England and which the lord pope has annulled.'[1] A personal submission was not enough. John de Lacy also had to abandon the cause for which he had been fighting, denounce the political programme of that cause, and publicly admit that it had been rendered invalid by a papal sentence. His charter of submission asserted that he did all this of his own free will, but in fact the words of the record were probably devised by the clerks of the King's household.[2] King John was trying to suffocate Magna Carta at birth and he had good reasons for doing so. One, perhaps, only impinged slightly on the fringes of his thought. Hitherto, if civil wars had been fought for any positive end, they had been fought on behalf of an individual, a Robert Curthose or a young King Henry, or in the interests of the participants in seeking land, office, and power. Now a civil war was being fought for a cause, a programme, not for one individual or even several, but for a document, a simple piece of parchment. The rebellion which King John faced was thus quite novel. It was the first of a long line which led through the Provisions of 1258–9

---

[1] *Foedera*, i, pt. 1, p. 137. For the date see *Rot. Litt. Claus.* i. 245.

[2] The form is repeated in the charter of submission of Gilbert fitz Reinfrey, who also made his peace some time in Jan. 1216 (*Foedera*, i, pt. 1, p. 136).

and the Ordinances of 1311 down to the Grand Remonstrance of 1641. Of all these Magna Carta was the ancestor and was so recognized by its progeny.[1]

As a new departure it was fumbling, half-blind. Its provisions often constituted little more than crude propaganda, or vague and platitudinous generalities, or administrative tinkering at once naïve and impractical. If at any stage it was drawn from a single coherent plan, this had long been lost in the complex interchange of arguments which preceded it. Those who fought for it were as hesitant as their programme was ill-formed. Scarcely one maintained his course undiverted, without considering surrender, from the beginning of the crisis in 1212 to the end of the civil war in 1217. They looked for precedents for what they were doing, but those they found were barely adequate. Their experience provided them with one great example of a war fought for a cause, and that was the Crusade. Somewhat ineptly now, for their king had taken the Cross, they described themselves as the Army of God and Holy Church. If they were opening up new vistas, they were determined to hide the fact, perhaps even from themselves.

The men who were responsible for the Great Charter of 1215 asserted one great principle. In their view the realm was more than a geographic or administrative unit. It was a community. As such, it was capable of possessing rights and liberties. Magna Carta was indeed a statement of these rights and liberties, which could be asserted against any member of the community, even and especially against the King. The durability of Magna Carta is to be explained by the general utility of this central concept. Once it was established, the rights it subsumed could be expanded, amended, and further defined. Judgement by peers could become trial by jury. *Per legem terrae* could become due process of law. That the constitutional history of England has been in Stubbs's words 'a commentary on this charter',[2] was a result of the Promethean quality of the Act of 1215.

For this many different men were in some degree responsible. Most obviously there was Stephen Langton, the Archbishop of Canterbury,[3] but there were other churchmen too, such as Bishop Eustace of Ely, and especially, perhaps, those clerks who stood

---

[1] See Miss Faith Thompson, *The First Century of Magna Carta* (Minneapolis, 1925), and her *Magna Carta* (1948).   [2] *Stubbs' Charters*, 9th edn., p. 291.

[3] See F. M. Powicke, *Stephen Langton* (Oxford, 1928).

by the rebel barons after the papal sentence of excommunication: Gervase of Heybridge, Simon Langton, and Elyas of Dereham, the Archbishop's steward. The claims of the loyalist barons and of the King's advisers have also been advanced, and certainly they cannot be excluded.[1] But the fight for the Charter was conducted by the rebel barons and none other. Without them the scene at Runnymede and all that it implied would not have occurred. The concept of the kingdom as a community may in some respects have been well worn, but to apply it as they did was revolutionary, for they made it more than academic. It was openly and expressly stated not so much in the Charter, which was seriously influenced by the King and drafted by his clerks, as in contemporary narratives and in documents which emanated more directly from baronial sources. However the rebel barons had acquired these views, it cannot seriously be doubted that they held them genuinely and tenaciously.[2]

The work of 1215 took root during the minority of Henry III at a time when all the essential operations of government were in the hands of a few great magnates, lay and ecclesiastical. Within fifteen years the myth of Magna Carta had already been created. The St. Albans chronicler, Roger of Wendover, writing after 1225 and probably before 1230, attributed both the Great Charter and the Charter of the Forest of 1225 to King John. The original and the reissues, and the respective backgrounds from which they had sprung, were now confused. The Charter was already venerable, a bulwark against tyranny, and was no longer what it had been either in content or in ethos. At first a revolutionary programme, it had become a statement of law. If the Charter of 1215 was the forbear of 1258 and 1311, then the Charter of 1225 was the forbear of the statutes of Merton and Marlborough and the legislation of Edward I. Magna Carta was at once a precedent for rebels and a precedent for lawyers, and later it was to be at its most dangerous to monarchical power when the rebels and lawyers were one and the same. This dual quality was perhaps its most important feature. Four of the provisions of 1215 still remain on the statute book.[3] No other rebellion can claim as much.

[1] See A. L. Poole, *From Domesday Book to Magna Carta* (Oxford, 1951), pp. 470–9.
[2] See J. C. Holt, 'Rights and Liberties in Magna Carta', *Album Helen Maud Cam*, i (*Studies Presented to the International Commission for the History of Representative and Parliamentary Institutions*, vol. xiii, pp. 57–69).
[3] Caps. 1, 13, 39, 40. Caps. 1, 13 and 39 were all amended to greater or less degree in the re-issues of the Charter, 1216–1225.

Some contemporaries, especially perhaps those closest to the crisis of 1215, took a rather different view. They saw in the rebellion not so much a great assertion of principle as a baronial bid for power and privilege,[1] a demand for a restoration of rights, property, and even office,[2] which culminated in a destructive and meaningless civil war.[3] This kind of emphasis is only to be expected, for the Charter was followed by many such restorations, especially to the leading rebels, and disputes over some of their claims contributed largely to the renewal of the civil war in the autumn of 1215. This has so impressed itself on some historians that they have seen Magna Carta as a document of feudal reaction[4] and the baronial leaders as 'feudal dynasts' hankering after heritable office and privilege like their predecessors in the reign of Stephen.[5] There were, indeed, may parallels with the events of Stephen's reign. Earl Ranulf of Chester's policies under John were largely determined by his desire to extend his interests into Lincolnshire and northwards from his earldom into Lancashire, just as were those of the earlier Ranulf who had captured King Stephen at Lincoln in 1141. In 1215, as in Stephen's time, men rebelled because of personal injuries and ambitions, and committed lawless acts in the process. These were occurrences common to any civil war. Nevertheless, in 1215 all these motives and actions only constituted one aspect of the crisis. There was more than this in Magna Carta, and it would be rash and inaccurate to argue that all that was self-interested and impermanent in it was the work of a reactionary group of rebel aristocrats, and that all that was constructive or high-principled was the contribution of others.

To look back, to seek precedents in the past, whether for an individual claim to land or for an assertion of legal principle was a natural, indeed an essential step for the opponents of King John in 1215. They were retrospective rather than reactionary. If we are disposed to rate some of them little higher than the turbulent men of Stephen's reign, we should note that the parallels with this earlier period are not all negative and destructive. Stephen's

---

[1] *Histoire des ducs de Normandie*, pp. 149–50.
[2] *Coggeshall*, p. 172; *Walt. Cov.* ii. 221; *Brut y Tywysogyon*, ed. T. Jones (Cardiff, 1952), p. 89.   [3] *Walt. Cov.* ii. 222.
[4] C. Petit-Dutaillis, *Studies supplementary to Stubbs' Constitutional History* (Manchester, 1908), i. 127 ff.
[5] J. E. A. Jolliffe, 'Magna Carta', *Schweizer Beiträge zur Allgemeinen Geschichte*, x (1952), 88 ff.; *Angevin Kingship* (London, 1955), pp. 335 ff.

second charter of liberties of 1136 was already approaching the atmosphere of 1215 when it released the afforestations of Henry I 'to the church and to the realm'.[1] Under Stephen, again, there was a London commune with which the new king made an agreement on oath.[2] Eighty years later King John's enemies likewise bound themselves together in a *conjuratio*. They insisted, too, on a general oath of obedience to the Twenty-Five, thus reinforcing these men with the 'commune of the whole land'.[3] When John de Lacy made his peace in 1216 he had to abandon not only the Charter, but also the oath he had sworn to the King's enemies.

Despite parallels with the reign of Stephen, there were important developments in the forms of political thought and action in the decades which preceded the Charter.[4] Nevertheless, there was little sign in 1215 of the spirit which later inspired the Song of Lewes. Men of knightly rank were important and influential enough; their interests were admitted in Magna Carta and especially in the charter of liberties of the earldom of Chester. But they did not succeed in putting forward their demands and schemes as a coherent political programme as their descendants did in 1259. In this matter the rebellion of 1215 stood midway between Stephen's troubled years and the situation in 1258–65.

Thus the main problem is the attitude of men of baronial rank and standing, especially the manner in which they correlated their assertion of principle with their reassertion of privilege. In some ways this is easy, for they viewed the law, quite correctly, as a system of rules whereby they could establish and defend their privileges. Law perpetuated right and title. Difficulties occurred when, for some reason like the chaos of Stephen's reign or the intrusion of a King John, this neat equation ceased to work. Magna Carta was not a universal panacea. When the civil war was over in 1217, one of the Twenty-Five, Roger de Montbegon, lord of the Lancashire barony of Hornby and of scattered manors in other counties, sought recovery of seisin in the Nottinghamshire manors of Clayworth, Oswaldbeck, and North Wheatley. He was faced with stubborn opposition and delaying tactics from the

[1] *Stubbs' Charters*, p. 144.
[2] J. H. Round, *Geoffrey de Mandeville* (London, 1892), pp. 247–9; Miss May McKisack, 'London and the Succession to the Crown in the Middle Ages', *Studies in Medieval History presented to F. M. Powicke* (Oxford, 1948), pp. 78–79.
[3] *Articuli*, cap. 49; Magna Carta, cap. 61.
[4] J. C. Holt, 'The Barons and the Great Charter', *E.H.R.* lxix (1955), 1 ff.

sheriff, Philip Mark. In 1220 the case developed into a complex argument in the shire court which involved many subsidiary matters. Among these, Roger was accused of holding stock which he had seized by distraint 'contrary to the peace of the lord king and the statutes of the realm'. A decision on his right to present a deputy in a duel was postponed 'since he was a great man and a baron of the lord king'. When the county court insisted on retaining some of Roger's own stock which had been distrained, he withdrew from the court exclaiming that if it would not restore his stock, then he would see to it himself. The Constable of Nottingham castle, who was in charge in the sheriff's absence, then asked him thrice 'by the counsel of the court and by several knights' that he should return to hear the consideration of the court. This he refused to do. *Superbe recessit*. It was said in the court that if he had not been a great man and a baron of the King, 'his person might well have been detained for so many transgressions'.[1] We may doubt whether Roger would have behaved in this way with John still on the throne. The thrice repeated summons might then have had a very sinister ring.

This report puts Roger de Montbegon's fight for the Charter in perspective. The judgement of a court was nice to have and was a good principle to assert, so long as it was in one's own favour. When a 'just', a favourable, judgement could not be obtained, then Roger was ready to deny and defy the authority of a shire court. Behind the formal provisions of Magna Carta we penetrate to a world in which county politics, as in the later Middle Ages, were dominated by the local barons, and in which powerful men tried to turn the law and the operations of government to their own ends. Magna Carta represented a combined attempt on a grand scale to bend the government to these men's will. Roger de Montbegon's behaviour represented a similar attempt by one particular man on one particular occasion.

The scene at Runnymede in 1215 was illuminated by many different streams of thought and experience: churchmen's views on the proper constitution of society; civilian and canonist doctrines of law; the development and practice of the English courts; the participation of barons and knights in all branches of the administration; the rapidly spreading literary tastes of epic and

---

[1] *Royal and other Historical Letters illustrative of the Reign of Henry III*, ed. W. W. Shirley (Rolls Series, 1862), i. 101–4.

romantic poetry. If the rebellion in 1215 no longer took the form it had under Stephen, if it amounted to an assertion of principle, this was not because the men of 1215 were less self-seeking than their predecessors. They were simply more sophisticated.

The following pages are devoted to a study of the rebellion against King John in northern England. The initial chapters are concerned with the social composition of the rebel party in this region: first, with the barons, who and what sort of men they were; then with the knighthood and gentry, and the extent to which they were dependent on the great magnates; lastly with the connexions which held all these men together as a group, distinguishing them both from loyalists in the north and from other groups of rebels based on other parts of the country. The next chapters are concerned with the Northerners' actions in the final years of John's reign: first, from the summer of 1212 to the beginning of 1215, with their leadership of the baronial movement against the King; secondly, with their gradual loss of influence as the rebellion widened in the months which preceded the settlement at Runnymede in 1215; lastly, with their conduct of the war which broke out in the autumn of that year. The final chapters are concerned with the causes and motives which underlay the rebellion: first, with the development of John's administration and its financial effects upon the northern landlords; secondly, with the legal implications of John's methods of government and with the baronial outcry for ancient rights, laws, and liberties; finally, with the reasons for the prominence of the north in the administrative and political history of the reign.

Much of this provides typical illustrations of the operations of King John's administration, of local reactions to it, and of the King's personal relations with the great magnates of his time. But we are not selecting the Northerners artificially, simply as a manageable sample. They are selected for us by contemporaries, in whose eyes they epitomized the rebellion against King John. These men, historians, annalists, administrators, and royal clerks, were the first to write and talk of Northerners. It is to the way in which they used this term that we turn first.

II

INIMICI NOSTRI OR THE ARMY OF GOD?

CONTEMPORARIES gave various titles to the men who rebelled against King John in 1215. Many were satisfied with the term *barones* or *barones Angliae*. But this was very loose and must have seemed inaccurate to those with detailed knowledge of events, for by no means all the great tenants-in-chief of the King were against him. Hence they sought greater precision, often referring to individual rebels, just as the government records of the period specified the rebels either by name or by such phrases as *barones contra nos* or *inimici nostri*. Another label was supplied by the rebels themselves, 'the Army of God and Holy Church'. This lacked brevity, claimed too much, and failed to stick. At least, it received only passing mention from ecclesiastical writers who were wary of baronial claims to represent both the Deity and their own order.[1] Between the extremes of this portentous title and the more general term *barones* there stood a third title, 'Northerner', and this quickly became the most popular nickname for the rebels. It was short. It was specific. It had, too, a graphic and perhaps derogatory quality, for it was used at the time by the King's supporters, and it painted the rebels with that touch of barbarity which Englishmen south of Trent are apt to attribute to their fellow countrymen of the north.[2] There is little to suggest that the Northerners so described themselves.

In the Latin chronicles the 'Northerners' usually appear as *Aquilonares* or *Norenses*. More rarely, the forms *Northanhumbrenses* or *barones Northanhumbriae* were used, but not normally in a restricted sense, for they were interchangeable with the more general term *Norenses*.[3] In the vernacular chronicles the word appears invariably as *Norois*. In the extant government records it

---

[1] This title appears in the treaty concerning the custody of London (*Foedera*, i, pt. 1, p. 133). See also *Walt. Cov.* ii. 220; *Coggeshall*, p. 171; *Chron. Maj.* ii. 586; Matthew Paris, *Historia Anglorum*, ii. 156.

[2] The disgust inspired by the Scottish invasions of the twelfth century may have had some effect here. See A. L. Poole, op. cit., pp. 270–1, 277. It is perhaps worth noting, too, that in the time of Henry II *Norenses* could still mean Norsemen. See W. de Gray Birch, *The Royal Charters of the City of Lincoln*, p. 18.

[3] *Coggeshall*, pp. 167, 170, 178–9.

appears once in the rolls of the Curia Regis as *Norenses*,[1] once in a letter written in March 1215 by Walter Mauclerc, John's agent at Rome, as *Boreales*,[2] and once in a royal letter patent in the more specialized form of *barones de partibus borealibus*.[3]

The term 'Northerner' had a history of its own which reflected the history of the rebellion itself. Despite the fact that it almost always appears in narrative sources written after the event, its changing sense can be followed closely. It first appears in the accounts of the years 1213 and 1214 given by the Barnwell, Coggeshall, and Dunstable chroniclers.[4] In these passages the term is used in a strictly limited manner. The 'Northerners' were so described because they came from the north. They drew the attention of these writers because of the recalcitrance of their opposition to the King and their refusal to support an expedition overseas on the grounds that they were not bound to do so on the terms on which they held their estates. The 'Northerners' thus appear as a distinct, definable group within the English baronage.

The most valuable and intelligent of these writers, the Barnwell chronicler, realized that the term came to present difficulties as more and more men joined the 'Northerners' in opposition to the King in 1215. In describing the baronial muster at Stamford in Easter week 1215, he stated that the rebels were called 'Northerners' because 'most of them came from northern parts'. Even so, he did not consider that the great rebels of the eastern and home counties, the Bigods, Mandevilles, and Robert fitz Walter, came under the title, for these, according to him, only joined the rebel army after the Stamford muster.[5] Further, after issuing this *caveat*, he persisted in using the term in the limited sense of his earlier passages, and, indeed, the word is almost always specifically associated in his work with northern men or events. The Coggeshall writer continued to use the word in this way too, but without exhibiting quite the same knowledge as his neighbour.[6] So also did the Dunstable annalist, although more rarely and with a weaker grasp than either of the other two of the complex events and shifting loyalties of the years following 1214.[7]

[1] *Curia Regis Rolls*, vii. 315.   [2] *Diplomatic Documents*, p. 29.
[3] *Rot. Litt. Pat.*, p. 129.
[4] *Walt. Cov.* ii. 217; *Coggeshall*, p. 167; *Annales Monastici*, iii. 40.
[5] *Walt. Cov.* ii. 219.   [6] *Coggeshall*, pp. 170, 177, 178–9.
[7] For example, he attributes the siege of Northampton, which followed the Easter muster, to the Northerners, the Welsh, and the Scots (*Annales Monastici*, iii. 43).

There is a wider variation in the works of writers who show no knowledge of the policy of the northern barons in 1213 and 1214, and who only came to use the term 'Northerner' in describing the events of 1215. They also, however, tended to connect the word with northern men either in naming individuals or in listing the rebel leaders. Thus, on the one occasion on which Roger of Wendover used it, he associated it with Lincolnshire and a Lincolnshire baron.[1] Similarly, in naming the opposition leaders, the author of the *Histoire des ducs de Normandie* first listed Robert fitz Walter, Saer de Quenci, Gilbert son of Richard of Clare, and Geoffrey de Mandeville. Then, he wrote, 'of those who were called Northerners, because their lands lay towards the north', there were Robert de Ros, Eustace de Vesci, Richard de Percy, William de Mowbray, and Roger de Montbegon.[2] This passage gives us a distinction between the two rebel groups identical to that made by the Barnwell chronicler, and also an almost impeccable list of the leading northern rebels. Nevertheless, the author of the *Histoire* did not stick to this. He used the term frequently, but almost always in the vaguest manner. Thus the *Norois* appear in the defence and abortive reliefs of Rochester castle in the last months of 1215, a campaign in which few northern men took part,[3] and, more surprisingly, in a rebel attack on Exeter in the spring of the same year.[4] This suggests that by May 1215, when this writer came to England in the company of Robert de Béthune, the term was already being used, especially by the royalist troops, as a general nickname for the rebels; not just for a section of them, but for all of them. Sometimes, indeed, this vague usage came to eclipse the original and more limited sense completely. Thus the annalists of Southwark and Merton described the war as one between the King and the *Norenses* and Magna Carta as a peace between the King and the *Norenses*.[5] To them the term had a simple evocative value and presented no problems. As a continuator of the *Gesta Regum* of William of Malmesbury put it: 'Although the barons came from diverse parts of the kingdom of England, yet they were all called Northerners.'[6]

[1] *Chron. Maj.* ii. 665.   [2] *Histoire des ducs de Normandie*, p. 145.
[3] Ibid., p. 160.
[4] Ibid., pp. 147–8.
[5] 'The Annals of Southwark and Merton', ed. M. Tyson, in *Surrey Archeological Collections*, xxxvi (1925), p. 49.
[6] 'Qui vero Barones, licet fuissent de diversis partibus regni Angliae, tamen

This debasement of the word 'Northerner' cannot have occurred in all minds at one and the same time. It did not occur at
all in the mind of the Barnwell chronicler. The Southwark annalist,
in contrast, may never have realized that the word had ever had
a specific sense. It is therefore impossible to establish a point prior
to which the term was always used accurately and after which it
was always used in an indeterminate and evocative sense. However, the three appearances of the Northerners in the surviving
government records provide a useful guide. These suggest that
the sense of the word was altering rapidly, at least for the advisers
and clerks of the King, in January and February 1215, at a time
when the old opposition of the Northerners was being heavily
reinforced from other quarters. At the beginning of March 1215
Walter Mauclerc wrote to King John from Rome, reporting on
his own negotiations and the activities of the baronial agents at
the papal Curia.[1] These agents were John fitz Osbert, a chaplain
of Richard de Percy, and John of Ferriby, a clerk of Eustace de
Vesci. They had been sent to Rome after the breakdown of negotiations between the King and the barons at London at the beginning of January.[2] They must have been fully cognizant of
baronial plans; their lords were themselves Northerners. Mauclerc
was an experienced agent and envoy, who stood high in the
King's counsels. This evidence is therefore very reliable. Mauclerc's report shows that these agents, and by inference he himself, still accepted a distinction between the Northerners and the
rest of the opposition baronage.[3] By March, of course, they were

omnes fuerunt vocati Norenses.' *Liber de Antiquis Legibus*, ed. T. Stapleton (Camden
Society, xxxiv, 1846), p. 201.
   There is a possibility that the use of the word became more widespread as time
passed. Although Wendover only used it once, and although Matthew Paris did not
add to this in the appropriate sections of the *Chronica Majora*, he did use the word
again very much later in his chronicle (see below, p. 13, n. 2) and also in the
marginalia of the *Historia Anglorum* (*Historia Anglorum*, ii. 180).
   [1] *Diplomatic Documents*, p. 29.
   [2] *Walt. Cov.* ii. 218. Mauclerc arrived in Rome on 17 Feb. and the others on 1 Mar.
The names of the two baronial agents are given incorrectly in *Foedera*. The error is
corrected by C. R. Cheney in *E.H.R.* lxvi (1951), 266 n.
   I have found no evidence on the date of Walter Mauclerc's departure. He was in
England, Poitou, and Flanders in the summer of 1214. His letter to John records that
he had been delayed by illness, so it is probable that he left London before January.
John strengthened his embassy at Rome, and presumably sent new information, by
the dispatch of Hugh, Abbot of Beaulieu, on 8 Jan. (*Rot. Litt. Pat.*, p. 126b).
   [3] 'Scio . . . quod magnates Angliae, scilicet Boreales, et, ut praedicti nuncii dicunt
Papae, omnes barones totius Angliae . . .'.

out of touch with English affairs, but, in all probability, the distinction they made was still current in England at the time they
left in January. The change came after their departure. On the
Curia Regis Roll of the Hilary term, 1215, it was noted that
judgement in a plea of advowson between the Abbot of Langley
and Roger de Cressy was postponed because Roger was 'one of the
Northerners who are in peace until the close of Easter'.[1] Roger's
estates lay mainly in Norfolk and Suffolk. Throughout the rebellion
he was associated with the lords of the eastern and home counties.
He had no important connexions with the rebel leaders of the
north. Further, the letters of protection issued for the barons after
the Epiphany negotiations at London covered all those who had
come to the discussions. They were not issued solely to the Northerners and, indeed, made no specific mention of them.[2] To the man who
wrote this entry on the roll any opponent of the King might be
a Northerner, and a Northerner might be any opponent of the
King. The word was losing its value as a precise term, and hence-
forth the government clerks fought shy of it, at least in their
official work. When the King wished to negotiate with the baronial
leaders in the north in February 1215, the letters of safe-conduct
were made out not to the 'Northerners', but to the 'barons of the
northern parts'.[3] This, if cumbersome, could not be misunderstood.

While the varying usages of the word 'Northerner' are important, the most significant feature of the evidence is that the word
was used at all, and used by so wide a selection of writers : a clerk
of the Curia Regis; a Fleming with King John's army; annalists
working independently at scattered monastic houses. The time
was one when men were becoming accustomed to labels of this
kind. At Oxford the scholars of the university were coming to be
divided into 'nations', the most prominent of which were the
Boreales and the *Australes*.[4] At Crowland the men of the Lincolnshire fens who so plagued the monks were known as the *Hoylandenses*.[5] But no label comparable to the word 'Northerner' was
ever applied in other rebellions of the twelfth and thirteenth

---

[1] *Curia Regis Rolls*, vii. 315.   [2] *Rot. Litt. Pat.*, p. 126b.
[3] Ibid., p. 129.
[4] C. E. Mallet, *History of the University of Oxford* (London, 1924), i. 40–41; *Rash-
dall's Medieval Universities*, ed. F. M. Powicke and A. B. Emden, iii. 56–57. The first
clear instance comes from 1248, but the division may possibly go back to 1214.
[5] *Historiae Croylandensis Continuatio*, printed in W. Fulman, *Rerum Anglicarum
Scriptores*, i (Oxford, 1648), p. 453.

centuries.[1] Further, however the word was used, in origin its sense was necessarily geographic. Contemporaries, in fact, felt that there was some important characteristic of the movement against King John which was peculiarly northern. They were not alone in this. Writing long after the rebellion, Matthew Paris commented on Geoffrey of Langley's visitations of the northern forests in 1250 by remarking that Henry III's oppression of the Northerners was so excessive that it seemed to stem from some long-nursed hatred.[2] Matthew was still recalling the part which the Northerners had played against King John.

This impression could have arisen in a very simple way. In 1213 and 1214 the majority of the King's most formidable opponents were northern men. Their refusal of overseas service and scutage in these years was striking and persistent; one contemporary even saw in the Poitevin scutage not only the occasion but the cause of the rebellion of 1215.[3] The prominence which some of them gave to the northern rebels and the widespread use of the word 'Northerner' may have resulted solely from the fact that they were the first in the field. The sense of the word may have widened automatically as increasing numbers from other parts of the country joined the movement in the winter and spring before Runnymede.

This view, however, only explains part of the evidence. As late as February 1215 the King was treating with the northern rebels as a distinct group on their own, just as, later, the Barnwell and Coggeshall writers maintained a distinction between the Northerners and the rest of the rebels. That the first consistent and open opposition to the King came from the north points to a bitterness of feeling and a willingness to take risks unparalleled in other parts of the country at this time. Ultimately the Northerners' course led to a complete rejection of the Angevin monarchy.

---

[1] For the use of the word 'Northerner' on a later occasion by Matthew Paris see below, n. 2. The author of the *Histoire de Guillaume le Maréchal* describes those who besieged Count John's men in Nottingham in 1194 as *Norois*, but he was writing after the civil war at the end of John's reign (*Histoire de Guillaume le Maréchal*, ed. P. Meyer, Paris, 1894, line 10181).

[2] 'Oppressio autem haec immoderata, qua rex Boreales afflixit, videbatur ab antiquo odio profluxisse' (*Chron. Maj.* v. 137).

[3] 'Hoc scutagium nec prelatis nec baronibus potuit imponi eo tempore. Propter illud enim divertentes se fere omnes barones a fidelitate Regis ejusdem, introducto in Angliam Ludovico primogenito Regis Francorum Philippi, capta Londonia submissisque sibi aliis civitatibus, eidem se subjecerunt' (*Red Book of the Exchequer*, ed. H. Hall (Rolls Series, 1896), i. 12).

Well before the southern rebels had formally recognized Prince
Louis of France, the Northerners had surrendered the three
northern counties of England to the Scottish crown and done
homage to Alexander II. Even at Runnymede there were signs
that some of the Northerners, like King John himself, were unwilling to accept the Charter as a just and permanent settlement.
The Northerners, in fact, provided not only the most extended
opposition to the King, but the most virulent, and also the most
radical attack on his policies and position.

Geographically, the word 'Northerner' requires qualification.
The dividing line between the north and the rest of England is
drawn, within limits, not on the ground, but in the mind and the
imagination. Its geographical location is thus highly subjective.
By the middle of the thirteenth century administrators were
taking the line of the Trent as a suitable division between the
responsibilities of the northern and southern chief foresters and
escheators. But, although this line was a natural boundary, it was
in some ways artificial. It placed Derby and Nottingham in the
north, but Newark and Lincoln in the south. If it had been applied
literally it would have cut across county boundaries. This, however, was rarely done, and sometimes, indeed, the phrases 'north'
and 'south of Trent' were interpreted in a very cavalier fashion.
In 1236, in an entry on the rolls headed *De escaetis regis ultra
Trentam*, Roger of Essex was appointed escheator, not only north
of that river, but in Lincolnshire, Warwickshire, and Leicestershire,
too.[1] When the Trent was not used as the boundary, then the north
tended to spread south of that river rather than vice versa. In
1229 Brian de Lisle's forestership included with the northern
counties, Lincolnshire, Rutland, Northamptonshire, Buckinghamshire, Essex, Cambridgeshire, Huntingdonshire, and Oxfordshire.[2] In 1399 the north parts of the Duchy of Lancaster included
Kenilworth, Leicester, Castle Donington, and Bolingbroke.[3]
More significantly still, men from south of the Trent often seem
to have considered themselves as Northerners. Those negotiating on

---

[1] *Cal. Pat. Rolls 1232–47*, p. 135. On the problem of the Trent boundary see
C. J. Turner, 'The Justices of the Forest south of Trent', *E.H.R.* xviii (1903), 112–13;
S. T. Gibson, 'The Escheatries 1327–41', *E.H.R.* xxxvi (1921), 218 ff.; E. R. Steven-
son in *English Government at Work*, 1327–36, ed. W. A. Morris and J. R. Strayer
(Cambridge, Mass., 1947), ii. 109 ff.

[2] C. J. Turner, loc. cit., p. 112.

[3] R. Somerville, *History of the Duchy of Lancaster* (London, 1953), i. 560 ff.

behalf of the *Boreales*, in a settlement with the *Australes* at Oxford
in 1274, included a William of Sleaford and a William of Boston.[1]

Lincolnshire is perhaps the chief debatable area. In John's
reign and earlier there were no fixed administrative procedures
which help to define its position. Sometimes it was included in the
judicial circuits of the midland shires south of the Trent; sometimes, in contrast, it went with the circuit of the northern shires.
While on the one hand the great diocese of Lincoln stretched
south to the Thames at Oxford and Dorchester, on the other,
John's journeys to Lincoln, more often than not, prefaced a royal
circuit of the northern counties. Tenurially, however, Lincolnshire had very strong ties with areas farther north. The great
honours of Chester, Lancaster, Durham, and Richmond all included Lincolnshire estates. The Yorkshire families of Mowbray,
Lacy, Vesci, Percy, Ros, and Brus all had interests in the county.
Conversely, the Gant and Aincurt baronies included Yorkshire
and Nottinghamshire lands and many Lincolnshire families of
second rank, the Kymes, Paynels, and Nevilles, held fees which
lay across the Humber or the Trent. This contributed to strong
social and political ties between Lincolnshire, Nottinghamshire,
and Yorkshire, the latter the less surprising if we remember the
important ferry passages at Ferriby and Barton on Humber. In
1205 and again in 1212 and 1213 important measures of vital effect
on John's relations with his subjects were applied in Yorkshire and
Lincolnshire concurrently and, on the last two occasions, by the
same agents and in these two counties alone. Hence men accepted
Lincolnshire as part of the north and Lincolnshire rebels as
Northerners. The Barnwell writer associated the Northerners with
the ebb and flow of civil war around Lincoln. The one Northerner
Wendover mentioned by name was Gilbert de Gant, the greatest of
the Lincolnshire rebels, and in a single sentence this latter writer
puts the issue beyond any doubt. In describing John's march from
Stamford to Lincoln in 1215 he writes of the King penetrating the
'north parts' to relieve his garrison at Lincoln.[2] This comes from
one who had spent the years of the civil war at Belvoir.

Any division between north and south must not be drawn too

---

[1] *Medieval Archives of the University of Oxford* (Oxford Historical Society, lxx,
1917), ed. H. E. Salter, p. 31.

[2] 'Deinde cum festinatione partes penetrans Aquilonis, castrum Lincolniae
audivit obsessum, quod summopere studuit visitare' (*Chron. Maj.* ii. 665).

clearly. It is a zone not a line. Nottinghamshire and Derbyshire south of the Trent, and Kesteven and the parts of Holland in Lincolnshire, roughly constitute the southern extremities of this zone. To the west it is easier to draw an artificial boundary, but only because of political factors peculiar to the rebellion of 1215. The Earls of Chester and Derby were loyal to the King, and hence there are few rebels recorded in the counties of Cheshire and Staffordshire. The line of the Mersey and the western slope of the Pennines marked the limits of the activities of the northern rebels here.

The vagueness of some of these boundaries produces problems of definition of almost scholastic proportions. Would a chronicler of the time have considered a particular rebel from Holbeach in the Lincolnshire fens, or one from Bingham wapentake south of the Trent in Nottinghamshire, as Northerners? If so, would one have seemed more 'northern' than the other? Such problems cannot be solved. Contemporary writers were not concerned with them.

They did, as we have seen, name individuals, sometimes deliberately, sometimes casually. In doing so they give us the names of those whose policy, throughout or on occasions, characterized the northern rebellion. Foremost among these were Eustace de Vesci, Richard de Percy, Robert de Ros, William de Mowbray, Gilbert de Gant, and Roger de Montbegon. In studying these men we can, in effect, outline a 'northern' attitude and policy, something quite distinct and characteristic, separating them from other groups of rebels. But, even with this small group, there were different reactions and lines of conduct and, if we work outwards from this central core, these variations become wider. Many Northerners followed the lead of de Vesci and his associates. But there were many, too, whose background and interests were divided between the north and other parts of the country; few of these behaved like de Vesci and the other recalcitrants. Even within the north there was no unanimity. Some, like Hugh de Balliol, stood by the King. Some were never quite sure whether their interests were best served by rebellion or not. Others deliberately sought an advantage in changing sides as immediate conditions dictated. Not all northern men, nor even northern rebels, were Northerners in the sense in which the Barnwell chronicler used the word.

III

THE NORTHERN BARONS

THE names of the rebels of 1215 have long been known, but the men who carried these names are indistinct to us. Of only one Northerner is there any kind of portrayal or personal description; William de Mowbray, we are told, was 'as small as a dwarf'.[1] For the rest, the formal equestrian figures on their seals are all that we have. Here and there throughout the north some of their work still stands, enigmatic and silent, in the great stone keeps which had become the fashion by their time. Their acts of charity are recorded, and also their quarrels. But the springs of their political actions lie hidden. Only a bare handful of their letters has survived from the civil war, and there is no record of their discussions and conferences, except from the work which preceded and reached completion at Runnymede. Yet behind the names were personalities, compounded at once of the traditions of their class and of individual intelligences and ambitions, expectancies, hatreds, and hopes. They were men, and they were none the worse for being barons; sometimes only their crimes have survived. To ignore this human quality is to tell a story which is at best arid, and at worst anachronistic. If the task of imagining what these men were like is difficult, it is none the less essential.

The contemporary narratives are not much help. The most that a baron usually merited was some brief obituary with a purely formal description like *vir nobilis et potens*.[2] We have passed the heroic age in which the great baron, a Geoffrey de Mandeville, a Robert of Gloucester, or a Strongbow, left the impress of his character on the pages of the annals. But, if this is missing, there is now a different imprint, the long, repetitive, and often wearisome story in roll and charter of the relations of each man with the central offices of government. We can never know what a William of Malmesbury might have told us about Eustace de

---

[1] *Histoire des ducs de Normandie*, p. 145.
[2] This description was applied, for example, by Wendover to Eustace de Vesci (*Chron. Maj.* ii. 666), and by Matthew Paris to Robert Grelley (*Historia Anglorum*, ii. 328).

Vesci, but from record we can still say much about his personal circumstances, even about his character.

Record gives us for each man a skeleton biography. It also reveals a great deal about the King's treatment of his barons. Indirectly, then, it brings us to the influences which, we may presume, led individuals to rebel; it leads us to make assumptions and draw conclusions about character and motive, in brief, to build up a picture of an individual. But, more important than this, it also reveals a pattern of typical baronial behaviour with which each individual may be compared. This pattern only helps us to see a part of these men's lives; it cannot tell us how they worshipped God, or how they used their leisure; but it brings us close to their interests and activities as landlords, to factors which must have had a deep influence on their political actions. The trail these men left through the rolls of Chancery, Exchequer, and Curia Regis did not represent a trivial aspect of their lives.

The typical baron of this time was an habitual litigant and a speculative gambler, expert in offering the King future payment for some present good. Land and office; wardship and marriage; franchise and litigation; these were fields of endeavour in which fortunes might be sought, won, and only too easily lost. Some men were compelled to gamble in this way, either by the King, or by social convention, or perhaps by family ties. Others seem to have done it simply from taste, perhaps from greed. Some men gambled in one field, others in another; some did it successfully, others disastrously. But only exceptional individuals avoided it, some because of luck or favour, some perhaps because of a wish to remain outside the field of battle, lost in rural anonymity. Of the rebels of 1215, many had suffered setback, failure, or defeat in these highly competitive fields; others had been denied fair access to them. Magna Carta may reveal some of their political assumptions and convictions, but the chief motives behind the rebellion are to be found elsewhere, in litigation in which royal influence told against them, in office which was refused them, in disseisins and monetary penalties inflicted on them, and in speculative proffers and costly compositions which led them deep into debt, sometimes to the verge of disinheritance or to a degrading dependence on the whim of the King. Scarcely one of the Northerners avoided some such calamity in the course of his life.

The quintessential deed of the Northerners was their refusal to serve overseas or pay scutage during King John's campaign in Poitou in 1214. Only a few men, the core of the resistance to the King in the northern counties, committed themselves clearly to this course. They were Eustace de Vesci, lord of Alnwick in Northumberland and Malton in Yorkshire; William de Mowbray, whose chief estates lay around Thirsk, Kirkby Malzeard, and Burton in Lonsdale in Yorkshire, in and around the Isle of Axholme in Lincolnshire, and around Melton Mowbray in Leicestershire; Peter de Brus, lord of Danby and Skelton in Cleveland; Richard de Percy, whose chief holdings lay in Yorkshire around Topcliffe and in upper Wharfedale and Craven; Roger de Montbegon, lord of Hornby in north Lancashire and of other lands in Nottinghamshire, Lincolnshire, and the West Riding of Yorkshire; and Robert Grelley, lord of Manchester. Of these, and these only, among the English baronage can we be certain.

This small group of northern lords was not, however, completely isolated. Their actions in 1214 were part of a campaign against the King which, in the case of Eustace de Vesci, can be traced back to the regicidal plot of 1212. With these earlier moves other men were certainly or probably associated; Richard de Unfraville, lord of Prudhoe, and Roger de Merlay, lord of Morpeth. These two had suffered the King's wrath and had surrendered hostages who were still in the King's hands in 1214. Although they rebelled later, they did not apparently resist the scutage, and many others, too, probably felt that they were under some similar constraint. The scutage of 1214 is not, therefore, a touchstone of baronial policies; those who resisted had to have the capacity as well as the desire to challenge the King. It is nevertheless a valuable guide, for there is no better witness to rebellious instincts than rebellion itself. It was to a rebellion that these northern lords were implicitly committing themselves.

Although few in number, they were by no means negligible politically. One of them, William de Mowbray, owed the service of nearly ninety knights to the King. Eustace de Vesci owed the service of thirty-six. Of the rest, two owed less than twenty and the others less than ten.[1] This, however, is an inaccurate guide to

---

[1] Brus, 16; Percy, 15 on half the Percy barony; Grelley, 12; Montbegon, 8; Merlay, 4; Unfraville, 2½. These figures are based on the returns to the inquest of 1212 printed in the *Book of Fees* for the Northumbrian baronies and on the Scottish scutage of 1211 for the rest, as are other similar figures given below.

their power and influence. Most of them held important mesne tenures. Further, knight service is a notoriously unreliable measuring rod of social and political importance, especially in the Border counties where the military service due from the baronies was relatively low, and where the strength and siting of castles and the possession of liberties added much to a man's influence. Richard de Unfraville owed service on only 2½ fees for his barony, but he was also master of the great Northumbrian franchise of Redesdale. His great-grandfather had been a friend of King David of Scotland and had acquired land there. His father, Odinel, was described by a Tynemouth annalist as 'the most powerful of the Northumbrian nobility'. His son, Gilbert, married Maud, Countess of Angus, and originated the Unfraville line of Earls.[1]

Most of these men were well on in years by the standards of the time. Eustace de Vesci must have been forty-seven or forty-eight when he was killed at Barnard Castle in 1216. William de Mowbray was four years younger.[2] Peter de Brus cannot have been under forty-one in 1215,[3] Robert Grelley was forty-one or forty-two,[4] and Richard de Percy was probably older than either of them.[5] Roger de Montbegon was at least fifty.[6] This was not a movement of young firebrands.

Eustace de Vesci, as the chroniclers also suggest, was undoubtedly the most remarkable of these northern lords. The records reveal him as a cautious, even parsimonious man who avoided the morass of debt in which so many of his friends played with abandon. His one major action in the royal courts concerned the tenure of the manor of Rotherham. Characteristically, he won it, after waging a duel, and kept his recorded expenses well below 100 m.[7] Thereafter he avoided any but small commitments of this kind.[8] His activities in other directions were equally restrained.

---

[1] *Monasticon Anglicanum*, iii. 311; J. Hodgson, *A History of Northumberland* (Newcastle, 1820), pt. ii, vol. 1, pp. 6 ff.

[2] They succeeded to their lands, in each case after minorities, in 1190 and 1194 respectively (*Pipe Roll 2 Richard I*, p. 21; *Pipe Roll 6 Richard I*, p. 160).

[3] *Early Yorks. Charters*, ii. 15. [4] *V.C.H. Lancs.* i. 329.

[5] *Complete Peerage*, x. 449 n.

[6] *V.C.H. Lancs.* i. 321.

[7] *Curia Regis Rolls*, i. 285–6; ii. 188; iii. 74, 161, 187, 228–9, 300; iv. 62; *Pedes Finium Ebor. regnante Johanne*, pp. 90–91 (for the duel), 95–97; *Pipe Roll 2 John*, pp. 109–10.

[8] He was amerced 300 m. in 1207 in a plea between him and Richard de Unfraville which concerned the custody of the heir of Henry Batail. This sum was pardoned (*Curia Regis Rolls*, v. 58–59; *Rot. Litt. Claus.* i. 99; *Pipe Roll 9 John*, p. 74).

He never speculated in the purchase of office or franchises. His one offer for land, a relatively low one of 100 m. and two palfreys, was made in 1210 for the seisin of the manor of Burton Leonard, to which in any case he had a sound title.[1] Eustace, we feel, expected real and certain returns for his money. Perhaps he took a keener interest in his offer of 100 m. and one palfrey in 1208 whereby he secured the confirmation of his right to have a fair at Rotherham and a port at Alnmouth near the centre of his Northumbrian lands.[2] Eustace might take political risks, but not financial ones. In the last complete Exchequer account before the outbreak of civil war, his total recorded commitments only came to 300 m.[3] and had never exceeded this amount significantly at any point in the reign.[4]

All this was unusual, not only in the underlying restraint exhibited by de Vesci, but also in his good luck. There was nothing in his family's history, or in his own before 1212, to make him immediately dependent on the King's good will. With others this was not so. Richard de Percy was uncertain from one year to the next of the title to most of his estates. A younger son of the marriage of Agnes de Percy and Jocelin de Louvain, he was faced throughout his life with the counter-claims of his nephew, William, the son of his elder brother, Henry, who had died in 1198. The Percy lands were divided between the two of them. William was a minor until at least 1212, in the custody of one of the King's most influential advisers, William Briwerre, whose daughter he ultimately married. Richard was thus committed to a long series of legal actions, first with William Briwerre, and then with William de Percy, which culminated in 1234 in a hearing before Henry III.[5] One thing only probably saved Richard from the almost certain financial consequences of such legal entanglements. His title to the Percy barony was identical to John's title to the English crown. Not even a William Briwerre could hope to oust him in these circumstances, nor could John sell his

---

[1] *Pipe Roll 12 John*, p. 40.

[2] *Rot. de Ob. et Fin.*, p. 423; *Rot. Chartarum*, p. 174.

[3] *Pipe Roll 16 John*, pp. 87–91.

[4] This does not include sums which he had pledged as a guarantor of other debtors.

[5] For an account of the Percy disputes and the descent of the estates see *Complete Peerage*, x. 449 ff. The best indication of the division of the lands at this time is given in a final concord of May 1218. See *Percy Cartulary*, no. 6, and *Yorkshire Fines 1218–31*, p. 1.

confirmations of Richard's position at more than a purely formal price. The implications might have been too dangerous.

What John might have done but for this is suggested by his treatment of William de Mowbray. Here there were no royal inhibitions. De Mowbray bore a name with ominously rebellious associations. He still carried the marks inflicted on his family's prestige by Henry II, who had destroyed the Mowbray castles of Kinardferry, Thirsk, Burton in Lonsdale, and Kirkby Malzeard after Roger de Mowbray's rebellion in 1173–4.[1] William still hankered after castles and was to claim York in 1215. The Mowbray fortunes were partly based on the acquisition from Henry I of the lands of Robert de Stuteville, who had been among Robert Curthose's supporters at Tinchebrai in 1106.[2] In 1200 William offered 2,000 m. for a royal judgement in the matter of the claims to his barony brought by William de Stuteville. The case ended in a compromise, but one very favourable to de Stuteville. Despite this, William de Mowbray's debt remained and ultimately he had to pay. He was forced into the welcoming arms of the Jews and an increasingly difficult financial situation.[3] Rebellion for him must have been an agreeable relief, at least until he was captured at Lincoln in 1217.

William de Mowbray was forced by circumstances into gambling on the success of legal action. Peter de Brus, in contrast, although not entirely free from pressure, speculated more of his own volition. Between 1200 and 1207 he made offers to the King of over £2,000 for land, wardships, and franchisal rights. The surprising feature of his career is not to be found in the size of this sum but in the fact that he was successful. At least he avoided the steadily accumulating burden of debt which was the usual end to such stories. Roger de Montbegon enjoyed a similar success. His one big gamble was the purchase of his wife, for whom he offered 500 m. in 1199.[4] He had supported Count John's rebellion in 1194 and had suffered temporary loss of estate as a result. Nevertheless, when John became King, Roger was not given the

---

[1] *Complete Peerage*, ix. 370. See a charter of Alice de Gant, wife of Roger de Mowbray, dated 10 Apr. 1176, 'in the year in which the *oppida* of Thirsk and Kirkby Malzeard were laid low' (*Monasticon Anglicanum*, v. 310). The Mowbrays continued to have some kind of manor house at Thirsk (*V.C.H. North Riding of Yorks*. ii. 59–60).

[2] *Complete Peerage*, ix. 367.

[3] For details see below, pp. 172, 173.   [4] *Rot. de Ob. et Fin.*, pp. 41–42.

advancement which he might have expected.[1] He was suspected of rebellion as early as 1205.[2]

These men were an influential element in the political affairs of the northern counties and the country as a whole. Four of them, Eustace de Vesci, William de Mowbray, Roger de Montbegon, and Richard de Percy, were members of the baronial committee of Twenty-Five set up under the security clause of Magna Carta. Eustace de Vesci had married an illegitimate daughter of William the Lion of Scotland and was a baron of Scotland.[3] He was frequently employed by John as an agent in his Scottish negotiations.[4] William de Mowbray's father had accompanied Richard I on the Crusade and had died at Acre in 1191. William was with Richard in Germany in 1193 and constituted one of the pledges for the payment of his ransom.[5] When, in 1208, King John sought aid in the work of reconstructing the moats at Lancaster castle, it was to Roger de Montbegon and Robert Grelley, along with Roger, Constable of Chester, and William Butler of Warrington, as the chief men in the county, that he addressed his letters.[6] Roger de Montbegon had been in charge of the Norman castle of Tillières in 1202[7] and earlier, in 1194, had been one of the leading defenders of Nottingham castle in support of Count John.[8] Robert Grelley survived the rebellion of 1215 to witness the re-issue of the Charter of 1225 and to act as a justice of the forest in Lancashire.[9] All of these men, along with many other northern lords, had been active in the defence of Normandy, sending their knights, or going themselves, to the last campaigns of Richard and John. They had all seen broader horizons than their own shires, and, we may presume, acquired a wider set of friendships than those created by their local background. In this they were

[1] It is incorrect that the remainder of the 500 m. which he had to proffer for the recovery of his land was still demanded when John came to the throne, as has sometimes been alleged. The sum of 40 m. outstanding in 1199 was still entered on the rolls, probably in accordance with the routine procedure of the Exchequer clerks. Roger never paid any part of it and it was finally pardoned by the King in 1210 (*Pipe Roll 12 John*, p. 152).

[2] *Rot. de Ob. et Fin.*, p. 275.

[3] He held the barony of Sprouston, Roxburghshire (*Liber S. Marie de Calchou* (Bannatyne Club, 1846), pp. 24, 172–3; Cronica Monasterii de Alnewyke, B.L. Harl. MS. 692, f. 207).   [4] *Rot. Litt. Pat.*, p. 91; *Hoveden*, iv. 89.

[5] *Complete Peerage*, ix. 372–3.   [6] *Rot. Litt. Pat.*, p. 87.

[7] Ibid., p. 18.   [8] *Hoveden*, iii. 240.

[9] *Patent Rolls 1216–25*, p. 570. On the family see an excellent account by James Tait, *Medieval Manchester and the beginnings of Lancashire* (Manchester, 1904), pp. 120 ff.

typical of their class at a time when the call of the crusade or of
military, administrative, or diplomatic business was frequent.

They were joined, as the rebellion developed, by others who
did not at first resist the campaign and scutage of 1214, but who
came to be associated with them in rebellion in 1215. Foremost
among these was Robert de Ros, one of the most interesting and
enigmatic individuals in the whole group. Robert had close
associations with Eustace de Vesci, but did not openly join the
rebellion until just before Runnymede. There, he became a
member of the committee of Twenty-Five. His estates consisted
of the barony of Wark-on-Tweed in Northumberland, the barony
of Helmsley in Yorkshire, and part of the estates of the Trussebut
family, which lay mainly in Yorkshire and Lincolnshire and
which he inherited through his mother. The total service due
from these lands was just over thirteen knights.[1] In 1215 Robert
was at least forty-six.[2] He was a man of considerable administrative and military experience. For the last two years he had been
sheriff of Cumberland, and his inheritance from the Trussebuts
included land in Normandy and the bailiwick of Bonneville-sur-
Touques.[3] He was a benefactor, and at his death a creditor, of the
abbey of Rievaulx, which his ancestor, Walter Espec, had
founded.[4] At Helmsley he had built one of the finest stone keeps
in Yorkshire,[5] and at Wark he held one of the crucial defences of
the northern border. He was a close acquaintance of the King;
during the Irish campaign of 1210 he was one of John's gaming
partners.[6] Like Eustace de Vesci he had married a daughter of
William the Lion and, like Eustace, was employed in embassies
to the Scottish king.[7] At times he seems to have had considerable
influence with John. In 1213 he was one of the baronial guarantors
of the King's agreement with Stephen Langton,[8] and in 1213 and
1214 he was partly responsible for John's instatement of William
de Fors, titular count of Aumale, in his English estates.[9] At other
times we find him plunging heavily with large proffers to the
King, usually seeking rights to which he had some claim. In 1205

[1] *Early Yorks. Charters*, x. 1 ff.   [2] *Pipe Roll 2 Richard I*, p. 67.
[3] *Rot. Scacc. Norm.* i. 127; ii. lxxvii.
[4] *Cartularium abbathiae de Rievalle*, pp. 26, 200. For the loan to the abbey see
Excerpta e Rot. Fin. i. 169.   [5] *Monasticon Anglicanum*, v. 280.
[6] *Rot. de Lib.*, p. 209.
[7] *Rot. Litt. Pat.*, p. 91; *Hoveden*, iv. 140.
[8] *Rot. Litt. Pat.*, p. 98b.   [9] Ibid., pp. 104b, 122b.

his lands were seized for a time by the King and probably only restored on the surrender of his younger son as a hostage.[1]

As this suggests, he was a man of curious vacillations. Nobody, perhaps not even Robert himself, ever knew quite where he stood. Despite his administrative experience, he had an unhappy knack of allowing prisoners to escape from his custody. His first essay in this field, in 1196, cost him a term of imprisonment and an amercement of 1,200 m., when Hugh de Chaumont, a French prisoner, fled from his charge with the assistance of one of Robert's sergeants.[2] There was a similar occurrence in 1207 when one Thomas of Beckering, accused of homicide, escaped from Robert's custody. This cost Robert an amercement of 300 m.[3] Beckering, we may note, was one of Robert's fiefs and Thomas probably the son of one of his tenants.[4] Robert's reliability was clearly questionable. In 1216 he was to surrender the town and castle of Carlisle to King John's agents without a fight. His reasons for doing so are obscure. The best possible excuse for him is that he held them by the King's bail and not by an act of war and therefore felt bound to surrender on request.[5] But, if this is so, we may also note that Robert apparently purloined arms and munitions pertaining to the castle.[6] By his later thirties Robert seems to have been attracted more and more to the religious life. Here, too, his progress was one of fits and starts. In February 1206 he was planning to go to Jerusalem but never apparently went.[7] In May 1212 he took religious vows, probably in the order of the Temple, to which he made grants in some of his Yorkshire lands.[8] This, however, was a very temporary move and piety did not finally triumph until December 1226, when, a few months before his death, Robert finally took the habit as a Templar.[9] He had already founded the leper hospital of St. Thomas at Bolton in Northumberland.[10] These pious works, however, were mingled with others not so pious. Robert seems to have

[1] *Rot. Litt. Claus.* i. 24b, 31, 99; *Rot. Litt. Pat.*, p. 59b.

[2] *Early Yorks. Charters*, x. 13–14.

[3] *Curia Regis Rolls*, v. 40; *Rot. de Ob. et Fin.*, p. 413; *Pipe Roll 9 John*, p. 72. This was later pardoned (*Rot. Litt. Claus.* i. 99).   [4] *Early Yorks. Charters*, x. 79 ff.

[5] See Robert's letter in *Rot. Litt. Claus.* i. 269.

[6] *Royal Letters of Henry III*, i. 38; *Rot. Litt. Claus.* i. 399b.

[7] *Rot. Litt. Pat.*, p. 59b.

[8] Ibid., p. 92b; *Rot. Litt. Claus.* i. 116b, 117b; *Cal. Charter Rolls*, i. 16, 27.

[9] *Early Yorks. Charters*, x. 15; *Rot. Litt. Claus.* ii. 166b.

[10] *Cal. Charter Rolls*, i. 30; *Monasticon Anglicanum*, vi. 693.

used the opportunity of the civil war to commit several disseisins in Yorkshire.[1] When, in 1220, the sheriff tried to execute sentence in one of these cases, Robert's men attacked his bailiffs with bows and arrows, put them to flight, and wounded them.[2] In 1226 the Templar could look back on a varied, indeed a chequered career.

Three other prominent men committed themselves to rebellion at about the same time as Robert: John de Lacy, who, like Robert, was placed on the baronial committee; Gilbert de Gant; and Nicholas de Stuteville. John de Lacy, Constable of Chester, was still a young man who had probably only come of age in 1213. He had engaged in youthful plots against the King as far back as 1209.[3] In 1213 he acquired his lands from the King on extremely stringent terms. Since then he had proved obedient, sailing with the royal army to Poitou in 1214 and taking the Cross along with the King in March 1215. By June 1215, when he finally rebelled, most of the burdens imposed in 1213 had been paid or pardoned. For the first time he had some freedom of action. Territorially and politically the de Lacys were one of the most important families in northern England. John held a total of just over 115 fees,[4] chiefly made up of the two great honours of Pontefract and Clitheroe, and of the baronies of Widnes and Halton which he held as Constable of Chester. His father, Roger de Lacy, had been a great figure, the defender of Château Gaillard in 1204, and an influential administrator and soldier in the northern counties and the Welsh Marches. John himself ended his days in 1240 as Earl of Lincoln in right of his wife Margaret de Quenci.[5]

Gilbert de Gant was of almost equivalent territorial power. He owed the service of some sixty-nine fees to the Crown.[6] The greater part of these lay in southern Lincolnshire with the *caput* at Folkingham. Through his uncle, Gilbert had acquired a somewhat fragile claim to the earldom of Lincoln. He was to press this claim successfully with Prince Louis, who girded him with the sword of the county in 1216,[7] but failed to get any recognition

[1] *Rolls of the Justices in Eyre for Yorkshire 1218–19*, cases 137, 301, 424, 425, 889, 894.
[2] *Curia Regis Rolls*, viii. 198.
[3] S. Painter, *The Reign of King John*, pp. 253 ff. Also see below, pp. 207–8.
[4] *Pipe Roll 14 John*, p. 3.
[5] *V.C.H. Lancs.* i. 306–7.
[6] *Pipe Roll 16 John*, p. 153.
[7] *Chron. Maj.* ii. 663.

earlier from John, for there were powerful counter-claims to the earldom from Ranulf, Earl of Chester.[1] The Gant barony had suffered a certain amount of delapidation at the hands of Henry II.[2] Gilbert was enmeshed with the Jews. By 1211 King John was pressing him for the repayment of *debita Judeorum* amounting to £800 and this sorry story of heavy indebtedness continued into the next reign.[3] Gilbert had strong reasons for rebelling. He was to direct the rebels' campaign in Lincolnshire until his capture at Lincoln in 1217.

Nicholas de Stuteville's fortunes were in an equally disturbing condition. He had succeeded to his lands in 1205 at the enormous fine of 10,000 m., which had been guaranteed by the surrender of Knaresborough and Boroughbridge to the King. He never recovered from the burdens John had imposed. By the beginning of the next reign his debts at the Exchequer stood at £10,000.[4] He had leased and ultimately sold part of his estates and by 1213 was in the hands of the Jews.[5] In 1214 he was being harried by his newly widowed daughter-in-law, Sybilla de Valoignes, who was bringing a plea of dower for a third of his possessions.[6] The war was to add to rather than subtract from Nicholas's problems, for he was captured by William Marshal at Lincoln and incurred a ransom of 1,000 m. Shortly after this he died.[7] In 1215 Nicholas held the baronies of Liddel in Cumberland and Rosedale in Yorkshire. He also held eight fees of the King in a group of manors in Yorkshire, of which the most important was Cottingham, and extensive mesne tenures of the Mowbrays.[8]

The policy of these men both before and during the civil war can be followed with some exactness. Behind them were a large number of barons, on the whole less important politically, who remain much more shadowy figures. In Northumberland there were Roger Bertram of Mitford; Richard Bertram of Bothal, who was still a minor in 1215 in the custody of his mother Mabel de Cler, who also joined the rebellion;[9] James de Cauz, who held

---

[1] *Complete Peerage*, vii. 671–5. Earl Ranulf's claims were recognized in 1217 when he was created Earl of Lincoln.

[2] Henry apparently seized three fees in Leicestershire following the forfeiture of William Peverel (*Book of Fees*, pp. 1158–9).   [3] See below, pp. 167, 173.

[4] See below, p. 173.   [5] See below, pp. 170, n. 1, 239.

[6] *Curia Regis Rolls*, vii. 178; *Early Yorks. Charters*, ix. 16–17.

[7] *Early Yorks. Charters*, ix. 15.   [8] Ibid. ix. 70–83.

[9] *Pipe Roll 16 John*, p. 66; *Rot. Litt. Claus.* i. 338; Richard was of age in or before 1219 (*Pipe Roll 3 Henry III*, p. 169).

half the barony of Bolam;[1] John le Viscunt, lord of Embleton; Gilbert de Laval, lord of the barony of Black Callerton; Jordan Heron, lord of Hadstone, and Adam of Tynedale. None of these men owed the service of more than five knights to the King. Gilbert de Laval was clearly suspected as a potential rebel as early as March 1215, when he had had hostages in the hands of the King.[2] John le Viscunt also surrendered hostages who were restored to him at Runnymede.[3] It is probable that all these men had joined the rebellion by the outbreak of the civil war in the autumn of 1215 at the latest. However, there is no clear reference to some of them as rebels until 1216[4] and, in many instances, the only evidence of their rebellion is provided by letters restoring their estates at the end of the war in 1217.[5]

In Cumberland the rebels came to number Richard Gernon, the holder, in right of his wife, of half the old Morville barony of Burgh by Sands; Richard son of Adam, lord of Levington; Adam son of Odard, lord of Wigton; Robert de Vaux of Gilsland; and probably Robert de Brus of Edenhall. Of these Robert de Brus was much the most important. Still a young man in 1215, he married a daughter of Earl David of Huntingdon and was one of the most important barons of Scotland, lord of Annandale and ancestor of the Earls of Carrick. In England he held Hartlepool of his cousin, Peter, and other important estates of the bishopric of Durham. He was among the men who recovered privileges at Runnymede.[6] Richard Gernon was a nephew of William Briwerre.[7] Letters restoring his estates were made out in 1217.[8] Richard of Levington and Adam son of Odard were restored at the same time.[9] Richard lived on to become a justice in Cumberland and Westmorland in 1236.[10] Robert de Vaux is of greater interest. He had joined the rebellion by the end of January 1216,[11] but certainly did not do so before the beginning of September 1215.[12] Since

---

[1] *Book of Fees*, p. 202. [2] *Rot. Litt. Claus.* i. 192b. [3] *Rot. Litt. Pat.*, p. 144.
[4] Roger Bertram had letters of safe-conduct of 26 Jan. 1216 (*Rot. Litt. Pat.*, p. 164).
[5] For Richard Bertram see *Rot. Litt. Claus.* i. 338; for Mabel de Cler, ibid. 338b; for James de Cauz, ibid. 326; for Jordan Heron, ibid. 341; for Adam of Tynedale, ibid. 341. [6] Ibid. i. 217b.
[7] *Pipe Roll 4 John*, p. 256. [8] *Rot. Litt. Claus.* i. 374b.
[9] Ibid. i. 374–5. On Adam see the *Register of the Priory of Wetheral*, pp. 144–6 n.
[10] On Richard and his family see J. Wilson in *Ancestor*, iii (1905), 80 ff., and T. H. B. Graham in *Trans. Cumberland and Westmorland Ant. and Arch. Soc.* N.S. xii (1912), 59 ff. [11] *Rot. Litt. Claus.* i. 246b. [12] Ibid. i. 227b.

July, John had been trying to establish him as sheriff of Cumberland in the place of Robert de Ros.[1] De Vaux's uncle had been a notable sheriff of the county under Henry II and was the founder of Lanercost priory.[2] Since then the wind had not blown so fair. Robert had suffered the temporary loss of his estates and imprisonment as a result of his inability to pay the heavy amercements which King John had placed on him. In the next reign he was driven to lease his estates in order to pay his debts.

In Yorkshire and farther south rebel barons were again numerous. Maurice de Gant was included in the letters of excommunication drawn up by the papal agents in the autumn of 1215.[4] He owed the service of 12½ knights for his lands in Yorkshire and also held estates in Lincolnshire. In 1213 Maurice had married Maud, the daughter of the important Oxfordshire baron, Henry d'Oilly, taking over with the lady her father's *debita Judeorum* which totalled over £750.[5] Like his uncle, Gilbert, he was captured at Lincoln in 1217. Henry de Neville was also involved in the rebellion. In Yorkshire his only tenure-in-chief consisted of the small barony of Bulmer which owed service on just over three fees, but he also held large mesne tenures both in this county and in Lincolnshire.[6] His sister, Isabel, was married to Robert son of Meldred of Raby and Brancepeth, co. Durham, a marriage from which the Nevilles of Raby descended. In 1216 Henry already held the castle of Brancepeth.[7] He was in rebellion by February of that year and had presumably joined the movement in 1215. This was also true of Gerard de Furneval,[8] lord of Hallamshire in right of his wife, Maud de Luvetot, and tenant of both the Paynel and Tickhill baronies.[9] Although Gerard made peace with the King in January 1216[10] and acquired the custody of Bolsover castle, he was in rebellion again by the following

[1] *Rot. Litt. Pat.*, p. 150.

[2] For the relationship between the two see T. H. B. Graham in *Trans. Cumberland and Westmorland Ant. and Arch. Soc.* N.S. xi (1911), 46. Also see below, p. 202.

[3] See below, pp. 248–9.

[4] *Chron. Maj.* ii. 644.

[5] *Pipe Roll 16 John*, p. 92, *Early Yorks. Charters*, vi. 35. See *Curia Regis Rolls*, ix. 334–6, for the detailed financial arrangements between Maurice and Henry.

[6] *Complete Peerage*, ix. 491 ff.

[7] *Rot. de Ob. et Fin.*, pp. 572–3.

[8] *Rot. Litt. Pat.*, p. 162b; *Rot. Litt. Claus.* i. 245b.

[9] See *Early Yorks. Charters*, iii. 5; vi. 209; *Book of Fees*, p. 32.

[10] *Rot. Litt. Claus.* i. 245b.

September[1] and was captured at Lincoln in 1217.[2] The civil war drew in two other men whose interests were divided almost equally between Yorkshire and Lincolnshire; Robert the Chamberlain of Wickenby and Duffield, whose service amounted to 1¼ fees;[3] and Hugh Paynel, who owed service on over 11 fees for his lordship of West Rasen and Drax. Hugh was in rebellion before the close of 1215.[4]

In Lincolnshire itself, the rebellion was supported by Simon de Chauncy, who owed service on five fees centred in Walesby;[5] Thomas and William de Scotigny who together held ten fees in eastern Lindsey;[6] Norman Darcy who owed the service of twenty knights for his barony, most of which also lay in Lindsey;[7] and Richard of Sandford, lord in right of his wife of the sixteen fees which had belonged to Hugh de Bayeux.[8] Two other important rebels had interests in Lincolnshire: Oliver de Aincurt, who was still only nineteen years old in 1215, a minor in the custody of the Bishop of Norwich; and Matilda de Caux of Laxton. Oliver's lands comprised a large barony owing service on thirty-five fees centred mainly in Lindsey and Nottinghamshire.[9] The Laxton barony owed service on 12½ fees, its lands lying in Lincolnshire and eastern Nottinghamshire. Matilda and her second husband, Ralf fitz Stephen, had acquired the hereditary forestership of the counties of Nottingham and Derby. Matilda was widowed in 1202. The King then retained the custody of the forest. Matilda also surrendered Laxton, the *caput* of her barony, and other Nottinghamshire lands as the price of her continued widowhood. The civil war was to end with her recovery of both the land and the office.[10]

---

[1] *Rot. Litt. Claus.* i. 288b.

[2] *Hoveden*, iv. 190; *Gervase of Canterbury*, ii. 111. He seems to have acquired the custody of Bolsover castle during his temporary peace with the King (*Patent Rolls 1216–25*, pp. 1, 71).

[3] *Early Yorks. Charters*, i. 471; ii. vi; Miss Kathleen Major in *Registrum Antiquissimum*, vii. 224; W. H. B. Bird, *Genealogist*, N.S. xxxii (1916), 73 ff.

[4] *Rot. Litt. Pat.*, p. 162.   [5] *Book of Fees*, pp. 159–60, 179, 190.

[6] Ibid., pp. 177, 156.   [7] Ibid., pp. 156–89.

[8] *Pipe Roll 13 John*, p. 58. William of Scotigny, Norman Darcy, and Simon de Chauncy can be shown to have been in rebellion before the spring of 1216 (*Rot. Litt. Claus.* i. 249, 249b, 258). For letters restoring Robert the Chamberlain, Thomas de Scotigny, and Richard of Sanford see ibid. i. 373b, 323b, 321b.

[9] Oliver was in rebellion by Dec. 1215 (*Rot. Litt. Pat.*, pp. 162–3).

[10] For letters restoring Matilda in 1217 see *Rot. Litt. Claus.* i. 316. For an account of her and her family see Miss Kathleen Major in *Registrum Antiquissimum*, vii. 209–17.

At its height the rebellion came to include a formidable proportion of the baronage of the northern counties. In Northumberland only two barons of any consequence stood by the King. These were Hugh de Balliol, lord of Bywell and tenant of the Bishop of Durham at Barnard Castle; and Hugh de Bolebec, lord of Styford and later sheriff of the county.[1] These two were close neighbours in the Tyne valley. In Cumberland the only man of baronial status who was not fully committed to the baronial cause was William de Fors, titular count of Aumale. North of the Eden and the Tees, only Robert de Vieuxpont, lord of Westmorland and an old familiar and sheriff of the King, took the same course as Balliol and Bolebec. In the Border counties, and in Durham too, the main hope for John's cause lay not in these three loyal barons, for by themselves they would have had a rough handling, but in the demesne castles, their castellans, and the royal sheriffs and custodians.

Farther south the baronage still divided in favour of rebellion, sometimes in as overwhelming proportion as along the Border. In Kendale and northern Lancashire John might reasonably have looked for support from Gilbert fitz Reinfrey, lord of Kendal. Gilbert owed his position to the grant by Henry II of the heiress to the barony. He had given good service to both Richard and John and in 1215 he was still sheriff of Lancashire.[2] Now he rebelled, his son was captured at Rochester, and Gilbert was severely punished for his defection when the King marched north in the winter of 1215. His action had left no serious check to the power of the rebels west of the Pennines southward to the bounds of the earldom of Chester and the fief of William Butler of Warrington. Ranulf de Blundeville, Earl of Chester, was to be the chief loyalist influence here, a staunch supporter not only of the King's interest, but also of the ancient claims of his family in the honour of Lancaster.[3]

East and south of the Pennines the situation was more varied. Some areas here were still dominated by the rebels. Indeed, if the movement had any single geographic centre, it was in and around the North Yorkshire Moors. Here was concentrated the power of

---

[1] See T. H. Hunter Blair in *Archeologia Aeliana*, 4th series, xxx (1952), 23.
[2] See W. Farrer, *Lancashire Pipe Rolls and Early Charters*, pp. 395 ff.
[3] For Ranulf's claims see J. H. Round in *E.H.R.* x (1895), 87 ff., and H. A. Cronne in *T.R.H.S.* 4th series, xx (1937), 103 ff., and *E.H.R.* l (1935), 670 ff.

Vesci at Malton, Mowbray at Thirsk, Brus at Skelton and Danby, Stuteville in Rosedale, Percy around Whitby, and Ros at Helmsley. Helmsley was one of the few rebel strongholds to hold out against the King during the civil war. Elsewhere, however, the King had better opportunities. The influence of the Earl of Chester spread across the midland counties into Lincolnshire, where he was the only secular lord who could match the power of Gilbert de Gant, and northwards into Yorkshire, where he was lord of most of the honour of Richmond. His sister was married to William de Ferrers, Earl of Derby, the most powerful landlord in western Derbyshire and eastern Staffordshire, and a power also in Nottinghamshire. De Ferrers was almost as consistent in his support of the Crown as was Ranulf of Chester. Together they were the chief allies of William Marshal at the battle of Lincoln in 1217.[1]

In many areas royalist and rebel forces were fairly evenly balanced. In Yorkshire the Lacy influence in the West Riding, based on the honour of Pontefract, was faced by the power of William de Warenne around Wakefield with his castles at Sandal and Conisborough. We may hesitate to pin William de Fors to any particular allegiance, so rapid were his changes of front, but he was on the whole for John after he had deserted the Twenty-Five in the summer of 1215. He was a powerful figure in both the West and the East Ridings, for he held the honours of Skipton and Holderness; his influence extended into Cumberland, where he held Cockermouth, and into the Lincolnshire fen country south and south-west of Boston. The Fossard lands around Doncaster were also a centre of royalist influence, for the heiress was married to the Poitevin, Peter de Maulay, one of the King's chief agents who held the important castellanship of Corfe. The neighbouring lordship of Bawtry was in the hands of Robert de Vieuxpont. At Lincoln the defence of the castle was vigorously conducted by that figure of Amazonian mould, the lady Nicolaa, heiress to the de la Haye barony and widow of Gerard de Camville, a notable sheriff of the county who had suffered deprivation in the cause of Count John in the squabbles of Richard's reign.[2] In 1216, in one of John's last acts, Nicolaa and Philip Mark, the castellan and

---

[1] *Chron. Maj.* iii. 18; see also a poem on the battle of Lincoln printed by T. Wright in *Political Songs in England* (Camden Society, 1839), p. 24.

[2] Kate Norgate, *John Lackland*, pp. 31, 33; *Hoveden*, iii. 134, 241.

sheriff of Nottingham, were made joint sheriffs of Lincolnshire.[1] This association of Norman aristocrat and Poitevin *parvenu* was characteristic of the co-operation which usually existed between loyalist barons and royal bailiffs in the final critical months of the reign.

In many ways the Northerners were typical members of their class. They were great landlords and keen business men, active enclosers and improvers of their lands, owners of vast sheep flocks, benefactors and patrons of great monasteries, founders both of religious houses and of market and municipal privileges. Their interests even extended into commerce and industry. Robert de Ros exported wool and leather from the Humber and imported wine.[2] Eustace de Vesci developed Alnmouth as a licensed port. The Unfravilles had iron works established on their lands within twenty years of Richard's death, and probably earlier.[3] Peter de Brus had a hand in the iron workings in Cleveland, one of the main centres of the development of the industry at this time. The Percys had forges at Spofforth.[4] The record these men left is not simply one of the purchase of feudal privilege.

In certain matters, however, their relations with the King marked them out. By and large they were the 'outs', excluded from the spoils of office, despite a family tradition of service to the Crown in many cases, despite the earlier administrative experience which some of them enjoyed, and despite the expectancy of office which their social position gave them. In addition many of them had personal wrongs, grievances, and problems to set right. William de Mowbray, Richard de Percy, Peter de Brus, Roger de Montbegon, Robert de Ros, John de Lacy, Gilbert de Gant, Maurice de Gant, Nicholas de Stuteville, Robert de Vaux, and Matilda de Caux were all in situations, or had been parties to transactions, which, in each case, could have become a deeply rooted grievance and ultimately a *casus belli*.

On the whole the rebellion was not one in which an active and adventurous landowning class broke the fetters which the monarchy had placed on its development; only occasionally, as,

---

[1] *Rot. Litt. Pat.*, p. 199b; *Patent Rolls 1216–25*, p. 117.

[2] *Rot. Litt. Claus.* i. 149b.

[3] J. Hodgson, *History of Northumberland*, pt. iii, vol. i, p. 85.

[4] For Peter de Brus see below, p. 180. For the rest see the recent summary of the evidence by H. R. Schubert, *History of the British Iron and Steel Industry* (London, 1957), especially pp. 100 ff. The Lacys, Bolebecs, and Stutevilles were also involved.

for example, in the case of the forest law, does such an interpretation illuminate the period. It was a rebellion rather of the aggrieved, of the failures; a protest against the quasi-monopoly of privilege by the King and his friends; at its most significant a call, not to break bonds, but to impose them on the most active and experimental administrative force of the day, the monarchy. It was a rebellion of the King's debtors. Peter de Brus, Roger de Montbegon, Robert de Ros, and John de Lacy had all owed large sums to him. William de Mowbray, Gilbert de Gant, Maurice de Gant, Nicholas de Stuteville, and Robert de Vaux, not to mention lesser men, were still seriously involved at the Exchequer. Some settled their accounts with the King only by opening new ones with the Jews, with monastic houses, or with the local bishop. In 1215 they all combined to attack the royal government and exercise of patronage which, in John's hands especially, had largely contributed to their plight.

IV

THE NORTHERN KNIGHTS

IN 1215 the knights were divided; their support was sought both by the King and the rebel barons. A superficial glance at Magna Carta might suggest that most of them were staunch supporters of the rising, for it benefited them in numerous ways. Moreover, part of the baronial programme depended on the knights for its execution and simply assumed their co-operation, as in cap. 48 of the Charter, which arranged for local inquiries by juries of knights, and in the writs of 19 and 27 June, which provided for these inquiries and for the seizure of the estates of those who refused to take the oath to the Twenty-Five.[1] But this is not the whole story. Some of the concessions to the knights in Magna Carta point to possible differences with their lords, as for example over the lords' right to aids.[2] Furthermore, King John, not the barons, was the first to make an open appeal for knightly support in his famous writ summoning four knights from each shire to a council at Oxford in November 1213.[3] He too assumed that he could rely on the knights for support, even those who held their fees of the great rebel lords.[4] After all, he was their liege lord.

Many knights simply followed their lords, either against or for the King. This was sometimes clearly recognized by contemporaries. In March 1216, for example, Walter de Clifford, sheriff of Herefordshire, reported on the rebellion in his county in reply to a general request for the names of all those who had risen in arms against the King.[5] He stated, in effect, that the whole county of Hereford had followed the lead of the Bishop of Hereford, Giles de Braose. They had rebelled when he rebelled and then

---

[1] *Rot. Litt. Pat.*, pp. 180b, 145b.

[2] On this and similar issues see below, pp. 176–7.

[3] *Stubbs' Charters*, 9th edn., p. 282.

[4] 'Rogerus de Braham posuit loco suo Johannem de Braham filium suum ad faciendum domino Regi servicium quod idem Rogerus facere debet domino Regi sicut alii milites de feodo Comitis Rogeri le Bygod' (*Rot. Litt. Claus.* i. 269b). This memorandum belongs to Mar. 1216, when a number of tenants of the Bigod fee surrendered following the fall of the Bigod castle of Framlingham (ibid. i. 254b–255).

[5] *Rot. Litt. Claus.* i. 270. The inquiry was followed on 17 Apr. by orders for the disinheritance of those who continued in rebellion (ibid. 270b).

made peace when he made peace. Only three men were still at war and they were with Reginald de Braose, the son-in-law of Llewellyn of Wales.[1] They were exceptions which proved the rule, for they achieved independence of the Bishop's faction ónly because they belonged to another. De Clifford saw the rebellion as one completely dominated by the baronage. He was the son and heir of a baron, indeed of a Marcher, but there is little reason to challenge his assessment of the situation in Herefordshire, and, indeed, a similar assessment could be made of the rebellion in many other parts of the country.

The rebellion revealed broadly feudal characteristics in that the tie of tenure was still a powerful bond, strong enough in many cases to determine the actions of the tenants of the great magnates. But it did not always function in a simple manner, for in certain circumstances tenants of a barony might band together against their lord or against a custodian placed in charge as a result of escheat or wardship. Moreover, the tenurial tie was not the only social determinant of political action. Sometimes its strength must have resulted from the compactness of a particular barony, from the fact that it was reinforced by complex bonds of association and common interest which were created by families living together for generations in the same environment and atmosphere. Some-times these ties of neighbourhood worked against and even over-rode the tenurial bond, and close neighbours took an identical political line despite tenure of different lords of opposing political interests. Occasionally, too, the tenurial bond was overridden by a tie of service, and men acted contrary to tenurial influences, perhaps because they held office of the King or under some baron of whom they held few or no estates.

The chief weakness of the tenurial bond, however, lay in its multiplication. A tenant who held of several different lords might well be presented with political choices. To hold of many different lords was, in some ways, to hold of none and to enjoy a measure of political independence. Multiple tenures of this kind were one of the main breaches in the unity of the barony, especially because they were frequently held by men of considerable standing and influence whose wealth, experience, and prestige outweighed that of many of the lesser tenants-in-chief. In terms of social and

---

[1] P.R.O., Ancient Correspondence, i. 10, printed by J. G. Edwards, *Calendar of Ancient Correspondence concerning Wales*, p. 1.

political influence there was no sharp distinction between the knight and the baron. If Walter de Clifford's letter misleads at all, it is in permitting the impression that the knights were automata, whose political allegiance could be commanded, rather than men of substance, who might have to be sought and won, and who might act along their own lines in pursuit of their interests and visions. It is a significant commentary on King John's rule in the north that where such men seem to have made an independent decision it was almost invariably for rebellion, and that where the political unity of the barony broke down it was almost always because tenants of loyalist barons rebelled and only very rarely because tenants of rebel barons sided with the King. When they could choose, the knights were against rather than for King John.

For the names of the under-tenants who rose in rebellion in and after 1215 we are mainly, although not entirely, dependent on the lists of *reversi* entered on the close roll at the end of the civil war in 1217. These and other sources name roughly 450 men and women who held land solely or mainly in the northern counties or who received writs of seisin directed to sheriffs or bailiffs in the north. These are numbers large enough to whet a statistician's appetite. But the size of the sample is misleading. Many of these men were so unimportant that it is difficult to establish where they held their land and of whom. In several cases it is plainly impossible. Nothing, for example, can be made of a Ralf son of William who received writs of seisin directed to the sheriff of Lincolnshire.[1] Equally difficult is a Richard of Burton, who shared his name with at least two men who lived at this time, in Yorkshire and Lincolnshire respectively,[2] but who was restored in Nottinghamshire,[3] a county in which there were two Burtons,[4] at neither of which can an eligible Richard be traced. Out of the total of 450 names over 120 have proved intractable for reasons such as these. They remain names and nothing more.

The lists of *reversi* must not be taken at their face value. They simply give the names of those on whose behalf letters of seisin were directed to the King's sheriffs and to royal and baronial bailiffs. To obtain such letters the repentant rebel had to submit

---

[1] *Rot. Litt. Claus.* i. 333b.
[2] *Early Yorks. Charters*, ii. 458–9; v. 49; *Danelaw Documents*, p. 297.
[3] *Rot. Litt. Claus.* i. 333b.
[4] Burton Joyce and West Burton, near Gainsborough.

to the Marshal, the Justiciar, or some other great man high in
royalist counsels, such as Peter des Roches; or else to some local
royalist or churchman who had the authority to accept such
submissions.[1] On submitting the rebel had to seal a charter of
fealty. These were made out to a form supplied by the Chancery
and some of them were probably drawn up blank in the Chancery
ready for the insertion of the grantor's name and the application
of his seal.[2] The process of submission was thus one of fairly
complicated record. Nevertheless, at the time, the loyalist barons
and royal officials were acting in great haste and under considerable political pressure. They began their work of pacification
where royal influence was strongest. Thus the earlier letters of
March and April 1217 deal largely with the southern and western
counties. Many were being sent to the midland shires by the
middle of June. East Anglia was being covered by the middle of
July, but many restorations here and most of those in the northern
counties were not ordered until October and November. By this
time the lists of *reversi* entered on the close roll had become inordinately long, and the Chancery staff must have been working
at great speed. Entries on the roll were being duplicated[3] and
names badly rendered.[4] The work probably got out of hand; the
last long lists were entered on the dorse of the roll;[5] the names of
men whom we know to have been in rebellion do not appear.[6]
The lists are certainly incomplete, and probably significantly so.
The earlier ones may possibly give an accurate indication of the
extent of rebellion in the south and west, but it cannot be argued
that this is so in the case of the later ones dealing with the east or

[1] Faulkes de Breauté, Richard Marsh, the elect of Durham, and the Archbishop
of York all enjoyed such authority. See *Patent Rolls 1216–25*, pp. 59, 69, 77, 90.

[2] P.R.O., Chancery Miscellanea, 34/8, contains a collection of twenty-three such
charters. They are all in common form. In the case of no. 10, submitted by Alice
Cokerel, the name seems to have been inserted after the rest of the document had
been written.

[3] For example, Robert de Laval (*Rot. Litt. Claus.* i. 338, 339b); Robert of Glanton
(ibid. 338b, 339b).

[4] Thus William of Eslington appears as William Deslint' and as William de
Elsintun' (ibid. 338, 338b).

[5] Ibid. 373b–376b.

[6] For example, Gilbert of Notton, steward of John de Lacy (P.R.O., L.T.R.
Memoranda Roll, 2 Henry III, m. 6, 1d); Roger de Aincurt, tenant of the Aincurt
fee (*Patent Rolls 1216–25*, pp. 74, 80; *Red Book of the Exchequer*, p. 524; *Book of Fees*,
pp. 981, 989); Engelram of Boynton (*Patent Rolls 1216–25*, p. 89); Walter of Sowerby
(ibid., p. 84); Robert of Everingham (*Rot. Litt. Claus.* i. 313).

north. They are not, therefore, of great use in illustrating the geographical distribution of the opposition to King John.[1]

There is another more important difficulty. A rebel would only seek letters of seisin if he had lost estates. A rebel holding land of loyalists in a predominantly loyal county might expect to lose his lands, but in those counties where most of the barons were in rebellion their tenants might well continue in secure occupation of their estates as long as they, too, joined the movement. It seems likely, therefore, that a considerable section of the rebels would not need to submit to the procedure of pacification and would probably only do so if required or compelled by some central or local official of the Crown.[2] By the final weeks of the war the sub-mission of a baron was probably frequently taken to cover the submission of his men and tenants.[3] Thus the lists of *reversi* give an entirely false impression in that they automatically under-estimate the strength of the rebellion in just those sections of the country where it was strongest. Only twenty writs of seisin were made out in favour of non-baronial landowners in Northumber-land.[4] Westmorland, in contrast, most of which formed the great

---

[1] Compare, however, Professor Painter's view, *The Reign of King John*, p. 298.

[2] For an earlier example of a rebel coming to the peace without making a fine, see the case of John de Fretney (*Foedera*, i, pt. 1, p. 144).

[3] See letters dealing with the men of William de Warenne (*Patent Rolls 1216–25*, p. 71).

[4] William Batail (*Rot. Litt. Claus.* i. 338b); writs also addressed to Yorkshire.

Roger de Belloc (ibid. 375); also Cumberland and Westmorland.

Thomas de Burgh (ibid. 338), whose main tenures were of Richmond and Lacy in Yorkshire and Cambridgeshire (*Early Yorks. Charters*, v. 149–53; iii. 318; *Yorks. Archeological Journal*, xxx. 311–17). He also held of the Crown by cornage in Cumberland and of the Clare honour in Suffolk (ibid.).

William of Eslington (*Rot. Litt. Claus.* i. 338, 338b). Mabel de Cler, widow of Robert and mother of Richard Bertram of Bothal (ibid. 338b); also Yorkshire.

Henry of Farlington (ibid. 375, 375b); also a tenant of the Bishop of Durham (*Book of Fees*, p. 24; *Early Yorks. Charters*, ii. 280; Surtees, *History of Durham*, ii. 348).

Roger fitz Walter (*Rot. Litt. Claus.* i. 327b).

Robert of Glanton (ibid. 338b, 339b).

William of Halton (ibid. 333).

Gilbert Hansard (ibid. 340), whose chief interests lay farther south in Durham (*Book of Fees*, p. 24; *Rot. Chartarum*, p. 23), Lancashire (*V.C.H. Lancs.* i. 323), and Yorkshire (*Rot. Chartarum*, p. 23; *Early Yorks. Charters*, ii. 58–59, 279).

Gilbert de Hauville (*Rot. Litt. Claus.* i. 338b).

Robert de Laval (ibid. 338, 339b), younger son of Gilbert de Laval (*Northumber-land County History*, ix. 140, 167).

Otuel de Lisle (*Rot. Litt. Claus.* i. 333), who also had land in Lincolnshire (*Book of Fees*, pp. 190, 189). [Note continued on page 40.]

lordship of the loyalist, Robert de Vieuxpont, and which figured much less in the rebellion than did Northumberland, received sixteen writs.[1] These sixteen writs probably give a fair impression of the extent of rebellion among the gentry of Westmorland. No such assumption can be made about the twenty writs for Northumberland. The rebel barons in this county would have been weak indeed if these few writs represented all the support they were able to muster.

The picture is further complicated by geographic variations in

William de Merlay (*Rot. Litt. Claus.* i. 341).
William de Mudden (ibid. 341b).
Alice de Stuteville (ibid.), mother of Roger de Merlay.
John of Tritlington (ibid. 338b).
Marmaduke de Tweng (ibid. 374b), whose chief interests lay in Yorkshire and Lincolnshire (*Early Yorks. Charters*, ii. 14; *Yorkshire Fines 1218–31*, p. 140; *Book of Fees*, pp. 156, 71).
Ivo de Vieuxpont (*Rot. Litt. Claus.* i. 305), who also held land in Northamptonshire (*Transactions of the Cumberland and Westmorland Antiquarian and Archeological Society*, N.S. xi. 271–2; *Honors and Knights' Fees*, ii. 342).
John of Weetslade (*Rot. Litt. Claus.* i. 341b).
[1] Margaret of Brankston (*Rot. Litt. Claus.* i. 375b).
Roger de Belloc (ibid. 375); writs also addressed to Cumberland and Northumberland.
Adam and Agnes of Derwentwater (ibid. 374b); also Cumberland.
Thomas of Hastings (ibid. 322), whose main interests lay in Yorkshire (*Early Yorks. Charters*, i. 113–14, 301–4, 312; *V.C.H. North Riding*, ii. 421; *Yorkshire Fines 1218–31*, p. 141).
Hugh de Hopeshall (*Rot. Litt. Claus.* i. 334b); also Yorkshire.
John of Lowther (ibid. 374b).
John of Newbiggin (ibid. 375).
Ada de Morville (ibid. 374b); also Cumberland.
Simon of Orton (ibid. 374b).
Wigam of Sandford (ibid. 375), also Yorkshire.
Henry de Redmain (ibid. 376), whose chief estates lay in north Lancashire and Kendale (W. Greenwood, 'The Redmans of Levens', *Transactions of the Cumberland and Westmorland Antiquarian and Archeological Society*, N.S. iii. 272 ff.).
Alan of Pennington (*Rot. Litt. Claus.* i. 376), whose chief estates were held of the honour of Lancaster and of Furness abbey in Lancashire and Cumberland (*Coucher Book of Furness*, ii, pt. ii, pp. 312–13, 563–4; Nicholson and Burn, *History of Westmorland and Cumberland*, i. 154, 485; *Lancashire Final Concords*, i. 13).
Ralf de Aincurt (*Rot. Litt. Claus.* i. 244, 376; *Rot. Chartarum*, p. 221b), a tenant of the barony of Kendal (*Records of Kendale*, i. 130–1; *H.M.C., 5th Report*, p. 329b).
Eudo of Carlisle (*Rot. Litt. Claus.* i. 374b); writs also addressed to Cumberland, Yorkshire, Lincolnshire, and Norfolk. A tenant of Robert de Brus in Cumberland and Scotland (*Register of Wetheral*, pp. 146–7; *H.M.C., Drumlanrig*, i. 39; *Pipe Roll 13 John*, p. 156), of Gant in Lincolnshire (*Book of Fees*, p. 1060), and possibly of Vesci (*Early Yorks. Charters*, i. 298; ii. 128).
Hugh de Vieuxpont (*Rot. Litt. Claus.* i. 375).

the structure of the barony. A Northumbrian barony was more of a tenurial and territorial unit than its counterpart in the plain of York or Lincolnshire. The contrast should not be drawn too sharply. Not one of the more important Northumbrian baronies formed a single, compact, distinct area of land.[1] Moreover, customary laws of descent, marriage contracts, sale, and mortgage had their effect in all counties impartially. By 1242-3 there were five separate tenures *in maritagio* held directly of the Balliol barony of Bywell.[2] Such developments affected the mesne tenures just as much as the tenures-in-chief. By the time of the first adequate surveys of 1242-3 a third or more of the tenants of any one Northumbrian baron were also holding land of another lord.[3] Probably these baronies had never shown the geometric simplicity of the textbook, for the circumstances of a frontier county were not normal.[4] But, whether they had done so or not, the passage of time and social change were slowly and with certainty destroying such unity as they had possessed.

Even so, to travel south from the Border was to journey from the simple to the complex. In Northumberland the estates of all but a few outstanding men were restricted to this one county. The influences which were breaking up these baronies, especially grants *in maritagio*, rarely crossed county boundaries; the marriage market, like the shire court at which much marriage business must have been privately discussed, was localized. Farther south the picture is very different. South of the Tees baronies might be scattered over several counties. The Lacy honour, for example, extended from Yorkshire into Lincolnshire, Nottinghamshire,

[1] See the excellent map of C. H. Hunter Blair, 'Baronys and Knights of Northumberland 1166-1266', *Archeologia Aeliana*, 4th series, xxx (1952), facing p. 16. Bothal and Morpeth approached this ideal more closely than the others. Compare W. Farrer's map of the honour of Lancaster in 1212, the frontispiece to his *Lancashire Pipe Rolls and Early Charters* (Liverpool, 1902).

[2] These were held by de Laval, fitz Robert, Bertram of Mitford, Bolebec, and Unfraville (*Book of Fees*, p. 1129).

[3] This is a rough estimate based on the returns printed in the *Book of Fees*. Five of the eleven Balliol tenants listed also held land of other lords; Adam of Perington, Robert of Heddon, Peter of Gunnerton, Otuel de Lisle, and Guy de Araynes (pp. 1120-1). Four out of twelve Bolebec tenants listed also held land of others; Richard of Kimble, Sybilla of Grandon, John of Middleton, and Otuel de Lisle (pp. 1113-14). These figures exclude barons and non-knightly tenants. For the other holdings of these men see *Book of Fees*, passim.

[4] There was, for example, no subenfeoffment in 1166 in two of the Northumbrian baronies, Bothal, and the newly created fief of Roger fitz Richard at Warkworth (*Red Book of the Exchequer*, p. 442).

Northamptonshire, and Oxfordshire.[1] These baronies were more diffuse, their dependencies lying cheek by jowl with those of others. Sometimes one or more mesne tenures intervened between the actual tenant of a manor and the lord of the barony of which it formed a part. Under-tenants frequently held of different lords, some of half a dozen baronies in as many counties; it was usual rather than abnormal for barons to hold extensive tenures of other baronies. Eustace de Vesci, as lord of Alnwick, held of no other Northumbrian baron. Eustace de Vesci, as lord of Malton, held seven fees of William de Mowbray in Yorkshire and Lincolnshire,[2] seven fees of the Fossard barony,[3] and other dependencies of the honours of Tickhill[4] and Knaresborough,[5] the bishopric of Durham,[6] the barony of Gilbert de Gant in Lincolnshire,[7] and the Bigod and Stuteville lands in Yorkshire.[8]

These varying tenurial conditions probably affect the evidence on the rebellion radically. The Northumbrian tenants of a rebel lord were in many cases dependent on him alone. Not many of them held land of the two loyalists in the county, Hugh de Balliol and Hugh de Bolebec. It is highly probable, therefore, that their rebellion lies hidden behind their lord's. Once he was reinstated in 1217, their reinstatement might well be automatic. Tenants in Yorkshire and Lincolnshire, in contrast, might often hold land close to strong loyalist centres, or near to tenants of loyalist barons, or perhaps of the loyalist barons themselves. They were more likely to require official reinstatement after the war. Thus, while only twenty writs of seisin were addressed to Northumberland, nearly 150 were addressed to Lincolnshire and nearly 200 to Yorkshire. These were counties of broad and fertile acres, certainly, on which men and manors were scattered more thickly than in Northumberland. But this alone does not account for the contrast nor do the figures show that rebellion was a more popular activity in Yorkshire and Lincolnshire than it was along the Border. We may well suspect distortion when we find, for example,

[1] *Book of Fees*, pp. 190–1; *Red Book of the Exchequer*, pp. 521–2; *Early Yorks. Charters*, iii. 189, 220–1, for Lincolnshire; *Book of Fees*, p. 990, for Nottinghamshire; ibid., pp. 18, 935, for Northamptonshire; ibid., pp. 449, 453, 456, for Oxfordshire.
[2] *Book of Fees*, pp. 192, 1460.
[3] *Early Yorks. Charters*, ii. 331; *Book of Fees*, p. 1099.
[4] *Book of Fees*, p. 32.   [5] *Early Yorks. Charters*, i. 392.
[6] *Book of Fees*, pp. 24, 28; *Red Book of the Exchequer*, p. 417.
[7] *Book of Fees*, pp. 162, 165.
[8] *Early Yorks. Charters*, i. 480; ii. 358; ix. 177 ff.

that only two of the *de veteri* tenants of the Bertram barony of Mitford acquired a writ of seisin. One was John fitz Robert, who was himself a baron with interests almost equally divided between Northumberland and the eastern counties. The other was Henry of Farlington who held estates additional to his Northumbrian lands in Yorkshire and Durham.[1] The instructions for his reinstatement were sent both to Northumberland and to Yorkshire.[2]

Despite these difficulties, the general impression of the evidence is that the great rebel lords were followed by the men whom they might reasonably regard as their particular tenants almost to a man. The lists of *reversi* do not provide an adequate sample for most baronies, but for apparently accidental reasons the picture is unusually complete for the barony of William de Mowbray. A list of the fees of this barony drawn up 1224–30 names seventy-eight tenants by knight service.[3] It has been possible to trace the policy of thirty-three of them during the civil war. In thirty cases these men or their ancestors were certainly rebels. Of the remaining three, one, Roger de Camville, held eight fees of the honour.[4] At one point in the civil war he was possibly in the King's peace;[5] otherwise there is no evidence about him. In the other two cases there is greater certainty. The first, Nicholas of Yealand, who held 3½ fees of the honour,[6] was certainly loyal to the King in 1216, although his goods had been seized earlier, at the outbreak of war in May 1215.[7] He also held land of the honour of Berkeley[8] and was the brother of the Lancashire loyalist, Adam of Yealand.[9] The second, John de Cundy, only held 1/12 fee of the Lincolnshire lands of the Mowbray honour.[10] In 1216 he enjoyed enough of the royal favour to acquire letters adding to his estates, in Rutland.[11] He was a royal sergeant, engaged on the business of the King's wine and horses[12] and was employed after the peace as a messenger to Poitou[13] and as an agent of the Treasury.[14] We may doubt whether William de Mowbray ever expected support from John de Cundy. Although his tenant, he was not his satellite. From the rest he probably expected, and certainly seems to have got, the succour and aid which a feudal lord would consider his due.

[1] See above, p. 39, n. 4.
[2] *Rot. Litt. Claus.* i. 375, 375b.
[3] *Book of Fees*, pp. 1460–2.
[4] Ibid., p. 1467.
[5] *Rot. Litt. Claus.* i. 258.
[6] *Book of Fees*, p. 1460.
[7] *Rot. Litt. Claus.* i. 213b, 265b.
[8] *Rot. Litt. Claus.* 283b.
[9] *Rot. Chartarum*, p. 190b.
[10] *Book of Fees*, p. 1462.
[11] *Rot. Litt. Claus.* i. 246.
[12] Ibid. 244, 220b.
[13] Ibid. 394.
[14] Ibid. 471b.

The situation in the Mowbray barony seems to have been typical, not only of most rebel, but also of many loyalist lordships. There is not a single example of a rebel holding land of the earldom of Chester *infra Limam* except where, as in the case of the Constable, John de Lacy, he also held baronies or important mesne tenures elsewhere. Ranulf of Chester, of course, enjoyed extraordinary powers and his good fortune in Cheshire may in part have been his own work, for he had granted his own charter of liberties to the men of his earldom. Nevertheless, other loyalists in the north could draw on almost equally unanimous support. Only one rebel has been identified who held his land wholly or mainly of Nicolaa de la Haye.[1] Not one was completely or even mainly dependent on William de Ferrers, Earl of Derby. Only one of the tenants of the Balliol lands in Northumberland, Otuel de Lisle, can be placed with certainty among the rebels.[2] De Lisle also held land in Lincolnshire of the Crown and of the rebel baron, Norman Darcy,[3] in addition to Northumbrian estates held of the rebel, John fitz Robert.[4]

Here and there, there was some leakage to the rebel side, but often only where competing tenurial attractions might be expected to have had this effect. In Westmorland and Furness, for example, most of the rebels were drawn, not from the tenants of the loyalist, Robert de Vieuxpont, but from the gentry of north Lancashire, Furness, and Kendale, the most prominent of whom were Alan of Pennington and Henry de Redmain, who was one of the Rochester garrison[5] and was steward of the renegade sheriff of Lancaster, Gilbert fitz Reinfrey.[6] Only three of the sixteen known Westmorland rebels seem to have held their land solely of de Vieuxpont.[7] Farther south, where the baronies were in general more fragmentary, where multiple tenures were very common, and where, as a result, rebel influence was often pervasive, this leakage was occasionally quite marked. Five of the Yorkshire

---

[1] Adam of Buckminster (*Rot. de Ob. et Fin.*, p. 579; *Book of Fees*, p. 186).

[2] *Rot. Litt. Claus.* i. 333. For his tenure of Balliol see *Book of Fees*, p. 1121.

[3] *Book of Fees*, pp. 189, 190. [4] Ibid., p. 1124.

[5] *Rot. Litt. Claus.* i. 241b.

[6] *Records of Kendale*, i. 4; Nicholson and Burn, *History of Westmorland and Cumberland*, i. 203; W. Farrer, *Lancashire Pipe Rolls and Early Charters*, p. 441.

[7] John of Lowther, Hugh de Vieuxpont, and Simon of Orton. Hugh de Vieuxpont cannot be fitted into the Vieuxpont pedigree, but Ivo de Vieuxpont's rebellion may be relevant. Alan of Pennington held land in Orton (Nicholson and Burn, *History of Westmorland and Cumberland*, i. 485).

rebels held all or most of their lands of the Fossard barony, which had come by marriage to Peter de Maulay.¹ While Ranulf of Chester had almost unbroken support from his men of Cheshire, five or six, at least, of the Lincolnshire rebels held all or most of their land of him.² In several cases it is reasonably easy to point to possible influences at work on these men. For example, the Fossard tenant, Walter of Sowerby, was associated with Adam, parson of the Stuteville manor of Cottingham, during the civil war.³ He was in fact the steward of Nicholas de Stuteville the younger.⁴ Despite his main tenure of the Fossard fee he was clearly a Stuteville satellite. In a similar manner, the rebellion of Gilbert of Benniworth, who held six fees of the Earl of Chester in Lincolnshire, is more easily understood in the light of his association in December 1215 with Simon of Kyme and Lambert, son of Thomas of Moulton,⁵ for Simon was, and Thomas had been, prior to his capture at Rochester, among the most prominent of the rebel knights in Lincolnshire. The Benniworths, furthermore, were tenants of the Kymes.⁶

Some of the loyalist lordships are exceptional in that they had only recently come into the hands of their lords as a result of royal favour. This may have contributed to the rebellion of tenants of the Fossard fee, for Peter de Maulay only acquired it in 1214.

---

¹ John of Bulmer (*Rot. Litt. Claus.* i. 375b; *V.C.H. North Riding*, ii. 109), also a tenant of Durham (*Rot. Litt. Claus.* i. 375b) and Percy (*Early Yorks. Charters*, ii. 130).

Roger and Durand of Butterwick (*Rot. Litt. Claus.* i. 375b; *Early Yorks. Charters*, ii. 374–8).

Hugh of Langthwaite (*Rot. Litt. Claus.* i. 327b; *Early Yorks. Charters*, ii. 331–2).

Walter of Sowerby (*Patent Rolls 1216–25*, p. 84; *Early Yorks. Charters*, ii. 383, 389).

² Gilbert of Benniworth (*Rot. Litt. Claus.* i. 255b, 332), who held nine fees of the Earl (*Honors and Knights' Fees*, ii. 135–6, 179), and also two fees of Hugh Paynel (*Book of Fees*, pp. 170).

William of Benniworth, Gilbert's son (*Rot. Litt. Claus.* i. 373b; *Honors and Knights' Fees*, ii. 180).

Walter Badvent (*Rot. de Ob. et Fin.*, p. 588) who held by service of falconry of both the Earl and the King (*Book of Fees*, pp. 161, 166, 168).

Hugh de Caux (*Rot. Litt. Claus.* i. 374b; *Book of Fees*, pp. 190–1; *Honors and Knights' Fees*, ii. 206–7).

Hugh of Harrington (*Rot. Litt. Claus.* i. 290; *Honors and Knights' Fees*, ii. 88–90; *Book of Fees*, pp. 1055, 1059, 1064, 1044), who was also a tenant of Richmond and Durham (*Book of Fees*, pp. 1020, 1080).

Possibly also Martin de Braybœuf (*Rot. Litt. Claus.* i. 334; *Honors and Knights' Fees*, ii. 185–6).   ³ *Patent Rolls 1216–25*, p. 84.

⁴ *Early Yorks. Charters*, ix. 19, 124.   ⁵ *Rot. Litt. Pat.*, p. 162.

⁶ *Danelaw Documents*, pp. 33–34.

In one important instance the tenants of a barony showed a united front, but it was against, not in support of, such a newly acquired lord. This was the honour of Richmond, the Yorkshire lands of which, excepting the Constable's fee and one other dependency, had been granted to Ranulf of Chester in 1205. These estates formed a compact area in the valleys of the Ure and Swale, and apparently provided all the prerequisites for the political domination of the lord of the honour. In fact, the knightly tenants of the honour, headed by Ruald fitz Alan, the hereditary Constable, rebelled almost to a man. They were determined about it too. They lost Richmond castle in the spring of 1215, recovered it at Runnymede, rebelled again in the autumn, and only surrendered when John himself came north at the beginning of 1216. Even then most of them rebelled again, for they ultimately received letters of seisin at the end of the war.[1] Several factors were probably at work here. Richmond was in a predominantly rebel area. Ranulf of Chester's extensive interests elsewhere probably meant that he was largely an absentee. Ruald fitz Alan had not been made dependent on him in 1205 and may well have been a source of rebellious policies. He came from a family which had suffered much at the hands of the Angevins and his own relations with King John had been far from good.[2]

---

[1] For a list of these men see *Rot. Litt. Pat.*, p. 163b, where the following are named: Ruald fitz Alan, Geoffrey fitz Geoffrey, Ranulf fitz Henry, Ralf de Werbyz, John fitz Alexander, Roger of Aske, Nicholas of Garriston, Nicholas of Stapleton, and Geoffrey Colburn.

We may add:

John Coleman, who was also a tenant of Vesci (*Book of Fees*, pp. 1026, 1040, 1086, and *Early Yorks. Charters*, v. 172–4).

Ranulf fitz Robert, who held twelve fees of the honour (*Patent Rolls 1216–25*, p. 118; *Early Yorks. Charters*, v. 297–303).

Thomas Crawe (*Rot. Litt. Claus.* i. 333; *Early Yorks. Charters*, v. 241–2).

Brian fitz Alan (*Rot. Litt. Claus.* i. 338b, 339b; *Early Yorks. Charters*, v. 196–204), who also held of a mediate Hansard tenure of Durham (ibid. v. 203–4), of a mediate Vesci tenure of Knaresborough (ibid. i. 392), and of Mowbray (*Yorkshire Archeological Journal*, xxx. 283).

Conan fitz Ellis (*Rot. Litt. Claus.* i. 373b; *Early Yorks. Charters*, v. 272–5; Miss Kathleen Major, 'Conan son of Ellis, an early inhabitant of Holbeach', *Associated Architectural and Archeological Societies Reports*, xlii, pt. 1, 1 ff.).

Ranulf fitz Pagan (*Rot. Litt. Claus.* i. 251).

Roger and Thomas de Lascelles (*Rot. Litt. Claus.* i. 337b, 374b; *Early Yorks. Charters*, v. 182–5; *Book of Fees*, p. 1019).

Hugh Malebisse (*Rot. Litt. Claus.* i. 323b, 261b, 330; *Early Yorks. Charters*, v. 23, 25), who was also a tenant of Percy in Lincolnshire (*Rolls of the Justices in Eyre for Lincolnshire and Worcestershire*, case no. 101; *Book of Fees*, p. 171).

[2] See below, pp. 179, 207.

For a time Richmond had been a royal escheat, and, indeed, the Lincolnshire lands of the honour were still in the custody of the Crown in 1215. Something similar to the situation at Richmond also occurred in other parts of the country where estates had come into the Crown's hands as a result of wardship, vacancy, or escheat. In Nottinghamshire and Derbyshire, for example, most of the rebels were tenants of the honours of Tickhill or Peverel, or, less frequently, of the archbishopric of York or the bishopric of Lincoln. Peverel was an escheat of long standing, now usually administered by the sheriff of Nottingham; Tickhill had only reverted to private lordship in May 1214, when it was granted to the claimant, Ralf, Count of Eu;[1] both the archbishopric of York and the bishopric of Lincoln had been in royal custody during the Interdict. Within these estates the balance was heavily on the side of the rebellion. Of thirty-two knightly tenants of the honour of Tickhill named in a survey of 1208–13,[2] the policy of seventeen has been traced during the civil war. Four were loyal: William de Cressy,[3] William Butler of Warrington, whose chief interests lay outside Nottinghamshire, and two important agents of the King, Robert de Vieuxpont and Philip of Oldcotes. All the rest were rebels. One of them, Richard de Furneaux, made his peace in the spring of 1216 and remained loyal thereafter.[4] Elsewhere, too, tenants of escheats clearly found rebellion attractive. In Lincolnshire the rebels included a considerable number of the

---

[1] For Ralf's claim, which lay through his wife, see Hunter, *South Yorkshire*, pp. 226–7. The grant included the castle, but Ralf did not apparently get control of it. Compare *Rot. Litt. Pat.*, p. 120, and *Patent Rolls 1216–25*, p. 90. Robert de Vieuxpont had charge of it in 1217.

[2] *Book of Fees*, pp. 32–33. [3] *Rot. Litt. Claus.* i. 276b.

[4] *Rot. Litt. Pat.*, p. 164b; *Rot. Litt. Claus.* i. 276b. He was also a tenant of the honour of Lancaster (*Book of Fees*, pp. 222–3, 226). The others included five barons: Eustace de Vesci, John de Lacy, Roger de Montbegon, Neal de Luvetot, and Gerard de Furneval; and also the following:

Ralf Salvein (*Rot. Litt. Claus.* i. 312).

John de Aincurt (ibid.).

Ralf of Willoughby (ibid. i. 322b).

Robert Chaworth (ibid. i. 258b, 313).

Roger de Mauluvel (*Rot. Litt. Claus.* i. 374), on whose tenure of Tickhill see also Thoroton, *Antiquities of Nottinghamshire*, pp. 391–2. He was possibly also a tenant, by marriage, of the bishopric of Durham (*Book of Fees*, p. 27; *Pipe Roll 11 John*, p. 139).

Fulk of Markham (*Rot. Litt. Claus.* i. 375b; Thoroton, *Antiquities of Nottinghamshire*, p. 385).

Robert fitz William of Alfreton (*Rot. Litt. Pat.*, p. 163), who was also a tenant of Peverel (*Honors and Knights' Fees* i. 152).

tenants of the honour of Richmond, headed by Alexander of Pointon who had been custodian of the Lincolnshire lands of the honour[1] and, in 1213, sheriff of the county.[2] Both in Lincolnshire and farther north, in Allertonshire and between Tyne and Tees, they included tenants of the bishopric of Durham, which, like Lincoln and York, had been in the hands of royal custodians.[3]

These movements will bear a number of complementary explanations. Tenurial influences probably did something to produce them. Many Richmondshire knights, for example, also held land of the honour in Lincolnshire and must have influenced the Lincolnshire tenants to join the rebellion. Moreover, many of the great rebel magnates appear as under-tenants of these large northern honours. Gilbert de Gant held upper Swaledale of the lords of Richmond; the tenants of Durham included Eustace de

---

[1] *Rot. Litt. Claus.* i. 22. For his tenure of the honour see *Red Book of the Exchequer*, p. 179; *Rot. Chartarum*, p. 66.

[2] Alexander was also a tenant of the barony of Creon and of Maurice de Gant (*Book of Fees*, pp. 195, 1028; *Early Yorks. Charters*, vi. 164). He was captured at Rochester (*Rot. Litt. Claus.* 241b).

Other Richmond tenants in Lincolnshire were:

Conan fitz Ellis, William of Holbeach, and Lambert d'Oyri (*Rot. Litt. Claus.* i. 373b; *Rot. Litt. Pat.*, p. 177b; *Rot. Litt. Claus.* i. 324). On these three, and their connexions with Fulk d'Oyri, see below, pp. 54–55, 58–59.

Osbert fitz Neal (*Rot. Litt. Claus.* i. 264b, 376; *Early Yorks. Charters*, v. 255–7), who was also a tenant of Henry of Clinton, Gilbert de Gant, and William de Percy (*Book of Fees*, pp. 183–6, 184, 399).

Joan of Mumby (*Rot. Litt. Claus.* i. 333; *Early Yorks. Charters*, v. 269; *Rolls of the Justices in Eyre for Lincolnshire and Worcestershire*, case no. 47).

Ralf of Trehampton (*Rot. Litt. Claus.* i. 340, 341; *Book of Fees*, p. 191).

Adam Paynel (*Rot. Litt. Claus.* i. 376; *Early Yorks. Charters*, v. 55–57), who also held one fee of the Paynels of Hooton Paynel (*Early Yorks. Charters*, vi. 264–6).

[3] Gilbert Hansard (*Rot. Litt. Pat.*, p. 163b; *Rot. Litt. Claus.* i. 340). For his tenure of Durham see *Book of Fees*, p. 24. For his other holdings see below, p. 57, n. 17.

Hugh de Capella (*Rot. Litt. Claus.* i. 323; *Book of Fees*, p. 28), who was also a tenant of Tickhill and the Earl of Chester (*Rot. Litt. Claus.* i. 358b; *Book of Fees*, pp. 979, 168).

Roger Daudre (*Rot. Litt. Pat.*, p. 163b; Surtees, *History of Durham*, i. cxxvii–cxxviii).

William of Layton (*Rot. Litt. Pat.*, p. 163b; *Rot. de Ob. et Fin.*, p. 290; *Curia Regis Rolls*, iii. 108–9).

Samson de la Pomeroy (*Rot. Litt. Claus.* i. 338b; *Early Yorks. Charters*, ii. 320).

John of Romanby (*Rot. Litt. Claus.* i. 376; *Book of Fees*, p. 24).

Henry and Walter Bek (*Rot. Litt. Claus.* i. 246, 314b; *Book of Fees*, pp. 28, 159, 164, 165, 167, 173).

Philip de Coleville (*Rot. Litt. Claus.* i. 327; *Book of Fees*, p. 24).

Henry of Farlington (see above, p. 39, n. 4).

Vesci, Peter de Brus, and Richard de Percy;[1] and Eustace, John de Lacy, and Roger de Montbegon were all tenants of the Tickhill fee in Nottinghamshire and south Yorkshire.[2] Such men were bound to pull more weight than a simple knight in the affairs of a great honour. Even so, the general drift to the side of rebellion is remarkable and it occurred where the balance between the King and the rebel barons was reasonably even, as, for example, in Nottinghamshire and eastern Derbyshire. Its root cause probably lay in the harshness with which King John and his men had administered escheats and custodies. The tenants of these estates had been given good cause to rebel and they took the opportunity to do so whenever possible. These knights, at least, were not following baronial direction; they were protesting against governmental policies.

However, the rebellion of these men still bore a feudal and tenurial stamp. In protesting against the administration of royal custodians, the knights were voicing their joint interests as tenants and, indeed, giving emphasis to the reality of tenurial ties. They were showing political independence, but of a kind which derived its strength in part from tenure of the same honour and from the mutual support of the tenants. This was especially so in the case of the honour of Richmond. But the case of Richmond also illustrates some of the problems and difficulties, for here tenurial bonds were strongly reinforced by the geographic homogeneity of the Yorkshire lands of the honour and possibly by older ties and loyalties, for the area had been, and was still described as, one of the ancient Yorkshire 'scirs'.[3] In brief, behind the bond of tenure lay the bond of neighbourhood, and although they reinforced each other in the case of Richmond, this was not always so and in fact could not be so in the case of baronies with scattered tenements. Where the two influences competed, there was no certainty in any particular case which would be more powerful.

This becomes apparent if we turn to examine northern society in a time of crisis, especially during John's great campaign against the northern rebels in the winter of 1215–16. This took him north from Nottingham at Christmas as far as the Border, then south

---

[1] *Book of Fees*, pp. 24–25.　　　　　　　　　　　[2] Ibid., pp. 32–33.
[3] For a writ addressed to the knights and free-tenants of the honour of Richmond and Richmondshire see *Rot. Litt. Pat.*, p. 51.

again through Yorkshire and Lincolnshire to Stamford and Bedford in the last days of February. The effects were catastrophic.
Castles were taken or surrendered; some men were captured and
ransomed, others felt compelled to negotiate; a considerable
number, fifty or more, made their peace. If hitherto we have been
compelled to examine northern society as something static, as
lists of names to be allotted to this or that fee, at this point we can
look at it as an organism, as composed of men making important
decisions affecting their lives and possessions in the crisis produced by the King's attack. The most significant sample of these
men is to be found in those who surrendered and made peace.

These included five men of baronial rank: John de Lacy, Roger
de Montbegon, and Gerard de Furneval, who made peace early
in January;[1] Henry de Neville who returned to the King's allegiance on 14 February;[2] and Gilbert fitz Reinfrey, whose son had
recently been captured at Rochester, and who came in on 22
January.[3] It was assumed at the time that the surrender of these
tenants-in-chief involved the surrender of their men. This is most
obvious in the case of Gilbert fitz Reinfrey, who had to hand
over the children of some of his tenants, including his steward,
Henry de Redmain, as hostages for his good behaviour.[4] Occasionally the magnates were able to influence the terms on which their
men surrendered. John de Lacy, for example, was instrumental in
securing a pardon of the arrears of the fine which Eustace of
Lowdham had made for the King's peace. Eustace was recorded
as having rebelled in John's company.[5] The Lacys had a mediate
interest in Lowdham,[6] a dependency of Tickhill. Eustace had been
deputy sheriff of Nottinghamshire to Philip Mark in 1214[7] and
later enjoyed royal favour,[8] but was now clearly under John de
Lacy's patronage. There are many similar illustrations of close
relations between lord and tenant. Tenants sometimes helped to
collect their lord's ransom. Sometimes letters of safe-conduct
provided specific cover both for lords and men. Throughout the
north, the tenants of the great honours bore the defence of the

[1] *Rot. Litt. Claus.* i. 244b, 245, 245b.
[2] *Rot. de Ob. et Fin.*, pp. 572–3.   [3] Ibid., pp. 570–1.
[4] *Rot. Chartarum*, p. 221b. Henry de Redmain had already been captured at
Rochester (*Rot. Litt. Claus.* i. 241b).   [5] *Pipe Roll Society*, N.S. xxxi. 144.
[6] *Early Yorks. Charters*, iii. 190–1.
[7] *Pipe Roll 16 John*, p. 156.
[8] *Cal. Charter Rolls*, i. 212; *Book of Fees*, p. 618.

great rebel strongholds. At Belvoir, in December 1215, the castle was surrendered by the knights and sergeants of the owner, William de Albini. They were persuaded by the King's threat that their lord, who had been captured at Rochester, would be starved to death if they attempted to resist.[1] At Richmond, a week later, there was yet another surrender by the knights of an honour.[2] At the end of February Peter de Brus' castle of Skelton was surrendered by a garrison consisting largely of his tenants, including his *camerarius*, Geoffrey de la Hoge.[3] In time of war castle guard was still a vital institution.

Examples of tenurial solidarity are easy to find. So also are examples of the opposite. Indeed, King John was able to win, or force, many northern gentry to his side, even those who had the strongest bonds of tenure and service with the rebel magnates. These surrenders were numerous; most of them occurred in February 1216, but records of them were still being entered on the Fine roll more than a month after the northern campaign had ended. They came from areas where the political effects of John's campaign were likely to last longest. There were none from the Border counties and only a dozen or so from Yorkshire and Nottinghamshire. The main mass came from Lincolnshire.[4]

There is no obvious trait common to all these men. Some of them held land on or close to the line of John's march to the Border and back. For example, the men of Melton Mowbray and Thirsk, through both of which John passed, submitted to him, although their lord, William de Mowbray, was still in rebellion.[5] John threatened to burn the houses of the men of Thirsk; it is scarcely surprising that men in this predicament surrendered, whatever the policy of their lords. But many surrenders came from men who were not apparently under such direct pressure. In Lincolnshire, for example, the surrenders came not only from Kesteven, through which John marched, but from the county as a whole, even from remote districts where the King's campaign can have had no immediate military results. They seem to have been a result of a general revival of the royalist cause within the

---

[1] For the names of these men see *Rot. Litt. Pat.*, p. 162. See also J. H. Round's notes to the miscellaneous Leicestershire charters in the Belvoir collection (*H.M.C. Rutland*, iv. 7–19). For John's threat see *Chron. Maj.* ii. 638–9.

[2] *Rot. Litt. Pat.*, p. 163b.

[3] Ibid., p. 167b. For Geoffrey see *Guisborough Chartulary*, i. 10, 18, 94, 178.

[4] *Rot. de Ob. et Fin.*, pp. 568–95.   [5] Ibid., pp. 568–9.

county. This still continued for a time after John's departure, for some of the later surrenders were made not to him, but to the sheriff, Ralf Ridel, and to Brian de Lisle.[1]

The surrenders came from a wide variety of men with diverse tenurial connexions, but a considerable proportion were made by men who had close connexions with leading northern magnates who were still continuing the fight against John. The King had clearly been able to make inroads into the feudal loyalties of these men. At least three of the Yorkshire knights who surrendered were Mowbray tenants.[2] Among the Lincolnshire men were John Coleman, who was the steward of Eustace de Vesci's Lincolnshire estates and held most of his lands of the Vesci barony;[3] John of Orby, who held his land in Orby and Addlethorpe as Gilbert de Gant's constable;[4] and William of Willoughby, who held just over one fee of the Gant honour and was Gilbert's steward.[5] Seven others held their land entirely or mainly of this same honour.[6] In Lincolnshire, indeed, those who surrendered were as often tenants of rebel lords as not. They made up a wide and often apparently random selection of the Lincolnshire gentry and were drawn from a thoroughly miscellaneous collection of the Lincolnshire baronies.

[1] *Rot. de Ob. et Fin.*, pp. 588–9.

[2] Richard de Wyville, who held half a fee in Slingsby, Sledmere, and Coulton (*V.C.H. North Riding*, i. 558–9); *Kirkby's Inquest*, pp. 113–15).
Ralf Beler, who held one fee at Kettleby in Leicestershire and a fraction of a fee at Thirsk (*Book of Fees*, pp. 1461, 1467; *Early Yorks. Charters*, iii. 437–8, 452).
Walter de Percy, who held half a fee of the honour (*Early Yorks. Charters*, ii. 91; *Book of Fees*, p. 1460), but who was mainly a tenant of Brus and Percy (*Whitby Cartulary*, ii. 698–700, 13; *Early Yorks. Charters*, ii. 90–91).

[3] *Rot. Litt. Claus.* i. 146; *Book of Fees*, pp. 1026, 1086. He was also a tenant of Richmond in both Yorkshire and Cambridgeshire (*Early Yorks. Charters*, v. 172–4).

[4] *Book of Fees*, p. 162. For his other tenures of Gant see ibid., p. 187. He was also a tenant of the Tattershall and Arsic baronies in Lincolnshire (ibid., pp. 163, 171) and possibly of fitz Ralph and Peverel in Nottinghamshire and Derbyshire (ibid., p. 998; *Honors and Knights' Fees*, i. 169; *Rolls of the Justices in Eyre for Lincolnshire and Worcestershire*, case no. 853).

[5] Ibid., case no. 11; *Book of Fees*, pp. 161, 165.

[6] Simon of Driby, who was also a tenant of Tattershall (*Book of Fees*, pp. 163, 182, 166).
Alan of Pointon (ibid., p. 180).
Ralf de Brueria (ibid., p. 187).
William of Well (ibid., p. 161), who was also a tenant of Richmond in right of his wife (*Early Yorks. Charters*, v. 267–8).
Robert de Amundeville (*Book of Fees*, p. 182).
Hugh of Threekingham (ibid., p. 180).
Walter de Birthorpe (ibid., p. 1028; *Lincolnshire Final Concords*, i. 192).

This conveys the impression of knightly independence, but in certain aspects it was a very restricted and artificial kind of independence, almost entirely the product of the King's campaign. There is nothing to tell us how far the northern magnates who retreated towards the Border were prepared for the surrender of the men they left behind; they may even have seen advantages in it. Those who surrendered revolted just as easily once John's attentions had been diverted elsewhere. The five barons who had made their peace all rebelled again after the invasion of Prince Louis in the spring. The gentry took the same course when the northern rebellion revived in the spring and summer. Practically all those who surrendered reappear among the *reversi* of 1217; their submission in 1216 had been purely temporary.[1]

Thus the significance of these surrenders lies not so much in the fact that they occurred as in the manner in which they occurred. In a few cases there was probably common action among the tenants of a particular honour. In the case of Richmond, the surrender of the castle seems to have produced a reaction among all the tenants of the honour, affecting not only Richmondshire, but also Lincolnshire, where many of the Richmondshire tenants also held fees. By the end of April 1216 only two tenants of the honour of any importance were still in rebellion in Lincolnshire.[2] Similarly, common action by tenants of the Gant honour probably underlay other Lincolnshire surrenders, especially in Kesteven around the *caput* of the honour at Folkingham.

However, these two examples seem to stand alone as possible illustrations of honorial influences. Elsewhere, there is often an impression of piecemeal action. Of the men who surrendered in Nottinghamshire and Derbyshire, one, Robert of Alfreton, was in negotiation as early as 7 January[3] and finally made his peace at the end of March.[4] He was closely followed, but apparently quite separately, by Walter of Stanton and Ivo de Heriz.[5] Meanwhile Robert de Lisurs and Ralf of Cromwell had made their peace on

---

[1] See below, p. 139.
[2] Geoffrey of Saltmarsh, who held his land by bail of the King or by his gift (*Book of Fees*, pp. 173-4).
Ralf of Trehampton (*Early Yorks. Charters*, v. 242; *Book of Fees*, p. 191; *Pipe Roll 3 Henry III*, p. 131).
No surrender is recorded for either of these men.
[3] *Rot. Litt. Pat.*, p. 163.
[4] *Rot. de Ob. et Fin.*, p. 591.   [5] Ibid., p. 592.

28 February.[1] These two were both tenants of the Bishop of Lincoln and close neighbours in the valley of the Trent, north of Newark.[2] Ivo de Heriz was a tenant of the honour of Peverel, Robert of Alfreton of both Peverel and Tickhill. Some of their lands lay cheek by jowl in the area between Alfreton and Chesterfield, an area dominated by the royal castle of Bolsover,[3] and around Bakewell in the Wye and Derwent valleys.[4] But if some bond, compounded part of tenure and part of neighbourhood, was at work in these instances, no such influences are apparent in the case of Walter of Stanton, who held one fee of the honour of Lancaster, with William Butler as his mediate lord, south of the Trent at Cropwell Butler.[5]

Sometimes where there was co-ordination it was of a kind which cannot be described in terms of baronial influence or honorial organization. In the Lincolnshire fens two of the more important rebels, Thomas of Moulton and Alexander of Pointon, had already been captured at Rochester.[6] In the early months of 1216 one of Thomas's sons, Lambert, and perhaps also Simon of Kyme and Gilbert of Benniworth, were trying to negotiate his release.[7] Simon of Kyme's son, Philip, was also a prisoner, presumably captured at Rochester.[8] These must have been severe blows to the Lincolnshire rebels and to the fenland gentry in particular. By the spring most of these last had come in to the King's peace. Fulk d'Oyri of Gedney and Walter of Pinchbeck were at peace on 5 March.[9] On 7 March Conan fitz Ellis, who held land in Holbeach and Whaplode, William of Holbeach, and Lambert d'Oyri were among those who received safe-conducts,[10] and all three were admitted to the peace on 18 April.[11] There were very close connexions among these men. Conan fitz Ellis's first wife was almost certainly a d'Oyri, possibly Fulk's sister; his fourth wife, Avice, survived him to marry Alan of Moulton, son of Thomas; one of his illegitimate daughters married William

---

[1] *Rot. Litt. Claus.* i. 249b, 250.

[2] *Book of Fees*, pp. 983, 984, 992; *Red Book of the Exchequer*, pp. 375, 516.

[3] *Book of Fees*, p. 530; *Honors and Knights' Fees*, i. 156; *H.M.C. Rutland*, iv. 180; Alfreton at Alfreton, Pinxton, and Blackwell, Heriz at Tibshelf and Ogston.

[4] Ibid.; Alfreton at Eyam and Monyash; Heriz at Over Haddon.

[5] *Rot. de Ob. et Fin.*, p. 592; *Book of Fees*, pp. 206, 531.

[6] *Rot. Litt. Claus.* i. 241b. [7] *Rot. Litt. Pat.*, pp. 161b, 162.

[8] Ibid., pp. 163b, 192b. [9] Ibid., p. 168b, 169.

[10] Ibid., p. 169.

[11] Ibid., p. 177b; *Rot. de Ob. et Fin.*, pp. 593-4.

of Holbeach.[1] William of Holbeach frequently acted as an attorney for Fulk d'Oyri and in 1216 was his steward, paying in part of the fine which Fulk proffered on making peace.[2] William was also a tenant of Thomas of Moulton.[3] In making peace he surrendered his son as a guarantee both for himself and his father-in-law, Conan fitz Ellis.[4]

In all this, complex influences seem to have been at work, economic and political, tenurial and family; but neither dependence on a particular barony, nor the distribution of the fenland manors between the great baronies seem to have affected these decisions in the slightest degree. Conan fitz Ellis held his land entirely of the honour of Richmond and was a cousin of the Constable, Ruald.[5] Fulk d'Oyri was the steward, and held his chief fenland estates of William de Fors, titular Count of Aumale,[6] who, although he had been a member of the Twenty-Five and was to rebel again later, had been supporting the King since August 1215. Walter of Pinchbeck held of the barony of Creon,[7] which had come by marriage to Oliver de Vaux, who had been, and still was, in rebellion against the King.

The political independence which men of knightly rank were showing had a secure basis in wealth and administrative experience. Among the Richmondshire rebels, for example, Ruald fitz Alan held thirteen fees, and Ranulf fitz Robert of Middleham twelve. These two could probably surpass many of the smaller barons in power and influence. They would require and deserve respect, not least from the lord of the honour. They were not, however, typical of their class, for they held their lands of one single honour. The knight who held of several different lords was on the whole more characteristic and was certainly a more significant social figure. Simon of Kyme, one of the most prominent men in Lincolnshire in the reigns of Richard and John, personifies this kind of tenant. In all, he held approximately thirty fees.[8] Of these, two, at the most, were held of the Crown.[9] The rest were held of

[1] Miss Kathleen Major, loc. cit., pp. 4–5.
[2] *Rot. Litt. Pat.*, pp. 174, 178b, 179b.
[3] Miss Kathleen Major, loc. cit., pp. 5–6.
[4] *Rot. de Ob. et Fin.*, pp. 593–4; *Early Yorks. Charters*, v. 274–5.
[5] *Early Yorks. Charters*, v. 272–3. His Holbeach properties were held of a mediate Mandeville tenure. See Miss Kathleen Major, loc. cit., p. 9.
[6] *Book of Fees*, p. 193.
[7] Ibid., pp. 193, 195, 1011.
[8] *Honors and Knights' Fees*, ii. 118.   [9] Ibid. ii. 123.

twelve different baronies, ranging from the great secular baronies of Gant,[1] Chester,[2] Peverel,[3] and Mowbray,[4] and the ecclesiastical lordships of Durham[5] and Lincoln,[6] down to the small Yorkshire barony of Arches.[7] There were others who differed from Simon, if at all, only in degree; in Lincolnshire, Thomas of Moulton, his close friend and associate,[8] Alexander of Pointon,[9] Theobald Hautein,[10] and Peter de Amundeville;[11] in Yorkshire and farther north, Robert de Percy,[12] Mauger and Robert Vavassor,[13] Thomas de Burgh,[14] Adam of Staveley,[15] Thomas of Hastings,[16] and Gilbert Hansard.[17]

[1] *Honors and Knights' Fees*, ii. 125; *Book of Fees*, pp. 162, 168, 179–80.

[2] *Honors and Knights' Fees*, ii. 120; *Book of Fees*, pp. 160–1, 167–9. This included six fees held of the Roumare honour.

[3] *Honors and Knights' Fees*, i. 183–4; ii. 120.

[4] *Book of Fees*, p. 1461.

[5] Ibid., pp. 159, 161; *Red Book of the Exchequer*, p. 416.

[6] *Book of Fees*, pp. 159, 171, 176; *Honors and Knights' Fees*, ii. 120.

[7] *Early Yorks. Charters*, i. 419, 421. Simon was also a tenant of the honours of Gloucester (*Red Book of the Exchequer*, p. 610; *Book of Fees*, p. 175), Percy (ibid., p. 154), Brus (ibid., pp. 166, 1098), Aincurt (ibid., p. 178), and de la Haye (ibid., p. 192). For an excellent account of the family see Farrer in *Honors and Knights' Fees*, ii. 117–27. There is additional material in F. M. Stenton, *Danelaw Documents*.

[8] Tenant of: (*a*) The honour of Lancaster in Lincolnshire and Suffolk, in some fees with Montbegon as mediate lord (*Book of Fees*, pp. 223, 597, 1009; *V.C.H. Lancs*. i. 322). (*b*) Richmond (*Book of Fees*, pp. 195, 1005, 1007–8). (*c*) Creon (Oliver de Vaux) (*Book of Fees*, p. 193). (*d*) Roumare (Earl of Chester) (*Honors and Knights' Fees*, ii. 163). (*e*) Prior of Spalding (*Book of Fees*, p. 193).

[9] Tenant of: (*a*) Creon (Oliver de Vaux) (*Book of Fees*, pp. 195, 1028, 1002, 1089). (*b*) Richmond (*Lincolnshire Final Concords*, i. 118, 140, *Book of Fees*, p. 194, 123; *Red Book of the Exchequer*, p. 179). (*c*) Maurice of Gant (*Early Yorks. Charters*, vi. 164).

[10] Tenant of: (*a*) Gilbert de Gant (*Book of Fees*, pp. 180, 1033, 1068). (*b*) Richmond (*Early Yorks. Charters*, v. 237–8). (*c*) Creon (*Book of Fees*, pp. 1027, 1033). (*d*) Bohun (*Rotuli de Dominabus*, pp. xlvi, 47, 55).

[11] Tenant of the bishopric of Lincoln, Aumale, Gant, Darcy, and Lancaster (C. T. Clay, in *Lincolnshire Architectural and Archeological Society Reports*, iii, pt. 2, 121–2).

[12] Tenant of: (*a*) Percy (*Yorkshire Fines 1218–31*, pp. 109–10; *Cal. I.P.M.* i. 205; *Whitby Cartulary*, ii. 707–8). (*b*) Fossard (de Maulay) (*Cal. I.P.M.* i. 205; *Book of Fees*, p. 1099). (*c*) Durham (*Pipe Roll 13 John*, p. 34; *Rolls of the Justices in Eyre for Yorkshire*, case 1125). (*d*) Knaresborough (*Early Yorks. Charters*, i. 392). Robert's exact connexion with the main Percy line is uncertain, but it was probably early twelfth century at the latest (see *Complete Peerage*, x. 436, and *Whitby Cartulary*, ii. 707).

[13] Mauger a tenant of: (*a*) Lacy (*Early Yorks. Charters*, iii. 224–5, 282–3). (*b*) Archbishopric of York (*Pipe Roll 16 John*, pp. 69–70). (*c*) Mowbray (*Early Yorks. Charters*, vii. 220–1). (*d*) Aumale (ibid.). (*e*) Percy (ibid. vii. 172). Robert a tenant of: (*a*) Percy (ibid. vii. 166–9). (*b*) Aumale (ibid.).

[14] Tenant of: (*a*) Richmond (*Early Yorks. Charters*, v. 164–6). (*b*) Lacy (ibid. iii. 318; J. W. Walker in *Yorkshire Archaeological Journal*, xxx (1931), 311–14). (*c*) Clare (ibid., pp. 312–15; *Early Yorks. Charters*, v. 165). Thomas also held directly of the Crown in Cumberland (*Yorkshire Archeological Journal*, loc. cit.).

[15] Tenant of: (*a*) Knaresborough (*Pipe Roll 16 John*, p. 67; *Early Yorks. Charters*, i. 392). (*b*) Mowbray (*Three Yorkshire Assize Rolls*, pp. 7–8). (*c*) Aumale (*Early*

These men represented descents of rank and merit in which marriage into baronial families was not uncommon. Ranulf fitz Robert of Middleham's mother was Helewise, a daughter of the great Ranulf Glanville;[1] there is some evidence that he himself married a daughter of Roger Bigod, Earl of Norfolk.[2] Thomas de Burgh was the grandson, and Roger de Montbegon the son, of two sisters, daughters of Adam son of Swain.[3] Both the Amundevilles and the Hauteins had a common ancestor in Agnes Grelley,[4] a great aunt of the rebel lord of Manchester. Such men provided a living demonstration of the absence of any sharp social distinction between the knightly and the baronial. This was as true in war as it was in family relationships. When Adam of Staveley was seeking the King's peace in February 1216, he was associated with Ranulf fitz Robert of Middleham and another important Richmond tenant, Brian fitz Alan of Bedale.[5] When he finally made his peace in 1217 he came in with Roger de Montbegon, Gilbert fitz Reinfrey, and Richard de Percy.[6]

Among men of this kind there were wealthy, energetic landowners and active, daring adventurers in the no-man's-land between business and politics. Ranulf fitz Robert so exploited the sheep country of Wensleydale that the monks of Jervaulx were driven to lodge a complaint in the King's court of which the burden was that Ranulf and his men had built houses, vaccaries, and a sty, pastured 2,000 sheep and ploughed up pasture, with the effect that the monastery's rights in the forest of Wensleydale had been reduced; they claimed a loss of 500 m.[7] Farther south, in Lincolnshire, Simon of Kyme and Thomas of Moulton were

Yorks. Charters, vii. 216–19). Adam also held directly of the Crown in Cumberland (*Bks of Fees*, p. 199).

[16] Tenant of: (*a*) Vieuxpont (*Whitby Cartulary*, i. 269–73; *V.C.H. North Riding*, ii. 421–2; *H.M.C., 10th Report*, iv. 320, 322). (*b*) Archbishopric of York (*Early Yorks. Charters*, i. 113–14). Thomas also held in chief of the Crown in Yorkshire (ibid. i. 301–3, 303–4, 312).

[17] Tenant of: (*a*) Durham (*Book of Fees*, p. 24; *Rot. Chartarum*, p. 23; Surtees, *History of Durham*, iii. 316), in some cases of Vesci and Lacy mediate tenures. (*b*) Montbegon (*Rot. Chartarum*, p. 23; *V.C.H. Lancs.* i. 323). (*c*) Jordan Heron (*Rot. Chartarum*, p. 23; *Book of Fees*, p. 1112). (*d*) Brus (*Rot. Chartarum*, p. 23; *Early Yorks. Charters*, ii. 58–59. (*e*) Vesci (*Early Yorks. Charters*, ii. 279).

[1] *Early Yorks. Charters*, v. 302.   [2] Ibid. 303.
[3] Ibid. iii. 318.   [4] C. T. Clay, loc. cit., pp. 115–17.
[5] *Rot. Litt. Pat.*, p. 165b.
[6] *Patent Rolls 1216–25*, pp. 102–3.
[7] *Curia Regis Rolls*, vii. 123–4. For a settlement of the case see *Yorkshire Fines 1218–31*, pp. 2–4.

engaged in such a hectic round of business and political speculation as to leave a long, involved story of litigation and debt on a
baronial scale in the rolls of the justices and the Exchequer. As a
result, Thomas suffered imprisonment, in 1208, and Simon fell
into the hands of the Jews.[1] But both were quite unrepentant, and
success ultimately came to Thomas at least. With Simon's aid he
purchased the widow and heiresses of Richard de Lucy of Egremont for himself and his sons, thus establishing the Moultons as
barons in Cumberland. From 1219 onwards he appears frequently
as a justice in eyre. When he died in 1240 he was a respected
justice of the Bench, who had been able to complete the family
foundation of the hospital of St. John at Skirbeck,[2] and who now
merited a dignified, if not uncritical, obituary from Matthew
Paris.[3] Thomas had raised the Moulton fortunes to unexpected
heights. But he was more than a particularly lucky or skilful
speculator in the purchase of privilege. In the parts of Holland he
was probably the most active of all secular landowners in the
dyking and enclosure of the fen. His father, along with Gerard
de Camville, Fulk d'Oyri, Conan fitz Ellis, and others, had organized in 1189, at the instigation of the Prior of Spalding, a notorious
attack on the marshland property of the monks of Crowland.[4]
Later Thomas himself, according to Matthew Paris, also invaded
the rights of Crowland,[5] and he was certainly actively engaged
in draining undertakings in the area.[6] In the early years of John's
reign he became involved in very expensive litigation against

---

[1] See below, pp. 182–3, 167–8.   [2] *Complete Peerage*, ix. 401.

[3] 'In ejusdem anni aestate Thomas de Muletuna, miles in armis cum juventus ei
arridebat, et cum provectioris erat aetatis, abundans possessionibus legisque peritus
saecularis, viam universae carnis est ingressus. Hic dum fines suos cupiebat ampliare,
abbatiae Sancti Guthlaci, cujus praedia suis erant contermina, multotiens intulit
dampnum et gravamen' (*Chron. Maj.* iv. 49).

[4] *Historiae Croylandensis Continuatio*, in A. W. Fulman, *Rerum Anglicarum Scriptores*,
pp. 453 ff. The attack was apparently provoked because the men of Holland·had so
reduced the marsh to arable that they were short of pasture land; hence they turned
to the property of Crowland. The invaders consisted of 'omnes potentiores de Ellou
wapentagio praeter paucos' and the chronicler alleges that they settled 3,000 men on
Crowland Marsh. The attack led to extended litigation in the courts in Richard's
reign.

[5] See n. 3, above.

[6] In a late twelfth-century agreement with the Prior of Spalding which concerned
the advowson of the church of Weston, the Prior granted to Thomas 20 acres in
Moulton Fen beyond the outer dyke, to enlarge Thomas's holding of the Prior, the
land to be dyked and enclosed whenever the Prior, Thomas, and his men of Moulton
should undertake it (Spalding Cartulary, B.L. Add. MS. 35296, f. 377d).

Gerard de Camville and Fulk d'Oyri over their various spheres of interest in the marshland between Spalding and Tydd. Alexander of Pointon was one of Thomas's guarantors in this action, along with the Prior of Spalding, Conan fitz Ellis, and others.[1] Conan, after whom Conan's newland and Conan's marsh were probably named, was also an encloser.[2] All these fenland gentry, along with the great religious houses of the area, had a common, if sometimes conflicting, interest in these activities.

Men of Thomas of Moulton's social position were normally very experienced administrators. Thomas himself was outstanding. He acted frequently as a royal justice; both before and after 1215 he appears as a sheriff. Simon of Kyme had been sheriff of Lincolnshire from 1194 to 1197. Alexander of Pointon and Robert de Percy were also employed as sheriffs for a time, in 1213.[3] Robert Vavassor had been deputy sheriff of Lancaster in 1197; Henry de Redmain was deputy for Yorkshire from 1210 to 1212. Simon of Kyme, Alexander of Pointon, Robert de Percy, Ranulf fitz Robert, and Robert and Mauger Vavassor all appear as justices of assize or gaol delivery under John or Henry III. Any one of these men might be called to fill a wide variety of administrative posts. Several of them, too, were intimately involved in the administration of baronial estates.[4] When King John drove these men into rebellion he was not playing with nonentities. Simon of Kyme, Thomas of Moulton, Alexander of Pointon, and Ranulf fitz Robert merited inclusion in the list of rebels who were excommunicated by name.[5] Thomas of Moulton survived the rebellion to witness the reissue of the Great Charter of 1225.

The society in which the battle for Magna Carta was fought and won was not one in which the great tenants-in-chief of the Crown dominated the political scene completely. When the barons promised to give their own men the privileges which they had received from the King, this was not just a matter of pious words, nor even just a skilful move to win the gentry to their side. It was

---

[1] *Rot. Litt. Claus.* i. 83; *Rot. de Ob. et Fin.*, p. 370.

[2] See the documents printed by Miss Kathleen Major, loc. cit., pp. 16, 19, 23.

[3] See below, p. 86.

[4] Simon of Kyme, for example, was steward of Gilbert de Gant in 1202 (*Earliest Lincolnshire Assize Roll*, p. 27); Theobald Hautein was steward of Robert Grelley (*Lincolnshire Final Concords*, i. 24; P.R.O., L.T.R. Memoranda Roll, 2 Henry III, m. 7).

[5] *Chron. Maj.* ii. 643, 644.

an act recognizing social facts, and especially the impossibility of ignoring these men. A Simon of Kyme or a Thomas of Moulton could obviously not be ignored, neither could the mass of smaller men who made up the society of the English counties and provided the voluntary service on which the whole scheme of local administration depended. When Roger de Montbegon's pretensions were challenged in the county court of Nottingham in 1220, the challenge came from such a man, John of Leek, who instructed Roger with some firmness in the proper processes of waging his law.[1] When the knights of Lincolnshire made a notable appeal to Magna Carta against the operations of their sheriff in 1225, the word was given to Theobald Hautein, who proceded to lecture the sheriff and the court on the terms of the Great Charter and claim special knowledge of what was in the mind of the King and the great men who advised him. Only when Theobald was driven to bring pressure on his fellows did he point out that some of them were stewards who would have to account for their actions in this matter to their lords.[2] Men like Theobald often were stewards; this must have added to their influence; but they were men of substance first and foremost, and sometimes their operations, as, for example, in the purchase of privileges from the King, specifically excluded the county magnates.[3] The social and political independence which Mr. McFarlane has seen these men enjoying in the fifteenth century, and Professor Treharne and Mr. Denholm-Young in the middle years of the thirteenth century, was not new at these dates. It was already developing in 1215 and at this point it owed much to the way in which the knights had been called increasingly into the King's government under Henry II and his sons. Its more distant origins are not our immediate concern, but it is not perhaps necessary to derive them from some new Rise of the Gentry. Gentry were always rising; it is their habit.

[1] *Royal Letters of Henry III*, i. 102, and see above, pp. 5–6.
[2] *Curia Regis Rolls*, xii. 434–5.   [3] See *E.H.R.* lxix (1955), 20–21.

V

THE TIES OF FACTION

WHEN the men who had defended Rochester castle fell into the King's hands in December 1215, they included Thomas of Moulton and his son, Alan, Alexander of Pointon, Philip, son of Simon of Kyme, Eustace de Mortain, a tenant of the honour of Peverel in Nottinghamshire, and William of Lancaster and Henry de Redmain, the one the son and the other the steward of Gilbert fitz Reinfrey, lord of Kendal.[1] The activity of the northern rebels was not confined to their own shires. Many influences cut across county and regional boundaries, blurring the distinctive characteristics of each locality and group of rebels. The most obvious of these was the widespread distribution of the lands of many English baronies.

Several of the northern rebel lords held estates outside the northern counties.[2] In some cases these southern holdings were large. A considerable portion of the Mowbray honour lay around Melton Mowbray. Although the estates which Maurice de Gant inherited from his mother lay in the north, those he got from his father, Robert son of Robert fitz Harding, lay in Gloucestershire and Somerset; his wife was the daughter of the important Oxfordshire baron, Henry d'Oilly.[3] Just as northern lords had southern interests, so the converse was also true. The lands of the Bigod Earls of Norfolk stretched into Yorkshire, while both the Clares and the Huntingfields had Lincolnshire estates.

In some instances this situation creates insoluble problems of definition. Maurice de Gant provides an excellent instance. He was active in the development of his northern lands and was

---

[1] *Rot. Litt. Claus.* i. 241, 241b; *Rot. Litt. Pat.*, p. 163b.

[2] In addition to John de Lacy, on whom see above, pp. 41–42, Robert de Ros held land in Northamptonshire (*Book of Fees*, p. 941; *Rotuli de Dominabus*, pp. 27–28; *Rot. Litt. Claus.* i. 34), Bedfordshire (*Book of Fees*, p. 867), and possibly also in Leicestershire (*Book of Fees*, p. 633; *Cal. I.P.M.* i. 257); Robert de Vaux had estates in Somerset, Suffolk, and possibly in Norfolk (*Book of Fees*, pp. 86, 914, 1324; *Rot. Litt. Claus.* i. 183b–184); Robert Grelley's holdings spread into Norfolk and Suffolk, Rutland, and Oxfordshire (James Tait, op. cit., pp. 12–13, 124–5; *V.C.H. Lancs.* i.328–9). [3] *Early Yorks. Charters*, vi. 31–38.

involved in extensive litigation over them.[1] He also fought along-side Gilbert de Gant at Lincoln in 1217 and was captured there.[2] But both his wives had southern interests and Maurice himself, for a time, was active in the southern counties during the civil war.[3] If a Northerner on some occasions, he was clearly not on others. Oliver de Vaux is in an equally complex position. He had married Petronilla de Creon in 1211[4] and thus acquired the barony of Creon which was centred chiefly in Kesteven and Holland.[5] Despite this contact with an area in which the rebellion was power-ful and closely organized, Oliver seems to have taken no part at all in the Lincolnshire rising. Perhaps his hereditary estates and ties in Norfolk were too attractive for him to develop new roots in another county in a short period of time.

Cases like these simply create difficulties of definition. More important was the existence of a number of men whose interests and activities bridged the gap between one area or political group and another. The best illustration of this is provided by one of the committee of Twenty-Five, John fitz Robert. John's father had been an important official of the Crown who had rapidly extended his lands in Northumberland.[6] When John succeeded to these estates in 1212, they amounted to six fees and included Warkworth, Rothbury, and the barony of Whalton.[7] He held further fees in Yorkshire.[8] John spent at least part of the civil war in the north, for he was in negotiation with the King in the com-pany of William de Mowbray, Eustace de Vesci, Peter de Brus, and other leading Northerners in May 1216.[9] He also married a Balliol.[10] Nevertheless, he must have spent a great deal of time in East Anglia too. Here the family held fees of the Bigod Earls of Norfolk, a tenure derived from John's great-grandmother, who had been a Bigod. John's father had founded the abbey of Langley.

---

[1] For his market charters for Bingley, 1212, and for Irnham, 1214, see *Rot. Char-tarum*, pp. 186b, 200b. See also below, p. 68.

[2] *Hoveden*, iv. 190, where he is incorrectly given as Gilbert's brother.

[3] He witnessed a charter of Louis dated 21 Nov. 1216 during the siege of Hertford (C. Petit-Dutaillis, *Étude sur la vie et le règne de Louis VIII* (Paris, 1894), p. 511).

[4] *Pipe Roll 13 John*, p. 1.

[5] The service of the barony is given variously at 22½ and 30 fees (*Pipe Roll 13 John*, p. 58; *Book of Fees*, p. 195).

[6] C. T. Clay, 'The Ancestry of the Early Lords of Warkworth', *Archeologia Aeliana*, 4th series, xxxii (1954), 65–71; *Rot. Chartarum*, pp. 116b, 133, 143.

[7] *Rot. Chartarum*, p. 187b; *Book of Fees*, p. 553.   [8] *Book of Fees*, p. 550.

[9] See below, p. 136, n. 8.   [10] Dugdale, *Baronage*, i. 108.

He himself was a half-brother of Roger de Cressy. He held fees of the Mandeville honour, and the manor of Clavering of the honour of Rayleigh;[1] from Clavering John's descendants derived their family name. These eastern connexions were so strong that both J. H. Round and Sir Maurice Powicke classed John with the rebels of the eastern and home counties.[2] Indeed, in 1213 and 1215 he was sheriff of Norfolk and Suffolk. But he was also sheriff of Northumberland from 1224 to 1227. As in the case of his father, Robert fitz Roger, who was also sheriff of these counties on different occasions, there seems to have been a genuine division of interest between the north and East Anglia.

Divided estates were not the only influence in dividing men's interests and activities. David, Earl of Huntingdon, had only secondary interests in northern England. But he was the brother of William the Lion of Scotland and had married Maud, sister of Ranulf of Chester. He was now an old man who had been knighted by Henry II as far back as 1170; he had carried one of the three swords at Richard's coronation, and helped to suppress Count John and his supporters in 1194. He was one of those Scots who found a southern climate welcome, for he died at Yardley in 1219 and was buried in Sawtry abbey.[3] In John's reign he was associated with Eustace de Vesci and Robert de Ros on Scottish embassies, and in 1212 the King had very strong suspicions that he was a party to the treasonable conspiracy of Eustace de Vesci and Robert fitz Walter.[4] If so, this was his last real political fling for, although apparently a rebel, he played no outstanding part in the civil war.

William de Albini of Belvoir was a more important and active figure. A member of the Twenty-Five and the commander of the baronial defence of Rochester, William held his chief estates in the vale of Belvoir and the surrounding country. He was also lord of nearly nine fees in Lincolnshire,[5] and of enfeoffed properties in Yorkshire.[6] His first wife was a sister of Richard de Unfraville, and his second was Agatha Trussebut, sister of Rose Trussebut, mother of Robert de Ros.[7] Robert and William, supported by

---

[1] *Book of Fees*, pp. 1462, 941.
[2] J. H. Round, 'King John and Robert fitz Walter', *E.H.R.* xix. 710; F. M. Powicke, *Stephen Langton*, pp. 127, 211.
[3] *Complete Peerage*, vi. 646–7.   [4] See below, p. 83.
[5] *Book of Fees*, pp. 155, 178, 182, 184, 185, 188, 191.
[6] *Early Yorks. Charters*, i. 460, 462.   [7] Ibid. i. 461.

Eustace de Vesci, co-operated in preserving the Trussebut estates to themselves by guaranteeing the price of the continued widow-hood of yet a third Trussebut sister, Hilary.[1] The lands which William held in right of his wife all lay in Yorkshire and Lincoln-shire.[2] William was acting as one of the bailiffs of the Lincolnshire ports in 1211 and 1212[3] and, according to the Barnwell chronicler, was made sheriff of Lincolnshire by the rebels in 1215.[4] His northern connexions were therefore very strong, and it may have been his influence in Lincolnshire which brought Thomas of Moulton and others south to share his fate at Rochester.[5] But apart from this, there is little evidence of his acting alongside the leading northern rebels. He had other associations. In 1203, for example, he was acting on Robert fitz Walter's behalf, selling and pledging fitz Walter's estates to raise his ransom after the fall of Vaudreuil.[6] He does not seem to have joined the rebellion until just before Runnymede.[7] Thereafter the rebel leaders seem to have been peculiarly concerned to ensure his continued support,[8] and he certainly justified their expectations by his energetic defence of Rochester. After King John's death he fined for his ransom and was released from his captivity at Corfe. He was given the custody of Sleaford castle and fought on the royalist side at Lincoln in 1217.[9]

The spread of territorial interests was only one of the factors which confused the Northerners with other groups. The political inconsistency, if not inconstancy, of certain individuals, had similar effects. Although King John retained the loyalty and support of his old friends and officials to a remarkable degree in the last years of the reign, there was some leakage to the ranks of the rebels, or at

---

[1] The three of them pledged 100 m. each of the fine of 300 m. and 2 palfreys made by Hilary, widow of Robert de Buillers, that she should not be compelled to marry (*Pipe Roll 5 John*, p. 104).   [2] *Early Yorks. Charters*, x. 25, 63.

[3] *Pipe Roll 13 John*, p. 59; *Pipe Roll 14 John*, p. 4; *Rot. Litt. Claus.* i. 127b.

[4] *Walt. Cov.* ii. 224.

[5] In 1211 and 1212 William was associated with Brian de Lisle and Gilbert fitz Reinfrey, father of William of Lancaster, as a custodian of the ports of Lincolnshire (*Pipe Roll 13 John*, p. 59; *Pipe Roll 14 John*, p. 4). William helped to pay the ransom which Thomas of Moulton incurred after his capture at Rochester (*Patent Rolls 1216–25*, p. 69), and had custody of Moulton's lands in June and Aug. 1217, perhaps as security for his assistance (ibid., p. 85; *Rot. Litt. Claus.* i. 313b). Prior to 17 Mar. 1217 William also seems to have had a wartime interest in the lands of Simon of Kyme (*Rot. Litt. Claus.* i. 301). Eustace de Mortain, another of those captured at Rochester, was a close neighbour of William de Albini for he held land at Gamston in right of the custody of the heir of Ranulf de Mersey (*Book of Fees*, 231).

[6] *Rot. Litt. Pat.*, p. 37b.   [7] See below, p. 107.

[8] *Chron. Maj.* ii. 614–5   [9] Ibid. iii. 6, 18.

least in some cases a lack of demonstrative eagerness, especially at the nadir of the King's fortunes after the landing of Prince Louis.

In the north two men stood out in this respect. One was Gilbert fitz Reinfrey, who owed his position to Henry II and his sons, for he was lord of Kendal by marriage to the heiress. He had been an extremely unpopular sheriff of Yorkshire in the years before 1213[1] and was still sheriff of Lancaster in 1215. Gilbert only joined the movement very late, probably not before Easter 1215.[2] He surrendered to the King in January 1216, probably because of the capture of his eldest son at Rochester.[3] However, he rebelled again and, when he finally made his peace in 1217, he came in with some of the most active of the rebels of north Lancashire and Craven.[4] Gilbert had clearly changed his spots and he suffered severely in the punishment exacted by King John.[5]

This was done with much greater success, indeed repeatedly, by William de Fors, titular Count of Aumale. In 1215 William was lord of Cockermouth and the honours of Skipton and Holderness. Although he owed much to the King's grace, he became a member of the Twenty-Five. By the middle of August 1215 he was working with the King once more.[6] He then joined the rebels again when Prince Louis landed in 1216, but returned to the Angevin allegiance before the end of the year.[7] This mercurial behaviour probably gave him a reputation of unreliability and bad faith which can have done him little good when his attempts to retain Castle Bytham and other lands which he had seized drove him into a desperate and solitary rebellion in 1220–1. In 1214 William had married a daughter of Richard de Muntfichet, another member of the Twenty-Five.[8] He was also a close friend of Robert de Ros, who held fees of his lands both in Holderness and Lincolnshire.[9] It was at Robert's request that William was permitted to come to England in 1213 and at his persuasion that

---

[1] See below, pp. 86, 229.

[2] As late as 2 Apr. 1215 a payment to him was ordered for fortifying his castles and holding them against the King's enemies (*Rot. Litt. Claus.* i. 193).

[3] See above, p. 61.

[4] Roger de Montbegon, Richard de Percy, and Adam of Staveley (*Patent Rolls 1216–25*, pp. 102–3).

[5] See below, pp. 137, 228.   [6] *Rot. Litt. Pat.*, p. 152.

[7] *Walt. Cov.* ii. 231; *Histoire des ducs de Normandie*, p. 174; *Rot. Litt. Pat.*, p. 199b; *Rot. Litt. Claus.* i. 295; *Patent Rolls 1216–25*, pp. 13–14.

[8] *Complete Peerage*, i. 355.

[9] *Early Yorks. Charters*, iii. 34; *Kirkby's Inquest*, p. 74; *Book of Fees*, p. 185.

William's claim to English estates was recognized.[1] In return, William seems to have done both himself and perhaps also Robert a good turn by acquiring the custody of Robert's lands when he suffered seizure during the civil war.[2] He must have been in the councils of the northern rebels on more than one occasion. He had every opportunity to betray such secrets as they had.

In the face of such political behaviour, it becomes extremely difficult to think of the rebels as a distinct, coherent group. It is even more difficult to imagine a particular set of rebels as such a group. What, for example, bound the Northerners together? Was there something which brought Peter de Brus closer to Eustace de Vesci than either was to Robert fitz Walter of Dunmow or Roger Bigod, Earl of Norfolk? Did Richard de Percy feel stronger ties with the northern renegade, Gilbert fitz Reinfrey, than with the East Anglian rebel, William of Huntingfield, or with William de Albini in the midlands? Did Thomas of Moulton and the *Hoylandenses* have any fellow feeling for the rebellious gentry of Nottinghamshire and Derbyshire and, if so, was this bond anything other than what they might feel for any rebel in no matter what part of the country? Were the differences between the Northerners as a whole and the rest of the rebels any sharper or wider than the differences between local groups within the north, or indeed within any other part of the country? Was there an almost endless series of specific, and in the last resort individual, differences and nothing more, or were there in addition generic differences and, in particular a genus 'Northerner' possessing common and distinct characteristics?

The evidence at this point is extremely difficult to use. It is easy, for example, to point to the numerous family ties between the leading rebels of the northern counties. Robert de Ros and Eustace de Vesci were both sons-in-law of William the Lion. Eustace's mother was a Stuteville, sister of Nicholas de Stuteville.[3] Nicholas's wife was also the widow of Robert de Gant and the mother of Gilbert de Gant.[4] Her mother, Sybilla de Valoignes, was grandmother not only to Gilbert, but also to Robert de Ros, and had also married the grandfather of Richard de Percy.[5]

---

[1] *Rot. Litt. Pat.*, pp. 104b, 122b.
[2] See letters of Jan., Mar., and Apr. 1216 (*Rot. Litt. Claus.* i. 246b, 256, 263b).
[3] *Early Yorks. Charters*, iii. 199; ix. 1. 7–8.
[4] Ibid. i. 461; ii. 433.   [5] Ibid. i. 461; *Complete Peerage*, x. 441 ff.

Robert de Ros's wife had earlier married a Brus.[1] The chain was endless. It tied the northern barons first to each other and then, less directly, to noble families in other parts of the land. Similar relations bound the lesser men. Even to compose pedigrees is to select and so convey a false impression. It is also hazardous to argue that any one kind of family tie was necessarily more significant politically than another.

Considerable importance has sometimes been attached to connexions of this kind,[2] but the dangers involved have been clearly indicated by Sir Maurice Powicke.[3] A family tie is in itself of little value as evidence. Indeed the Barnwell chronicler emphasized the fact that families were divided internally in 1215.[4] There were some notable instances of this. The Marshal stayed with the King; his son joined the rebels. If there was some possibility of collusion between the two in this case,[5] this was certainly not so between the Percy uncle and nephew, Richard and William, the former of whom was among the leaders of the northern rebellion, while the latter, a ward of William Briwerre, stayed loyal to the King. Here the issue was the possession of the Percy honour, and the nephew profited temporarily from his uncle's rebellion by obtaining a grant of his portion of the estates.[6] The Vieuxpont family was similarly divided. Robert, lord of Westmorland, remained loyal; his brother Ivo, who was probably the older of the two, rebelled. In this case it may be that Ivo felt that he had the better claim to the lordship of Westmorland, which Robert now enjoyed by the King's gift.[7]

In these cases the civil war coincided with family feuds. They were probably exceptional, and the existence of a few such prominent instances may be all that lies behind the remarks of the

---

[1] *Early Yorks. Charters*, ii. 15.

[2] See J. H. Round, in *E.H.R.* xix (1904), 707 ff., also S. Painter, *The Reign of King John*, pp. 291–3.   [3] F. M. Powicke, *Stephen Langton*, p. 212.

[4] *Walt. Cov.* ii. 220.   [5] See S. Painter, *William Marshal*, pp. 185–6.

[6] See above, pp. 21–22.

[7] For the Vieuxpont claim to Westmorland see below, pp. 220–1. Dodsworth makes Ivo the elder brother (Bodleian Library, Dodsworth MS. 33, f. 55), but a pedigree of the family drawn up by Richard Gascoigne reverses the order (Dodsworth MS. 105, f. 122). Ivo apparently acquired the paternal inheritance of the family in Northumberland and Northamptonshire (*Trans. Cumberland and Westmorland Antiquarian Archeological Society*, N.S. xi. 271, 272; *Honors and Knights' Fees*, ii. 342). This is more convincing evidence of Ivo's seniority than that which suggests the opposite, namely that Robert acquired the continental possessions of the Norman branch of the family which sided with Philip Augustus.

Barnwell writer. In contrast, some relationships, especially when they included grants of land *in maritagio*, clearly brought families into closer touch. Robert Grelley's fees held of John de Lacy derived from his grandmother, Maud, who was the daughter of William son of Nigel, the first Norman Constable of Chester.[1] Roger de Montbegon's two fees held of de Lacy derived from his father's marriage to Matilda, one of the daughters and coheiresses of Adam son of Swain, a twelfth-century tenant of the Lacy honour.[2] Peter de Brus's family likewise held fees of the Mowbrays as a result of a twelfth-century marriage between a Brus and a Mowbray tenant.[3] Family ties had been, and still were, remoulding the tenurial structure of northern society.

The results, however, were not always the same. Sometimes those who benefited from the marriage of heiresses combined to preserve the spoils. Thus the Trussebut marriages led William de Albini and Robert de Ros into co-operative action.[4] But families could also be brought into too close a contact and become involved in lengthy and expensive litigation over the division of the spoils of some long past, but not forgotten, marriage, or the respective portions of well-endowed coheiresses. Examples of such actions are a commonplace of the legal records. Some must have acquired the status of *causes majeures* in the gossip of northern society. Maurice de Gant, Gilbert de Gant, and Nicholas de Stuteville, for example, all had common connexions in Robert de Gant, who died in 1191, or in his second wife and widow, Gunnora. Maurice was Robert's grandson of his first wife; Gilbert his son of his second wife; Nicholas the husband of this second wife. From 1200 onwards Maurice pressed claims to the manor of Saltby, first against Nicholas and Gunnora, and then against Gilbert. It was not until 1209, after a duel had been waged between Maurice and Gilbert and the champions had duly appeared, that the matter was at last settled by agreement.[5] Maurice's claim originated in his grandmother, Alice Paynel, Robert de Gant's first wife. The pursuit of other of her possessions also led him into a large number of subsidiary actions between 1208 and 1211.[6] An equally important and even more lengthy action was

---

[1] James Tait, op. cit., pp. 134–5.   [2] *Early Yorks. Charters*, iii. 317–19.
[3] *Early Yorks. Charters*, i. 415, ii. 15.   [4] See above, pp. 63–64.
[5] Gilbert quitclaimed Saltby to Maurice and Maurice confirmed it to Stephen de Gant, Gilbert's brother. For details see *Early Yorks. Charters*, vi. 36, 150–1.
[6] *Curia Regis Rolls*, v, vi, *passim*.

being fought in Cumberland over the tenure of the baronies of Allerdale and Copeland among the heirs general of William son of Duncan and Alice de Romilly. Here the main protagonists were Baldwin de Béthune, William de Fors, Reginald and Richard de Lucy, and Robert de Courtenay; from 1213 Thomas of Moulton and his sons also developed an interest in some of the estates in question. Claim and counter-claim absorbed the time of the King's justices and depleted the resources of the participants from 1199 on to beyond 1225, when, despite several attempts at agreement, some of the principals were still vigorously quarrelling.[1] By this time the case had engaged the interest of a succession of husbands of the various heiresses and had been passed down from father to son.

In default of supporting evidence, a family tie should never be assumed to create a political alliance. All that can be argued is that where political alliances already existed, then they might be strengthened by family ties. This is an assumption in nine cases out of ten, but nevertheless a reasonable one. Further, the most important family tie politically, marriage, was itself a product of political and social circumstances. To emphasize its importance simply leads back in the end to the way society was organized. The great men held estates of each other. They worked together in governing and defending the country. They were brought together in musters, the ceremonial gatherings of the court, the regular meetings of the shire, and the royal progresses throughout the land. The knights served alongside each other as coroners, foresters, jurors, and on the multitude of commissions which the government of the Angevins had called into being. More traditionally, they and the great men of the country combined to endow and enrich the local monasteries. Every surviving cartulary is a witness to the members and the tenantry of the founding family, along with their friends and neighbours. Men of the same class living in the same part of the country were automatically brought together. Co-operation in politics and intermarriage both came back to this common origin. The effect was to produce a society of more or less discrete groups, of which the basis was partly social, partly administrative, and partly tenurial. Sometimes these groups operated as political units too: the gentry of Holland, the knights of Richmond, the men of the Kent and Lune estuaries, or the tenants of the great Nottinghamshire escheats and wardships.

[1] *Early Yorks. Charters*, vii. 13-22.

To argue that there was also in the north a larger grouping, the Northerners, first requires the projection of these arguments on a wider screen. Just as gentry from different parts of the shire met in the county court, so barons from different northern counties met when the King travelled north or on some other great occasion. They were therefore more likely to build up close ties among themselves than with other magnates living in the south, whom they were bound to see less frequently; it was more usual for an important northern baron to marry a wife from the northern counties than it was for him to seek one farther south. Proximity counted. But these factors by themselves are insufficient to explain what happened in 1215. They could not by themselves create some overriding political feeling throughout the north which might subordinate the separate interests of local groups; they simply created circumstances in which such feelings and policies could develop and spread. These feelings and policies never swamped the north completely. They were always to some extent in competition with the desire of particular groups to go their separate ways, and their impact must always have been lessened by geographic disunity and bad communication. They were never so potent, so attractive, or so deeply founded in the *genius loci* as to wean more than a handful of the King's friends and agents in the northern counties to the side of the rebels.

The evidence thus presents a curious picture of political action at different levels. The chroniclers used the term 'Northerner' quite easily. When they named Northerners they placed barons of Yorkshire and Northumberland alongside those of Lancashire, and showed no hesitation in applying the label to a Lincolnshire figure like Gilbert de Gant. On the other hand, it is perfectly clear that Gilbert de Gant's chief activity during the rebellion was confined to his own county. It seems unlikely, too, that his continual attempts to seize Lincoln castle ever received any significant support from men whose interests lay mainly outside Lincolnshire, except in the final disastrous campaign of 1217. There are other illustrations of this fragmentation of policy. The barons of Northumberland acknowledged Alexander II's lordship of the Border counties on 22 October 1215, the barons of Yorkshire not until 11 January 1216, probably only as they were fleeing north from the wrath of King John.[1] During this campaign especially,

[1] See below, p. 131.

groups and individuals tended to go their own way in the face of his attack. It may be argued that all this occurred in time of war, when men were seeing to the defence of their own castles and protection of their own estates; war necessarily localized affairs. But even so, it is clearly unwise to pretend that the northern group was either monolithic in composition or single-minded in policy.

Yet it was still a group which was compounded of policies and loyalties capable of overriding the local differences within the north. It would be quite impossible, for example, to make geographical or tenurial distinctions between those northern tenants-in-chief who led the resistance to the Poitevin scutage and those who only seem to have joined the movement later. The first group, the recalcitrants, held estates widely scattered throughout the north. Vesci, Mowbray, Percy, and Brus had their main estates in Yorkshire. Grelley's and Montbegon's interests were centred in Lancashire. Vesci was a dominant figure in Northumberland, Mowbray an important one in Leicestershire. All of them held lands of varying importance in Lincolnshire. Those who followed them into rebellion later had equally scattered possessions. John de Lacy's interests stretched from Cheshire and Lancashire in the west to Pontefract in Yorkshire and then into Nottinghamshire, Lincolnshire, and farther south. Robert de Ros had lands in Northumberland, Yorkshire, and Lincolnshire in addition to southern estates. Nicholas de Stuteville's possessions ran into Cumberland, Westmorland, Lincolnshire, and other counties, in addition to his chief holdings in Yorkshire. Gilbert de Gant, although mainly interested in Lincolnshire, was lord of eleven fees around Filey and Bridlington, where his family had founded the priory, and of four fees held of the honour of Richmond in Swaledale. Tenurially the two groups were closely interlocked. Eustace de Vesci held estates of the apparently more moderate Gilbert de Gant[1] and Nicholas de Stuteville.[2] Simon of Kyme held land of the apparently more radical Peter de Brus and Richard de Percy.[3] Stuteville held of Mowbray;[4] Montbegon and Grelley of Lacy.[5]

In part the Northerners were the product of the rebellion and the civil war; a political crisis and armed action necessarily canalized

[1] *Books of Fees*, pp. 162, 165. [2] *Early Yorks. Charters*, ii. 358; ix. 177 ff.
[3] See above, p. 56, n. 7. [4] Ibid. ix. 200 ff.
[5] See above, p. 68.

policy and opinion. But in part, too, the rebellion and civil war were the conscious creation of the Northerners. The common bond between them was more than an accidental, temporary alliance of a time of chaos. It had been forged before the war started, partly of the local ties already existing in northern society, but partly also of the common relations of the northern aristocracy with the King's government. These were most obvious in the financial relations of the baronage and gentry with the King and his Exchequer. Here, groups were being formed which were distinctly northern in composition, which were more than local groupings in that they covered the whole or most of the north, and which were political in character in that they excluded all or most of the King's officials and close supporters. That evidence which touches most closely on the financial exploitation of the county families by the Crown is also that which most clearly illustrates the incipient community of action of these families. This is highly significant. It is also what we might expect, for the Northerners' characteristics, as contemporaries saw them, were their recalcitrance and determination either to control King John or be rid of him.

It is well known that John's government led to the imposition of large monetary charges of many different kinds on the wealthier men of the land. When this occurred the debtor was frequently expected to provide some kind of security for repayment. Usually this guarantee was provided by personal pledges: by the debtor's tenants or by interested parties, or simply by his friends, who each took responsibility for part of the principal's debt. These procedures were important. A promise might not be accepted as remitting the King's wrath or as purchasing some privilege until these guarantees had been provided. Local officials of the King might be asked to investigate the ability of the pledges to pay should the principal fail.[1] The fine rolls, and more rarely the pipe rolls, were littered with long lists of the names of such pledges.[2] A baronial or knightly debtor, seeking guarantors among his friends, must have been a regular feature of the local scene, especially of the shire courts.[3]

---

[1] See the letters of Matthew Mantel to the King (*Rot. de Ob. et Fin.*, p. 445).

[2] For example, the dorse of the fine roll of 9 John (ibid., pp. 443–64).

[3] For the seeking and presenting of pledges at the shire court see the proffer of Peter de Brus (ibid., p. 110).

The resulting lists of pledges do not always provide a rigid forecast of the lines of political division which became visible in 1215. Much depended on who the debtor was, how the debt was incurred, how big it was, and who was interested in the proffer which usually initiated it. Nevertheless, the support which northern landowners were giving to each other in financial matters stands out quite clearly, especially towards the end of the reign. When Roger de Montbegon proffered 500 m. for his wife in 1200, Eustace de Vesci stood as pledge for 300 m.[1] When Peter de Brus offered £1,000 for the manor and forest of Danby in 1201, pledges were taken immediately for the payment of the first 700 m. Eustace de Vesci and Robert de Ros guaranteed 200 m. each and they, along with William de Stuteville, then sheriff of Yorkshire, undertook that Peter would find other pledges for the remainder of the debt.[2] Vesci and de Ros also acted together along with William de Albini to preserve the widowhood of Hilary Trussebut.[3] Similar mutual support is still quite apparent lower down the social scale. When, in 1206, William de Lande, a tenant of the Darcy barony,[4] offered 50 m. and a palfrey for the hand of Joanna, widow of Thomas and mother of Norman Darcy, his pledges were: Eustace de Vesci; John Malherbe, half-brother of Roger de Montbegon and uncle of Olivia, wife of Hervey, the head of the junior Darcy line;[5] Philip fitz John, a knight of William de Mowbray,[6] who received the writs executing Magna Carta in Yorkshire[7] and was excommunicated by name in 1215;[8] and a certain Robert of Kent.[9] Norman Darcy and William de Lande made peace simultaneously in 1217.[10] When the later rebel, Ralf of Willoughby, tenant of the archbishopric of York and the honour of Tickhill in Nottinghamshire, and of the Gant honour in Lincolnshire,[11] offered 100 m. and two palfreys in 1207 for a stay of judgement, he was backed by five other future rebels, namely, Simon of Kyme, Thomas of Moulton, Simon de Chauncy,

---

[1] *Pipe Roll 2 John*, p. 110.   [2] *Rot. de Ob. et Fin.*, pp. 109–10.

[3] See above, pp. 63–64.

[4] *Book of Fees*, p. 156. He also held fees of Tattershall and Camville (de la Haye) (ibid., pp. 166, 179).

[5] For these connexions see *Early Yorks. Charters*, iii. 257, 318; v. 292; *Yorkshire Archeological Journal*, xxix. 295.   [6] *Book of Fees*, p. 1461; *Rot. de Lib.*, p. 45.

[7] *Rot. Litt. Pat.*, p. 180b.   [8] *Chron. Maj.* ii. 644.

[9] *Rot. de Ob. et Fin.*, p. 349.   [10] *Rot. Litt. Claus.* i. 322b.

[11] *Red Book of the Exchequer*, pp. 491, 593; *Rot. de Ob. et Fin.*, p. 418; *Book of Fees*, pp. 33, 179.

Alexander of Pointon, and Walter of Birthorpe, who was another Gant tenant;[1] three others also assisted.[2] Simon of Kyme's activities were widespread. In 1206 he supported Norman Darcy's proffer for the Darcy barony.[3] In 1213 he guaranteed the whole 1,000 m. which Thomas of Moulton offered for the custody of the daughters of Richard de Lucy of Egremont.[4] When Thomas purchased the shrievalty of Lincolnshire in 1205 for 500 m. and 5 palfreys, Simon headed the list of pledges with the guarantee of 100 m., a figure which only Gilbert of Benniworth among the remaining pledges could equal. This list included not only these two future rebels, but also William Picot, Gerard of Howell, Henry de Neville, Peter of Beckering, Walter of Pinchbeck, Richard of Sandford, Robert of Bassingham, and John Coleman, who between them guaranteed 140 m. and a palfrey. Only Walter of Coventry, steward of the Lincolnshire lands of the Earl of Chester and later a loyalist, seems out of place.[5] A parallel offer of 500 m. which Thomas made in his legal battles for the control of the fenland around Fleet was backed, amongst others, by Bartholomew of Moulton, his uncle, Alexander of Pointon, Walter Bek, Hervey Darcy, and Simon de Chauncy.[6]

The group which constituted pledges for a debt might often be highly localized; but this was not always so, especially in the case of the larger debts. When Richard de Lucy offered 300 m. for his inheritance in 1200, the guarantors included not only Hugh de Morville, William de Stuteville, and other Cumberland landowners, but also Richard de Unfraville who had no stake at all in the county.[7] Certain cases provide extreme instances. The pledges of the 1,200 m. which Henry fitz Count proffered for the land of William de Tracy in 1202 were to be sought in sixteen different counties and were taken from men of vastly different origins and interests: William Marshal, Eustace de Vesci, William de Braose, Ranulf of Chester, William, Earl of Salisbury, David, Earl of Huntingdon.[8] But this general scattering of the pledges is rare; it is unusual to find any of the later rebels of the East Anglian and home counties, for example, coming in to support

---

[1] *Lincolnshire Final Concords*, i. 192; *Book of Fees*, p. 1028.
[2] *Pipe Roll 9 John*, pp. 11–12.   [3] *Pipe Roll 8 John*, p. 104.
[4] *Rot. de Ob. et Fin.*, pp. 482–3.   [5] Ibid., pp. 369–70.
[6] Ibid., p. 370.   [7] Ibid., p. 45.
[8] *Pipe Roll 4 John*, p. 252; *Rot. de Ob. et Fin.*, pp. 278–80. Compare the proffer of Geoffrey de Lucy (ibid., pp. 458–9).

the proffers of the Northerners. In 1206 Robert fitz Walter, Geoffrey de Say, Roger de Cressy, and Adam of Newmarket stood beside Gilbert de Gant, the Abbot of St. Mary's, York, and Hugh Paynel to pledge a debt of Gerard de Furneval;[1] but Gerard had land in Essex and Hertfordshire in addition to his northern lands, and his father's English connexions had been with these southern counties.[2] Such widely scattered groups of pledges, in fact, appear just where we might expect them on other grounds. Normally a northern debt entailed northern pledges.

In the early years of the reign these pledges might often include officials and intimates of the King. Richard de Lucy's proffer of 1200 was supported by William de Stuteville,[3] one of the most influential of the Angevin officials in northern England. William again appeared, along with another northern sheriff, Hugh Bardolf, as one of Peter de Brus's guarantors in 1201.[4] When Richard Malebisse fined in 1199 to recover estates seized when he rebelled with Count John in 1194, his pledges included, on the one hand, Peter de Brus, Robert de Ros, and Marmaduke de Tweng, a tenant of the Brus and Percy fees,[5] and, on the other, Gilbert fitz Reinfrey and another curialist, Robert of Thornham.[6] This kind of mixture is common in the list of pledges of this time. But the further into the reign, the less frequent it becomes. The last clear recorded case was in 1209 when William de Mowbray was being pressed for the payment of debts arising from the proffer of 2,000 m. made in 1201 to defend his lands against the claims of William de Stuteville. William had already sought some kind of assistance in paying this debt, probably soon after it had been contracted. These original guarantees were provided partly by his tenants and partly by William de Humez, Constable of Normandy, Eustace de Vesci, and Nicholas de Stuteville, who was in the odd position of carrying a burden imposed, albeit indirectly and unwittingly, by his own brother. William de Mowbray was now required to find guarantees for a further 800 m. Eustace de Vesci acted once more, along with Robert de Ros and Roger de Montbegon, each providing 100 m. William of Well, a tenant of Gilbert de Gant, pledged 50 m. The remaining sum of 450 m. was

---

[1] *Curia Regis Rolls*, iv. 88–89.
[2] *Early Yorks. Charters*, iii. 6; *Book of Fees*, pp. 14, 124.
[3] *Rot. de Ob. et Fin.*, p. 45. [4] Ibid., pp. 109–10.
[5] *Early Yorks. Charters*, ii. 14; *Yorkshire Fines 1218–31*, p. 140; *Book of Fees*, pp. 156, 71. [6] *Rot. de Ob. et Fin.*, p. 41.

guaranteed by five curialist lords, William de Warenne, Roger de Lacy, Constable of Chester, Robert de Vieuxpont, Hugh de Gournay, and Saer de Quenci.[1] The exaction of this debt placed de Mowbray in difficult straits; it is probable, too, that it was a current scandal. Perhaps William was driven to exceptional measures; perhaps he was able to draw on unusually widespread sympathy in his plight. Perhaps, although there is nothing to prove it, the aid given by such a man as Robert de Vieuxpont was inspired by something more sinister than sympathy. Sometimes Robert's embrace was not so much affectionate as suffocating.[2]

By the time these arrangements were made they were becoming exceptional. Like debtor, like pledge. Immediate circumstances might occasionally alter this general rule; when the future loyalist, Hugh de Balliol, borrowed £200 from the King in Poitou in 1214, repayment was guaranteed by many future Northumbrian rebels, including Richard de Unfraville, Roger de Merlay, Roger Bertram, John fitz Robert, and Gilbert de Laval.[3] Here the political allegiances of the civil war were not foreshadowed. But such examples are rare. Normally the close mutual support of men like de Vesci, Peter de Brus, and Robert de Ros is paralleled on the opposing side by co-operation among the King's agents and intimates. The mutual exclusiveness of the two groups is best seen in the proffers of the obvious *parvenus*, the men rising rapidly through the social and administrative grades to high office and great influence. When Brian de Lisle offered 300 m. for the hand of the widow of Norman de Camera, his pledges included Geoffrey fitz Peter, the Justiciar, William Briwerre, Hugh de Neville, the Chief Forester, and curialists and members of the household like Peter fitz Herbert, Reginald of Cornhill, and Fulk de Cantilupe.[4] When Brian proffered two palfreys to the King in 1210, Peter de Maulay and William, Earl of Salisbury were his backers.[5] When Robert de Vieuxpont offered 500 m. for the custody of the land and heirs of William son of Ranulf and the marriage of William's widow, Heloise de Stuteville, he was backed by William Briwerre, William de Cahaignes, William de Cantilupe, and Saer de Quenci. Earl Richard of Clare also helped, but the only future

[1] *Pipe Roll 11 John*, pp. 126, 130.
[2] This is not unduly cynical. For Robert's relations with Nicholas de Stuteville see below, p. 239.
[3] *Pipe Roll 3 Henry III*, p. 170.
[4] *Rot. de Ob. et Fin.*, pp. 240–1.   [5] *Pipe Roll 12 John*, p. 9.

northern rebel to do so was Adam of Staveley.[1] When the political objectives and effects of such offers were blatant, then the dividing lines were hard and fast. When, in 1214, John accepted a proffer from Peter de Maulay for the hand of Isabel of Thornham, the heiress of the Fossard barony, not one single Northerner lent a hand. The chief guarantors were Ranulf of Chester, William de Ferrers, Earl of Derby, Savaric de Mauleon, Reginald de Pontibus, William, Earl of Salisbury, and Hubert de Burgh.[2] In this transaction a Eustace de Vesci or a Peter de Brus would seem quite out of place.

All these lists of pledges place before us the slow emergence of the genus 'Northerner'. No doubt the political programmes and discussions of the crisis drew tighter bonds. The Northerners might well come to feel, as Benjamin Franklin felt at a later date and in a different revolution, that if they did not all hang together then they would all hang separately. But these emotions could only bind a society already closely knit, in which individuals had already acted in close support of each other. The mutual confidence and trust which must have existed between Eustace de Vesci and Peter de Brus in 1214 and 1215 cannot be dissociated from Eustace's financial support of Peter in 1201. Simon of Kyme and Thomas of Moulton were not just random Lincolnshire rebels; they were a well-tried partnership. William de Mowbray, Nicholas de Stuteville, and Robert de Ros were all connected in business. In all this the Northerners were distinguished both from the baronage in other parts of the country and from the King's men in their own counties.

The men who had pledged each others' debts in time of peace came to negotiate and fight together in time of war. Robert de Ros, William de Mowbray, Eustace de Vesci, Peter de Brus, and others all treated together with the King in 1216;[3] Gilbert de Gant, Gilbert fitz Reinfrey, William de Mowbray, and Robert de Brus all shared in owing 200 m., after the war, to a certain Henry of Boulogne.[4] But they did not constitute a monolothic party. William de Mowbray, Peter de Brus, Richard de Percy, and Eustace de Vesci, all of whom had resisted the Poitevin scutage in 1214, considered surrendering in 1216. One of those who resisted the scutage, Roger de Montbegon, did in fact surrender.

[1] *Pipe Roll 11 John*, p. 96.   [2] *Pipe Roll 16 John*, p. 94.
[3] See below, pp. 135–7.   [4] *Pipe Roll 3 Henry III*, p. 197.

Gilbert de Gant, in contrast, who accepted the King's demands in 1214, never treated at all in 1216. Richard de Unfraville, a probable associate of de Vesci in 1212, failed to join him in 1214, but did so in 1215. The variants are numerous. Some men, Eustace de Vesci especially, were perhaps more prominent, more consistent than the rest. But not even Eustace can be looked upon as a party leader. The clue lies not in the group, but in the opinions and policies expressed within and by the group. These, more than anything else, gave the Northerners their identity. But it followed that these policies might be openly expressed first by some individuals and then by others. Some men might differ from the generally accepted views for a time, others feel that their relations with the court might require a judicious silence, others, in time of war, that their friends would understand if they surrendered to *force majeure*. But, if Northerners tended to come and go, their policy was expressed continuously. This policy was characteristic and distinct, and it was their own.

VI

THE REBELLION

KING John was unprepared for rebellion in the summer of
1212. The success of his campaigns in the last three years
in Scotland, Wales, and Ireland had suppressed actual or
potential opposition at home. There is no sign of any relaxation
in his administrative and financial measures. The justices of the
forest were beginning a new eyre;[1] demands were being made for
the payments of Jewish debts in the King's hands;[2] on 1 June a
great inquiry was initiated into feudal tenures and services.[3] On
the Continent John's diplomatic activity was reaching a climax in
his new alliances with the princes of the Low Countries. All, in
fact, was ready for the long-delayed campaign for the recovery of
the Angevin lands.

By writs of 15 June nearly forty English towns were ordered
to provide men ready to cross the sea with the King;[4] then the
fine bubble of expectation burst. A Welsh invasion of the Marches
compelled the King to abandon his continental plans. Instead he
arranged to muster his army at Chester on 19 August to deal with
the Welsh.[5] On his journey to Chester John suddenly learned of a
baronial plot against his life. On 16 August, while he lay at
Nottingham, he ordered the dispersal of the army at Chester and
hastily summoned mercenaries to his side.[6] He had lost the
political initiative and was never to regain it completely for the
rest of his life. The firm policy with which he had treated the
baronage hitherto became henceforth a patchwork of harshness,
political blackmail, and concession.

The chroniclers suggest that the crisis was less sudden than the
King's activities indicate. Wendover commented in an exaggerated

---

[1] *Walt. Cov.* ii. 207; *Pipe Roll 14 John*, pp. xxiii–xxiv.

[2] *Chron. Melsa*, i. 375; *Memorials of Bury*, ii. 23.

[3] *Book of Fees*, p. 52. [4] *Rot. Litt. Claus.* i. 130b–131.

[5] *Rot. Litt. Claus.* 131–131b. No summons of tenants by military service is recorded, but compare the letters dismissing the levies (*Rot. Litt. Pat.*, p. 94).

[6] It should be noted that some authorities have confused the chronology of this
period and postdated the crisis to September. See Miss Kate Norgate, *John Lackland*,
pp. 169–70, and S. Painter, *William Marshal*, p. 171. Painter gives a correct version
in *The Reign of King John*, p. 267.

style that almost all the magnates had become the King's enemies by this time.[1] Other writers told of a country uneasy with alarms and rumours. The Barnwell chronicler wrote of a great panic hue and cry, the whole countryside pursuing non-existent male-factors;[2] the Bury annalist heard stories that a French inva-sion was imminent, and wilder tales of the rape of the Queen and the murder of young Prince Richard at Marlborough;[3] others again thought that the King's subjects had been absolved from their allegiance by the Pope.[4] Much of this may constitute a retro-spective attempt to explain the events of 1212. Writers soon enough explained the actions of Robert fitz Walter and Eustace de Vesci, the two men whose participation in the plot was both certain and notorious, on personal grounds for which there is little warrant in strictly contemporary sources.[5]

These stories suggest an increasing *malaise* affecting a wide area of the country. The most obvious indication of this was provided by Peter of Wakefield, who, some time during the summer, was already prophesying the downfall of the King. Nevertheless, there is nothing to connect the plot of 1212 with any earlier baronial resistance to the King. Since the destruction of William de Braose

[1] *Chron. Maj.* ii. 535: 'idem rex tot fere habuit hostes quot habuit magnates'.
[2] *Walt. Cov.* ii. 206.　　　　　　　　　　[3] *Memorials of Bury*, ii. 23.
[4] See C. R. Cheney in *Studies in Medieval History presented to F. M. Powicke*, pp. 115–16.
[5] The famous story of John's attempted seduction of Eustace's wife appears in a continuation of the chronicle of William of Newburgh written by a monk of Furness at the end of the thirteenth century (*Chronicles of Stephen, Henry II and Richard I*, ii. vii, 521). Here Eustace is given the name of his grandfather, Eustace fitz John. The mistake was corrected by Knighton who expanded the story (*Chronicon*, i. 193–4). The associated story of John's attempts on fitz Walter's daughter has a much earlier source—the *Histoire des ducs de Normandie* (pp. 119–21), and Robert may indeed have alleged this as a bid for sympathy during his exile in France. The tale was ex-panded and embroidered in the chronicle of Dunmow (*Mon. Angl.* vi, pt. i, 147b). The *Histoire* provides a further explanation for Robert's flight in telling of his at-tempts to protect his son-in-law, Geoffrey de Mandeville, from John's vengeance after Geoffrey had killed a sergeant of William Briwerre in a squabble over lodgings (pp. 116–19). The details of this make good reading but are not convincing and are not supported elsewhere. Matthew Paris came closer to reality in connecting Robert's flight with the King's intervention in his dispute with the Abbot of St. Albans over their respective rights in the priory of Binham, Norfolk (*Gesta Abbatum*, i. 220–9). Paris's story is partly confirmed in the *Curia Regis Rolls* (vi. 52, 55–56, 133–4, 273, 284). The case was unfinished when Robert fled, in particular the settlement of damages. However, it cannot be assumed, as Paris suggests in this work, that King John's support of St. Albans was the only, or even the main, cause of Robert's flight. Compare the more usual story of Robert's complicity in the August plot which Paris repeated in the *Chronica Majora* (ii. 534).

there may have been bitter feeling, but there is no sign that there had been open or covert opposition of any importance. John's ignorance of baronial plans up to 16 August suggests that there was very little to arouse his sensitive suspicion earlier, and, indeed, the details of the plot could scarcely have been decided before July when John changed his plans to an expedition against the Welsh. His opponents were probably goaded into action partly by the opportunity offered and partly by the inquest into tenure and service ordered on 1 June. This inquiry was being executed as the baronial plot matured; many of the surviving returns are thorough and detailed; something important was being planned, and yet John, like his predecessors in 1086 and 1166, did not divulge his intentions. Its coincidence with his plan for a continental campaign, however, cannot but have suggested to the barons that some new urgency in the exaction of feudal service was imminent. The King had gone too far.[1]

The details of the plot soon became well known. The King's opponents planned to murder him in Wales or desert him in the face of the enemy and let the Welsh do their work for them. They then went on to elect a new king;[2] one chronicle, the Annals of Dunstable, names the candidate—Simon de Montfort, the leader of the Albigensian crusade.[3] All this points to extensive support

---

[1] John's intentions in ordering the inquiry were further obscured by the fact that the political crisis of 1212 prevented him from carrying them out. Earlier returns printed in the *Book of Fees* show a considerable interest in the knights' fees held of escheats, wardships, and ecclesiastical estates in royal custody (*Book of Fees*, pp. 16–51), and in 1211 the Exchequer clerks seem to have been taking great care to state the number of fees on which scutage was being paid (S. K. Mitchell, *Studies in Taxation under John and Henry III*, pp. 104–5). Closely similar inquiries to that of 1212 were carried out on the occasion of the campaign of 1242 (*Book of Fees*, pp. 637 ff.).

The writ ordering the 1212 inquiry demanded a return of alienations from land formerly held in chief of the King (ibid., p. 52). This may have been intended as a preliminary to royal resumptions, or at least to *quo warranto* proceedings and the sale of confirmations. Compare a closely similar writ ordering investigations into alienations from the lands of the honour of Lancaster in 1205 (*Rot. Litt. Claus.* i. 55).

Painter considers that there was little connexion between the inquiry and the plot of August (*The Reign of King John*, pp. 209–11), contending that as the returns were arranged hundred by hundred, they could not have been used easily for estimating the total military service of a baron and hence cannot have greatly concerned men of this rank. This argument assumes that the form in which we have the returns represents the ultimate intention of the inquiry. In the returns of 1242 the information was usually presented by hundreds and then recast under each tenancy-in-chief at the end of each county section. This may well have been intended in 1212.

[2] *Walt. Cov.* ii. 207.　　　　　　　　　[3] *Annales Monastici*, iii. 33.

and organization, and John's reaction indicates that he suspected such. There are even indications that the plotters had made arrangements for local announcements of their success at the critical moment. In the Michaelmas term of 1212 some of the King's household knights accused an unimportant Cornish tenant, Baldwin Tyrel, of fortifying a house and 'denouncing' the King's death. The details of the charge were that he had announced that the King had been murdered in North Wales or was so surrounded by his enemies that escape was impossible.[1] Baldwin seems to have been a little too hasty.

On the whole, however, the conspirators covered their tracks effectively. Only Robert fitz Walter and Eustace de Vesci seem to have felt that their complicity could be proved beyond doubt. They fled, were appealed in the county courts, and eventually outlawed. Nine of fitz Walter's tenants or associates were outlawed with them and two others were imprisoned.[2] Two clerks who were to play important roles later were involved: Gervase of Heybridge, shortly to be, if not already, Chancellor of St. Paul's;[3] and John, the incumbent of the church of de Vesci's manor of North Ferriby, who had acted frequently as Eustace's attorney.[4] This group probably constituted a small proportion of the total number of conspirators. There is little to suggest that fitz Walter and de Vesci were the only barons prepared to take action against the King. There is no evidence that the two were close friends or connected in any way;[5] they did not even flee together, for Robert went to France and Eustace to Scotland.

---

[1] *Curia Regis Rolls*, vii. 168–73, 94, 257. The case was a complicated one; no conclusion to it is recorded and it was eventually referred to the King. Baldwin claimed that he had already accused some of the knights concerned with false arrest and holding him to ransom and that the charges against him were a malicious retaliation. Baldwin's alleged announcement is not dated. The earliest dated incident in the case is 6 Nov. 1212, but the evidence presented does not in any way exclude Baldwin having made this announcement as early as August.

I have been unable to trace where Baldwin Tyrel's estates lay. The case was first heard in the hundred courts of Truro and St. Austell. It may be relevant that Robert fitz Walter held fees along the Fowey estuary (*Book of Fees*, p. 393; *Red Book of the Exchequer*, p. 539).

[2] *Rot. Litt. Claus.* i. 165b; *Rot. Litt. Pat.*, p. 101b.

[3] On Gervase see H. G. Richardson in *E.H.R.* xlviii (1933), 252 ff.

[4] *Rot. Litt. Claus.* i. 165b; *Rot. Litt. Pat.*, p. 96b, *Curia Regis Rolls*, v. 311; vi. 50, 241.

[5] Tout's statement (*D.N.B.* vii. 220) that the estates of Robert's wife, Gunnora de Valoignes, lay mainly in the north is incorrect. Compare *Book of Fees*, pp. 578–9, and J. H. Round in *E.H.R.* xix. 710.

The plot cannot be treated as the private enterprise of these two. The reason for their prominence is that they were found out.

It is impossible to decide how many other people were involved in the conspiracy. It is easy, however, to follow John's suspicions and train of thought. His first reaction was to demand guarantees of loyalty. As early as 24 August Richard de Unfraville had agreed to surrender his castle of Prudhoe and his four sons as hostages for his faithful service. He also accepted liability both in life and possessions should a charge of treason be proved against him.[1] On the 25th the King ordered Earl David of Huntingdon to surrender his castle of Fotheringhay to Hugh de Neville and other royal agents; the whole *posse* of Northampton was mustered in case the Earl resisted.[2] Robert fitz Walter's sister, Alice Peche, had to surrender her daughter and other hostages.[3] Later evidence points to others being involved. In 1213 two Northumbrian barons, Roger de Merlay and Robert de Muschamps, had hostages in the hands of the King.[4] Gilbert de Laval may also have surrendered hostages at this time.[5] Hugh de Balliol, too, had been deprived, for a time, of Barnard Castle and his lands and chattels.[6] Farther south hostages had been taken from Geoffrey de Say and Adam of Newmarket,[7] and Earl Richard of Clare and his son, Gilbert, surrendered charters as a pledge of faithful service.[8] Although a connexion between this later evidence and the conspiracy is not stated and cannot be proved, it is highly probable in most cases. The King's suspicion ranged widely; even his old distrust of William Marshal was temporarily revived.[9]

In the face of rebellion John acted with remarkable speed. Letters of 20 August ordered Robert fitz Roger to transfer the county of Northumberland to William de Warenne, Philip of Oldcotes, and Aymer, Archdeacon of Durham.[10] Whether Robert

[1] *Rot. Litt. Claus.* i. 122b.

[2] *Rot. Litt. Pat.*, p. 94b; *Rot. Litt. Claus.* i. 122–122b.

[3] *Rot. Litt. Pat.*, p. 101b. [4] Ibid., pp. 99, 106.

[5] *Rot. Litt. Claus.* i. 192b. [6] Ibid. i. 129.

[7] Ibid. i. 124; *Rot. Litt. Pat.*, p. 105.

[8] *Rot. Chartarum*, p. 192. Compare ibid., p. 197, where Richard's daughter, Matilda, appears as a hostage in the spring of 1213.

[9] On 17 Aug. Geoffrey de Lucy was ordered to send eighteen ships along the coast of North Wales as a demonstration against the Welsh. He was given the following warning: '—semper vobis praecaveatis ne a terra vel potestate Willelmi Comitis Marescalli malum vobis possit evenire' (*Rot. Litt. Claus.* i. 122).

[10] *Rot. Litt. Pat.*, pp. 94, 94b. Warenne first denied complicity in the plot.

had been implicated or was being suspected is uncertain; he had seen many years in the Crown's service and his recent health had not been good. By the 26th, ten days after John had heard of the plot, William de Warenne and Philip of Oldcotes had garrisoned Eustace de Vesci's castle of Alnwick with their own troops.[1] The King stayed at Nottingham and then at Kingshaugh until 28 August, mustering his forces, collecting money and provisions, hastening the construction of siege machines.[2] He then moved quickly north. Meanwhile, Reginald of Cornhill, sheriff of Kent, was busy sending on Flemish knights to join the King at York.[3] By 3 September John was at Durham. He stayed there three days and then moved south, reaching Nottingham again on the 9th. His journey was not so much a royal progress as a military expedition. Later, probably on 17 September, when he disbanded his troops at Northampton, over £400 was disbursed to nearly sixty English and foreign knights.[4] In addition, the great northern castles were made ready for war. At the end of the financial year, over £1,300 had been spent on fortification at Scarborough, Norham, Durham, Bamburgh, and Newcastle.[5] £200 had also been spent on providing provisions and munitions at Scarborough and Pickering, and further sums for Knaresborough, Bolsover, Newark, and the Peak.[6] At Newcastle and Bamburgh the garrisons were reinforced, chiefly with men provided by William de Warenne and Philip of Oldcotes.[7]

In the autumn of 1212 northern men must have become well accustomed to the sight of royal troops and trains of fodder and armaments. In all probability the promptness of the King's reaction had prevented open rebellion. As yet many men were undecided, unwilling to commit themselves. William, son of Robert de Ros, John fitz Robert, William de Albini, Nicholas de Stuteville, and Henry de Neville, along with several lesser men, were with the troops John had taken north.[8] William de Mowbray met the King at Northallerton on 1 September.[9] John came north again in the new year, this time on a much more leisurely journey lasting nearly six weeks and bringing him as far north as Alnwick. This time many northern men attended him

---

[1] *Pipe Roll 14 John*, p. 48.   [2] *Rot. Litt. Claus.* i. 122.
[3] *Pipe Roll 14 John*, p. 12.
[4] *Pipe Roll 17 John and Praestita Roll 14–18 John*, pp. 90–1.
[5] *Pipe Roll 14 John*, pp. 26, 46–47.   [6] Ibid., pp. 27, 169–70.   [7] Ibid., p. 48.
[8] *Praestita Roll, 14–18 John*, pp. 90–1.   [9] *Rot. Chartarum*, p. 187b.

or met him: William de Mowbray once more, Roger de Merlay, Peter de Brus, Richard de Unfraville, Robert de Ros, whose son had been in the King's company during his earlier journey, Simon of Kyme, and Thomas of Moulton.[1] Whether any of these men, apart from Richard de Unfraville, had been a party to the plot, we do not know. We cannot know either how far they discussed the political situation with the King. It is certain, however, that John's journeys north, especially the second one, led him to make important concessions. Eustace de Vesci gained nothing from his actions, but his friends and neighbours did.

The change in John's policy was noted by three chroniclers. According to the Bury annalist, the King swore that he would eject foreigners from his counsels and rely on the advice of native-born magnates;[2] for this story there is no satisfactory corroboration. The Barnwell chronicler stated that the King's treatment of his subjects became gentler. In the face of adversity his actions were 'memorable and praiseworthy'. He remitted the new forest exactions and made his foresters swear that they would limit their exactions to the amount customary in the reign of his father. He also restrained the keepers of the ports from making new demands, and, 'so it is said', treated widows more favourably and looked to the keeping of the peace in temporal matters.[3] In a further passage this writer described royal investigations into the behaviour of the sheriffs and new limitations on their exactions.[4] The Dunstable annalist, too, stated that a strict inquiry was made into the actions of the sheriffs as a result of which some were arrested and others fled.[5]

The new tone of John's policy was set while he was at Nottingham. On 18 August he summoned the sheriffs to his side. They were each to bring six knights of their shires who were to do 'what we tell them'.[6] The sheriffs were also informed that all who owed *debita Judeorum* to the King, barons excepted, were to come before him 'because we wish by the Grace of God to relax their

---

[1] Ibid., pp. 190–190b. [2] *Memorials of Bury*, ii. 24.
[3] *Walt. Cov.* ii. 207.
[4] Ibid. ii. 214–15. The chronicler places these inquiries after the arrival of the papal legate, Nicholas of Tusculum, in Sept. 1213. In all probability, however, he has misdated them for he states that the King's measures came to nothing because of the general muster ordered to meet the threatened invasion from France. This occurred in Apr. and May 1213. This passage, therefore, is best referred to the early months of 1213. For record evidence confirming this see below, p. 86.
[5] *Annales Monastici*, iii. 35. [6] *Rot. Litt. Claus.* i. 132.

debts'; the nearer they were, the sooner they were to come to the King.[1] A month later John's attention turned to the forest. On 25 September Alexander of Pointon and John of Birkin, neither of whom were normally involved in the forest administration, were appointed to inspect all forests north of Trent to see how they were kept, supervise the agistment of demesne woods, and report on the profits from pannage.[2] The most obvious and sweeping concessions, however, concerned shrieval administration. On 30 January 1213, while at Fenwick, John ordered the transfer of Cumberland from the chief forester, Hugh de Neville, to Robert de Ros.[3] On 25 February similar orders provided for the replacement of Hubert de Burgh and his deputy, Robert Aguillon, in Lincolnshire, by Alexander of Pointon, and of Gilbert fitz Reinfrey, in Yorkshire, by Robert de Percy.[4] Letters of the same date were sent to the men of Yorkshire and Lincolnshire stating that the King had heard many complaints, 'which have moved us not a little', of the extortion of the sheriffs and their men. They were now to report all such excesses which had occurred since the last Irish expedition to a commission of four so that the King might correct them. The commission consisted of Robert de Ros, William de Albini, Simon of Kyme, and Thomas of Moulton.[5] These men, the new sheriffs, and the investigators of the northern forests, all rebelled in 1215. None of them belonged to the privileged, expert group of royal familiars. In using them and in listening to complaints John was trying to provide a safety valve.

The King's reactions to the plot of 1212 point conclusively to the north as the chief centre of trouble. John's first move was to march to Durham. It was on northern men, or men with northern connexions, that his demand for security of good behaviour

----

[1] *Rot. Litt. Claus.* i 132. It is probable that new steps were also taken in the matter of baronial *debita Judeorum*. On 24 Dec. 1212 the sheriff of Yorkshire was ordered not to trouble Robert de Ros concerning such a debt until the King had details of it and had issued further instructions (*Rot. Litt. Claus.* i. 128). See also *Rot. de Ob. et Fin.*, p. 519, where the *debita Judeoram* of Henry de Neville were put in respite in return for service in Poitou.

For a further discussion of some of these measures see below, pp. 168–9.

[2] *Rot. Litt. Claus.* i. 125. A further writ of 15 May 1213 ordered that four knights from every northern county should report to Brian de Lisle (Hugh de Neville's deputy) to execute what he would tell them of the King's business. None of the four were to be verderers (ibid. i. 129b). 　　　　　[3] *Rot. Litt. Pat.*, p. 96b.

[4] Ibid., p. 97. 　　　　　　　　　　　　　　　　　[5] Ibid.

largely fell. The northern castles were made ready for war with great urgency and at great cost; there was no comparable effort on castles in other parts of the country. It was in the north, too, that the concessions noted by the chroniclers were put into effect; there is nothing comparable in other counties. There is no reason to think that John had blundered in piecing together the situation. He is in effect our prime authority because he was concerned with saving his skin and his crown, and with salvaging his continental plans. He could not afford to blunder.

Even so, John's actions at this time suggest an optimistic mood. While he dealt with the north, he left his subordinates to punish the Welsh.[1] He never abandoned the projected continental campaign. By 15 November he was busy again arranging for the muster of shipping for an expedition in the spring,[2] and in March 1213 final orders were made for the concentration of a fleet at Portsmouth.[3] By this time John must have felt satisfied that there would be no further conspiracy or rebellion and that the northern counties were securely under the control of his castellans. His difficulties now arose from facts which could not entirely be foreseen. First, he was thrown on the defensive by Philip Augustus's obvious intention to invade England. From 21 April to the end of May, when the French fleet was destroyed, John and his armies had to await a possible attack in Kent. Secondly, the settlement of John's dispute with the Pope, the terms of which the King had decided to accept in November 1212, came to include the restoration of Robert fitz Walter, Eustace de Vesci, and their associates.[4] Thirdly, in these new circumstances, baronial opposition to John's continental plans was openly and generally expressed and could not be broken down immediately. All this happened at one and the same time. The formal submission to the papal legate was made on 13 May. John accepted papal vassalage on 15 May.[5] Letters patent of 27 May provided a safe-conduct for the return of fitz Walter and de Vesci.[6] By the summer resistance to service overseas had become so strong that John had to abandon his schemes for this year.

The King's policy in the north in the winter of 1212–13 was effective enough. The army of Kent is one of the few examples

[1] *Brut y Tywysogyon*, ed. T. Jones, pp. 86–88; *Rot. Litt. Claus.* i. 121b–122.
[2] Ibid. i. 127b.   [3] Ibid. i. 133.   [4] *Selected Letters of Innocent III*, pp. 130 ff.
[5] *Foedera*, i, pt. 1, pp. 111–12.   [6] *Rot. Litt. Pat.*, p. 99.

of a general muster of the feudal service of England. All the
important northern magnates, with the single exception of
Nicholas de Stuteville, answered the summons.[1] But the King,
unwittingly and unwillingly, had produced a situation which was
potentially disastrous. For a full six weeks the English baronage
lived within the confines of a single county, and this in the worst
possible atmosphere from the King's point of view, that of the
boredom and unease of an army waiting to repel invasion.
During this time they were spectators of the King's humiliating
concessions to the Pope. The chroniclers suggest that they became
increasingly restive. They were credulous of Peter of Wakefield's
prophecies, which were now becoming somewhat ominous with
a French invasion probable.[2] There are hints of some renewal of
the plans of 1212. According to Wendover, John feared that he
might be deserted on the field of battle or handed over to his
enemies.[3] Wendover, too, believed that some of the barons were
now in touch with King Philip of France[4] and a similar rumour
came to the ears of the Barnwell writer.[5] But, except for Robert
fitz Walter, who was still in France, there is no clinching evidence
on this point.[6]

It is probable that the chroniclers exaggerated. When the
French threat had passed and John was once more pressing forward with his plans, the baronial reaction to his demands for
service overseas was clearly not the product of a well co-ordinated
plan. The King was simply faced with an increased obstinacy
which varied from individual to individual and from one part of
the country to another. Only in the north were men committing
themselves to outright and open resistance. The excuses advanced
were threefold. In the first instance, the magnates refused to
accompany the King until he had been absolved from the papal
sentence of excommunication. This story appears only in the
chronicle of Wendover,[7] but it is not inherently improbable, for
John was planning his expedition for June[8] and at the beginning
of July he wrote urging Langton to return to England as soon as

---

[1] *Praestita Roll 14–18 John*, pp. 92–8.
[2] *Walt. Cov.* ii. 209, 211; Wendover suggests that fear of Peter's prophecy was one
of the reasons for John's submission to the Pope (*Chron. Maj.* ii. 541).
[3] Ibid.   [4] Ibid. ii. 540.   [5] *Walt. Cov.* ii. 211.
[6] *Histoire des ducs de Normandie*, pp. 119–21, 124–5.
[7] *Chron. Maj.* ii. 549.
[8] See letters to Jordan Foliot (*Rot. Litt. Claus.* i. 143).

possible.[1] Secondly, the barons argued that their resources had been so exhausted by expeditions within the kingdom that they could not sustain a campaign on the continent.[2] Finally, the Northerners argued that they were not bound to serve overseas by the terms on which they held their lands.[3] Collectively these arguments forced the King to withdraw. On 17 August he wrote to his ally, the Count of Toulouse, explaining that he had been delayed *per magnam venti quantitatem*.[4] Four days later he was making preparations for sailing on 2 February 1214.[5]

The first two of these arguments were makeshift. They necessarily lost cogency as time passed. The first, indeed, became irrelevant after 20 July when the King was absolved by Stephen Langton. The case presented by the Northerners was quite different. This was more than an excuse; it was a rebellion by implication. They were denying their primary responsibility as military tenants of the King. They were hitting John where it hurt most, for they were striking at the end towards which the whole of his external and internal policy had been directed. Their actions were deliberately provocative.

Overseas service was not so much the real issue between the King and the northern magnates as the issue on which they chose to fight. Only on one earlier occasion are there signs of similar resistance from them. On 2 January 1204, in a council at Oxford, John was granted a feudal aid for the purpose of the defence of Normandy.[6] This was to be levied at $2\frac{1}{2}$ m. on the knight's fee and appears in the pipe rolls as a scutage. In the event there was no full-scale expedition in this year although a small force of knights was dispatched under the command of the Count of Aumale.[7] John proceeded to collect the levy. This was reasonable in that it was an aid to which consent had already been given. But he also used it as an opportunity to levy heavy fines *pro servicio*,[8] a move which would have had many precedents if the levy had been a normal scutage but which had none in the case of a feudal

---

[1] *Ibid*. i. 164.   [2] *Walt. Cov*. ii. 212; *Coggeshall*, p. 167; *Chron. Maj*. ii. 551.

[3] *Coggeshall*, p. 167. The Barnwell chronicler gives a similar reason for the refusal of scutage in 1214 and also states that the Northerners had prevented the expedition sailing in 1213 (*Walt. Cov*. ii. 217).   [4] *Foedera*, i, pt. 1, p. 114.

[5] *Rot. Litt. Pat.*, p. 103b.   [6] *Chron. Maj*. ii. 584.

[7] *Rot. Litt. Pat.*, p. 41b.

[8] The amount assessed as scutage came to approximately 750 m. The fines assessed totalled approximately 5,050 m. See S. K. Mitchell, *Studies in Taxation under John and Henry III*, pp. 64–65.

aid. In the north it seems to have met resistance. On 1 April the Northumbrian barons were excused their contributions.[1] This concession was also extended to Lincolnshire,[2] and none of the leading Yorkshire barons accounted for the levy at the Exchequer.[3]

This levy was an unusual one. It occurred, moreover, at a time when the northern counties were unsettled politically for other reasons.[4] Apart from this instance, the men who resisted John's demands for service and scutage in 1213 and 1214 had performed their service with remarkable consistency earlier. Eustace de Vesci, William de Mowbray, Robert de Ros, Richard de Percy, Peter de Brus, Robert Grelley, and Roger de Montbegon, all received quittances on their scutage for John's expeditions prior to the loss of Normandy and again for his campaign in Poitou in 1206. So regular was these men's service that it was only in 1204 and again in 1205, when a proposed campaign was cancelled, that they were required to pay scutage, and in the latter case they accounted without demur. Only two of them, William de Mowbray and Robert de Ros, had interests in Normandy of any importance.[5] In effect only the smaller men, who did not normally send their service and who bore the main weight of heavy fines *pro servicio*, had to face serious financial demands and even so they normally managed to meet the account.[6] Thus there are strong

---

[1] *Rot. Litt. Claus.* i. 25; *Pipe Roll 6 John*, pp. 45–46.

[2] *Pipe Roll 6 John*, pp. 50–51; compare ibid., pp. 45–46.

[3] Ibid., pp. 189–90.   [4] See below, pp. 205–7.

[5] The Mowbrays held lands at Montbrai and Château Gontier which amounted to just over eleven fees in 1172 (F. M. Powicke, *The Loss of Normandy*, p. 504). For Robert de Ros see above, p. 24.

[6] S. K. Mitchell has noted the important point that the smaller tenants-in-chief suffered most. Their fines *pro servicio* were heavier; they served less frequently; they often paid fines when the greater barons simply paid scutage (*Studies in Taxation under John and Henry III*, pp. 39, 57, 66, 73, 79). Further, they probably did not enjoy the opportunities, available to the greater men, to recover these sums, or expenses incurred on expeditions, from their own tenants, either by levying scutage or by some other means.

Between 1199 and 1206 Eustace de Vesci was only assessed with 40 m., Robert de Ros with 60 m., William de Mowbray with 129½ m., Richard de Perci with 20 m., and Peter de Brus with nothing at all (*Pipe Roll 7 John*, pp. 18, 62, 232). In contrast, Roger de Merlay, responsible for four fees, was quit on three occasions and assessed with 118 m. on three others (*Pipe Roll 4 John*, p. 201; *Pipe Roll 5 John*, p. 87; *Pipe Roll 7 John*, p. 17). Richard de Unfraville, responsible for 2½ fees, was quit on one occasion and assessed with 254 m. on the others (*Pipe Roll 1 John*, p. 122; *Pipe Roll 3 John*, p. 250; *Pipe Roll 4 John*, p. 201; *Pipe Roll 5 John*, p. 87; *Pipe Roll 6 John*, p. 45). John le Viscunt, responsible for three fees, was quit twice and charged with 80 m.

reasons for thinking that the refusal of service in 1213 and 1214 was not aimed against overseas service as such. In 1201, according to Howden, some of the earls refused to serve overseas until their rights had been restored.[1] The Northerners, likewise, were now refusing service in order to force concessions from the King.

The claim which they advanced was sufficiently familiar and had just that shred of legality to make it attractive. Men were coming to think that military service should be limited, that any service outside the kingdom was contrary to custom, that foreign service should be restricted to the payment of scutage,[2] or that it should be limited to the old possessions of the Norman monarchy and not include the Angevin lands.[3] There were additional considerations in the north which were closely connected with forms of tenure peculiar to that area alone. The most important of these was cornage or noutgeld. This tenure, the chief feature of which was the payment of customary rent, can be traced in all the Border counties and in Durham. In Northumberland all the great baronies were held both by cornage and knight service.[4] In Cumberland all the baronies but three were held by cornage alone.[5] When the barons of Cumberland defined their military responsibilities in reply to the inquest of June 1212, they stated that they were liable for service against the Scots, *in eundo in anteguarda et in redeundo in retroguarda*.[6] Earlier John had expected cornage tenants to fine

in the remaining levies (*Pipe Roll 3 John*, p. 250; *Pipe Roll 4 John*, p. 201; *Pipe Roll 5 John*, p. 87; *Pipe Roll 7 John*, p. 17). By Michaelmas 1206 all these demands had been met except for 15 m. still owed by Richard de Unfraville (*Pipe Roll 8 John*, pp. 215–16).

[1] *Hoveden*, iv. 161. Many tenants-in-chief did in fact serve in the end on this occasion. See S. K. Mitchell, op. cit., pp. 34–40.

[2] See the arguments of St. Hugh of Lincoln and Bishop Herbert of Salisbury in 1197 (*Magna Vita Sancti Hugonis*, pp. 249–50). These are discussed by J. H. Round in *Feudal England*, pp. 528 ff., and by Miss Helena Chew in *The Ecclesiastical Tenants-in-Chief*, pp. 38 ff. Compare the reaction of the knights of Bury in 1198 (*The Chronicle of Jocelin of Brakelond*, ed. E. H. Butler, pp. 85–86).

[3] This would seem to be the point of cap. 7 of the 'unknown' charter where Normandy and Brittany are excepted from the general prohibition against overseas service. Compare the admittedly contentious source of some ten years later, the *querimonia* of Faulkes de Breauté, which states the following: 'Saepe autem in Anglia fuerat deceptatum, an homines terrae regem in Pictaviam prosequi tenerentur, et post deceptationem contra regis voluntatem negaverunt omnino prosecutionem ipsam fieri debere' (*Walt. Cov.* ii. 269). The writer was referring here to the events of 1213–15.

[4] J. Hodgson, *History of Northumberland*, pt. 1, vol. i, p. 260.

[5] The exceptions were Copeland, Gilsland, and Edenhall (*Book of Fees*, p. 197).

[6] Ibid., p. 199.

ne transfretent on the occasion of campaigns overseas,[1] but there can be little doubt that the customary responsibilities of these tenants were limited to service on or over the Border. Cornage was never equated with knight service, and in 1224, on the occasion of the siege of Bedford, Richard of Levington, who held by cornage, successfully upheld a claim that he could not be asked to serve elsewhere in England, let alone abroad.[2] In 1213 those Northerners who held by cornage, and by cornage alone, had a sound, arguable case in refusing John's demands. However, only a few men, all of them from Cumberland and none of them of great importance, were in this position. The rest had no legal case at all. Their conduct was a compound of bravado and chicanery; they had learned much from John and were matching his ingenuity with their own, for in basing their resistance on tenure they were not so much defying the King as claiming that his demands were unlawful. Implicitly, they were asking for judgement in a court. Thus, when John attempted to suppress them, Stephen Langton could intervene to insist that they should have it.

In the face of a general resistance to a campaign in 1213 John resorted once more to the policy of concession which he had applied in the north in the previous winter. Whereas earlier, however, his concessions had been on matters of detail and had been firmly allied to military preparations, he now began to gamble; he promised general reform. He was able, as a result, to launch his campaign in 1214. If he had succeeded abroad, he would probably have been able to ignore his promises; in the event he failed, and they could not be ignored. For the nature of these promises we are almost entirely dependent on the chroniclers. The first was made when the King was absolved on 20 July. Coggeshall thought that it simply involved the restoration of ancient liberties;[3] Wendover went into greater detail and stated that John swore that he would recall the good laws of his predecessors, in particular those of King Edward, and destroy all evil customs, that he would judge all men according to the just judgements of his court, and that he would restore to all men their

---

[1] Tenants in drengage and thegnage faced similar demands (*Pipe Roll 3 John*, p. 257; *Pipe Roll 6 John*, pp. 4–5, 45, 144; *Pipe Roll 8 John*, pp. 73–74).

[2] *Rot. Litt. Claus.* i. 614b. For accounts of the military responsibilities of cornage tenants see James Wilson in *V.C.H. Cumberland*, i. 318 ff., and F. W. Maitland, 'Northumbrian Tenures', *Collected Papers*, ii. 96–109.

[3] *Coggeshall*, p. 167.

rights.[1] That some oath, at least a renewal of the coronation oath, was made by the King on this occasion is almost certain.[2] In a second instance the King was not directly involved. While he was still vainly trying to muster forces at Portsmouth, Geoffrey fitz Peter and Peter des Roches met the Archbishop, bishops, and magnates at St. Albans and ordered on his behalf that the laws of Henry I were to be maintained by all and that evil customs were to be ignored. For this, Wendover is the sole authority[3] as he is again for the celebrated and dramatic scene in which Langton, after preaching at St. Paul's on 25 August, read the charter of liberties of Henry I to the assembled magnates.[4]

In some ways this evidence, particularly Wendover's, is of doubtful value. His story of the meeting at St. Paul's he admitted was rumour.[5] Coggeshall made no reference to the charter of Henry I until he came to describe the negotiations which ended at London in January 1215.[6] The Barnwell chronicler also considered that it was not until these later discussions of 1214–15 that Henry's charter came to play a part in the quarrel.[7] Neither Langton's actions at this time nor the sermon he preached on this occasion suggest that he was prepared as yet to enter on a conspiracy with potential rebels.[8] But, whatever is accepted of the detail of the chroniclers' stories, one feature of their evidence is significant. They were not as yet writing of baronial demands, but in the main of royal promises and instructions. When John gambled, he did it very thoroughly.

John was probably willing to take this gamble. In addition, however, he was almost compelled to do so, in that his opponents now had the protection of the church. In letters patent of 19 July in which he ordered the restoration of de Vesci and fitz Walter, the King emphasized that Stephen Langton could quash the whole agreement with the church if these instructions were not carried

---

[1] *Chron. Maj.* ii. 550.
[2] See Walter Mauclerc's report from Rome (*Diplomatic Documents*, pp. 28–30).
[3] *Chron. Maj.* ii. 551.   [4] Ibid. ii. 552, 554.
[5] 'ut fama refert.'   [6] *Coggeshall*, p. 170.
[7] *Walt. Cov.* ii. 218.
[8] The sermon was printed by G. Lacombe in *Catholic History Review*, xv (N.S. ix) (1930), pp. 408–20. On certain points, especially the restoration of property to the church, Langton showed some concern to present the King's actions since his absolution in a favourable light. He clearly believed that a period of peace and order was necessary for the proper convalescence of the church. This is inconsistent with any suggestion that he deliberately encouraged rebellion.

out properly.[1] During the last year of the Interdict the ecclesiastical and secular opposition to the King had come much closer together. William fitz Walter, Archdeacon of Hereford, and Gervase of Heybridge were among those who had been exiled with Robert fitz Walter.[2] Fitz Walter is said to have met the nuncio, Pandulf, in France; somebody at least persuaded Innocent III that he and de Vesci had rebelled because of the Interdict, for their exile was included in the matters touching the Interdict in the Pope's terms of 27 February.[3] Eustace de Vesci, too, was acquiring important connexions within the church. He had been followed into exile by John, parson of Ferriby. When Eustace was restored John of Ferriby and Elias of Dereham were authorized to receive the monetary compensation due for the loss of his estates.[4] Elias of Dereham was Stephen Langton's steward. In him there is a direct link between Eustace and the Archbishop, and Langton was bound both by his position and by his opinions to intervene in any major political crisis. Indeed his first important action on returning to England, the absolution of the King, was accompanied by royal promises of reform. The situation had swung against John. The readmission of de Vesci and fitz Walter was in itself an important defeat. The baronial opposition had gained the prestige of an equivalent victory and enjoyed greater moral backing than ever before. In 1212 they had pinned their hopes on regicide. They now turned to less primitive methods of dealing with the King.

Despite these setbacks, however, John's judgement of the temper of the country was sound. He continued preparations for his campaign throughout the autumn, and his promises at least achieved their end for in February 1214 the long-delayed expedition sailed at last. Only in the case of the northern magnates did his policy fail. They had made it clear that their opposition to the proposed campaign was more than temporary. Further, in Eustace de Vesci, who was probably back in England in the summer, John faced perhaps his most bitter opponent. On the very day on which a safe-conduct was provided for de Vesci, the King ordered

---

[1] *Rot. Litt. Pat.*, p. 101.

[2] *Rot. Litt. Claus.* i. 165b.

[3] *Selected Letters of Innocent III*, p. 133. Innocent later wrote to his legate, Nicholas of Tusculum, ordering him to declare null and void all conspiracies which had been formed because of the quarrel between the kingdom and the priesthood (ibid., p. 165 and note).   [4] *Rot. Litt. Claus.* i. 146.

the complete destruction of his castle of Alnwick.[1] His Yorkshire
castle of Malton was also razed.[2] The only compensation Eustace
received for his exile and the subsequent seizure of his lands was
£100,[3] in the circumstances a paltry sum amounting to perhaps
a quarter of the annual revenue of his lands.[4] Eustace is the only
one of all the rebels whom we know received the compliment of
a personal letter from the Pope ordering him to cease troubling
the King.[5]

John's reaction to the situation in the north was very similar
to what it had been a year earlier. By September it must have been
clear that his northern opponents were not going to submit. He
marched north to Durham with the intention of suppressing
them, but was followed as far as Nottingham by the Archbishop,
who insisted that he could take no action without the judgement
of a court.[6] The Northerners' arguments were now bringing in
their rewards. John stayed in the north for three weeks but
achieved little; there is not even an indication that he met any
of his opponents. He then changed his tactics completely. On
1 November he met the Northerners at Wallingford. Through the
mediation of the papal legate, the Archbishop, and the magnates
lay and ecclesiastical, some kind of agreement was reached between them. Of this the chroniclers tell nothing except that the
King promised to restore the Northerners' ancient liberties.
Whatever the details of the settlement they soon lost immediate
importance for the King failed to keep his word.[7]

The Northerners' success was brief. Whatever the concessions
gained from the King on 1 November, they were revoked by him
within a week. In general letters patent of 7 November, which

---

[1] *Rot. Litt. Pat.*, p. 99.
[2] *Pipe Roll, 16 John*, p. 86.
[3] *Rot. Litt. Claus.* i. 146.
[4] Eustace's landed revenues were valued by local juries at £287. 1s. 8d. in 1219
(*Book of Fees*, pp. 246–50, 286). This was almost certainly an underestimate. In
1184–5 the Vesci estates yielded a gross income of £578. 3s. 4d. when in the hands
of royal custodians (*Pipe Roll 31 Henry II*, pp. 8–9). They were farmed at nearly £400
in 1186–8 (*Pipe Roll 33 Henry II*, pp. 12–13; *Pipe Roll 34 Henry II*, p. 4).
[5] *Foedera*, i, pt. 1, p. 126.
[6] *Walt. Cov.* ii. 212; *Coggeshall*, p. 167; *Chron. Maj.* ii. 551–2.
[7] This account is based on two sources which are apparently mutually independent, the Dunstable annals (*Annales Monastici*, iii. 40) and Coggeshall (p. 167).
Coggeshall alone gives the form of agreement and mentions the mediation of the
Archbishop, bishops, and magnates. The Dunstable annals alone give the place and
date. John was in fact at Wallingford on 1 Nov.

Stubbs has made famous,[1] John ordered that the knights of the shire who had already been summoned to Oxford for the 15th should now come armed; the barons were to appear in person and unarmed. It may be that the original summons of these men was made in execution of the agreement reached on the 1st, but, if so, it had clearly collapsed. The threat of force was blatant. Further, the additional summons of four knights from each shire suggests that in the face of baronial criticism, the King was turning to other groups for an endorsement of his policies.

This writ marked a *volte face* in the King's policy towards the northern magnates. John was able to carry it through because of his success in other parts of the country. The general promises of reform of which the chroniclers wrote were only one part of his concessions. They were supplemented by specific arrangements with individual barons, most significantly with the great lords of the eastern and home counties who were to predominate in baronial counsels at Runnymede in 1215. John had been suspicious of some of these men following fitz Walter's treason. Now his relations with them became noticeably easier. In the spring Earl Richard of Clare's daughter was in the King's hands as a hostage.[2] On 21 July John ordered her release.[3] Later, on 20 November, he made a grant to Richard's son, Gilbert, in the lands of Amaury, Count of Evreux, in Marlow and Hambleden, Buckinghamshire.[4] His dealings with two other men, Geoffrey de Mandeville and his old enemy, Robert fitz Walter, are more significant chronologically. On 4 November, three days after his settlement with the Northerners and three days before he broke it, he ordered the commissioners investigating ecclesiastical damages in Norfolk to assess Robert's losses too.[5] Like Eustace de Vesci, Robert hitherto had been given only £100 for his pains.[6] This new order must have raised his hopes of receiving reasonable compensation. On 4 November, too, the King instated Geoffrey de Mandeville in the whole of his inheritance and gave him custody of all the wards and custodies which had been in the charge of his father, Geoffrey fitz Peter; the Tower of London alone was excepted from the grant.[7] The custody of one of these wards, the

---

[1] *Stubbs' Charters*, 9th edn., p. 282. [2] *Rot. Chartarum*, p. 197.
[3] *Rot. Litt. Pat.*, p. 101b. [4] *Rot. Litt. Claus.* i. 155.
[5] Ibid. i. 154b, 164b. [6] Ibid. i. 146.
[7] *Rot. de Ob. et Fin.*, pp. 502–3. The custody of the Tower was given to the Archdeacon of Huntingdon on 3 Nov. (*Rot. Litt. Pat.*, p. 105b).

heir of Adam of Cockfield, was granted to Thomas de Erdinton at the end of December, but in return John wrote to Geoffrey de Mandeville stating that he had allowed Geoffrey 300 m. at the Exchequer 'as agreed upon between us'.[1] A month later de Mandeville's marriage to Isabella of Gloucester was being arranged.[2] These moves, and similar *détentes* affecting other parts of the country,[3] must have altered John's position radically. It is unimaginable that he would have made them without a *quid pro quo*. In all probability they represented the final stages in the political isolation of the northern opponents of the proposed campaign in Poitou. Eustace de Vesci and Robert fitz Walter, who had suffered the same fate in 1212, were to react very differently to the Poitevin campaign in 1214.

John tried similar methods in the north, but with less success. Sometime in the summer of 1213 he granted the custody of the daughters of Richard de Lucy of Egremont to Thomas of Moulton, a grant which eventually established the Moultons in Cumberland.[4] On 20 September, while he was at Tickhill, he also gave John de Lacy possession of his inheritance and acquitted him of all the debts of his father, Roger.[5] In both these cases, especially the last, the King drove a hard bargain, but at least these men followed him to Poitou. In general in the north, however, concession was no longer producing results, and in the end the King reversed the administrative arrangements which had followed the plot of 1212. On 25 January 1214 Alexander of Pointon was instructed to hand over the custody of Lincolnshire to one of the King's familiars, John Marshal.[6] By April Robert de Percy had been replaced as sheriff of Yorkshire by another

---

[1] *Rot. Litt. Claus.* i. 140b.   [2] Ibid. i. 162b; *Rot. Litt. Pat.*, p. 109b.

[3] Geoffrey's marriage was part of a general rearrangement of forces in the Welsh Marches involving a pacification of the Marcher baronage.

John's suspicions of William Marshal lessened towards the end of 1212 (S. Painter, *William Marshal*, pp. 173 ff.). In Oct. 1213 William was permitted to fine for Haverford castle (*Rot. Litt. Pat.*, p. 105; *Rot. de Ob. et Fin.*, p. 499) and in Jan. 1214 received custody of the castles of Cardigan, Carmarthen, and Gower (*Rot. de Ob. et Fin.*, p. 522; *Rot. Litt. Pat.*, p. 109b).

In July 1213 Walter de Lacy was restored to all his English and Marcher lands except Ludlow (*Rot. Litt. Claus.* i. 147). He recovered Ludlow town in October as part of some kind of agreement with the King (ibid. i. 173b, 175); Ludlow castle was not restored to him until Apr. 1215 (*Rot. Litt. Pat.*, p. 132).

[4] *Rot. Chartarum*, p. 197; *Rot. de Ob. et Fin.*, pp. 482–3.

[5] *Rot. de Ob. et Fin.*, pp. 494–5.

[6] *Rot. Litt. Pat.*, p. 109; *Rot. Litt. Claus.* i. 162.

trusted royal agent, Peter fitz Herbert.[1] When the King sailed to Poitou the north was still unpacified; the northern castles were still kept in readiness for instant action.[2]

John sailed on 9 or 10 February. He did not return to England until 15 October. There is a mass of material dealing with the military and financial administration of the campaign. There are two fragmentary lists in the close rolls, one naming those who sent their service, the other those who were to have their scutage.[3] These are supplemented by the scutage accounts and the accounts of those who received payments during the campaign (*prestita Pictavensa*) on the pipe roll for 16 John. From 1214 also comes the first surviving scutage roll, which records the names of those who undertook to perform service or pay scutage and hence were given a licence to collect it themselves.[4] Finally, a fragment of a muster roll survives covering some of the southern counties and part of the honour of Leicester.[5]

These records provide a complete and impressive confirmation of the evidence of those two writers who thought that the Northerners played a special part in the resistance to John's plans. Indeed, if the Coggeshall and Barnwell chroniclers erred at all, it was in being too general rather than too specific. They were right in arguing that the resistance to the campaign and scutage came from the northern magnates. Even in the north, however, many of those who rebelled in 1215 were not yet prepared to refuse the King's demands.

The most important feature of the evidence lies in the reaction of the barons of the midland, eastern, and home counties. Many of these men, even those who later found a place on the committee of Twenty-Five, served in Poitou or sent their service. Saer de Quenci, Earl of Winchester, sent his son,[6] was allowed to collect his scutage[7] and was quit by writ on the Warwickshire and Sussex accounts in the pipe roll.[8] Roger Bigod, Earl of Norfolk, sent his

---

[1] Peter was given custody of Pickering castle, which normally went with the shrievalty, on 8 Apr. (*Rot. Litt. Pat.*, p. 113). At Michaelmas he accounted for the shire for half the year (*Pipe Roll 16 John*, p. 85).

[2] See orders of June and July for the replacement of perishable foodstuffs at Scarborough and Knaresborough (*Rot. Litt. Claus.* i. 207, 208b).

[3] *Rot. Litt. Claus.* i. 166, 200b–201.   [4] *Pipe Roll 17 John*, pp. 105–8.

[5] P.R.O., Chancery Miscellanea, 5/11. I am obliged to Miss Patricia M. Barnes, of the Public Record Office, for bringing this document to my notice.

[6] *Rot. Litt. Claus.* i. 201.   [7] Ibid.

[8] *Pipe Roll 16 John*, pp. 114, 167.

knights and was acquitted by writ of his scutage.[1] Richard de Muntfichet, William de Lanvallei, William de Mandeville, William of Huntingfield, and Geoffrey de Say all had to account for *prestita Pictavensa*[2] and were all allowed their scutage.[3] Even where there is no evidence of the performance of service, there was no difficulty in the matter of scutage. Geoffrey de Mandeville was allowed to collect his scutage and paid part of what was due from the honour of Gloucester.[4] Earl Richard of Clare and William de Albini were both allowed to collect.[5] The scutage roll also records that Robert fitz Walter's scutage was put in respite until the second week in September, when the account for the scutage was due.[6] There is little hint in any of this of an exceptional or critical situation.

Many northern men followed the same line of action. John de Lacy, Nicholas de Stuteville, Maurice de Gant, Robert de Vaux, and Thomas of Moulton all accounted for *prestita Pictavensa*.[7] Robert de Ros and Simon of Kyme sent their sons. Robert also paid part of his scutage, but Simon was quit by writ.[8] John fitz Robert was also quit by writ on the Northumberland account,[9] and Norman Darcy and Simon de Chauncy on the Lincolnshire account.[10] The collection of scutage was not an insuperable difficulty in all northern counties. Letters were sent to the sheriffs of Northumberland ordering them to collect scutage from all tenants-in-chief by knight service.[11] They later accounted for the sums due from many of these men, including Richard de Unfraville, Roger de Merlay, Adam of Tynedale, Gilbert de Laval, and Roger Bertram.[12] On the Lincolnshire account Gilbert de Gant and Thomas de Scotigny paid part of what they owed.[13] So did Hubert fitz Ralph of Crich on the account for Nottinghamshire and Derbyshire.[14]

---

[1] *Rot. Litt. Claus.* i. 166, 201; *Pipe Roll 16 John*, p. 177.
[2] Ibid., pp. 9, 13, 176.
[3] Ibid., pp. 10, 34 and *Rot. Litt. Claus.* i. 200b–201b.
[4] *Pipe Roll 17 John*, p. 107; *Pipe Roll 16 John*, p. 60.
[5] *Pipe Roll 17 John*, pp, 106, 108						[6] Ibid., p. 106.
[7] *Pipe Roll 16 John*,. pp. 95, 140, 152; *Rot. Litt. Claus.* i. 201.
[8] *Pipe Roll 16 John*, pp. 66, 95, 152, 153, 161; *Rot. Litt. Claus.* i. 201b.
[9] *Pipe Roll 16 John*, p. 66.
[10] *Rot. Litt. Claus.* i. 200b–201; *Pipe Roll 16 John*, 153.
[11] *Pipe Roll 17 John*, p. 107.						[12] *Pipe Roll 16 John*, p. 66.
[13] Ibid., pp. 152, 153.
[14] Ibid., p. 161.

Some men, however, were adamant in the face of the King's demands. The most prominent were Eustace de Vesci, Peter de Brus, Richard de Percy, Roger de Montbegon, Robert Grelley, and William de Mowbray. None of these men appeared on the scutage roll. None of them accounted for *prestita Pictavensa*. None of them accounted for their scutage. On the account of the archbishopric of York, the custodian, Brian de Lisle, paid the scutage on a quarter fee held of the archbishopric by William de Mowbray,[1] but this is the only payment recorded at the time against any one of them.[2] Their action was decisive, and John and his officials saw its implications only too clearly. In July, in a rather undignified letter, John wrote home from Poitou asking all those who were not serving or involved in government business at home to come to his aid, and promising that any rancour he had towards them would be allayed if they complied.[3] This plea awoke no response. The new Justiciar, Peter des Roches, tried more direct methods. One of the last entries on the roll of letters close issued under his name is an undated and mutilated entry dealing with the scutage of Eustace de Vesci, Roger de Montbegon, and Robert Grelley. Their stock had been distrained 'pro scutagio'. The sheriffs responsible were now to restore it until 15 October.[4] This, coincidentally, was the day John landed at Dartmouth. Peter was shelving the problem. This time there was no hope of browbeating or crushing the King's opponents.

Like John, the Northerners were gambling, they on the failure of his campaign, he on its success. The Northerners won. The road from Bouvines to Runnymede was direct, short, and unavoidable. On 16 August, probably shortly after he had heard of the defeat of his allies, the King sent home two agents with secret instructions for the Justiciar and his associates and orders to castellans throughout the country dealing with the 'keeping of our castles and our person'.[5] By September Peter des Roches' instructions were sounding a new note of panic. Thus, on the 7th, Philip of Oldcotes was ordered to fortify the castles in his custody

---

[1] *Pipe Roll 16 John*, p. 70.

[2] On the pipe roll of Easter 1215 the sheriff of Northumberland accounted for the scutage of Eustace de Vesci and paid it out of his surplus. This account, however, was not in fact drawn up until Michaelmas 1219. The surplus on the 1219 account was transferred to the 1215 account (*Pipe Roll 17 John*, p. 39; *Pipe Roll 3 Henry III*, p. 168.   [3] *Rot. Litt. Pat.*, p. 118b.

[4] *Rot. Litt. Claus.* i. 213b.   [5] Ibid. i. 202.

'as seems best to him and according to the rumours he hears'.[1] John and his officials expected disaster. They did not miscalculate.

The first effect of the King's failure was to broaden the opposition to the Poitevin scutage. The day of account which had been given to the sheriffs was 9 September. This too was the day when those barons who had received licences to collect were to account either by payment or by producing a quittance.[2] When the accounts came to be held they were the occasion of a widespread demonstration against the King. No account was possible for Yorkshire. After the civil war it was noted on the roll for 1214 that the account had been put in abeyance until 1218, but no payments had been made when the roll of 1219 was completed.[3] There was no account in 1214 for Lancashire. This first appears on the roll of Easter 1215, but all that was done was to note the quittance due to John de Lacy.[4] The outstanding sums were still due in 1219.[5] After the north, the difficulties were greatest in the eastern and home counties. No payment was recorded against Earl Richard of Clare[6] or Robert fitz Walter.[7] There was no account for Norfolk and Suffolk. This was inserted on the 1214 roll in 1217 or 1218.[8] The quittances due to Earl Roger Bigod, William, Earl of Arundel, Hubert de Burgh, and others were then noted and the sheriff accounted for six small payments, but there was still no payment from the rest, and their scutage was still owing in 1219.[9] On the Essex and Hertfordshire roll the items were entered ready for account, but no payments were made; the Exchequer clerks did not record whether the tenants-in-chief accounted for their scutage or still owed it, the appropriate space simply being left blank.[10] In the end the administration of the account broke down completely. Blank entries similar to those on the Essex and Hertfordshire account appear on the rolls of almost every county. They even appear against the names of such notable supporters of the King as William de Warenne,[11] Peter des Roches,[12] Warin fitz Gerald,[13] and William Briwerre.[14] In some instances similar entries were made against men who also accounted for *prestita*

---

[1] *Rot. Litt. Claus.* i. 212.
[2] *Pipe Roll 17 John*, p. 108.
[3] *Pipe Roll 16 John*, p. 95; *Pipe Roll 3 Henry III*, pp. 205–6.
[4] *Pipe Roll 17 John*, p. 58.
[5] *Pipe Roll 3 Henry III*, p. 154.
[6] *Pipe Roll 16 John*, p. 177.
[7] Ibid., p. 10.
[8] Ibid., pp. 176–7.
[9] *Pipe Roll 3 Henry III*, p. 44.
[10] *Pipe Roll 16 John*, pp. 9–10.
[11] Ibid., p. 166.
[12] Ibid., p. 10.
[13] Ibid.
[14] Ibid., p. 177.

Pictavensa and had received a quittance on their scutage.¹ All this stands in striking contrast to the customary neatness and exactness with which the exchequer officials had done the preliminary work of preparing the accounts and noting the number of fees on which scutage was due.

The renewed resistance in the eastern and home counties was significant. There were signs in the summer and autumn of 1214 that good relations between the government and the East Anglian baronage were wearing thin. Geoffrey de Mandeville had made the enormous offer of 20,000 m. for the hand of Isabella of Gloucester. Payment was due in four instalments, the last at Michaelmas 1214.² Geoffrey did not keep these terms, and in February the seizure of the honour of Gloucester was ordered.³ These lands were restored in August,⁴ but Geoffrey was still in a precarious position, for, apart from this fine, Geoffrey son of Geoffrey de Say was renewing the old claims of his family to the Mandeville barony.⁵ Meanwhile the King was still suspiciously resentful of Robert fitz Walter. In a letter dealing with the election of a new abbess at Barking, addressed to Peter des Roches at the end of August, John directed that Robert's sister was not to be chosen under any circumstances.⁶ Once the King and those who had accompanied him were back in England, the baronial campaign developed more rapidly. According to the Coggeshall and Barnwell writers, the Northerners were now insisting on the confirmation of the charter of Henry I.⁷ According to Wendover, the King's opponents met at Bury St. Edmunds and swore that they would compel him, if necessary by force, to accept this demand.⁸ Wendover's evidence is of dubious value.⁹ If true, it

---

¹ See the instance of William de Cahaignes (*Pipe Roll 16 John*, pp. 103, 105; *Rot. Litt. Claus.* i. 201).
² *Pipe Roll 16 John*, p. 10; *Rot. de Ob. et Fin.*, pp. 520–1.
³ *Rot. Litt. Claus.* i. 163b. ⁴ Ibid. i. 209b, 210, 211b.
⁵ Geoffrey backed his claim with the proffer of 15,000 m. in July (ibid. i. 168b). Geoffrey de Say senior, who died in May 1214, had also brought an action claiming the Mandeville honour in the Hilary Term, 1214 (*Curia Regis Rolls*, vii. 110–11). For the nature of the claim see *Complete Peerage*, v. 118 ff., 126.
⁶ *Rot. Litt. Claus.* i. 202b. ⁷ *Walt. Cov.* ii. 217–18; *Coggeshall*, p. 170.
⁸ *Chron. Maj.* ii. 582–3.
⁹ The passage presents two obvious problems:
1. It partially duplicates the story of the St. Paul's meeting of 25 Aug. 1213. Although he had transcribed the charter of Henry I in his description of this first incident, Wendover now goes out of his way to provide a summary of it. On the earlier occasion the barons had apparently sworn to fight to the death for the charter;

could only mean that the centre of rebellion was already shifting to the eastern and home counties. In fact the great lords of this area only came into the open very slowly. Fitz Walter himself cannot have committed himself publicly until the last few weeks of the year. He and Roger Bigod were associated with William Marshal, Peter des Roches, and others in a meeting held at Bury on 28 June to determine the disputed election to the abbacy.[1] On 22 November both fitz Walter and Richard de Muntfichet, along with many loyalist lords, witnessed a royal grant to the church of St. Paul's dated at the New Temple at London.[2] Fitz Walter, Richard of Clare, Geoffrey de Mandeville, and Richard de Muntfichet were all at London when the King and the magnates met for discussions there in the second week of January.[3] Those present were given a safe-conduct until Easter.[4] One East Anglian magnate, Roger de Cressy, came under its terms; he, and presumably men of similar origins, were soon being described as 'Northerners'.[5] Nevertheless, they did not all jump at once. A notification of this safe-conduct was addressed on 14 January to William Marshal and Roger Bigod.[6] Roger cannot yet have cast his lot with the King's opponents.

There is perhaps no greater tribute to John's ability as a politician and administrator than the energy and skill with which he faced the situation. Throughout the winter months he made rapid preparations for the impending civil war. He had brought

now there was yet another confederation in a slightly different form (*Chron. Maj.* ii. 552, 554, 582–3).

2. Wendover is the sole contemporary source. The story reappears in a slightly condensed form in the fourteenth-century *Cronica Buriensis* (*Memorials of St. Edmund*, iii. 10–11), but it does not appear in the contemporary Bury writers. It is particularly surprising that there is no hint of it in the narrative of the election of Abbot Hugh. This, although probably written in its present form in the middle of the thirteenth century, is based on a very detailed contemporary account of a man who witnessed many of the events he described and who took a keen interest not only in the history of his own house, but also in the activity of the local magnates. He notes the texts on which Langton and the papal legate preached when they visited Bury (*Memorials*, ii. 39, 42) and gives a magnificent account of the visit of the King on 4 Nov. 1214, when John sat in the chapter house to settle the disputed election (ibid. ii. 95–101). He could scarcely have been ignorant of a baronial *conjuratio* sworn on the high altar of the abbey. This is exactly the kind of event which would have interested him. Nowhere, however, does he even hint of anything similar to the events described by Wendover.

[1] *Memorials of St. Edmunds*, ii. 74–77.
[2] *Cal. Charter Rolls*, i. 154.
[3] *Rot. Chartarum*, pp. 203–204b.
[4] *Rot. Litt. Pat.*, p. 126b.
[5] *Curia Regis Rolls*, vii. 315.
[6] *Rot. Litt. Pat.*, p. 126b.

mercenary forces back from Poitou. At the end of October they were dispatched to several royal castles throughout the country; Faulkes de Breauté was in charge of their distribution and pay.[1] Letters of 21 November provided for the construction of siege machines at Nottingham and Knaresborough.[2] Work was being done on the defences of at least ten castles.[3] Even weaker defences were now considered of value; at the end of March the bailiffs of Peter de Maulay at Doncaster were instructed to erect a palisade behind the ditch surrounding the town and barricade the bridge.[4] After the failure of the discussions at London in January these measures were being pressed on even more rapidly. Twenty sergeants had been sent to Philip Mark at Nottingham on 30 October.[5] More reinforcements were sent to him on 28 January[6] and a further six knights on 17 February.[7] Philip of Oldcotes was being similarly reinforced.[8] When Geoffrey de Neville was placed in charge of Scarborough castle on 29 March he had at least sixty sergeants and ten crossbowmen under his command. The garrison of the castle after 18 April consisted of at least ten knights, seventy-two sergeants, and thirteen crossbowmen.[9] Brian de Lisle, constable of Knaresborough, and Gilbert fitz Reinfrey, sheriff of Lancaster, were also busy fortifying the castles of their bailiwicks and holding them against the King's enemies.[10] Meanwhile foreign troops were beginning to pour into the country. John was expecting the knights and men of Savaric de Mauleon as early as 8 February.[11] Hubert de Burgh, Seneschal of Poitou, was dispatching knights to England in March.[12] By April he and the Chamberlain, Geoffrey de Neville, had received a loan of 1,100 m. from the Templars to pay for their transit.[13] In January John had gained respite from answering the baronial demands until Low Sunday. He was making very good use of his time.

---

[1] *Rot. Litt. Claus.* i. 176, 178b; *Rot. Litt. Pat.*, pp. 126b, 127.

[2] *Rot. Litt. Claus.* i. 178–178b.

[3] Colchester (*Rot. Litt. Claus.* i. 179b, 182b, 193, 195), Corfe (ibid. i. 178b, 185), Winchester (ibid. i. 185b), Wallingford (ibid. i. 187b), Oxford (ibid. i. 188), Hertford (ibid. i. 189b), Tower of London (ibid. i. 191), Mountsorrel (ibid. i. 194), Berkhampstead (ibid. i. 195), Northampton (ibid.).   [4] Ibid. i. 192b.

[5] Ibid. i. 176.   [6] Ibid. i. 183b.   [7] Ibid. i. 188.

[8] On 20 Feb., 3 and 31 Mar. (ibid. i. 188b, 189b, 192b).

[9] *Rot. Litt. Pat.*, p. 131b; *Rot. Litt .Claus.* i. 214b.

[10] *Rot. Litt. Claus.* i. 193.   [11] Ibid. i. 187b.

[12] *Rot. Litt. Pat.*, pp. 130–130b.   [13] *Rot. Litt. Claus.* i. 194.

In addition to these military measures the King was trying hard to adjust the political balance in the north in his own favour. In October 1214 he instated William de Fors in his English inheritance.[1] William had been with the King in Poitou[2] and was presumably considered a good political investment. John's probable intentions here, admittedly obscured in the event by William's waywardness, were to establish a strong royalist influence at Cockermouth and in Holderness, and especially at Skipton in the Aire Gap. In May he had also acknowledged the claims of Alice, Countess of Eu, to the honour of Tickhill and granted the honour to her husband, Ralf de Lusignan.[3] Earlier still, in April, he had given the hand of Isabel, daughter of Robert of Thornham, to Peter de Maulay, the castellan of Corfe.[4] Peter offered 7,000 m. for the marriage[5] and, as a result, acquired a position of considerable territorial influence in Yorkshire. At Doncaster his men controlled one of the strategic points in the county. Letters of 1 February 1215 instructed all royal officials to protect Peter's lands while he was in the King's service and acquitted him of suit at shire and hundred, of sheriff's aid and of all pleas and complaints.[6] On 29 April his debts to the King were excused until further notice.[7] Doncaster was to remain a centre of royalist influence throughout the civil war.

During 1214 and the early months of 1215 John was making several arrangements of this kind affecting different parts of the country.[8] He was also working hard to retain the loyalty of those who were still probably wavering between him and his opponents. Foremost among these in the north were Robert de Ros and John de Lacy. Robert was still sheriff of Cumberland. He was present at the negotiations at London in January 1215 and on the 14th appeared as one of the guarantors of the safe-conduct given to the barons who had attended.[9] A day later John granted him three manors of the royal demesne in Cumberland, until such time as he could recover his lost Norman estates,[10] and the fee farm of the manor of Aldwark in Yorkshire.[11] On 13 April Robert was granted

---

[1] *Rot. Litt. Pat.*, p. 122b; *Rot. Chartarum*, p. 201b.

[2] *Rot. Litt. Claus.* i. 200b.

[3] *Rot. Litt. Pat.*, p. 116; *Complete Peerage*, v. 162–3.

[4] *Rot. Litt. Pat.*, p. 113b. [5] *Pipe Roll 16 John*, p. 94.

[6] *Rot. Litt. Pat.*, p. 128. [7] *Rot. Litt. Claus.* i. 197b.

[8] See S. Painter, *The Reign of King John*, p. 282.

[9] *Rot. Litt. Pat.*, p. 126b. [10] Ibid., p. 128. [11] *Rot. Litt. Claus.* i. 183.

the farm of Carlisle as a contribution towards his expenses in keeping the castle.[1] Robert adhered to the baronial cause in June, but John did not attempt to remove him from his shrievalty until 24 July.[2] John de Lacy seems to have sold his support more dearly. He is named as one of those who took the Cross along with the King on 4 March.[3] On the next day he received a pardon for all his debts, including those of his father, Roger.[4] These included over £2,800 which he still owed from the fine he had made for his baronies in 1213.[5] With several northern sheriffs and castellans, he was warned by letters of 23 April to be ready to receive secret instructions from Peter des Roches,[6] and as late as 31 May royal letters provided for the protection of those whom de Lacy vouched to the King's peace.[7] De Ros and de Lacy were not the only ones to be wooed. The King was even bestowing material expressions of his benevolence on men whom he had earlier suspected of treason. On 14 April Roger de Merlay was given a licence to empark his wood of Nether Witton.[8] On the 23rd the custodians of the bishopric of Durham were instructed to lend Richard de Unfraville 60 m.[9]

These and similar measures did much to limit the slow leakage of men to the ranks of the opposition. It is impossible to follow the spread of rebellion in detail. On 12 May, after the baronial defiance, the King directed his men to seize the lands of his enemies,[10] but only a dozen or so subsequent recorded writs were aimed at individual rebels.[11] Most prominent among these were Robert fitz Walter, Robert de Vere, Henry de Bohun, and William of Huntingfield. Other evidence shows that Roger de Cressy, Saer de Quenci, and William Malet were also involved by the latter part of May.[12] None of this evidence, however, deals with the northern counties, for by now John was losing touch with his northern castellans and supporters. Their only recorded achievement was the considerable one of forcing the surrender of Richmond castle from Ruald fitz Alan.[13] This gap in the evidence cannot be filled. The chroniclers name some of the rebels, but only the most obvious, such as Robert fitz Walter, Geoffrey de Mande-

[1] *Rot. Litt. Claus.* i. 194b.
[2] *Rot. Litt. Pat.*, p. 150.
[3] *Gerv. Cant.* ii. 109.
[4] *Rot. Litt. Pat.*, p. 129b.
[5] Pipe Roll 16 John, rot. 8, m. 2d.
[6] *Rot. Litt. Pat.*, p. 134.
[7] Ibid., p. 142b.
[8] *Rot. Litt. Claus.* i. 195.
[9] Ibid. i. 196b.
[10] Ibid. i. 204.
[11] Ibid. i. 200.
[12] *Rot. Litt. Pat.*, pp. 141b, 138b.
[13] Ibid., pp. 131, 132, 143b.

ville, and Eustace de Vesci. The one detailed list, that which
Roger of Wendover gave of the men who met at Stamford at
Easter,[1] is thoroughly unreliable and was largely compiled from
the later letters excommunicating the rebels which Wendover
included in his chronicle.[2]

Despite this difficulty, one important point is certain. Until the
baronial capture of London on 17 May created a landslide, the
King was managing to retain the loyalty of many of those who
figured on the baronial side at Runnymede. John assumed that he
had the support of Robert de Ros as late as 13 April,[3] of John fitz
Robert as late as 17 May,[4] and of John de Lacy as late as 31 May.[5]
William de Albini, another of the Twenty-Five, had been one of
the guarantors of the safe-conduct of January[6] and probably only
joined the movement after the fall of London.[7] The fall of London
was probably also decisive in the case of William de Fors; the first
sure indication of his temporary junction with the King's opponents is his inclusion in the Twenty-Five. When the rebels

---

[1] *Chron. Maj.* ii. 585.

[2] Ibid. ii. 643, 644. The objections to Wendover's evidence at this point are as
follows:

1. It conflicts with the evidence of the Barnwell writer, who states that Robert
fitz Walter and Geoffrey de Mandeville joined the rebel army after the muster at
Stamford during the march on Northampton (*Walt. Cov.* ii. 219).

2. It reflects the papal letters of excommunication and those of the executors of
the papal mandate. Where the names are common to both Wendover's list and these
letters, those in the first part of his list are, with one exception, to be found in the
papal letters, those in the second part of his list are usually to be found in the executors' list, which dealt on the whole with less important men. More significantly, the
names of Robert de Vere, Fulk fitz Warin, William Malet, and William de Montagu
appear in the same contiguous order in both Wendover's list and the papal letters of
excommunication. The odds against this happening accidentally are very long.

3. Wendover's list has some independence. The names of John fitz Alan, Gilbert
de Laval, Gilbert de Gant, John fitz Robert, and Robert of Brackley do not appear in
either of the letters of excommunication. But in the case of one of these, John fitz
Robert, Wendover's knowledge was inaccurate, for John was still on the King's
side. So also were John de Lacy and Robert de Ros, both of whom he names.

4. The one really important man named in the letters of excommunication, but
omitted in Wendover's list, is William de Albini, lord of Belvoir. As Wendover was
prior of Belvoir at the time, William de Albini's exclusion from the list of the muster
probably reflects accurate knowledge. Wendover, in fact, states that he only rebelled
after the baronial capture of London (*Chron. Maj.* ii. 587-8).

These arguments assume, of course, that the names listed in the letters of excommunication are given correctly. Wendover is the only source for them. Apart from
his acknowledged unreliability, there is no reason for doubting them.

[3] See above, pp. 105-6.   [4] *Rot. Litt. Pat.*, pp. 136b-137.

[5] See above p. 106.

[6] *Rot. Litt. Pat.*, p. 126b.   [7] *Chron. Maj.* ii. 587-8.

came face to face with John at Runnymede, there were many whose open support of the baronial cause was only a few months old. In some cases its duration could be counted in weeks, even days. This new accession of strength to the rebels, along with the loss of London, compelled the King to negotiate. But, at the same time, it provided him with opportunities. John was expert in the policies involved in the principle of 'divide and rule'.

VII

RUNNYMEDE

IN June 1215 the barons proceeded to choose twenty-five of
their number for the commission envisaged in cap. 60 of
Magna Carta. The names of the Twenty-Five survive in the
Chronica Majora of Matthew Paris.[1] Paris had some source of
information on the events of John's reign which had not been
available to earlier surviving writers, either at St. Albans or elsewhere.[2] His list of the Twenty-Five seems to be accurate.[3] It is a
significant commentary on the speed with which the opposition
to the King had developed since 1214. Three members of the
Twenty-Five had been guarantors of the safe-conduct given to
the barons in January.[4] Two certainly, and probably a further
four, had only turned against the King within the last month.[5]

---

[1] *Chron. Maj.* ii. 604–5.

[2] For example, he added the name of Conan fitz Ellis to Wendover's list of the
Stamford confederates (ibid. ii. 585). He also included what appears to have been a
list of some of those who took the oath to the Twenty-Five (ibid. ii. 585).

[3] Where strictly contemporary evidence survives, it confirms Paris's list. Thus
thirteen of the Twenty-Five and no others are named as the baronial parties to the
treaty dealing with the custody of London (*Foedera*, i, pt. 1, p. 133). Compare the
four named in what is clearly a writ authorized by the Twenty-Five (*Bulletin of the
John Rylands Library*, xxviii. 443).

The names of the Twenty-Five are also given in a late thirteenth-century collection
of English law and custom, which includes extracts from the laws of Edward the
Confessor and William I, Glanville, the charters of liberties of Henry I, John, and
Henry III and the statutes of Marlborough and Westminster I. The names are here
inserted by a later hand in the margin of the last section of the 1215 Charter (B.M.
Harl. MS. 746, f. 64).

In some respects this second version reads the better of the two. It does not, like
Paris, make William Marshal the younger an earl, but this was perhaps a pardonable
error on Paris's part. It also gives Roger de Montbegon correctly (*Mumbezon*; compare Paris's Roger de Mowbray, *Munbrai*), and William de Lanvallei correctly (compare *Chron. Maj.* ii. 605, n. 3). In contrast the Harleian MS. reads *Robertus de Roys*
for Paris's *Robertus de Ros*.

For a discussion of both lists see Blackstone's Commentary (*Law Tracts*, ii. xxxii).
His views have rightly been accepted by all subsequent authorities. See, for example,
McKechnie, *Magna Carta* (1914), p. 469, n. 2.

[4] Saer de Quenci, Robert de Ros, William de Albini (*Rot. Litt. Pat.*, p. 126b).

[5] John de Lacy, John fitz Robert, Robert de Ros, William de Albini, and William
de Fors (see above, p. 107). Saer de Quenci was probably not known to be a rebel
as late as 6 May, the day after the baronial defiance, for he was then referred to as

Eleven, at least, had either served in Poitou or sent their service.[1] Both territorially and politically, the old northern opposition of 1213 and 1214 was now submerged in a much wider flood of protest. The balance on the committee lay heavily with the magnates of the eastern and home counties and their friends and associates.[2] Even Gilbert de Clare and Hugh Bigod, the sons of the Earls of Clare and Norfolk, found a place. Gilbert de Gant, in contrast, did not, even though he was present at Runnymede.[3] Only eight of the Twenty-Five had major territorial interests in the north. Four of these, William de Fors, John de Lacy, Robert de Ros, and John fitz Robert, were recent recruits to the rebellion. The other four, Eustace de Vesci, William de Mowbray, Roger de Montbegon, and Richard de Percy, were the only members of the committee who had openly resisted the Poitevin scutage prior to the defeat at Bouvines. Two of their associates in this resistance, Peter de Brus and Robert Grelley, both men of importance, were not members.

There is no evidence to suggest that Peter or Robert were embittered by their exclusion. To argue as much would perhaps put an anachronistic reading on their attitude, for the medieval baron was more willing to rebel than to burden himself with the administrative drudgery which a rebellion, once successful, necessarily involved. Nevertheless, the composition of the committee represents a marked dilution of the opposition to the King, a dilution in the sense that the old recalcitrant element of 1214 was now in a small minority. Those of the committee who had fought the Poitevin scutage were even outnumbered by those who had sided with the King into the early months of 1215 and beyond.

There is, therefore, the problem of the relationship between the old opposition and the new. These men were not all equally committed to fighting the King. William of Aumale returned to the King's side within two months; John de Lacy was to sur-

dilectus et fidelis in a writ of computate allowing him expenses incurred in repairs to Kenilworth castle (*Pipe Roll Society*, N.S. xxxi (1955), 129).

[1] Saer de Quenci, Roger Bigod, Richard de Muntfichet, William de Lanvallei, William of Huntingfield, Geoffrey de Say, John de Lacy, Robert de Ros, John fitz Robert, William de Fors (see above, pp. 98–99), and William Malet (*Rot. Litt. Claus.* i. 201).

[2] For the importance of this group see J. H. Round, 'King John and Robert fitz Walter', *E.H.R.* xix (1904), 707–11; F. M. Powicke, *Stephen Langton*, pp. 207 ff.

[3] *Rot. Chartarum*, p. 210b.

render under humiliating terms in the winter of 1215, and Robert de Ros was to yield the vital fortress of Carlisle to royal agents in January 1216. They were not all agreed on the terms they were demanding from the King. The dilution of the opposition was accompanied by a dilution in its demands, so much so, that when the final settlement was drawn up in Magna Carta it proved unacceptable not only to King John, but also to the more determined of the rebels. There may well have been incipient divisions in the baronial ranks much earlier. When, at London in January, John asked for respite until Easter before answering the baronial demands, there were mixed reactions. According to the Barnwell chronicler, some were prepared to agree; others objected, fearing treachery on the King's part.[1] From January until June the King played his hand skilfully, now negotiating with a section of the baronage, now making offers to individuals, now suggesting a form of general settlement which might satisfy the more moderate of his opponents and retain waverers on his side. In the end he gained something from the passage of time, for the terms he procured in June were in some respects easier than those which he would have had to accept, and indeed had himself offered, earlier.

The period between January and June was one of repeated, almost continuous negotiation.[2] Throughout, a vital role was played by two men who must have had a moderating influence on both parties, Archbishop Stephen Langton and William Marshal, Earl of Pembroke.[3] One or both of them appear in all the exchanges between the two parties. The exact chronology of the earlier part of the negotiations is very difficult to follow, probably because not all the relevant letters were enrolled. Apparently John's first move was to attempt a settlement with the Northerners. On 19 February he gave them a safe-conduct to come to Oxford on the 22nd to speak with William Marshal, Stephen Langton, and his fellow bishops.[4] This was very short

[1] *Walt. Cov.* ii. 218.
[2] See C. R. Cheney, 'The Eve of Magna Carta', *Bulletin of the John Rylands Library*, xxxviii (1956), 311 ff.; J. C. Holt, 'The Making of Magna Carta', *E.H.R.* lxxii (1957), 401 ff. In my discussion of Professor Cheney's paper I inadvertently implied that he considered the *Articuli* to be baronial in origin. He does in fact emphasize that they reflect wide interests, especially the influence of Langton and men of moderate opinion (loc. cit., pp. 325, 330).
[3] See F. M. Powicke, *Stephen Langton*, pp. 102 ff.; S. Painter, *William Marshal*, pp. 178 ff. [4] *Rot. Litt. Pat.*, p. 129.

notice, and there is no evidence that the proposed meeting ever took place. A further gathering, perhaps of no more than the King's supporters, occurred at Oxford on 14 April.[1] During the interval between these two arrangements a settlement suitable to the King was almost achieved, and this despite his artful performance of crusading vows on 4 March. Letters of 13 March were sent to the barons and bachelors of Poitou who were coming to England, thanking them for the eager response to the King's summons and ordering them to return home 'because the business for which they had been required was concluded'.[2] The early weeks of March also saw a marked slackening in the measures the King was taking against the outbreak of war, in the preparation of his castles and the disposal of his troops at home.

What there was to justify John's optimism at this point is not clear. A possible explanation is suggested by his letters of 29 May in which he outlined the course of his negotiations with the barons to Pope Innocent III. After he had taken the Cross, the King apparently suggested that he should abolish the evil customs of his own reign and his brother's. He further promised to submit the customs of his father's reign 'if any of them were burdensome' to the judgement of his faithful men. These concessions proved unacceptable to the barons and John at once asked the Archbishop to excommunicate his opponents. This the Archbishop refused to do.[3] John's letter does not permit a dating of this offer except within the rather wide limits of 4 March and the early days of May. If it was in fact made in March, and the enrolled writs suggest no other suitable time, the King's letters of the 13th suggest that it came very close to acceptance and may perhaps have been accepted for a time by some of the barons.

At least one further offer was made by the King before the final settlement at Runnymede. This was on 10 May when he promised that he would deal with the barons 'by the law of our realm or by the judgement of their peers in our court'. He agreed to submit the issues between them to a committee of eight, four to be chosen by each side, with the Pope as supreme arbiter. He also

---

[1] *Memorials of St. Edmund*, ii. 124–5.

[2] *Rot. Litt. Pat.*, p. 130. Similar letters were sent to the Seneschals of Gascony and Poitou and to the Chamberlain of Poitou, who were responsible for the transit of the troops. Some of them had got as far as Barfleur; these were ordered to stay there and await orders from the King carried by Aymer de Sacy (ibid., p. 130b).

[3] *Foedera*, i, pt. 1, p. 129.

promised special treatment to Geoffrey de Mandeville and Giles de Braose, Bishop of Hereford, by offering them the judgement of the King's court on the fines they had made for the Gloucester and Braose honours.[1] The barons had already defied the King on 5 May. On 12 May the King took the decisive step of ordering the seizure of the rebels' estates.[2] His promises had proved to be of no avail.

John was forced to go far beyond these promises in his ultimate surrender at Runnymede. By then the fall of London had altered the situation radically. But in one respect his final concessions were not so wide as he had envisaged earlier. His first offer, which we may associate with the *détente* of March, took the year 1189 as a suitable dividing line between good and evil custom. In Magna Carta, in contrast, when a distinction was necessary between the reigns of the three Angevin kings, 1199, the beginning of John's reign, became the crucial year. This meant that the crusader's respite which John was claiming was applied not only to the afforestations and unlawful disseisins of Henry II, but also to those of Richard I.[3] This was a comparatively slight gain, perhaps, but it is a significant indication of the comparative moderation of some of the sections of the Great Charter.

This feature of the Charter stands out more remarkably by the side of some of the earlier baronial demands. These had originated in the cry for the confirmation of the laws of Henry I and Edward the Confessor and for the destruction of evil customs. The criticism of the whole machine of Angevin government which this demand implied was far deeper and wider than the limitations imposed on that machine by the Great Charter.[4] Similarly, the confirmation of the charter of Henry I would have had disastrous effects on at least one branch of the royal administration, for it would probably have entailed the limitation of the forest to the bounds existing in 1087.[5] This would have meant vast deforestations. One surviving document, the so called 'unknown' charter, gives a clear indication of the way in which some of the barons were glossing these demands. At almost every point its provisions are much more sweeping than those of the Great Charter. It

---

[1] *Rot. Litt. Pat.*, p. 141. See also *Rot. Chartarum*, p. 209b.
[2] *Rot. Litt. Claus.* i. 204.   [3] *Magna Carta*, caps. 52, 53.
[4] J. C. Holt, 'The Barons and the Great Charter', *E.H.R.* lxix (1955), 1–24, especially 18 ff.
[5] Cap. 10.

demands that wardships should be placed in the hands of knights of the fee concerned,[1] a point only conceded in Magna Carta in cases where the royal custodian had wasted the estate.[2] It limits overseas service to Normandy and Brittany and provides for a reduction in the amount of service.[3] This finds no mention in Magna Carta. It places restrictions on the levying of scutage which again have no parallel in the 1215 version of Magna Carta.[4] It provides for the deforestation of all areas brought within the forest since 1154.[5] In Magna Carta this was only applied to John's afforestations, the crusader's respite covering those of his two predecessors.[6] Finally, in two sections, it deals with the administration of the forest law.[7] Magna Carta simply provided for investigations by juries into the administration of the foresters and promised subsequent destruction of evil customs.[8]

We do not know precisely when all these demands originated. Wendover would have us believe that Henry I's charter was being discussed as early as the summer of 1213, but we cannot be sure that this was so until the winter of 1214–15.[9] There has also been a wide variation in the dates which modern authorities have attributed to the 'unknown' charter. One point is certain; all these projects preceded Magna Carta. It is perhaps too easily assumed that they were ill-considered, far-reaching schemes which were later forgotten as the more practical and moderate ideas represented in the Charter gained ground. In fact, we do not know exactly how these early plans developed into the Charter. What might be one of the vital links in the evidence, the Brackley schedule, has not survived. It is probable, however, that these and other radical demands were still live issues when the terms of the Charter were being settled by the King and the assembled baronage at Runnymede. The Charter was not so much cast in a new-found mould of sober deliberation as hammered out on the anvil of political conflict.

Part of this conflict is illustrated by the important differences between the Charter and the preliminary terms laid down in the *Articuli*.[10] A further sector of the debate is perhaps revealed by the repetitive language of cap. 2 of the Charter—'scilicet heres vel heredes comitis de baronia comitis integra per centum libras:

---

[1] Cap. 3.   [2] Cap. 4.   [3] Cap. 7.   [4] Cap. 8.
[5] Cap. 9.   [6] Caps. 47, 53.   [7] Caps. 10, 12.   [8] Cap. 48.
[9] See above, pp. 92–93.   [10] See *E.H.R.* lxxii. 403–4.

heres vel heredes baronis de baronia integra per centum libras'—
which seems to reflect an original intention to distinguish between
the reliefs of a baron and an earl, perhaps by putting the baron's
relief at the lower figure of 100 m. to which it was reduced in
1297.[1] It is also arguable that no great interval of time separated
the 'unknown' charter from the *Articuli* and Magna Carta.[2] Seven
of its twelve sections are repeated, in effect, in the *Articuli* and
later in the Charter.[3] Further, to some extent, the *Articuli* reflect
the order in which these sections occur in the 'unknown' charter.[4]
The most striking exception to this is cap. 1 of the 'unknown'
charter. This clause is also distinct in that it is cast in the third
person singular—*concedit rex Johannes*; the remaining clauses
employ the archaic first person singular. Cap. 1 summarizes the
principles of justice later elaborated in caps. 29 and 30 of the
Articuli and caps. 39 and 40 of the Charter. But it is also similar
in intent to the concession John had offered in his letters patent
of 10 May. Its position at the head of the document and its different formulae may therefore result from the fact that the King had
already granted the principle of cap. 1 when the demands contained in the 'unknown' charter were first put together.

The form in which the document has survived, as a contemporary transcript made by a French clerk, makes the late date
which this argument would suggest, or indeed any other date,
highly conjectural. However, there is some significant evidence
in support of it. First, the 'unknown' charter is the only surviving
document to place a limitation on overseas service, and this the
geographic one of confining it to Normandy and Brittany. In

---

[1] The point was appreciated by Bémont, *Chartes des libertés anglaises*, pp. 27, 47 n.

[2] For arguments on the dating see W. S. McKechnie, op. cit. (1914), pp. 171 ff.,
and the later authorities listed in *E.H.R.* lxxii. 413 n.
The choice of dating is very much determined by the attitude taken to the formulae
of the document. If it is accepted as a grant which was in fact made by John, then
Nov. 1213 is the only likely date for it on our present evidence, for this is the only
well recorded occasion of an agreement between the King and his opponents prior
to Runnymede. A more distant possibility might be Mar. 1215. See above, pp. 111–12.
If it is taken as a set of petitions or demands which have been recast, and badly
recast, into the form of a grant, then a wider range of dating is possible, for it could
then belong to any of the discussions between the two parties. This second assumption seems preferable.

[3] Caps. 1, 2, 3, 4, 5, 6, 11.

[4] Caps. 2, 3, and the first sentence of cap. 4 and cap. 6 of the 'unknown' charter
become caps. 1, 2, 3, and 4 of the *Articuli*. The second sentence of cap. 4 becomes
cap. 17 of the *Articuli*, but cap. 8 of Magna Carta. Cap. 5 of the 'unknown' charter
is covered in caps. 15 and 16 of the *Articuli* and caps. 26 and 27 of the Charter.

1225 the writer of Faulkes de Breauté's protestation stated that a prohibition of service in Poitou had been one of the *articuli* for which the country had risen against King John.[1] Secondly, Wendover, as is well known, committed the cardinal mistake of attributing the Charter of the Forest to 1215. The more reputable author of the *Histoire des ducs de Normandie* also erred in stating that John promised at Runnymede that no man should lose life or limb for any wild beast that he took. Neither the *Articuli* nor the Charter dealt with the administration of the forest except to provide for local inquiries into evil customs.[2] But the 'unknown' charter did do so.[3] Indeed its final sentence is identical with the promise which the *Histoire des ducs de Normandie* attributes to King John.[4]

There were probably many demands and proposals made between 1213 and 1215, some perhaps rapidly forgotten, others seriously maintained and not submerged until the general settlement at Runnymede. Of these the 'unknown' charter is one chance survival. Another is probably reflected in Roger of Wendover's version of Magna Carta. Wendover's knowledge of the 1215 Charter was very slight. He had probably seen the preamble, or some kind of draft of it, for he embodied some of its phrases in his own version and used it as a source for his list of those who were on the King's side at Runnymede.[5] The rest of his version, however, to the final clause, is a copy of the reissue of 1225. In this section he made one significant error, for he put the relief of a baron not at £100 but at 100 m., a point which, as we have seen, was probably a topic of debate in 1215.[6] This could have been a slip of the pen, but there are matters in the last section of Wendover's version which could not have been. This section consists of the *forma securitatis* of the 1215 Charter. In the middle of it he inserted material which is peculiar to him alone. First he combined caps. 50 and 51 of the Charter in such a way that they provide not just for the removal of John's alien administrators from office, as in the authentic document, but also for their exile from the country. He also made the otherwise unwarranted insertion of the name of Faulkes de Breauté among those of the Poitevins. Secondly, he followed up this section with a unique

---

[1] *Walt. Cov.* ii. 269. [2] Cap. 39; cap. 48. [3] Caps. 10, 12.

[4] 'Et concedo ne homo perdat pro pecude vitam neque membra.' Compare '—jamais ne feroit pierdre home menbre ne vie por bieste sauvage k'il presist' (*Histoire des ducs de Normandie*, p. 150).

[5] *Chron. Maj.* ii. 589–90. [6] See above, pp. 114–15.

clause which lays down that the custody of four castles, Scarborough, Nottingham, Kenilworth, and Northampton, should be in the hands of trustworthy castellans who should take an oath to do with their castles as the Twenty-Five instructed them.[1] Historians have frequently regarded the *forma securitatis* as the most radical section of the Charter. If this sentence were in the authentic document, it would be regarded as the most radical sentence of the most radical section. In its insistence on a positive control of the choice of royal agents it smacks more of 1258 than of 1215.

Wendover was an inventive, muddled, dramatic writer whose reliability is often questionable.[2] It is possible that he inserted the name of Faulkes de Breauté, from whom St. Albans had suffered much, among the Poitevins with the eye of memory very much on the events of 1223–4 and Faulkes's downfall and exile. Indeed, the careers of John's foreign agents during Henry III's minority may have led him to combine caps. 50 and 51 of the Charter in his own more stringent version. But the section dealing with the custody of the four castles can scarcely be completely spurious. It rings true. Its phrases fit in with the rest of the *forma securitatis*. The four castles named were all of great strategic importance and in the spring of 1215 the barons had already tried, unsuccessfully, to take Northampton. Wendover had the inventiveness to produce this on his own, and the events of the 1220's could be taken as providing him with a reason for doing so, but it is very doubtful whether he had the intelligence to do it without giving himself away. It is perhaps significant that his greater successor, Matthew Paris, made no alteration in Wendover's version at this point when he reproduced it in the *Chronica Majora*, although he had access to an authentic version of the 1215 text and inserted many of its clauses in the 1225 version on which Wendover had chiefly relied. More strikingly still, the *forma securitatis*, as Wendover gave it, was the only section of the Charter which Paris gave *in extenso* in his shorter and later chronicle, the *Historia Anglorum*.[3]

---

[1] 'Et ad melius distringendum nos, quatuor castellani, de Norhantun, scilicet, et Kenillewurthe, de Nithingham, et de Scardeburc, erant jurati (predictis) viginti quinque baronibus quod facient de castris predictis quod ipsi praeceperint et mandaverint, vel major pars eorum. Et tales semper castellani ponantur in illis castris, qui fideles sint, et nolint transgredi juramentum suum' (*Chron. Maj.* ii. 603).

[2] V. H. Galbraith, *Roger of Wendover and Matthew Paris* (Glasgow, 1944)

[3] *Historia Anglorum*, ii. 158–9.

In all three works, one of Wendover and two of Paris, the additional material takes almost the same form and appears at the same point in the *forma securitatis*.[1] Thus there are grounds for believing that one or both of the St. Albans writers had access to a version of the *forma securitatis* which included the section on castles and perhaps also the more stringent version of caps. 50 and 51. Two considerations seem to support this view. First, Wendover's version of the *forma securitatis* was not an integral part of his version of the Charter; in his chronicle the Charter of the Forest intervenes between the two. This suggests that it was derived from a separate and distinct document which did not include the rest of the clauses of the Charter. Secondly, the *Histoire des ducs de Normandie* gives strong support to the St. Albans chroniclers. In discussing the barons' demand for the establishment of the committee of Twenty-Five, the author stated that they wanted the King to agree that he could not make any man a bailiff except by the Twenty-Five.[2] It is difficult to escape the conclusion that some such demand was being pressed.

The evidence presents several variations, of which Magna Carta was only one, on the baronial theme of good and ancient custom. It is clearly important to know which section of the orchestra was playing which tune. The Charter itself was produced at a time when the ranks of the opposition had been swelled by a large number of new recruits. If, as has been argued elsewhere,[3] the immediate predecessor of the Charter, the *Articuli*, was drawn up on 10 June, this document must have been subject to political pressures closely similar to those which produced the Charter. Who took part in these preliminary discussions we do not know, except that Stephen Langton was certainly present and possibly also Saer de Quenci.[4] But in all probability the political balance on the baronial commission which arranged matters with the King on 10 June was little different from that which was revealed some nine days later in the composition of the Twenty-Five. The greater moderation of the *Articuli* and the Charter was a product of the less marked

---

[1] In the *Historia Anglorum* Paris gave the castle clause in full, but condensed Wendover's version of caps. 50 and 51 to 'Et nos amovebimus omnes alienigenas a terra'.

[2] 'Et si vorrent encore avoec tout chou que li rois ne peust jamais metre en sa tierre bailliu, se par les xxv non' (*Histoire des ducs de Normandie*, p. 150).

[3] *E.H.R.* lxxii (1957), 401 ff.   [4] Ibid., pp. 405–6.

recalcitrance of those who now predominated in the baronial party.

The earlier demands for the confirmation of ancient laws and the charter of Henry I were, in contrast, produced at a time when the opposition was still predominantly northern. The Northerners still seem to have been the most influential element as late as January 1215, for, when the barons dispatched agents to Rome, they sent John of Ferriby, a protégé of Eustace de Vesci, and John fitz Osbert, a chaplain of Richard de Percy.[1] Further, there is a strong case for associating many of the variant demands of 1215 with the northern opposition to the King. The 'unknown' charter especially bears an unmistakably northern stamp. First, as has frequently been noted, the Northerners were the members of the opposition most likely to demand the restrictions on overseas service contained in cap. 7. Secondly, the radical sections on the forest are more likely to have sprung from the north, where there was extensive forest in every county except Lincolnshire, than from the east, where there was no forest at all except in Essex. Finally the clause concerned with scutage was probably connected with earlier objections which had been made in the north to this burden. This clause laid down that if there was a scutage it should be levied at the rate of one mark per fee, but that, if the burden of an army occurred, more might be taken by the advice of the barons of the realm.[2] The obvious object of attack here was any scutage levied at a higher rate than a mark per fee, particularly, perhaps, the Poitevin scutage of 3 m. If the obscure phrases of the rest of the clause can be related to any particular situation, it is to what had happened in 1204. Then there had been a scutage—at 2½ m., levied by baronial consent. It had been followed by demands for personal service; the *gravamen exercitus* had been imposed and 'more' had been 'taken'; John had levied fines *pro servicio*, but not, as far as we know, by the advice of the barons of the realm. In Northumberland, Yorkshire, and Lincolnshire, as we have seen, these demands had to be relaxed.[3]

---

[1] See above, p. 11.

[2] 'Et si scutagium evenerit in terra, una marca argenti capietur de feodo militis; et si gravamen exercitus contigerit, amplius caperetur consilio baronum regni.'

I cannot accept Hubert Hall's suggestion, accepted by both Petit-Dutaillis and McKechnie, that *gravamen* is an error for *allevamen*. The text of the document is quite clear at this point. It is not very likely that a scribal error would lead to the insertion of a word exactly opposite in sense to that originally intended.

[3] See above, pp. 89–90.

Whether disgruntled with the comparative moderation of the
Great Charter, or angered by other features of the settlement of
which we know little or nothing, it seems certain that some
at least of the northern rebels were very loath to accept the newly
agreed peace. A considerable number of them benefited from the
restitution of property, hostages, and rights to which the King
had been compelled. Hostages were restored to John de Lacy,
Ruald fitz Alan, and John le Viscunt.[1] Ruald also recovered
Richmond castle which had been lost in the fighting in the spring,[2]
and Fotheringhay castle, which had been taken into the King's
hands in 1212, was now restored to Earl David of Huntingdon.[3]
Letters ordering the restoration of estates were made out in favour
of Eustace de Vesci, Gilbert de Gant, Robert Grelley, Roger de
Montbegon, and Robert de Brus.[4] Eustace also regained the
liberty of having his dogs in the forest of Northumberland, and
Robert de Brus his privilege of holding a market and fair at
Hartlepool.[5] The settlement embodied in the Charter thus yielded
an immediate return for some. Others, however, had less cause
for satisfaction. William de Mowbray tried to use this period of
compulsory royal beneficence to pursue ancient family claims to
the custody of the shire and castle of York. The King quickly
questioned the validity of the claim, and de Mowbray's bid
failed.[6] Nicholas de Stuteville, too, was nursing a grievance in the
loss of Knaresborough and Boroughbridge under the terms of
the fine he had made for his brother's lands in 1205. The Charter
provided no immediate recompense in this kind of case unless it
came under the fines made *injuste et contra legem terrae* of cap. 55.
The barons presumably decided that it did, for Nicholas tried to
recover these estates on the renewal of the war in the autumn,
after the baronial committee of Twenty-Five had adjudicated
them to him.[7]

The Barnwell chronicler sketches a situation much more serious
than these individual grievances by themselves suggest. He
thought that some of the Northerners had cut adrift from the
meeting at Runnymede and then reopened hostilities using the
excuse that they had not been present at the settlement. He also

[1] *Rot. Litt. Pat.*, pp. 143b, 144.   [2] Ibid., pp. 143b, 148b.
[3] Ibid., p. 144.   [4] *Rot. Litt. Claus.* i. 215, 215b, 217b.
[5] Ibid. i. 216b, 217b.   [6] *E.H.R.* lxxii (1957), 408–9.
[7] See the letters sent to Robert de Ros, the baronial sheriff of Yorkshire, printed
by H. G. Richardson, *Bulletin of the John Rylands Library*, xxviii. 443.

mentioned attacks on the King's manors in the north and the harrying of the northern forests, with the slaughtering of game and felling of timber.[1] There is insufficient evidence on the precise whereabouts of individuals for this account to be checked in detail. Some of the Northerners were still at Runnymede on 20 June.[2] Nevertheless, this writer has no equal among contemporaries in his ability to analyse complex political changes. His account clearly implies that some of the northern rebels were openly and actively dissatisfied with the turn negotiations took at Runnymede. It gains considerable support from the surviving record evidence.

The royal forests constituted one of the critical problems during the summer. On this issue, the terms of the Great Charter differed markedly from the demands of the 'unknown' charter. Here, too, there was certainly active disapproval of the Charter, for Stephen Langton and his colleagues, probably at the King's request, later issued letters patent stating that it had never been intended to interpret the Charter in such a way that it became impossible to maintain the King's forest rights.[3] It also seems that the settlement at Runnymede had little effect in restoring peace to the north. In the week prior to the meeting at Runnymede, some of the Northerners had apparently seized control of Lincoln and were preparing to attack the castle.[4] After the meeting no serious effort seems to have been made to apply those terms of the Charter which were concerned with the restoration of the pre-war *status quo*. Over a month after the peace, on 23 July, letters patent were addressed to the barons of Yorkshire, ordering the restitution of lands, castles, prisoners, hostages, and chattels which had been seized or surrendered.[5] These letters covered all such acts done since as well as before the firm peace of 19 June. By the second week of August the King was obviously anticipating open war. Letters of the 11th ordered William of Duston, castellan of Scarborough, to receive William de Fors and his associates as a reinforcement to the garrison.[6] The King was busy, too, in making

---

[1] *Walt. Cov.* ii. 222.

[2] William de Mowbray, Eustace de Vesci, Roger de Montbegon, Robert Grelley, and Gilbert de Gant all witnessed a royal grant to Philip fitz John on the 20th (*Rot. Chartarum*, p. 210b).   [3] *Foedera*, i, pt. 1, p. 134.   [4] *Walt. Cov.* ii. 221.

[5] *Rot. Litt. Pat.*, pp. 150–150b. There is no indication that this writ was addressed to any other county.

[6] Ibid., p. 152. William's defection seems to have been rewarded. On 31 Aug.

new dispositions of his agents in the north.[1] But already it was clear that neither these men nor the leading Northerners were ready to give that instant response to royal instructions which John had been able to exact earlier. The restoration of Richmond castle to Ruald fitz Alan had been ordered on 21 June.[2] These instructions had to be repeated on 8 July, the two royal custodians, Robert de Vieuxpont and Philip of Oldcotes, now being informed that they were not to destroy the fortress.[3] This was probably effective, for Ruald recovered the castle by the autumn. Robert de Ros, still sheriff of Cumberland, was not so easily overawed. Letters of 24 July ordered him to surrender his custody of Carlisle and the shire and forest of Cumberland to Robert de Vaux.[4] But he was still in charge of Carlisle in January 1216.[5]

By the first weeks in August the north was dissolving into civil war. The responsibility for this seems to have lain with the barons rather than with the King. The record evidence does not suggest that the situation was yet so serious in other parts of the country. Indeed, the baronial leaders met the bishops and the King at Oxford between 17 and 23 July to discuss claims arising from the Charter which were still unsettled.[6] A further meeting was arranged at Oxford for 16 August.[7] This time the barons apparently came armed.[8] John did not attend, but sent envoys on the 20th.[9] There were no open acts of war until September.[10]

John ordered that he was to have the manor of Driffield, which his grandfather had held under Henry II (ibid., p. 154). See also letters of 2 Sept. dealing with William's rights in Craven (*Rot. Litt. Claus.* i. 227b).

[1] Letters of 13 Aug. ordered the transfer of Yorkshire from William of Duston to William de Harcourt (*Rot. Litt. Pat.*, p. 152b; *Rot. Litt. Claus.* i. 225). William of Duston had been in charge since 2 July (*Rot. Litt. Pat.*, p. 146b). Letters of 25 July had already placed Lincolnshire in the hands of Walter of Coventry, the steward of the Earl of Chester (ibid., p. 150b). Letters of 13 Aug. ordered the transfer of the castle of the Peak to Ranulf of Chester (ibid., p. 153). This was not carried out. On the same day Philip of Oldcotes was ordered to hand over Durham castle to Robert de Vieuxpont (ibid., p. 152b; *Rot. Litt. Claus.* i. 225).

[2] *Rot. Litt. Pat.*, p. 143b.   [3] Ibid., p. 148b.

[4] Ibid., p. 150.   [5] Ibid., p. 163b.

[6] H. G. Richardson, 'The Morrow of the Great Charter', *Bulletin of the John Rylands Library*, xxviii (1944), 422 ff.; S. Painter, *The Reign of King John*, pp. 337 ff.

[7] *Walt. Cov.* ii. 222–3.   [8] Ibid.

[9] *Rot. Litt. Pat.*, p. 153.

[10] The papal commissioners gave instructions to the Archbishop and bishops to excommunicate the King's opponents on 5 Sept. (see F. M. Powicke in *E.H.R.* xliv. 93). On 13 Sept. John wrote to the Pope informing him that the barons were in rebellion (*Rot. Litt. Pat.*, p. 182). The first confiscation of rebel lands was ordered on 17 Sept. (*Rot. Litt. Claus.* i. 228).

It cannot be argued that the increasingly chaotic situation in the north was the main factor in leading to the final breach. Some modern authorities have regarded the meeting at Oxford in July as a serious attempt by both parties to complete the execution of the Charter's terms,[1] and have argued that John had not yet determined to break the agreement of June. There is little, almost nothing, to support this contention. The chronicle evidence portrays two mutually suspicious and hostile parties and emphasizes, often unwittingly, that Magna Carta, especially the security clause, had placed John in a totally unacceptable position. Thus the Barnwell writer wrote of the strengthening of the walls of London, and the fortification of baronial castles, the King all the while staying near his own strong points.[2] Matthew Paris imagined a king driven to the verge of madness by his rage.[3] To Coggeshall the peace was nothing more than a *quasi pax*.[4] The Dunstable annalist also emphasized its impermanence.[5] Meanwhile the *Histoire des ducs de Normandie* presents a picture of a king stricken by gout, brusquely informed that he had to appear with the Twenty-Five to do judgement, and finally being carried before them when they refused to sit in his chamber.[6] The detail and circumstances of these and other stories may be discounted or ignored, but the general consensus of chronicle opinion cannot be so treated.

In a less obvious way the surviving records tell the same story. As early as 6 July the baronial leaders at London were informing their friends of their fears of a *coup de main* against the capital.[7] They had reason to be suspicious. The King was slow to execute some of the terms of the Charter, especially cap. 50, which provided for the removal of the aliens. Geoffrey de Martigny was

---

[1] H. G. Richardson, *Bulletin of the John Rylands Library*, loc. cit., and 'The Morrow of the Great Charter; an Addendum', ibid. xxix (1945), 184 ff. Compare S. Painter, op. cit., pp. 337 ff.

Mr. Richardson's case came to include the erroneous supposition that the *triplex forma pacis* to which the papal commissioners made favourable reference in the letters of the 5th was in fact the Charter (*Bulletin of the John Rylands Library*, xxix. 193). This view was corrected by Professor Painter (op. cit., pp. 344–6) and Professor Cheney (*Bulletin of the John Rylands Library*, xxxviii. 316 ff.), both of whom equated the *triplex forma pacis* with earlier papal proposals of March.

The criticisms of baronial conduct which the letters of the 5th contain must then be taken as criticisms of, among other things, their exaction of the Charter.

[2] *Walt. Cov.* ii. 222.
[3] *Chron. Maj.* ii. 611–12.
[4] *Coggeshall*, p. 172.
[5] *Annales Monastici*, iii. 43.
[6] *Histoire des ducs de Normandie*, p. 151.
[7] *Foedera*, i, pt. 1, p. 134.

ordered to surrender his custody of Northampton castle by letters patent of 2 July.[1] Gloucestershire, which had been in the hands of Engelard de Cigogné, was transferred to Ralf Musard on 8 July.[2] But it was not until 19 July that Andrew de Chanceaux, Engelard's colleague as sheriff of Herefordshire, was ordered to surrender that county and Hereford castle.[3] Peter de Chanceaux, also, was only ordered to surrender Bristol castle on 20 July.[4] Philip Mark, now one of the most important of the King's foreign agents and condemned like the other Poitevins in the Charter, was never removed from his crucial position as sheriff of Nottinghamshire and constable of Nottingham castle.

If the barons had grounds for their suspicions, so had the King for his. The barons had refused to guarantee their fealty in writing.[5] The Twenty-Five were exacting full remission from him under the terms of cap. 52 of the Charter. More dangerously still, cap. 55 levelled a threat of investigation into all fines which had been made with the King *injuste et contra legem*. By September this threat had materialized, for it is only on the basis of this clause that the Twenty-Five could have lawfully questioned the King's right to retain Knaresborough and Boroughbridge in pursuance of Nicholas de Stuteville's fine of 1215. John's plight is revealed, almost casually, but in a manner as convincing as all the strident notes of Wendover, by a letter of 5 July in which he informed the Barons of the Exchequer that he had granted the manor of Laughton to Brian de Lisle to maintain him in the royal service. The grant was to last, not as in the usual formula *quamdiu nobis placuerit*, but *quamdiu illud ei warantizare potuerimus*.[6] It was with some justice that the papal agents argued in September that the barons had deprived the King of the proper control of his lands.[7] No King of mettle could bear for long a situation in which a grant to a loyal supporter might be called in question.

John showed little sign of doing so. When Geoffrey de Martigny was ordered to hand over Northampton castle on 2 July, he was also instructed to come to the King with his knights and sergeants and all their equipment except the heavy siege machines.[8] On 10 July the sinister combination of Hugh de Boves, Faulkes de Breauté, and Theodore the German, all foreign military experts,

[1] *Rot. Litt. Pat.*, p. 146b. [2] Ibid., p. 148b.
[3] Ibid., p. 149b. [4] Ibid. [5] Ibid., p. 181. [6] *Rot. Litt. Claus.* i. 219.
[7] *E.H.R.* xliv (1929), 92. [8] *Rot. Litt. Claus.* i. 218.

was with the King at Clarendon.[1] On the 16th Faulkes and Geoffrey de Martigny were with him at Freemantle.[2] Meanwhile, John was mustering his ultimate financial resources. Letters of 24 June were directed to religious houses at which the King had deposited his jewels and plate, ordering them to return them to him as quickly as possible.[3] By 7 July most of his treasure had come in.[4] More treasure was received from Hugh de Neville at Marlborough on 4 July[5] and on the 6th at Devizes an acknowledgement was given for the receipt of over 9,000 m. in cash which had been brought up from Corfe.[6] Orders were still going out for the payment of the King's garrisons.[7] The tempo had slackened since the days before Runnymede, but there is nothing in this evidence to suggest that John was resigned to his fate. By the end of the conference at Oxford in the third week of July, at the latest, he must have taken the decisive step of asking the Pope to annul the Charter.[8]

The conference itself did little but indicate a deadlock. King Alexander of Scotland sent agents, probably to press his claims under the Charter. Letters of safe-conduct were made out to cover the attendance of the Welsh princes.[9] Some of the English barons were still putting forward demands; orders were drawn up for the transfer of Colchester to one of the Twenty-Five, William de Lanvallei.[10] It is possible, too, that John was submitting to baronial pressure when he dismissed Engelard de Cigogné and Peter de Chanceaux from their offices. But the transfer of these positions to Hubert de Burgh and Philip de Albini, both loyal agents, suggests that while the King was prepared to execute the letter of the Charter, he was still keeping a firm control on local government and the royal castles.[11] There is little to illustrate common

---

[1] *Rot. Chartarum*, p. 213.   [2] Ibid.   [3] *Rot. Litt. Pat.*, p. 144b.
[4] Ibid., pp. 145–158b.   [5] Ibid., p. 147.   [6] Ibid., p. 148.
[7] Ibid., p. 147b, orders of 5 July for the payment of the garrison of Scarborough; *Rot. Litt. Claus.* i. 221, writs of *computate* of 15 and 19 July for the payment of the garrison of Dorchester and for the fortification of Sherborne.
[8] The bull annulling the Charter was dated 24 Aug. Thirty days at least should be allowed for the transit of John's request for the annulment. See L. Landon, *The Itinerary of Richard I* (Pipe Roll Society, N.S. xiii), pp. 184 ff.
[9] *Rot. Litt. Pat.*, p. 150.   [10] Ibid., p. 151.
[11] I am unable to follow H. G. Richardson and Painter in arguing that these and other changes were made *per consilium* (H. G. Richardson, loc. cit. xxviii. 423; S. Painter, op. cit., p. 337). The only hint that this was so lies in a note on the memoranda roll of 1217–18 that Hubert de Burgh was made sheriff of Norfolk and Suffolk (by letters patent of 24 July; *Rot. Litt. Pat.*, p. 150) *when* the council was held at

action between the King and his opponents. Indeed, the one piece of evidence which we may attribute to this conference with some certainty, the letters of Langton and the bishops dealing with the forest, indicates that there were important differences in the interpretation of the original agreement of June.[1] Within a fortnight of the end of the Oxford meeting John was heading deliberately for war. On 9 August he took the provocative step of asking Langton to surrender Rochester castle to Peter des Roches.[2] On the 13th Richard Marsh was sent to Poitou to collect mercenary forces.[3]

The evidence for the period between the conference at Runnymede and the renewal of war is in many ways unsatisfactory. The narrative sources are sometimes confusing and always vague where precision would be most welcome. The records are often suggestive and secretive rather than certain or clear. Much was

Oxford. It does not follow that this was done by the advice of the council as Richardson and Painter assume.

Throughout the summer John was switching his officials about rapidly. These moves seem to have been inspired partly by the necessity to remove some at least of the Poitevins from office, where he could afford to do so, and partly by strategic and administrative convenience. The changes which occurred in the third week of July are in no way exceptional. Some were very much in the King's interest. See, for example, letters of 18 July ordering William de Albini to transfer Sauvey castle to Hugh de Neville (*Rot. Litt. Pat.*, p. 149) and the orders to Robert de Ros to surrender Carlisle and Cumberland to Robert de Vaux (ibid., p. 150). Admittedly Robert de Vaux rebelled later, but he was not, like de Ros, a member of the Twenty-Five.

[1] I cannot accept H. G. Richardson's attribution to this meeting of the undated agreement on the custody of London (*Foedera*, i, pt. 1, p. 133) and the letters of the archbishops and bishops which stated that the barons had refused to give John written guarantees of their fealty (*Rot. Litt. Pat.*, p. 181). The first seems to me to belong to the Runnymede meeting itself. It alone of all the surviving documents imposed a time limit (15 Aug.) for John's execution of the terms of the Charter. Hence it was an essential feature of the original settlement. It is significant that the Barnwell chronicler thought that 16 Aug. was the date fixed in June for the final settlement of outstanding issues (*Walt. Cov.* ii. 223). The second, the episcopal letters on the barons' fealty, should probably be allocated to the closing days of the meeting at Runnymede. The bishops' letters on the forest, in contrast, are probably later, since they imply that some experience had already been gained at the time they were drawn up of the difficulty of applying the Charter's forest clauses in practice.

It should be noted in support of Richardson's case that the bishops named are identical in both letters. However, the letters were not enrolled together. The one on the forests was enrolled with the London agreement on the dorse of the close roll membrane covering 11–19 July (*Rot. Litt. Claus.* i. 268b–269). The one on fealty was enrolled on the dorse of the patent roll membrane covering 28 June to 3 July. As I have suggested elsewhere (*E.H.R.* lxxii. 412 n.), it is hazardous to argue from this to the actual date of composition of these documents.

[2] *Rot. Litt. Pat.*, p. 181b.
[3] Ibid., pp. 152b–153.

being conveyed by word of mouth between the King and his officials which only bore fruit in the rolls in a meagre letter of credence on behalf of a royal familiar. Nevertheless, one point seems reasonably clear. If the King and the more refractory of his opponents were agreed on anything, it was on the unacceptability of the Charter. On the King's side there was intransigence, first perhaps concealed, then soon openly expressed in action. On the baronial side some seem to have been unwilling to accept the Charter as adequate right from its inception, and to have resorted to self-help and lawlessness, actions which in the end could only lead to civil war. A caucus of the baronial committee might continue to operate from London, make judgements and negotiate with the King, but the initial cracks in the baronial party at Runnymede must have been widened further with the return of most of its members to their own homes. Between these two extremes of opinion, moderate men balanced along an increasingly precarious course. In July and August Langton was still negotiating on behalf of the barons and protecting them from the wrathful bulls of Pope Innocent. But he also felt that he had to testify that the barons had refused letters of fealty and he tried to protect the King's interests in the royal forests. Langton's exile saved him from the most awkward of dilemmas, that of choosing between two parties of which one could not attract complete and uncritical support, and the other did not deserve whole-hearted opposition.

Others, however, could not avoid the choice. The Archbishop's brother, Simon Langton, gave himself to the baronial cause. William de Fors, in contrast, had already re-entered the royal fold in the first fortnight in August. In the arguments which preceded the renewal of war most of the advantages lay with the King, for the fragmentation of the baronial party and the unwillingness of some of his opponents to accept the Charter gave him a chance to argue that he had kept his part of the bargain while the barons had not kept theirs. This was the burden of the letters of the archbishops and bishops on the barons' fealty and the forest clauses of the Charter. It was John's continual plaint. When he wrote to Langton and the barons at Oxford on 15 July excusing his delay in coming, he sent agents 'to do what we ought to do and to receive from you what you ought to do'.[1] To the later

---

[1] *Rot. Litt. Pat.*, p. 149.

gathering in August he apparently wrote complaining that he had made all the concessions he had promised, only to suffer enormous damages at the hands of the magnates.[1] By September the letters of the papal commissioners covering the bull *mirari cogimur* were presenting the opposition as a group of irresponsible men who had pressed unlawful demands upon the King by force, seizing control of his capital, punishing his agents, depriving him of his dignities and the control of land in his gift, and imposing new customs upon the country.[2] The wheel had come full circle; it was John's opponents who were now on the defensive. Those who had attacked his system of government as founded in unlawful innovation, now faced the same charge. It was a telling charge against men who had forced the security clause and other innovations on the King. It could be brought all the more easily when the Charter had not produced that unity of purpose which Langton and his like must have hoped to see.

[1] *Walt. Cov.* ii. 223.   [2] *E.H.R.* xliv. 87–93.

VIII

THE CIVIL WAR

THE first civil war in 1215 had begun with the baronial muster at Stamford, the formal defiance of the King, and the march on London. The second civil war into which the country slid in the autumn had no such dramatic opening. Indeed, the first move, the siege of Rochester, was the King's. At London there was some attempt to maintain the organization created by the security clause of the Charter,[1] but the baronial effort was now much dispersed. The geography of the land, the decentralization of the King's treasure, the delegation of administrative authority to almost independent royal agents, the distribution of mercenary troops throughout the royal castles, all tended to produce, not one civil war, but many, of which the setting, strategic forces, tactical problems, and personnel varied from one region to another.

Even within these regions there was often no common pattern, for the *foci* were the great stone-built castles, each generating its own particular local conflict. Occasionally some kind of uniformity throughout a region might be produced by the presence of the King or some marauding campaign by Faulkes de Breauté and the royal mercenaries. But of strategy in the larger sense there was little, except that required by external intervention either from France or from Scotland. It was around such intervention, or the threat of it, that the few more extended and organized campaigns revolved. This apart, there was great diversity in the activity and policies of the rebels. The surprising feature of their behaviour is not that they worked together on occasions, but that they worked together at all. Some may wish to attribute this to an overriding hatred of the King, and this no doubt played a part, but it does not provide a complete explanation, for the rebel armies did not disintegrate on John's death. Other factors were clearly at work: a determination to fight for the

---

[1] See the baronial letters concerning Knaresborough printed by H. G. Richardson in *Bulletin of the John Rylands Library*, xxviii. 443. See also the Scottish evidence discussed below, pp. 131-3.

Charter, perhaps; a fear of the agents of the King, both before and after his death; but possibly first and foremost local loyalties, the social ties and common interests of the *patria*.

One of the first effects of the war was to isolate the north almost completely. To the geographical factors of distance and difficulty of access was now added a *cordon sanitaire* consisting of the earldom of Chester to the west, and the royalist castles in Lincolnshire, Nottinghamshire, and southern Yorkshire. Lincoln, Newark, and Nottingham, and to a lesser extent Tickhill, were crucial to John's conduct of the war, for they cut the enemy forces in two. Bamburgh, Newcastle, and Scarborough, along with Norham and Durham, gave him control of the north-east coast, while William de Fors at Skipton, Robert de Vieuxpont at Appleby, and Hugh de Balliol at Barnard Castle could hinder passage across the Pennines. The only serious weakness in John's position lay in his failure to dislodge Robert de Ros from the custody of Carlisle castle before the outbreak of war.

In these circumstances the northern rebels could scarcely interfere in matters farther south. Only a few of them are known to have served under William de Albini in the defence of Rochester.[1] They may have planned to reinforce the relieving armies, but there is no evidence that they did in fact do so.[2] John, too, was content to leave the conduct of the war in the northern counties in the hands of his lieutenants. From the beginning of September until 10 December he remained within the boundaries of Kent. During the whole of this period scarcely one surviving administrative or military instruction of real importance issued from the Chancery to the King's northern agents. John was busy at this time ordering the seizure of rebel lands and their transfer to his own supporters and agents. Over thirty important grants of this kind were made before Christmas. Most of them dealt with land in the southern or western counties. Some of the rebels of the eastern and home counties were affected,[3] as were some of the few northern rebels who held land in the southern counties.[4] But there were only two

---

[1] See above, p. 61.

[2] Coggeshall believed that John forged letters purporting to come from Robert fitz Walter and the rebels at London directing the Northerners to delay coming south (*Coggeshall*, p. 177). On 21 Nov. John was planning to reinforce the garrison at Lincoln (*Rot. Litt. Pat.*, p. 159b). Rochester fell on 30 Nov. (*Chron. Maj.* ii. 625).

[3] See letters dealing with lands belonging to Robert fitz Walter, Richard of Clare, and Geoffrey de Mandeville (*Rot. Litt. Claus.* i. 228, 231; *Rot. Litt. Pat.*, p. 161b).

[4] See letters dealing with lands belonging to Maurice de Gant in Gloucestershire, Somerset, and Oxfordshire (*Rot. Litt. Claus.* i. 232b, 238); with estates of Roger de

important grants affecting Lincolnshire[1] and only three, two of which were insignificant, affecting the area north of the Trent.[2]

But for the Scottish invasion, the northern counties would probably have seen little fighting apart from isolated actions between small groups of rebels and the northern castellans. However, Alexander II of Scotland had already been pressing his claims against John as early as the conference at Oxford in July, probably in an attempt to reverse the harsher features of the Anglo-Scottish agreements of 1209 and 1212. It is also probable that Alexander was reviving the ancient Scottish claims to the shires of Northumberland, Cumberland, and Westmorland. The rebel barons now proved only too willing to acknowledge these claims in return for military support. According to the chronicle of the great Border house of Melrose, Alexander laid siege to Norham castle on 19 October. On the 22nd the rebel barons of Northumberland did homage to him. Their action was copied by the Yorkshire rebels on 11 January 1216.[3]

Some of the details of these arrangements are supplied in two calendars of Scottish muniments drawn up in 1282 and 1291.[4] In the enigmatic entries of these valuable and much neglected records there is a catalogue of part, at least, of the extensive correspondence which must have passed between Alexander and the English rebels. Robert de Ros and Eustace de Vesci, both of whom had married daughters of William the Lion, seem to have been the chief men on the English side, for their letters to Alexander were listed separately, and, when the calendars were written, there still survived at Edinburgh the staff with which Eustace de

---

Montbegon in Sussex and of Robert Grelley in Oxfordshire (ibid. i. 241), and with a manor of Gilbert fitz Reinfrey in Berkshire (ibid. i. 237).

[1] All Simon of Kyme's lands within the county were granted to Geoffrey de Neville. Daniel de Gant received a similar grant of the estates of Alexander of Pointon (ibid. i. 233b, 234b).

[2] Letters ordering that William de Ferrers, Earl of Derby, should have all the lands held of his fee by enemies of the King were addressed to the sheriff of Nottinghamshire and Derbyshire as well as to southern sheriffs (ibid. i. 233b). For the other two letters, sent to Yorkshire and Northumberland respectively, see ibid. i. 236b, 242b.

[3] *The Chronicle of Melrose*, pp. 61–62. This is the sole source for these dates. It places the homage of the 22nd at Felton. However, the inventory of Scottish records mentioned below (pp. 131–3) refers to a staff with which Eustace de Vesci invested Alexander with the shire of Northumberland while he was laying siege to Norham (*Acts of Parliament of Scotland*, i. 112).

[4] The sections of interest occur in *Acts of Parliament of Scotland*, i. 108, 111–12. The two lists partly duplicate each other.

Vesci had invested Alexander with the shire of Northumberland during the siege of Norham. The two acts of homage which the Melrose chronicle records were probably formal recognitions of the Scottish claim to the three Border counties. These counties were adjudged to Alexander by the barons of England, presumably by the Twenty-Five, or some of them. The men of Carlisle were informed of this judgement and of arrangements for the transfer of their town.[1] Other letters clearly show that the baronial leaders in the south now accepted Alexander as an intermediary between themselves and the rebels of the Border counties.[2] Alexander's part of the bargain is more obscure. He reached an agreement with the barons of England on certain marriages, and it is highly probable that he was required to make a large payment to the rebels' war chest.[3] Who, John might well have asked, was selling justice now?

These arrangements with Alexander had probably been completed by the end of November.[4] At first sight, they appear to spring from a wild irresponsibility, to constitute a withdrawal of the frontier from the line for which the English monarchy, and often the northern baronage too, had fought successfully since the reigns of Rufus and Henry I. But this was probably not so clear at the time. Alexander acquired the lordship of these northern counties, but almost certainly as fiefs of the English crown. The transaction was made to appear as a lawful exercise of the judicial authority which the Charter had given the barons. The homage which the Northerners paid to Alexander was not inconsistent with the liege-lordship of the English crown. Indeed, Prince Louis sent letters presumably confirming the transfer of the three shires,[5] and in 1216 both the Northerners and Alexander marched south to do homage to Louis as King of England. The

[1] The canons of Carlisle accepted these arrangements, and Alexander proceeded to intervene in the pending election of a new bishop. See the English complaint to the Pope of 26 Apr. 1217 (*Patent Rolls 1216–25*, p. 111).

[2] Letters of the barons of England were sent to the barons of the three Border shires via Alexander (*Acts of Parliament of Scotland*, i. 108).

[3] The Scottish documents included an excuse presented by certain Scottish agents, and guaranteed by certain English magnates and by other forms of security, dealing with the depositing of a sum of money at the Temple at London. There are also references to letters of the citizens of London (ibid. i. 108).

[4] They were clearly coincident with the siege of Norham. This began on 19 Oct. and, according to the Melrose chronicle, lasted for 40 days (op. cit., p. 61).

[5] *Acts of Parliament of Scotland*, i. 108.

Northerners were not trying to place themselves outside the range of the English crown in so far as they held land in the Border shires. They were introducing the King of Scotland as a buffer between themselves and their old masters.[1]

King John was bound to react violently. As the autumn wore on his presence in the north became more clearly necessary, for he could scarcely expect his agents and the few loyal barons to hold on for long against the rebels and the Scots combined. Already there were signs that a landslide might begin at any moment. Robert de Vaux, whom John had tried to promote to the custody of Carlisle and Cumberland in July, joined the rebels sometime during the autumn.[2] More significantly, one of the King's most reliable agents hitherto, Gilbert fitz Reinfrey, lord of Kendal and sheriff of Lancaster, had gone over to the rebel side. Gilbert's son, William of Lancaster, was among those captured when Rochester fell in December.

John moved as soon as Rochester had fallen. Before the year was out he had taken Belvoir and Castle Donington. On New Year's day he was at Doncaster, a day later at Pontefract, and by 4 January he had reached York. He went on to Alnwick which he reached on the 11th and to Berwick which he reached on the 14th. After a stay of ten days he moved south again by easy stages, arriving at Lincoln on 23 February. The campaign was not isolated. While the King was in the north, other royal armies were raiding into East Anglia and attacking rebel castles there. Overhanging both expeditions was the constant threat of Prince Louis' invasion from France.[3] This made speed essential. It also reduced the effectiveness of John's onslaught, for the rebels could readily appreciate that he could only stay in the north for a limited period.

John's initial military successes in the north were considerable enough for many of the chroniclers to write of them as a trium-

[1] This argument assumes that in 1216 Alexander did homage to Louis for his English fiefs and for the Border counties, not for the kingdom of Scotland. John had been able to assert a general liege-lordship over William the Lion in 1212. It is very doubtful, however, whether Alexander would continue to acknowledge this in the circumstances of 1216.   [2] *Rot. Litt. Pat.*, p. 150; *Rot. Litt. Claus.* i. 246b.
[3] Louis did not land until the end of the third week in May (*Coggeshall*, p. 181; *Histoire des ducs de Normandie*, p. 169; *Chron. Maj.* ii. 653), but the threat was a long-standing one. According to a letter later added to the chronicle of Howden the first proposed date for his expedition was the octave of Hilary and French troops did in fact arrive in London as early as December. (*Hoveden*, iv. 189–90; C. Petit-Dutaillis, *Étude sur la vie et le règne de Louis VIII*, pp. 89–90.)

phant demonstration of his strength.[1] For a few weeks' effort the
list of castles gained was a long one. Belvoir and Castle Doning-
ton were followed by Richmond,[2] Kendal, and Brancepeth. In
Northumberland Morpeth, Mitford, and probably Prudhoe were
all taken or surrendered.[3] By the end of the first week in February
Carlisle was in the hands of Robert de Vieuxpont,[4] and when the
King turned south again into Yorkshire Peter de Brus' castle of
Skelton fell with its garrison.[5] By this time, too, royal agents
had been given instructions to take charge of Manchester and
Moulton.[6] Even in their purely military aspects, however, these successes were far from complete or decisive. The two most important Northumbrian castles in the hands of the rebels were Alnwick
and Wark-on-Tweed, both constant challenges to the neighbouring fortresses of Norham and Bamburgh. Neither of these fell,
although the King put the two vills to the fire.[7] In Yorkshire
Helmsley held out throughout the whole campaign, despite its
proximity to Pickering and Scarborough.[8] The rebels can scarcely
have expected to lose such strongholds as Richmond or Carlisle,
but there is more than a hint that the ease of the King's advance
owed something to a deliberate policy of withdrawal. Roger of
Wendover later wrote that Castle Donington had been left un-
occupied.[9] This was not in fact so, but it may well have been left
only lightly garrisoned.[10] The Melrose chronicler, too, speaks of a
policy of scorched earth, of the rebels deliberately wasting their
own estates before the King's advance.[11] In some ways the rebels

---

[1] *Chronicle of Melrose*, p. 62; *Walt. Cov.* ii. 228–9; *Coggeshall*, pp. 178–9; *Chron.
Maj.* ii. 636–7, 639–41. The more exaggerated stories of the atrocities committed by
the King's armies should be compared with the statement of a jury in 1228 that
neither John nor his agents took anything from the fee or liberty of the Chapter of
Ripon during the war (*Memorials of the Church of Ripon*, ed. J. T. Fowler, i. 59).

[2] *Rot. Litt. Pat.*, p. 163b; *Rot. Litt. Claus.* i. 245.

[3] Morpeth and Mitford were granted to Philip of Oldcotes at the end of January
(*Rot. Litt. Claus.* i. 246b). Only in the case of Mitford is it certain that he actually
got control (*Pipe Roll 3 Henry III*, p. 170). This castle later passed into the
hands of Hugh de Balliol. See below, pp. 244–6.

According to the *Histoire des ducs de Normandie*, John also gave Styford to Philip
of Oldcotes, but there is no evidence to show that its owner, Hugh de Bolebec, was
ever a rebel; he was certainly still loyal at the end of Jan. 1216 (*Histoire des ducs de
Normandie*, p. 164; *Rot. Litt. Claus.* i. 246b).

Prudhoe was in the hands of Hugh de Balliol in 1217 (*Patent Rolls 1216–25*, p. 119).

[4] *Rot. Litt. Claus.* i. 247b.　　　　　　　　[5] *Rot. Litt. Pat.*, p. 167b.

[6] Ibid., p. 164b, 165; *Rot. Litt. Claus.* i. 313b.

[7] *Chronicle of Melrose*, p. 62.　　　　　　　　[8] *Chron. Maj.* ii. 642.

[9] Ibid. ii. 639.　　[10] *Rot. Litt. Pat.*, p. 162b.　　[11] *Chronicle of Melrose*, p. 62.

and their Scottish allies behaved with remarkable confidence and resilience. On 15 February, when the royal army was moving from Kirkham to York, the King was negotiating with rebel knights in arms as near as Beverley.[1] In the second half of January, when his headquarters were at Berwick, the King harried the Scots as far north as Dunbar;[2] before the end of February the Scots were retaliating, laying siege to Carlisle and ravaging the monastery of Holm Cultram.[3] By the spring, the rebels farther south were besieging York.[4] It was probably at this time that the new sheriff, Geoffrey de Neville, turned to the desperate remedy of releasing the prisoners from York gaol.[5]

If the military results of John's campaign were indecisive, its political achievements were very largely temporary. At the outset much clearly depended on the extent to which John could compel or persuade the northern rebels to make their peace. All he got in the end was the temporary surrender of the weaker brethren and those whom he caught. The opening phases of the campaign saw the surrender of two members of the Twenty-Five, Roger de Montbegon and John de Lacy. A few other barons and a considerable number of lesser men in Yorkshire, Nottinghamshire, Derbyshire, and Lincolnshire had also made their peace by the time the campaign ended.[6] Meanwhile many men were negotiating for terms and, as Prince Louis' invasion came closer, John listened to the repentant rebel in a readier and more lenient mood. By April and early May he was coming close to agreement even with the most obdurate of the northern rebels.

These moves were often ill-organized, bearing fruit simply in the issue and reissue of safe-conducts. Robert Grelley obtained one in January and another in March.[7] Simon of Kyme collected two in December, one in January, and a fourth late in February.[8] Other letters dealt with Maurice de Gant and Roger Bertram.[9] In several important cases matters went farther. By February John was making efforts to bring Peter de Brus back to his allegiance. The Prior of Guisborough was sent to him on the 6th, and on the 15th an embassy headed by Aymer, Archdeacon of Durham, was

---

[1] *Rot. Litt. Pat.*, p. 165b.

[2] *Chronicle of Melrose*, pp. 62–63; *Histoire des ducs de Normandie*, p. 164.

[3] *Chronicle of Melrose*, p. 63.　　　　　　　　　　　　[4] *Coggeshall*, p. 180.

[5] *Rolls of the Justices in Eyre for Yorkshire, 1219*, nos. 459, 499, 631, 901, 1034, 1059, 1081.　　　　[6] See above, pp. 49 ff.　　　　[7] *Rot. Litt. Pat.*, pp. 162b, 169.

[8] Ibid., pp. 162, 163b, 166b.　　　　　　　　[9] Ibid., pp. 162b, 163, 164.

directed to both Peter and Robert de Ros.[1] In the latter case John insisted that Robert should surrender Carlisle, as had been ordered as long ago as July, before he received a safe-conduct.[2] Robert's reply is preserved on the dorse of the close roll. In it he stated that he was ready to surrender the town and castle of Carlisle and had already ordered his constable to do so, adding that he was willing to discuss terms of peace as soon as he received a safe-conduct.[3] What happened in the end we do not know. John certainly got Carlisle, but there is no indication that de Ros was offered such terms that he made his peace. Nor is there any sign that Peter de Brus, his associate in the letter of the 15th, surrendered.

When John moved south again at the end of February he left Robert de Vieuxpont and Brian de Lisle with special powers to negotiate on his behalf and to arrange the surrender of rebels.[4] He had not lost all hope of obtaining further surrenders and he engaged in a new bout of negotiation in April. On the 9th a safe-conduct was made out for William de Ros, who was acting for his father, Robert, and for Eustace de Vesci.[5] On the 12th safe-conducts were made out for Robert, Eustace, and Peter de Brus.[6] By the 14th John seems to have expected some kind of settlement in the north, for the three Border counties, which the rebels had surrendered to Alexander of Scotland, were excluded from general letters ordering the disinheritance of all those who failed to submit within a month of Easter.[7] Negotiations were still proceeding at the beginning of May, for letters patent of the 7th make it clear that the King had met delegates of the leading northern rebels at Dover on the previous day.[8] Then the story ends. Within two weeks Prince Louis was in the country.

If, at the beginning of January, John hoped to drive the northern rebels from the field, he missed his aim by a wide mark. There are clear signs that he recognized this failure for what it was. At first, the terms he imposed on the men he captured or received into his peace were severe enough to suggest that he was full of

[1] *Rot. Litt. Pat.*, pp. 165, 165b.   [2] Ibid., p. 163b.   [3] *Rot. Litt. Claus.* i. 269–269b.
[4] *Rot. Litt. Pat.*, pp. 164b, 167b.   [5] Ibid., pp. 175–175b.
[6] Ibid., p. 176.   [7] *Rot. Litt. Claus.* i. 270b.
[8] *Rot. Litt. Pat.*, p. 180. These letters are on a very badly damaged portion of the roll. They give no hint of the form negotiations were taking. They were addressed to Robert de Ros, William de Mowbray, Eustace de Vesci, Peter de Brus, John fitz Robert, Richard de Percy, Richard de Unfraville, Roger de Merlay, Roger Bertram, Ranulf fitz Robert, and Bartholomew fitz ——. The latter half of the last name has been lost through damage.

confidence and righteous indignation. William de Albini's ransom after his capture at Rochester was 6,000 m.[1] When John de Lacy surrendered he made over his brother as a hostage, and gave the King a charter of fealty in which, among other things, he agreed to accept the disinheritance of his family as the appropriate punishment should he break this new agreement.[2] Gilbert fitz Reinfrey seems to have received very special treatment as a trusted royal agent who had failed his master. He had to surrender his castles, hand over ten hostages, submit to the threat of disinheritance if he broke his fealty, and make a payment of 12,000 m.[3] Many of the lesser men also had to surrender hostages and charters of fealty[4] and were compelled to buy the King's grace and benevolence.[5] By April and May, however, John had ceased to dictate and had begun to woo. He was now making special provision for the restoration of Roger de Montbegon's lands in Clayworth, Nottinghamshire, and of Henry de Neville's lands in Harworth. One of the newly restored knights in Lincolnshire, William de Lande, received a royal grant of twenty librates of the lands of one of his fellow rebels, Roger de Lascelles. The really big fish, John de Lacy, was basking in the shallows of the royal favour, digesting the wardship of the Aincurt fee which the King had just granted him.[6] He had also been granted all the lands which enemies of the King held of his fee.[7] De Lacy had now become an important intermediary between John and the remaining northern rebels. These last were now being offered far better terms than those imposed in January. On 12 April the King wrote to John de Lacy, Gerard de Furneval, and Geoffrey de Neville, guaranteeing that he would exact no money if Robert de Ros, Eustace de Vesci, and Peter de Brus came to them to make peace. John now said that he preferred faithful service to cash.[8]

---

[1] *Pipe Roll. 3 Henry III*, p. 126.

[2] *Foedera*, i, pt. 1, p. 137. See also above, p. 1.

[3] *Rot. de Ob. et Fin.*, pp. 570–1; *Rot. Chartarum*, p. 221b.

[4] *Rot. de Ob. et Fin.*, pp. 570–95.

[5] Fulk d'Oyri proffered 500 m. (*Pipe Roll 3 Henry III*, p. 126); Richard de Wyville, 200 m. (ibid., p. 196); Ruald fitz Alan 200 m. and the payment of an old debt of the same amount (*Rot. de Ob. et Fin.*, p. 569). Most of the proffers were lower than this and rarely exceeded 50 m. For the Lincolnshire fines see *Pipe Roll 3 Henry III*, pp. 125–6; for the Yorkshire fines, ibid., pp. 195–6.

[6] *Pipe Roll Society*, N.S., xxxi. 143; *Rot. Litt. Pat.*, p. 180b. All these arrangements were made on 15 to 18 May.

[7] *Rot. Litt. Claus.* i. 266b. [8] *Rot. Litt. Pat.*, p. 176.

In the end the successes John had achieved in January and February were of little effect. The landing of Prince Louis and a great resurgence of the northern rebels brought all to nothing. By June and July the King was preparing for a general withdrawal. On 1 June Brian de Lisle was told to hold Bolsover, if he could, but otherwise to destroy the fortifications.[1] On the 5th Ranulf of Chester was given similar instructions for dealing with Richmond.[2] Farther south royal agents were ordered to hand over the two episcopal castles of Newark and Sleaford to the Bishop of Lincoln, with instructions that they were to be destroyed if the Bishop's agents would not accept them.[3] Orders for the destruction of Newark, one of the key points of the Trent–Humber system, were in fact issued, although they were soon countermanded.[4] By August Lincoln was being attacked by a force under Gilbert de Gant, who had now been recognized as earl of the county by Prince Louis. The castellan, Nicolaa de la Haye, was able to buy a truce.[5] Farther north, the Yorkshire rebels were recovering lost ground.[6] Meanwhile Alexander of Scotland was laying siege to Carlisle. The town fell on 8 August and the castle sometime later.[7] Alexander then marched up the Eden and crossed Stainmore, gathering rebels to him as he went, skirmished with the garrison of Barnard Castle, where Eustace de Vesci was killed, and in the last days of the month and the first week of September marched into southern England to meet Prince Louis at Dover, where both he and the Northerners gave the French prince their homage and fealty.[8] Apart from the few castles he had

---

[1] *Rot. Litt. Pat.*, p. 184b. Nine days later Brian was ordered to transfer Bolsover to Gerard de Furneval who had made his peace with the King in Jan. (ibid., p. 187). Gerard got control of it, but refused to surrender it in Aug. when he went over to the rebels once more. He was still in charge of the castle in the next year. See ibid., pp. 192b, 193, 199, 199b; *Rot. Litt. Claus.* i. 288b; *Parent Rolls 1216–25*, pp. 1, 71.

[2] *Rot. Litt. Pat.*, p. 186b.   [3] Ibid., p. 187; *Rot. Litt. Claus.* i. 291b.

[4] *Rot. Litt. Claus.* i. 284b.   [5] *Chron. Maj.* ii. 663; *Walt. Cov.* ii. 230.

[6] *Chron. Maj.* ii. 663.

[7] *Chronicle of Melrose*, p. 63. This states that the castle did not fall on this occasion. Nevertheless it was in the hands of the Scots in Sept. 1217 (*Patent Rolls 1216–25*, p. 93).

[8] *Walt. Cov.* ii. 230; *Chronicle of Melrose*, p. 63; *Chron. Maj.* ii. 666. Wendover places the homage to Louis in August, but it almost certainly occurred in Sept. The author of the *Histoire des ducs de Normandie* discussed the homage at Dover after dealing with events which occurred in the second week in Sept. (*Histoire des ducs de Normandie*, p. 179). The Barnwell chronicler gives a confused and inconsistent account of both John's and Alexander's movements, but his evidence also suggests that the homage occurred in mid-September (*Walt. Cov.* ii. 231).

gained in the early months of the year, John was now in a worse position than before. Nevertheless, his last convulsive actions showed a sound strategic grasp. His last great raid north to Lincoln and Newark so strengthened the royalist garrisons in this area and so threatened the estates of the northern rebels, that the danger of united action between King Alexander and Prince Louis and of the concentration of all the rebel forces against the royalist garrisons in the south quickly vanished. Alexander and the Northerners turned sharply about.[1] John made no greater contribution to his son's succession than in dying where he did—

> Summus honos mors illa fuit, culmenque decoris
> Attulit, in nullo quod erat superatus ab hoste,
> Et tot erant hostes; victus victore superno,
> Invictusque suos hostes moriendo momordit.[2]

Before he died he had already realized the inadequacy of the arrangements he had made in the winter with those rebels who had surrendered. As early as April he had ordered the seizure of the estates not only of the confirmed rebels, but also of those who surrendered and rebelled again.[3] He was also instructing his agents to get better guarantees in future from those whom they admitted to the peace.[4] In fact even the most stringent conditions, the surrender of hostages and charters of fealty, were of little avail in the changed military circumstances of the spring. John de Lacy, who had handed over both, was once more in rebellion by the summer,[5] and it is probable that most of those who had made their peace took similar action at this time; practically all had joined the rebels once again before the war ended in 1217. The initial victories of Prince Louis also led to the defection, usually temporary, of men who had hitherto been staunch supporters of the King, in the north of Peter fitz Herbert, who had been sheriff of Yorkshire in 1214 and 1215, elsewhere of the Earls of Salisbury,

---

[1] *Histoire des ducs de Normandie*, p. 179. Compare the Barnwell chronicle, which states that Alexander and the Northerners were cut off from their lands by John's attack and only returned after his death (*Walt. Cov.* ii. 232–3). This writer is confused; Wendover, too, presents a muddled chronology (*Chron. Maj.* ii. 665–7); the sequence of events given in the *Histoire* is probably nearest to the truth, despite the relatively restricted field it covers.

[2] *Political Songs of England*, ed. Thomas Wright (Camden Society, 1839), p. 21. This is a poem on the battle of Lincoln, surviving in a fourteenth-century MS.

[3] *Rot. Litt. Claus.* i. 259. Letters to the sheriff of Lincolnshire.

[4] *Rot. Litt. Pat.*, p. 185. Letters to John Marshal.

[5] Ibid., p. 180b; *Rot. Litt. Claus.* i. 289.

Arundel, and Surrey, and John fitz Hugh.[1] William de Fors, barometric in his reactions to the political atmosphere, also decided that his fortunes once more lay with the rebels.

These were sinister developments. Equally disturbing was the increasing disorganization of the administration. The financial difficulties of the royal castellans were increasing.[2] The problem of the sequestered estates placed such a burden on the royal memory and the overworked chancery officials that chaos quickly followed. Order and counter-order led sometimes to the grant of the same lands separately to two different men,[3] sometimes to the continued interference of sheriffs and bailiffs in estates already transferred to the King's supporters.[4] Sometimes differences arose because one man was given fees of an honour which had been granted to another.[5] There were signs, too, that the King was losing control of his officers. As far back as 13 August 1215, Brian de Lisle had been ordered to surrender the castle of the Peak to Ranulf of Chester.[6] Letters of 21 June 1216 expressed the King's surprise that this had not been done. Brian was now instructed to transfer the castle to William de Ferrers, who had been empowered to take it by force if Brian failed to surrender.[7] Brian still refused to budge. These orders were repeated twice in August,[8] but Brian did nothing and the matter became the subject of repeated mandates after the King's death.[9] Ultimately, Brian and the Earl of Derby seem to have engaged in private war.[10] This shabby story of insubordination was one of the symptoms of the King's declining power to compel. Others like Brian were following the path of disobedience towards a semi-independent power: at Nottingham, Brian's neighbour, Philip Mark; in Northumberland, the sheriff, Philip of Oldcotes. The control of

---

[1] For Peter fitz Herbert see *Rot. Litt. Claus.* i. 280. For the others see *Walt. Cov.* ii. 231; *Histoire des ducs de Normandie*, p. 174; Annals of Waverley, *Annales Monastici*, ii. 285; *Rot. Litt. Pat.*, pp. 187b–188; *Rot. Litt. Claus.* i. 285, 286, 295.

[2] On 29 May and 14 June Brian de Lisle was ordered to send 100 m. to Geoffrey de Neville for the maintenance of Scarborough (*Rot. Litt. Pat.*, pp. 184b, 187b), but nothing seems to have been done, and at the end of the month the King ordered Philip of Oldcotes and Hugh de Balliol to give what financial aid they could to Geoffrey to enable him to maintain his men and castles (*Rot. Litt. Claus.* i. 276).

[3] *Rot. Litt. Claus.* i. 260. A letter to Philip of Oldcotes.

[4] See a letter dealing with land of Robert Grelley (ibid. i. 274).

[5] See letters dealing with the land of Robert de Vaux (ibid. i. 246b, 259b).

[6] *Rot. Litt. Pat.*, p. 153.   [7] Ibid., p. 188b.

[8] Ibid., pp. 192b, 193.   [9] *Patent Rolls 1216–25*, pp. 1, 4, 7–8.

[10] For the disseisin of one of Brian's men by the Earl see *Rot. Litt. Claus.* i. 294b.

these men and their like was an urgent task for William Marshal and his colleagues once peace had been re-established.

It is probable that when John died the northern rebels represented a more powerful and better organized body of opposition than they had done before the winter campaign of 1216. They had lost castles, and by the summer they had lost that inveterate rebel, Eustace de Vesci, but they had staged a great counter-attack, which, in the homage done to Louis at Dover, had given a unity to the actions of all John's opponents. John's death, the growing consolidation of the power of the loyalist barons, the increasing rivalries around Prince Louis, the reissue of Magna Carta in November 1216, diverted them scarcely at all from their rebellion.[1] Two things seem to have turned them towards surrender. First, their ranks were severely thinned in the rebel disaster at Lincoln in May 1217. Among the captured were William de Mowbray, Nicholas de Stuteville, Gilbert and Maurice de Gant, Robert Grelley, Oliver de Aincurt, and William, son of Robert de Ros.[2] On these surrender was enforced. Secondly, probably by the end of May and certainly by June, the proposals to restore the territorial *status quo*, later confirmed at Kingston, had become widely known.[3] Once the Northerners knew that their lands would be secured they began to trickle to the Marshal's side. The first move was made by John de Lacy, one of the few important men to escape the disaster of Lincoln, and one who had already tried to compromise. Safe-conducts of 23 May were granted to him and his men with a promise of full restoration of their estates.[4] By 9 August he had submitted.[5] Meanwhile two of the Northumbrian rebels, Roger Bertram and John fitz Robert, had made their peace at the end of July.[6] A safe-conduct was made

[1] Prior to the battle at Lincoln in May 1217 only Fulk d'Oyri and Robert de Mesnil, a Yorkshire tenant of the Archbishop of York, had made their peace (ibid. i. 295, 301b).

[2] Wendover gives the names of Gilbert de Gant, William de Mowbray, Oliver de Aincurt, and William de Ros (*Chron. Maj.* iii. 22). A note at the end of Howden's chronicle adds Robert de Mowbray, Robert Grelley, Simon of Kyme, Gerard de Furneval, and Maurice de Gant, who is incorrectly placed as Gilbert's brother (*Hoveden*, iv. 190). The continuator of Gervase of Canterbury adds Stephen de Gant, Nicholas de Stuteville, and Eustace de Stuteville (*Gerv. Cant.* ii. 111). This information is largely accurate. None of those named can be shown to have been active after the date of the battle.

[3] F. M. Powicke, *King Henry III and the Lord Edward*, i. 13–17.

[4] *Patent Rolls 1216–25*, p. 112.

[5] *Rot. Litt. Claus.* i. 318.   [6] Ibid. i. 316, 316b.

out for Richard de Percy under the date of 20 July and another for Roger de Montbegon under the date of 11 August.[1] Final negotiations were opened with these two, along with Gilbert fitz Reinfrey and Adam of Staveley, on 10 October;[2] letters of 31 October and 2 November ordered the restoration of their lands.[3] At about the same time Robert de Ros, Richard de Unfraville, and Roger de Merlay all submitted,[4] and by the end of the first week of November, when the last long list of *reversi* were entered on the close rolls, practically all northern rebels had made their peace. Officially the revolt was over. It remained to resolve the local rivalries, the territorial and personal conflicts, which had been part of it. To these the return of peace made little difference.

[1] *Patent Rolls 1216–25*, pp. 80, 85.   [2] Ibid., pp. 102–3.
[3] *Rot. Litt. Claus.* i. 338, 339, 339b.
[4] Ibid. i. 341b; *Patent Rolls 1216–25*, pp. 106, 119.

IX

THE LOSS OF NORMANDY AND ITS CONSEQUENCES

KING JOHN commanded the minds of those who wrote about his reign. To them, he was a central dominating figure. The chronicles, once raised above annalistic form, become *gesta regis*. Even though no writer gave this title to his work, John stands out from almost every page written about the period. This was affected little by the attitude men took towards his character and ability, towards the qualities of kingship which he enjoyed. Wendover might concoct a picture of a ruler, part madman, part evil genius, part idle voluptuary, but even this compound of monkish prejudice and inhibition had a masterful, satanic quality about it. Wendover protested too much; his chronicle is still a chronicle about John. We may not be able to say much about the King's character, so veiled is it behind fable, invention, and hostile criticism. But at least it impressed men. It might lead one to condemn him as 'John nature's enemy', thus, in effect, raising an image of some new Attila. Others, at the height of John's power, might say that England had not seen such a king since the days of Arthur. The extreme hostility of the first view and the extreme adulation of the second both reflect the awe John inspired, the authority he exercised, the majesty he enjoyed, and the good or evil which he did. He was not a weak man. It was not purely because of his quarrel with Rome that sixteenth-century minds found him so attractive. There was also an authoritarian quality in him which appealed to this later age.

But if John was masterful, he was also mastered. To contemporaries he might appear as a creative or destructive, but nevertheless dynamic, force. Wendover might attribute the great calamities of his reign, the loss of Normandy, the quarrel with the Church, the quarrel with his barons, to his own sloth, irreligion, and tyranny. Taking a more classical, less moralistic, pattern, the Barnwell chronicler might say that he was unlucky and find a parallel for him in Marius. Both writers paid scant attention to the fact that John was dragged along by problems not of his own creating, was committed to or hustled into policies which were not of his own invention, and was finally broken by the impossibility of the task which faced him. Whatever John's abilities, they were as nothing besides the restricting, almost oppressive limitations which hemmed them round.

Continental scholars have often pointed out that Magna Carta followed inevitably on John's defeat at Bouvines in 1214. They are right in two senses. First, Bouvines stripped John of any defence against the English barons; he had now been defeated in the end towards which the whole of his administrative and diplomatic effort had been directed. Secondly, the unrest among the English baronage which achieved its final explosive form in Magna Carta was an unavoidable product of the manifold ways in which English resources had been exploited since the early years of the reign of Henry II to support Angevin policy and possessions on the continent. To this general policy John was committed by birth and position just as his brother and father had been. That he failed in the defence of Normandy was important, for it subjected him to criticism. We may perhaps doubt whether this criticism was justified, for King Philip's financial accounts for the year 1202–3 suggest that French resources available along the Norman frontier were already far greater than anything John could bring to bear. But the detailed allocation of blame or excuse to the King or others is of little real significance. John's most decisive action was not that he lost Normandy, the Touraine, and the old Angevin influence in the Midi, but that for ten furious years he devoted all his efforts to regaining what he had lost. He was a true son of Eleanor of Aquitaine. To argue that he should have accepted the decision of 1204 is unrealistic. Not even his son, Henry III, was prepared to abandon the old Angevin claims until 1259, and he only did so then under the pressure of events in England.

Thus, in the chronology of John's reign, 1204, not 1199, is the crucial date. The great mass of the chronicle evidence obscures this, for most writers were looking back from the period after the Interdict, the failure abroad, and the final civil war at home. Their accounts of the early years of the reign were frequently coloured by later events. If John, in their eyes, behaved like a monster, then it must have been a monster who ascended the throne in 1199; the whole conflict came to be viewed in terms of a single, dominating character. Perhaps in some respects the record evidence also encourages this view, for the great mass of Chancery material first survives, and in some cases was first produced, from John's accession or the years immediately following. It gives us our first sight of the detail of many administrative processes; it is only too easy to imagine that this first sight coincides with the actual origin of these processes. In the chronicles a truer appreciation of John's early years as king is found in those writers who died before Normandy was lost and the Canterbury election in dispute. Roger of Howden and Ralf de Diceto, although critical at times of John and mindful of his rebellion against Richard, never show that uncomprehending hostility which Wendover, for example, displays. To them John was a human being, albeit fallible, rather than a limb of Satan. Similarly, it is well to remember that the sudden increase in record material must be attributed, if to any single person, to Hubert Walter, John's Chancellor, Richard's Justiciar, Glanville's *protégé*, a statesman schooled in the court of Henry II. With John in Normandy in the early years of the reign, Hubert simply carried on where he had scarcely stopped in 1199. His death within a year of the fall of the last English strongholds across the Channel simply emphasized the new situation which had arisen in 1204. John had to face new problems without the old master's advice. England was now governed more immediately by the King than it had been in his earlier years, large parts of which had been spent in Normandy, or in the reigns of Richard I and Henry II. This had its effect in many ways: in the expansion of the financial control of the Chamber, in the increasing use of the small seal, in the increasing decentralization of financial operations to the great royal castles, in the closer supervision by the King of the judicial work of the *curia regis*. John was not just the power behind the administrative machine. He was often the machine itself.

It would be a mistake to imagine that 1204 marked a rough dividing line between lawful and reasonable government on the one hand, and increasingly harsh tyranny on the other. The government of Henry II and Hubert Walter had already placed heavy burdens on the country.[1] Since 1194 especially, with the

---

[1] J. H. Round drew attention to the heavy reliefs, amercements, and *oblata* which appear on the rolls of the later years of Henry II (*Pipe Roll 22 Henry II*, pp. xxii ff.; *Pipe Roll 23 Henry II*, pp. xxiii, xxv–xxvi; *Pipe Roll 28 Henry II*, pp. xxi ff.).

dual burdens of King Richard's ransom and the crisis in the
Norman wars, the strain had become intolerable;[1] England paid
dearly for the vainglorious military luxury of Château Gaillard
and King Richard's soldierly energy. These years, too, witnessed
an inventiveness in fiscal administration scarcely rivalled at any
period in English medieval history. During Hubert Walter's
tenure of the justiciarship and chancery, the first effective customs
system was started, the administration of the Jews and *debita
Judeorum* was completely overhauled, there were attempts to levy
an accurately assessed tax on landed revenues in the carucage of
1198, the same year saw a new forest eyre, and the Archbishop
made frequent excursions into sectors of the country's economy
with the Assize of Weights and Measures, the enforcement of
Exchequer control over the Cornish stannaries, and the recoinage
ordered in 1204. All these measures were quite separate from the
additional burdens required by Richard's ransom. In some ways,
too, John's accession added to the load, for he followed the
customary policy of a new king in insisting that his men should
seek confirmation of their privileges.[2] The pipe rolls of 1199 and
1200, and the inordinately long charter roll of the first year, bear
witness to his energy and success in this direction. If it was not a
monster who had succeeded to the throne, neither was it a philan-
thropist prepared to forget his traditional rights.

But if the administration up to 1204 was harsh and burdensome
enough, it was severely conditioned by the situation in France
and the increasingly desperate state of Angevin fortunes. It
became more and more necessary to sacrifice thoroughness to
speed. In financial terms, the complete execution of a measure,
which would take time and energy, was sometimes sacrificed for
an immediate, if smaller, yield. Thus the reassessment of the
carucage planned in 1198 was never carried out in full; many
counties paid fines to escape assessment and the recorded yield of
the tax in the first two years of its collection barely exceeded
£1,000.[3] Similar payments were again taken for the carucage of

---

[1] See Lady Stenton's comments in *Pipe Roll 9 Richard I*, p. xiii.

Howden commented on the forest eyre of 1198 with the following: 'His igitur
et aliis vexationibus, sive juste sive injuste, tota Anglia a mari usque ad mare
redacta est ad inopiam. Sed his nondum finitis, supervenit aliud genus tormenti ad
confusionem hominum regni' (*Hoveden*, iv. 62–63).   [2] *Curia Regis Rolls*, i. 331.

[3] *Pipe Roll 1 John*, pp. xix–xx. See also S. K. Mitchell, *Studies in Taxation under John
and Henry III*, pp. 7–9.

1200.[1] Perhaps these measures were not designed to do anything more than compel such payments; almost certainly this was one of the motives behind the Assize of Weights and Measures.[2] But, with some exceptions, the projects of these years compare unfavourably with what followed after 1204. The Thirteenth of 1207 raised over £60,000.[3] Most of what we know of the Seventh of 1203 is contained in four notices in the records. One states that it was assessed,[4] but two consist of writs excusing the Count of Aumale and William Marshal from paying the tax.[5] It is unwise to argue from the absence of evidence in the pipe rolls, particularly when the Chamber and special *ad hoc* exchequers were at work behind the scenes, but, even so, there is a striking contrast between the tenor of these entries and what happened in 1207. This reappears in contemporary reactions to these fiscal measures. Many of the earlier ones aroused discontent. The Assize of Weights and Measures was unpopular in the cloth towns;[6] Archbishop Geoffrey of York resisted the carucage of 1200;[7] the Cistercians resented the efforts made to exact money from them. But there was nothing at this time to rival the outburst of resistance which the tax of 1207 produced. For all his power during later years, John never tried to repeat it.

In the last years of the Norman war English resources became inadequate for the task. Tremendous sums were being drafted to the King in Normandy.[8] By 1202 he was raising forced loans, seeking aid both from the Cistercians and his Irish subjects.[9] The Justiciar was collecting debts and amercements directly, rather than wait for the slower processes of the normal account at the Exchequer.[10] It was usual at any time for the King to sell land and privileges. By 1203 and 1204 this was being done so rapidly that it threatened a dangerous diminution of the rights and property of the Crown. After the loss of Normandy the King enjoyed a tarnished reputation. Men might point—

> Al rei Joan que pert sa gen,
> Que non lor secor pres ni loing,[11]

---

[1] *Pipe Roll 2 John*, pp. xiv–xv.   [2] *Pipe Roll 4 John*, pp. xx–xxi.
[3] *Rot. de Ob. et Fin.*, p. 459.   [4] *Pipe Roll 6 John*, p. 256.
[5] *Rot. Lib.*, pp. 43, 47–48. See also S. K. Mitchell, op. cit., pp. 62–63. The fourth reference is to an amercement for concealment in 1210 (*Pipe Roll 12 John*, p. 192).
[6] *Hoveden*, iv. 172.   [7] Ibid. iv. 139–40.   [8] *Pipe Roll 5 John*, p. xi.
[9] *Rot. Litt. Pat.*, p. 14; *Rot. Chartarum*, pp. 133b–134. See also S. K. Mitchell, op. cit., pp. 61–62.   [10] *Pipe Roll 4 John*, pp. xiii, xviii–xix.
[11] *Political Songs of England*, ed. T. Wright (Camden Society, 1839), p. 5.

but John had tried to succour his men and was to try to do so again. Any second occasion, however, was not to suffer from the financial difficulties of 1202–4. Whatever else was ill-conceived in the Poitevin campaign of 1214, it certainly did not lack financial resources. John had learned this lesson; so well, indeed, as to provoke rebellion by the way in which he had treated his realm in accumulating the treasure for war. In this lies the great contrast. In the less provident measures of the years up to 1204 men could find opportunities for profit. They could evade accurate taxation by cash payments; above all, they could exploit the urgency of the King's financial needs to buy privileges, land, and perhaps even office. After 1204 this was not so easy. John was not now forced into such a giving mood. Further, he could devote all his energies to the government and exploitation of his realm. Prior to 1204 there had been many political safety valves, for men who could buy privileges easily were unlikely to fight for them. One by one, these were now shut down.

The most obvious of these safety valves in the years before 1204 lay in John's willingness to sell office and the eagerness of his subjects to buy. The records of these years are scattered with such transactions. In 1201 the custody of Yorkshire with the town of York was given to William de Stuteville in return for offerings totalling £1,133.[1] The agreement laid down that the King could retain castles, forest, and demesne in his own hands and increase their yield as much as he could.[2] Presumably de Stuteville felt that he could make the office prove worth while, despite this limitation. But he was not the only man to benefit from John's policy. The King proceeded to transfer the farms of many of the Yorkshire demesnes, Pocklington, Scalby, Pickering, Scarborough, and Driffield, to the men of the manor. They gained control; in return they had to pay increments over and above the ancient farms.[3] He made similar plans for his Northumbrian demesnes of Newcastle, Newburn, Corbridge, and Rothbury, only to cancel them and leave these estates in the hands of the sheriff.[4] In some northern counties there was a veritable auction. The men of Penrith, Langwathby, and Salkeld made a bid to farm their vills at the ancient renders plus increments totalling £11. John accepted the offer and then cancelled it because the sheriff of

[1] *Pipe Roll 3 John*, pp. xvi–xvii, 158–9.   [2] *Rot. de Ob. et Fin.*, p. 109.
[3] *Rot. Chartarum*, p. 85b.   [4] Ibid., pp. 86b–87b; *Pipe Roll 3 John*, p. 249.

Cumberland, William de Stuteville, made a higher bid and offered increments of £20.[1] Many of these arrangements were made during a royal progress through the northern counties which was extremely burdensome and drew the hostile criticism of chroniclers. This was just, but it obscures the way in which others besides the King used his journey to their own profit.

These transactions were not atypical. In one field the sale of privileges was particularly prominent. In 1201 John accepted an offer from the men of Surrey for the confirmation of the partial deforestation of their county which they had bought from Richard I in 1190.[2] Then in July 1203, at the height of his financial difficulties, John authorized the Chief Forester, Hugh de Neville, to sell forest privileges 'to make our profit by selling woods and demising assarts'.[3] Hugh responded well. The spring of 1204 alone saw nine important deforestations; three in Yorkshire,[4] one in Lincolnshire,[5] and part or all of the New Forest of Staffordshire, Brewood (Salop), and the forests of Cornwall, Essex, and Devon.[6] At the same time many individuals acquired licences to assart or other privileges within the forest bounds.[7] If English landowners were having to reach deep into their pockets to support the King's failing cause in Normandy, they were at least doing it in these cases in a way which ensured a substantial return. If any one man was winning these privileges for them, it was Philip Augustus.

Most of the magnates were closely involved in John's last campaigns. There is some hint in the chronicles that John's demands for military service were occasionally refused. But these incidents, as they are reported, suggest that the refusal of military service was used as a bargaining counter to attain other ends,[8] or that it sprang from political and strategic considerations.[9] Most of the great barons, even those Northerners who led the opposition to the Poitevin scutage in 1214, served with remarkable regularity

[1] *Pipe Roll 3 John*, pp. 254–5.

[2] Ibid., p. 229; *Pipe Roll 2 Richard I*, p. 155.   [3] *Rot. Litt. Pat.*, p. 31b.

[4] Ryedale, Wharfedale, and Hertfordlythe (*Rot. Chartarum*, pp. 121, 123, 132b–133). See map 2.

[5] This affected the vills of Surfleet, Gosberton, Quadring, and Donington (ibid., p. 128). See map 2.   [6] Ibid., pp. 122–3; *Foedera*, i, pt. 1, p. 89.

[7] See grants to Robert Vavassor, Alan of Wilton, and Thomas de Burgh, all in Yorkshire (*Rot. Chartarum*, pp. 122b, 127b; *Rot. Lib.*, p. 104).

[8] *Hoveden*, iv. 161.

[9] See the arguments of the magnates in 1205 (*Chron. Maj.* ii. 490; *Coggeshall*, pp. 152–4; *Gerv. Cant.* ii. 98).

in these earlier years. In doing so, some of them were of course defending their own Norman possessions, but, in addition to this, service in Normandy could be highly profitable. It normally entailed a grant of letters of protection and the postponement of legal actions as long as the service lasted.[1] Frequently it was accompanied by a temporary quittance from suit at shire and hundred and freedom from sheriff's aid.[2] These were the elementary, almost automatic, concomitants of service in Normandy. There were much greater bargains to be obtained. Robert fitz Walter was given the right of free passage for his ships passing up and down the Seine;[3] several other magnates received similar quittances of toll at Les Andelys and elsewhere.[4] While Saer de Quenci was engaged with Robert fitz Walter in the defence of Vaudreuil in 1203, he received a royal quittance of 300 m. and 260 livres Angevin which he owed to the Jews and of a year's interest on another 300 m.[5] The Earl of Arundel and William de Braose were among others who got similar concessions.[6] Hugh de Balliol, Gerard de Furneval the elder, and Saer de Quenci also received quittances or respites on debts owed to the King.[7]

Sometimes the only link between these concessions and military service is the admittedly weak one that they were made while the recipients were with the King in Normandy. Frequently, however, there were closer connexions. In 1205, for example, during the muster at Portsmouth at which the King was vainly trying to persuade his men to follow him across the Channel, Peter de Brus received a pardon of 300 m. which he owed at the Exchequer.[8] Saer de Quenci, Gerard de Furneval, and Peter fitz Herbert had similar concessions during the same muster.[9] It is difficult to avoid the conclusion that in these cases John was trying to buy service and support for his proposed campaign. Sometimes a financial concession to a baron was stated categorically to be a *quid pro quo* of this type. In 1203 Geoffrey de Say was pardoned the payment of interest on *debita Judeorum* for as long as he remained in the

---

[1] See, for example, *Rot. Litt. Pat.*, p. 41b; *Curia Regis Ro ls*, iii. 77, 211; iv. 182.

[2] See, for example, *Rot. Litt. Pat.*, pp. 2, 2b, 30b, 27b; *Rot. Lib.*, p. 34.

[3] *Rot. Norm.*, p. 78.   [4] Ibid., pp. 79–84.

[5] Ibid., p. 61; *Rot. Lib.*, p. 38; *Rot. Litt. Pat.*, p. 30.

[6] *Rot. Litt. Pat.*, pp. 16, 30b, 22b; *Rot. Lib.*, p. 48.

[7] *Rot. Lib.*, p. 65; *Rot. Litt. Claus.* i. 38b–39.

[8] He was also pardoned another 100 m., but not at the time of the Portsmouth muster (*Rot. Litt. Claus.* i. 22, 38b).   [9] Ibid. i. 38b–39.

King's service with horses and arms.[1] In the same year two Lincolnshire barons, William de la Mare and Thomas Darcy, were both pardoned their *debita Judeorum* by order of the King. In return Thomas agreed to provide the service of three knights at his own pay for a whole year, and William the service of three knights and five sergeants for nine months;[2] in both cases this service was additional to that which was due from their baronies. Rather different arrangements were made in 1206 with another Lincolnshire baron, Peter de Scotigny, on the occasion of the first Poitevin campaign. Here the King acquitted Peter of most of his debts at the Exchequer as long as he was overseas in the royal service with horses and arms.[3] At the time of the second Poitevin expedition, which was being planned in 1213, arrangements of this kind, involving either a complete pardon of a debt or a temporary relaxation in the terms of payment, had become common.[4]

Edward I was not the first English king to obtain specific contracts of military service from his barons. Under Edward perhaps the techniques were more sophisticated and their use more widespread than under John. But there was little alteration in principle over the course of the thirteenth century. John was already evolving a form of service which fell midway between feudal service, even feudal service at the new reduced quotas, on the one hand, and the purely mercenary service of a Mercadier or a Cadoc on the other. Like Edward, John, in a tortuous way perhaps, was using his barons as mercenaries. The implications of this are important. John might have met serious objections if he had relied solely on the feudal responsibilities of his vassals. His supplementary measures probably made men readier to discharge their feudal duties, and then led them to accept additional military responsibilities. They were given a stake in the war, even though the war proved increasingly disastrous and even though they were unable to profit from loot and ransoms as their descendants did in France a century and a half later. The narrative evidence suggests that where critical feelings were aroused these were directed not against the war as such, but against continued failure, against John's apparent inability or unwillingness to do anything decisive,[5] against his tactical errors and the behaviour of his

[1] *Rot. Lib.*, p. 48.   [2] Ibid., pp. 42, 44.
[3] *Rot. Litt. Claus.* i. 72b.   [4] *Rot. de Ob. et Fin.*, pp. 474–519 *passim*.
[5] *Chron. Maj.* ii. 482; *Histoire des ducs de Normandie*, pp. 104–5.

mercenaries,[1] and against disasters like that at Vaudreuil. Roger de Lacy's defence of Château Gaillard still awakened a response. As late as 1205, when the magnates, headed by the Archbishop and William Marshal, persuaded the King to abandon his projected expedition across the Channel, the knights in his army and the sailors in the fleet protested bitterly.[2] Some of John's men still retained sufficient interest in the war to trust his leadership. They must still have felt that victory was not out of reach.

The loss of Normandy in 1204 marked a break, a change in the problem facing King John, but it did not produce sudden and violent changes in policy. John does not seem to have accepted the need for a breathing space until after his attempted expedition of 1205 and the first Poitevin campaign of 1206. Although there were some important administrative innovations in these years, it was not until 1207 and subsequent years that his whole energy was concentrated on the exploitation of his kingdom. There was a similar lag in the mental readjustments of his subjects. Frequently they engaged in transactions with the King which seemed to assume the continuance of the relatively easy-going atmosphere of the early years. Some failed to grasp that the King might become much more stringent in his demands, especially in his demands for the payment of the large proffers for privileges which they had made. Hitherto it had sometimes been possible for them to perform extra service in Normandy in order to settle these debts. But now this alternative method of payment was removed just at the time when the King was becoming more troublesome and insistent. Despite this, some continued to gamble heavily in the traffic of wardships, marriages, and offices. Many got themselves into increasing financial difficulties as a result; some suffered the penalties of disseisin and imprisonment. The final crisis of 1215 was produced not only by John's skill and perseverance in seeking his financial advantage, but also by the eagerness with which some plunged into the net he cast and the clumsiness which enmeshed them ever more closely in their financial subjection to the King.

The first and most obvious developments after 1204 occurred in the financial administration of the shires and the royal demesne. John removed some of his old sheriffs, transferred others to

---

[1] *Histoire de Guillaume de Maréchal*, lines 12019–43, 12531–50, 21595–606.
[2] *Coggeshall*, pp. 153–4.

different counties, and introduced a considerable number of new men into local government. At the same time he tried to alter the character of the shrievalty by appointing the sheriffs as custodians, who ceased to farm their shires and were expected to account for the total yield, for variable 'profits' over and above the normal farm. Here he was applying techniques which had already been well proved in the administration of custodies and escheats;[1] there was therefore some tradition and experience behind them, and it may be that the new moves were one of the last administrative measures of Hubert Walter. In theory, at least, the sheriff, if not a salaried official, was now an official who could expect the payment of his expenses, for he was no longer expected to retain any portion of his county's revenue.[2] In practice this rarely happened. The new system was difficult to operate, for it posed insoluble problems of account before an already overburdened Exchequer. There was no method of checking the variable receipts of a sheriff with any accuracy. In many counties the new moves were abandoned in favour of the older methods of requiring a fixed increment in addition to the ancient farm. But, where the custodian principle worked, it usually worked well, and in certain counties John continued to use it until the final years of the reign.[3]

Whether these new methods were effective or not, their introduction accompanied and in part produced a markedly disturbed atmosphere in local government. It was no longer so easy to buy and retain the control of shire and demesne farms. In 1199 and again in 1204 the men of Lancashire had made a proffer that Richard de Vernon might be their sheriff.[4] In 1205 Richard was replaced by Gilbert fitz Reinfrey, who remained sheriff until 1215.

[1] See the pipe rolls of the later years of Henry II and especially *Rotuli de Dominabus* (Pipe Roll Society), *passim*. See *Pipe Roll 31 Henry I*, p. 63, for a *superplus* of 1,000 m. paid on the shires in the custody of Richard Basset and Aubrey de Vere.

[2] In Feb. 1215 John ordered a payment to Peter fitz Herbert for the custody of Yorkshire and various castles, adding that as Peter accounted for the 'profits' of the shire it was right that he should be credited with his reasonable expenses (*Rot. Litt. Claus.* i. 187b).

[3] See Miss Mabel H. Mills, 'Experiments in Exchequer Procedure', *T.R.H.S.* 4th series, viii. 151 ff. I am unable to accept Painter's view that there was a general abandonment of the new system because of political difficulties facing the government in 1207-8 (*The Reign of King John*, pp. 122-3). Where the system was abandoned, as it was in several counties in 1207-8, the reasons for abandonment were probably administrative and financial, not political.

[4] *Rot. de Ob. et Fin.*, p. 38; *Pipe Roll 6 John*, p. 6.

The men who had acquired the farms of the Yorkshire demesnes in 1201 also lost them, either for a short period or for the remainder of the reign. The men of Pocklington were in debt on their account for the manor by 1203.[1] The farm was transferred to Robert de Stuteville. Robert was in debt on the farm in 1204[2] and was deprived of it before the last quarter of the financial year of 1204-5. He suffered disseisin and the arrears of the account were met from the sale of his chattels; Pocklington was transferred to the sheriff.[3] Meanwhile the farm of Pickering had been transferred to Robert de Vieuxpont,[4] and in 1208 the men of Scarborough also seem to have lost control of their farm for a time.[5] Where the control of local government could still be acquired, it was on terms which were more and more burdensome financially. William de Stuteville's proffer for Yorkshire in 1201 had brought him the county at the cost of sacrificing control of the castles, forest, and demesne. In 1205, when Roger de Lacy acquired the shrievalty, John went further. He now tried to exact 'profits'. De Lacy seems to have resisted, but the King partly won his point for de Lacy fined for the 'profits' and agreed to pay £200 over and above the farm. He never paid this until he lost the shrievalty in 1209. He was then charged with the sum for the last five years and paid over £600 of it.[6] The next sheriff, Gilbert fitz Reinfrey, accounted for the 'profits' properly, and the results were substantial. Between 1210 and 1212 the 'profits' of Yorkshire never fell below £580, and in the first year, 1210, exceeded £700.[7] Largely through this, the normal income for which the sheriff accounted in 1212 was nearly twice the figure for 1204[8] and more than treble that of 1199.[9] Extraordinary results were sometimes achieved when the same methods were applied to the administration of demesnes and escheats. In 1206 the sheriff of Yorkshire was credited with an allowance of £22 for the manors of Knares-

---

[1] *Pipe Roll 5 John*, p. 199.   [2] *Pipe Roll 6 John*, p. 193.
[3] *Pipe Roll 7 John*, pp. 41, 46; *Pipe Roll 8 John*, p. 192.
[4] *Pipe Roll 6 John*, p. 193; *Pipe Roll 7 John*, p. 41.
[5] *Pipe Roll 10 John*, p. 140.
[6] *Rot. de Ob. et Fin.*, p. 273; *Pipe Roll 11 John*, p. 125.
[7] *Pipe Roll 12 John*, p. 149; *Pipe Roll 13 John*, p. 33; *Pipe Roll 14 John*, p. 27.
[8] £1,090. 5s. 6d. as against £550. 9s. 6½d. These and other figures given below include the gross farm of the shire, less recurrent allowances and items under the heading *in terris datis*, plus increments and 'profits' on the shire, where they occur, and farms, increments or yields of *terrae datae* for which separate accounts were made either by the sheriff or some other custodian.   [9] £321. 19s. 8d.

borough and Boroughbridge, which were in the hands of Brian de Lisle.[1] This sum was the ancient farm of these manors for which the sheriffs of Yorkshire had accounted before Henry II had granted them, first to the Morvilles and then to the Stute-villes.[2] In the same year, 1206, Brian de Lisle's account as cus-todian of these lands amounted to nearly £540.[3]

Yorkshire illustrates the King's policy at its most demanding. Elsewhere, he was still prepared, at a price, to make arrangements whereby local men got complete or partial control of the shrieval office.[4] In some counties, too, such as Cumberland and Lancashire, there was little increase in yield after increments had been imposed in the early years of the reign. In some cases, such as Northumber-land, revenues actually fell as a result of an alienation of demesne lands for which no administrative improvement of what was left could compensate.[5] In other cases, even where there was no startling expansion of revenue, there was clearly a new spirit in the sheriff's relations with the Exchequer, a new stringency, part threat, part fact. In the case of Nottinghamshire and Derbyshire 'profits' of £100 were agreed between John and the sheriff, Robert de Vieuxpont, in 1208.[6] Thereafter 'profits' were not mentioned until 1214 when the Exchequer had been considering the 'profits' which should have been paid over the previous six years.[7] It is probable that Philip Mark, who had been sheriff for most of this period, was only saved from answering awkward questions by the advent of civil war. In the case of Lincolnshire, one sheriff, Thomas of Moulton, met with disaster. His proffer for the shrievalty of Lincolnshire in 1205 included an agreement to pay an increment of 300 m. on the farm of the county.[8] Within three years he had run into debt on the terms of his proffer and on his shire accounts. He was amerced, deprived of his shrievalty, and imprisoned. Such arrangements as Thomas made with the King had not been abnormal in the early years of the reign. He was not

---

[1] *Pipe Roll 8 John*, p. 191.   [2] *Early Yorks. Charters*, i. 390–1.
[3] *Pipe Roll 8 John*, pp. 217–18.
[4] For example, Cornwall in 1208 and Dorset and Somerset in 1210 (*Pipe Roll 10 John*, p. 183; *Pipe Roll 12 John*, p. 75).
[5] £166. 19s. 2d. in 1199 as against £127. 11s. 11d. in 1211.
[6] *Rot. Litt. Claus.* i. 104b; *Rot. Chartarum*, p. 184. This was an interesting case in which 'profits' and increments became confused, the same charge of £100 appearing under each of these labels on different occasions.
[7] *Pipe Roll 16 John*, p. 158.
[8] *Rot. de Ob. et Fin.*, p. 338; *Pipe Roll 8 John*, p. 88.

excessively in debt on his accounts. In earlier years he could probably have avoided such severe disciplinary action. Now it was almost as if he were being used as an example to the rest.

Thomas of Moulton's difficulties are illuminating. He was the local candidate for the shrievalty; his proffer was backed by a large group of Lincolnshire gentry.[1] He could not therefore ride rough-shod over local interests. In addition there is something to suggest that his bargain was uneconomic. The increment of 300 m. to which he had agreed was the one which Simon of Kyme had been returning at the end of Richard's reign. It was reduced to 200 m. when Gerard de Camville became sheriff in 1199. Lincolnshire, admittedly a very wealthy county, already carried the very large farm of £969. 1s. 8d., more than twice that of Yorkshire. It may well be that the 100 m. additional increment which Thomas had to carry made just the difference between a reasonable gain on the transaction and no gain at all. The sheriffs who followed him, Hubert de Burgh and his deputy, Richard Aguillon, were expected to account for 'profits', but, in fact, all they did from Michaelmas 1209 onwards was return the increment which Thomas had agreed earlier.[2] There is little evidence available on their administration of the county, but they were not bound by the local ties which had limited Thomas's freedom of action, and in the end complaints were made against them. In 1213 they were replaced as sheriffs and inquiries held into their activities.[3] We may imagine that they had proceeded to recoup themselves by exploiting the county in their charge. This, indeed, must have been the general reaction of sheriffs throughout the land. Ultimately the shires carried the burden, for no sheriff, given a free hand, was going to work at a loss or indeed at anything but a considerable profit. The game was not worth the effort on any other terms. As the yield produced by the sheriffs of Yorkshire increased, so there were hints after Roger de Lacy's death that his administration would not bear investigation, and then direct evidence of administrative malpractice under Gilbert fitz Reinfrey.[4] The rising curve of royal income was accompanied by a rising curve of shrieval corruption. It is not surprising that Gilbert's activities, like Hubert de Burgh's, came under investigation in 1213.[5]

[1] See above, p. 74.   [2] *Pipe Roll 11 John*, p. 70.
[3] See above, pp. 85–86.   [4] See below, pp. 229–233.
[5] The complaint against Gilbert came from Yorkshire alone, not from his other

If there was a contrast between John's early and later years in his handling of shire government, there was an even sharper one in the administration of the forest. Here, the sale of privileges had been adopted as a principle in 1203 and had led to extensive deforestations in the course of 1204.[1] These relaxations were emphasized not only by what followed but also by what had preceded them. They were in fact sandwiched between the forest eyre of 1198 which was still proceeding when John came to the throne and the new forest eyre begun in 1207 and 1208. The forest eyre of 1198 was burdensome, as Howden indicated;[2] it led men to seek freedom from forest regulations or compelled them to fine for a confirmation of privileges already theirs. In 1200 the men of Lancashire offered £200 and ten hunters for the confirmation of their forest charter[3] and in the same year the Abbot of St. Mary's, York, and the men of Ainsty wapentake offered £300 to be quit of the forest.[4] The eagerness with which men bought forest privileges in 1204 may have been accentuated by their experience of this eyre.

There was a further difference between the administration of the forest and the administration of the shires. In the latter instance the new methods depended for their success on the particular sheriff and perhaps also on the particular county in question. As a result, there was great variation in the extent to which the new methods were adopted and in the resulting increase in revenue. In the case of the forest this was not so. All forests equally came under the searching investigation of Hugh de Neville and his associates. The new eyres of 1207-8 were striking and violent in their effects. They affected, almost simultaneously, all counties into which the forest law extended.

The new forest eyre was begun in 1207 and most of its work was completed by 1209.[5] The long accounts for forest pleas on

shire of Lancashire where the 'profits' he produced barely exceeded the old increment which the county had borne in Richard de Vernon's time. It is worth noting that Gilbert had much stronger local ties in Lancashire, especially in the northern part of the county, than he had in Yorkshire.

[1] See above, p. 149.

[2] *Hoveden*, iv. 63; *Pipe Roll 1 John*, p. xix; *Pipe Roll 2 John*, p. xvi.

[3] *Pipe Roll 2 John*, p. 237. For the charter, granted by John when Count of Mortain, see W. Farrer, *Lancashire Pipe Rolls and Early Charters*, pp. 418-19.

[4] *Rot. de Ob. et Fin.*, p. 54.

[5] *Pipe Roll 9 John*, pp. xxiii-xxvi; *Pipe Roll 10 John*, p. xxii; *Pipe Roll 11 John*, pp. xxv-xxvi.

the pipe rolls seriously underestimate its effects, for some of its work bore fruit not in the forest amercements but in the *nova oblata*,[1] and many payments probably went directly through the hands of Hugh de Neville, who had his own Exchequer of the Forest which had earlier been situated at Nottingham.[2] Despite this, the sums assessed as forest amercements were impressive enough, over £1,300 in Yorkshire[3] and nearly £600 in Northumberland.[4] The whole operation received frequent, sometimes extended notice in the narrative sources. According to the *Histoire des ducs de Normandie* the beasts of the forest enjoyed such protection that they pastured the fields like sheep. If chased, they only deigned to flee at a trot and stopped when their hunters stopped.[5] This idyllic picture of a benevolent, all-powerful, kingly gamekeeper was very far from the truth. But it is significant that the author of this work turned to the forest law to illustrate the strength of John's rule at this time. Other writers were more critical. The continuator of Ralph Niger's chronicle noted that all mastiffs within the forest were killed.[6] According to the Dunstable annalist, the King ordered the destruction of all ditches, hedges, and assarted houses, 'even the old ones', throughout the county of Essex; eighty foresters were imprisoned and eventually allowed to ransom themselves.[7] Wendover apparently drew on, and distorted, some source similar to the Dunstable annalist at this point. According to him, the King ordered the destruction of hedges and ditches throughout every royal forest. For good measure, he also stated that John forbade the taking of birds.[8]

We cannot say whether these statements represent some new severity in the articles of the forest eyre of 1207 for they have not

[1] In the case of Nottinghamshire and Derbyshire the *nova oblata* suggest that the eyre had begun as early as 1207, but no pleas of the forest appear on the rolls until 1209 and 1210 (*Pipe Roll 9 John*, p. 124; *Pipe Roll 11 John*, pp. 118–19; *Pipe Roll 12 John*, p. 15).

[2] See J. C. Holt, 'Philip Mark and the Shrievalty of Nottinghamshire and Derbyshire', *Trans. Thoroton Society*, lvi (1952), p. 10. Hugh's account to 24 June 1207 included £5,500 arrears of debtors in addition to approximately £9,400 for his custody of the forests of England during nearly six and a half years (*Memoranda Roll 10 John*, p. 64; *Rot. Litt. Pat.*, p. 78b).

[3] *Pipe Roll 10 John*, pp. 156–8; *Pipe Roll 11 John*, pp. 122–3.

[4] *Pipe Roll 9 John*, pp. 3–4; *Pipe Roll 10 John*, p. 55; *Pipe Roll 11 John*, pp. 176–7.

[5] *Histoire des ducs de Normandie*, p. 109.

[6] B.L. MS. Bibl. Reg. 13 A xii, f. 88v.

[7] *Annales Monastici*, iii. 31. Compare *Pipe Roll 11 John*, p. 27.

[8] *Chron. Maj.* ii. 524, 525.

survived.[1] After the conclusion of the eyre a breathing-space could reasonably have been expected, but this, if it occurred, was brief. The Barnwell chronicler noted new forest exactions in 1212.[2] This new eyre was cut short, but its trail in the pipe rolls suggests that it was even more searching than that begun in 1207.[3] Over £550 was assessed on Nottinghamshire and Derbyshire and the bailiwick of Brian de Lisle,[4] and over £400 on Cumberland.[5] Yorkshire was assessed with approximately £1,250, most of this coming from penalties placed on towns and vills; £200 was levied on the shire.[6] The administration of the forest was among the first to be relaxed after the outbreak of treason in 1212.[7] It was a vital issue in the political conflicts of 1215. It was the only administrative field to require a special charter of liberties of its own. The execution of this charter of 1217 was to prove a quarrelsome business for a century to come.

The bare and fomal entries in the pipe rolls give but a schematic impression of the conflicting interests and passions which the royal forest aroused. The forest was the King's private perquisite. 'In forestis etiam penetralia regum sunt et eorum maxime delicie.' Forest offenders were punished at the King's pleasure. The forest law derived solely from the King's will and bore no relation to the custom of the realm. The justice of the forest law was relative, not absolute.[8] All this ran counter to the views men were coming to hold on the proper organization of the kingdom, and what they did, in effect, in 1215 and 1217 was to put the forest law for the first time on the same footing as the custom of the realm.[9] As in his father's day, hunting lodges were often the seats of John's government. His love of hunting was so well known that critics readily contrasted it with an alleged lack of martial ardour.[10] Sometimes he enforced the forest law in person, and on

---

[1] What seem to be articles of the regard for John's reign appear in *Register of the Priory of Worcester*, ed. W. H. Hale (Camden Society, xci), pp. 96a–97b.
[2] *Walt. Cov.* ii. 207.   [3] *Pipe Roll 14 John*, pp. xxiii–xxiv.
[4] Ibid., pp. 165–7.   [5] Ibid., p. 156.
[6] Ibid., pp. 16–18, 38–39.   [7] See above, pp. 85–86.
[8] *Dialogus de Scaccario*, ed. Charles Johnson, pp. 59–60.
[9] This was so in so far as the Charters covered all matters of forest administration.
[10]   Mais ama l'bordir e l'cassar
             E bracs e lebriers et austors,
             E sojorn; per que il faill honors,
             E s'laissa vius deseretar.

(*Political Songs of England*, ed. T. Wright (Camden Society, 1839), p. 4.)

occasions mercilessly. In 1200 the amercements of the forest in Nottinghamshire and Derbyshire were levied *coram rege*.[1] In 1206 the Abbot of Furness compounded for an enormous amercement of the forest of 500 m. which had been imposed *per os regis*.[2] Even when he sold privileges, the King seems to have expected that payments should be made for their confirmation at almost every eyre. The men of Ainsty wapentake, which was deforested in 1190, had to pay for confirmations in 1200[3] and 1208[4] and were still amerced *pro transgressione* in 1212.[5] What the King had given away, he was prepared to recall.

The forest regulations, especially those of an economic character which dealt with purprestures and assarts, touched the local landowner at a vulnerable spot. The forest stood in the way of any expansion of arable or any improvement of land within the bounds by hedging, ditching, draining, building, or destruction of trees and undergrowth. Many of the forest privileges bought and many of the amercements imposed were concerned with these practices of assarting and wasting. In 1206 the custodians of Knaresborough accounted for over £90 which they had accumulated either from proffers to hold assarts or from the sale of corn from assarts from within the forest of Knaresborough.[6] In the next year the yield of the corn of assarts was over £50.[7] The lists of the amercements of the forest eyres only give a limited amount of information on this crucial question of assarting. Full returns appear in the rolls of the regarders, but only fragments of these survive for John's reign.[8] Where they do survive they present an impressive picture of agrarian expansion at the expense of the King's rights. In successive regards of the forest of Pickering 300 acres and 160 acres of assarts were recorded. In successive regards of the forest between Ouse and Derwent the acreage was over 80 and over 100.[9]

In these and other forest matters the local landowner often possessed a distinct advantage. Very frequently the foresterships

[1] *Pipe Roll 2 John*, p. 18.
[2] *Rot. de Ob. et Fin.*, p. 365.
[3] See above, p. 157.
[4] *Rot. de Ob. et Fin.*, p. 434.
[5] *Pipe Roll 14 John*, p. 39.
[6] *Pipe Roll 8 John*, p. 218.
[7] *Pipe Roll 9 John*, p. 125.
[8] See P.R.O., Treasury of Receipt, Forest Proceedings, 249, rots. 1, 2, 9, 10, 11, 18, for records of the regard for Leicestershire, Rutland, and Northamptonshire which appear to belong to John's reign. These consist of long single membranes filled with charges for assarts or waste.
[9] Treasury of Receipt, Forest Proceedings, 235.

were the hereditary right of local families. Hence the enforcement of the law, between eyres and the roving inspections of Hugh de Neville or, perhaps, Brian de Lisle, was in the hands of men who had strong local connexions, who were probably prepared to turn a blind eye to the depredations of their friends and who were certainly eager to profit from their position at the King's expense, if they could. The amercements they had to face, when caught, figure prominently in the records of the forest eyres. In 1201, in Yorkshire, Alan of Thornton and Alan Boie were in trouble for keeping the forest badly and owed 100 m. and 300 m. respectively as a result.[1] In 1209 Richard de Lucy of Egremont had to offer £100 as a fine for the recovery of land and chattels which had been seized for faulty custody of the forest.[2] In the same year Richard of Laxton proffered 200 m. for the same purpose,[3] and in Yorkshire William of Cornbrough, forester of Galtres, the enormous sum of 1,000 m.[4]

In the case of the Yorkshire forest of Galtres, the situation behind such an amercement can be traced in some clarity and detail. In the early years of the reign this forest had been in the hands of Richard Malebisse.[5] In 1204 he had to proffer £100 for the seisin of his land and chattels which had been taken into the King's hands because of a report that he had kept the forest badly.[6] The full catalogue of Richard's misdeeds still survives.[7] An inquest had discovered that he had taken 250 of the King's oaks for the construction of his castle at Wheldrake. He had also sold trees from the King's demesne woods to the value of over 140 m.; the proceeds had apparently gone into his own pocket. Richard seems to have escaped rather lightly. The next forester, William of Cornbrough, was not so lucky. He may have felt the brunt of the King's wrath because he had failed to improve an administration which clearly required it after Richard's activity. It is also possible that his heavier penalty reflected the increased severity of John's later years. But when all excuses for him have been made, it is also apparent that this forest, far from improving, had actually deteriorated in his hands. A report on his activities,

---

[1] *Rot. de Ob. et Fin.*, pp. 107, 108.   [2] *Pipe Roll 11 John*, p. 95.
[3] *Rot. de Ob. et Fin.*, p. 392.   [4] *Pipe Roll 11 John*, p. 139.
[5] Richard's descendants later alleged a grant of the forestership in fee by Richard I (*Patent Rolls 1247–58*, p. 627).
[6] *Pipe Roll 6 John*, p. 188.
[7] P.R.O., Chancery Miscellanea, 11/1/1a, 1b.

this time by Brian de Lisle and Robert de Percy, also survives.[1]
They stated that the forest was badly kept and much wasted,
particularly the demesne woods of Easingwold and Huby.
William of Cornbrough had admitted that 426 oaks had been
taken, but only 65 of these could be traced. The beasts of the
forest were much reduced in number, wood was being cut without
the view of the verderers, cattle were being pastured within the
bounds. There had, in fact, been a wholesale attack by local
interests on the King's rights, an attack which the local forester
had been unable to prevent or in which he had joined. Matters
had gone so far that the recovery of royal rights was impossible.
In 1230 Easingwold and Huby were deforested and granted to
a royal sergeant at a farm of £5 per annum.[2]

In the matter of the forest, men did not wait for 1215 and the
Charter of the Forest of 1217. Long before these great events,
they had been helping themselves. When John took the offensive
in 1207 with his new eyre, some revival of royal rights was obviously needed. But at best it could only have temporary effects.
The feebleness or recalcitrance of the local forester, the continual
invasion of the King's rights by local landowners, the simple fact
that it is often easier to poach than protect game and almost
always easier to destroy a tree than preserve it, all told against the
King. The eyre must have been bitterly resented. Even if the King
was within his rights, it must nevertheless have appeared to the
local landowners as a sudden and violent intrusion into their affairs.

The amercements recorded in the pipe rolls for the two eyres
begun in 1207 and 1212 consist in the main of small payments
levied on a wide section of the population. Where larger payments
were involved these were sometimes levied on the shire or wapentake and frequently on the township or vill. However, it should
not be imagined that these royal investigations were of little importance to the baronial or knightly landowner. In Derbyshire, in
1200, Hubert fitz Ralf of Crich owed 100 m. to be quit of an
appeal.[3] In the same year Henry fitz Hervey of Ravensworth owed
the same sum to be quit of an amercement imposed on him in
Richard's time.[4] In 1208, in Northumberland, Robert Bertram
of Bothal owed nearly £250 *pro foresta*.[5] In the next year, in York-

---

[1] *Chancery Miscellanea*, 11/1/11.   [2] *Cal. Charter Rolls*, i. 122–3.
[3] *Rot. de Ob. et Fin.*, p. 109.   [4] *Rot. Chartarum*, p. 101b.
[5] *Pipe Roll 10 John*, p. 55.

shire, Robert and Mauger Vavassor were amerced 100 m. and 50 m. respectively and William de Stuteville of Cowesby was charged with 100 m. for default.[1] Sometimes a lord might find the preservation of his own forest rights a difficult matter in the face of royal policy. In 1209 Nicholas de Stuteville the younger made a proffer for the perambulation of the bounds between his own forest and the forest of Pickering. The only immediate effect of this was that the Crown recovered the forest of Farndale.[2] A year later the knights and men who held land in the forest between Ouse and Derwent had to pay for a confirmation of their right to pasture animals and to take timber within the bounds.[3]

In these cases the interests of the local barons and gentry were directly and closely involved. This was probably so, too, in many other cases where their names do not appear, the amercement falling on township, wapentake, or shire. In assarting especially they must have been deeply concerned because this activity required a considerable outlay, both in time and money. On occasions they paid heavily for assarting or waste; in 1209, in Northumberland, for example, Roger de Merlay had to pay 60 m. for wasting woods.[4] Sometimes, too, they obtained licences to assart, Robert de Ros for 200 acres in Northumberland in 1201,[5] Richard Malebisse for 80 acres at Wheldrake in 1200.[6] But we may suspect that many a vill had to bear the sentences of the justices of the forest for breaches of the law organized by their lords. Even so, the lords occasionally appear as the culprits. The roll of assarts for Pickering shows them paying the annual charges of 1s. or 6d. an acre on their assarts like any ordinary freeholder or group of villagers: Robert de Stuteville 10s. for 20 acres of new assart in Middleton, Warin de Vesci his share of 6s. for part of 12 acres in Knapton. These seem like pin-pricks perhaps; there is nothing of the dramatic in them; but we may wonder whether the regular exaction of these sums from a Stuteville or a Vesci was either politic or worth while.

The increasingly stringent supervision of the forest which was enforced from 1207 onwards contributed, with other measures like the experiments in the administration of the shires, to a male-

---

[1] *Pipe Roll 11 John*, pp. 122, 123.
[2] Ibid., pp. 138, 123. For Farndale see map 2.
[3] *Pipe Roll 12 John*, p. 216.
[4] *Pipe Roll 11 John*, p. 176.
[5] *Rot. Chartarum*, p. 101b.
[6] *Rot. de Ob. et Fin.*, p. 55.

volent, oppressive quality in government not experienced hitherto on such a scale. When the crisis came at the end of the reign, however, the rebel magnates were not simply attacking methods of government which had proved generally burdensome and which they considered unjust. Very frequently, royal policies affected them directly and disastrously. Through the simplest operations of the Exchequer baronial families could be driven to penury, loss of estate, and deprivation. When they fought in 1215, they fought above all for themselves.

John's policies in these matters are most clearly illustrated in his administration of *debita Judeorum*, those debts, originally owed at usury to Jews, which had escheated to the Crown on the death of the creditors, and which were now payable by the baronial or knightly debtor to the King. The most ancient of these debts, and a recurring feature of the pipe rolls in the early years of the reign, were the debts of Aaron of Lincoln. Aaron had died in 1186. For five years his affairs had been administered by a special exchequer which had collected an unknown quantity of his *debita*. Between 1191 and 1193 the outstanding sums, totalling £15,000, were entered on the pipe rolls.[1] Those which still survived on the pipe rolls in John's early years represented the hard kernel of unwillingness or incapacity to pay. Little was being done in most cases to collect the debts; many had already been passed down from father to son. This, in any case, was a period when the payment of these debts was sometimes pardoned or relaxed in return for service on the continent. In 1207 John stopped all this. In November he instructed the Barons of the Exchequer to seize all the lands which Jollan de Amundeville held at the time he contracted his debt with Aaron, £272 of which was still owing to the King. Quite casually, John also ordered that similar distraint should be made on the lands of all those who owed debts of Aaron.[2] The King was aiming here not so much at the dispossession of the debtors as at tightening the screw, at using distraint on land or the threat of distraint as a method of compelling payment. The change was apparent enough. Jollan's debt first appeared on the pipe roll of 1191 as nearly £270 owed on the security of his manors of Barrow and Kingerby and an additional 10 m. under a separate

---

[1] J. Jacob, 'Aaron of Lincoln', *Trans. Jewish Historical Society*, iii. 168; *Pipe Roll 3 & 4 Richard I*, pp. xiii–xiv.
[2] *Rot. Litt. Claus.* i. 98b.

bond.[1] By 1207 he had clearly done nothing of any consequence towards paying. In 1209 his son, Peter, took over the estates and the debt, which now stood at £264. He agreed to pay it off at £10 per annum[2] and did so until the rebellion came to provide relief. By the end of the 1214 account he had reduced the debt to £222, which was still owing in 1219.[3] The £50 John was able to collect between 1207 and 1214 compares very favourably with what had come in earlier. He was becoming impatient with these veterans among debtors.

John's actions were potentially dangerous to himself. In re-examining the problem of *debita Judeorum* he was entering treacherous country full of ugly scenes and vistas, of pogroms, cheating, traffic in mortgages, and dispossession, a country in which baron and knight were involved in an obscure and unwholesome conflict with the rapacity of the Jew, the acquisitiveness of monastic houses, and the interest of the King as the residuary legatee to whom, in the end, the profits of usurious transactions descended. In 1190 riots against the Jews were widespread. At York they had been led by indebted gentry and needy crusaders, who in a fine blend of religious prejudice and financial self-interest had finished by burning the bonds of the Jews in the middle of the Minster. This was indeed a peculiar and spectacular offering before the Almighty.[4] In 1203 John felt compelled to complain of the bad treatment which the Jews were receiving at London.[5] In 1215 the rebel barons tore down the houses of the Jews to repair the walls of the city.[6] Where there was no open violence of this kind there was sometimes passive resistance to a Jew's lawful financial demands.[7]

[1] *Pipe Roll 3 Richard I*, p. 19.   [2] *Pipe Roll 11 John*, p. 68.
[3] *Pipe Roll 16 John*, p. 147; *Pipe Roll 3 Henry III*, p. 119.
[4] See the account of William of Newburgh in *Chronicles of Stephen, Henry II and Richard I*, i. 312 ff.; Hoveden, iii. 33–34; *Chron. Melsa*, i. 243–4, 250–2.
[5] *Rot. Litt. Pat.*, p. 33.
[6] *Coggeshall*, p. 171. For archaeological evidence in support see *Stow's Survey of London*, ed. C. L. Kingsford (Oxford, 1908), i. 38.
[7] In 9–10 John, Matthew Mantel had pledged the manor of Standon, Herts., to Moses son of Brun. The Jew, however, could not obtain full seisin of the estate because Matthew's sergeant would not see that the men of the vill swore fealty to him, and the men would not accept him. He then obtained a writ directing the sheriff to give him full seisin, and the sheriff was also ordered to sell the stock and chattels. When he tried to execute this, however, he only found four oxen and six draught animals. No corn was found, and there was no purchaser for the few animals which had been seized (*Curia Regis Rolls*, v. 169).

Few men were unscathed by the financial operations of the Jews. The mortgage was the normal resource of any landowner who required cash quickly.[1] The Jew was the obvious source of loans. The rates of interest he charged were high, frequently rising to 40 per cent.[2] Once in his hands it was difficult to escape; one loan tended to succeed to another.[3] Relief might come in various ways. The debtor might be able to evade his responsibilities by legal or political chicanery, although the Crown, as the protector and residuary legatee of the Jew, was watchful in preserving both his and its own rights. There was little leakage of this kind after 1194 when the system for registering the debts was reorganized. Sometimes a monastery might step in to pay off debts in return for a grant of land by the debtor. There were many arrangements of this kind, an unknown number covered by charters which purported to be perfectly normal grants in free alms.[4] The practice was so widespread in the Cistercian order that it had to be forbidden by the Chapter. Even so, the critics of these monks among the secular clergy, like Walter Map and Gerald of Wales, were able to jibe at their financial methods, and Richard I, in a celebrated *bon mot*, was said to have allocated the sin of Greed to their order.[5] It is certain that some Cistercian houses benefited frequently from the debtor's plight. William Fossard lost the manor of Wharram to the monks of Meaux by transactions of this kind; in return for the grant the monks paid Aaron of Lincoln 1,260 m. for bonds to the value of 1,800 m.[6] The chronicle of this abbey provides a dry, unenthusiastic record of the religious life, but a convincing picture of the advantages which accrued to active landowners with resources available and the determination to exploit the ill fortune or bad planning of their neighbours.

[1] See, for example, licences granted to various men who were going on the crusade in 1201–2 (*Rot. Litt. Pat.*, pp. 3b–4b; *Rot. Lib.*, p. 25). Robert de Ros obtained a similar licence when he was planning to go to the Holy Land in 1207 (*Rot. Litt. Pat.*, p. 59b). For licences to pledge land granted to men who were faced with the payment of ransoms see ibid., pp. 37b, 59b, 64.

[2] C. Roth, *History of the Jews in England*, pp. 106–7.

[3] This accumulation of debt is well illustrated by some of the entries among Aaron's debtors. William Fossard's debts of approximately £500, for example, appear as six distinct items, those of Alan fitz Ruald, totalling £46, as three distinct items (*Pipe Roll 3 & 4 Richard I*, p. 22).

[4] F. M. Stenton, *Danelaw Documents*, pp. li–liii.

[5] Gerald of Wales, *Opera*, iv. 54. For a review of the evidence of Gerald and Walter Map, but one favourable to the Cistercians, see D. Knowles, *Monastic Orders in England*, pp. 663–77.   [6] *Chron. Melsa*, i. 173–8.

Relief of this kind was only relative. It involved the surrender of land and this might be a bitter blow. William Fossard's successors refused to accept this depletion of their inheritance without a fight. Legal actions followed his death in 1194, and the monks were not secure in their possession until the early years of John's reign.[1] Finally, relief could be expected when the Jew died. The collection of the debt then devolved on the Exchequer or the King's justices of the Jews. Either might be relatively lenient and dilatory. In this lay the danger for John in 1207. He was reorganizing an administration which had been relatively lax, perhaps too sympathetic and genteel. He was beginning to press men who, by definition, were already among the more hard pressed financially. He might drive them further into debt, ultimately towards penury. But in hustling them along this road the King would meet resistance. Men would nurse grievances, object, and perhaps in the end fight.

From 1207 onwards John began to impose extraordinarily heavy tallages on the Jews culminating in 1210 in the Bristol tallage of 66,000 m.[2] The St. Albans chroniclers, among others, have given considerable notoriety to John's imprisonment and treatment of the Jews on this last occasion,[3] but they failed to notice the really crucial development. To make up this enormous sum, the King took the debts of the Jews into his own hands and made efforts to collect them directly from the debtors. Hitherto the Crown had only had a direct interest in the debts of dead Jews. Now John was trying to collect the debts of all Jews, those alive as well as those dead. He was threatening a general foreclosure.[4] There is little indication of how far he pressed this line of action immediately. What seem to be some of the results, however, quickly appeared on the financial records. In the Exchequer account of 1211 it was revealed that Gilbert de Gant owed *debita Judeorum* amounting to 1,500 m. This sum was reduced to 1,200 m. on condition that he paid it off in two years.[5] Simon of Kyme was another perennial debtor who was now brought to heel. In John's reign he was still trying to cope with the debts of his father, Philip, including some which had been owed to

[1] Ibid. i. 232, 290–1.   [2] C. Roth, op. cit., pp. 35–36.
[3] *Chron. Maj.* ii. 528.
[4] *Select Pleas, Starrs, and Records from the Rolls of the Exchequer of the Jews,* ed. J. M. Rigg (Selden Society, xv), p. 3.
[5] *Pipe Roll 13 John,* p. 61; *Pipe Roll 14 John,* p. 109.

William Cade.[1] Philip also seems to have been involved with Aaron of Lincoln,[2] and Simon, for a time, had been in the hands of Aaron's brother, Benedict.[3] In 1200 Simon was involved in leasing land in Thornton, Yorkshire, to the monks of Kirkstall.[4] In 1211–12 he was found to owe *debita Judeorum* amounting to £853. 12s. 4d. capital and £419. 11s. 6d. interest. He compounded for £1,000 to be paid off in three years.[5]

These are striking examples because of the size of the sums involved. Equally impressive was the organization behind the routine collection of the *debita* after the revolutionary step of 1210. The King persevered with his demands on to 1212. According to the Bury annalist, Richard Marsh, the Chancellor, was collecting *debita*, both capital and usury, in this last year.[6] The Meaux chronicle noted that about the same time the King was demanding that all who owed any debt to the Jews, of whatever kind, should compound for it with him.[7] The King's policy is illuminated by the fortunate survival of a roll of receipts of *debita Judeorum*.[8] This document is incomplete in that it does not cover the whole country, or any one financial year completely for any part of the country. Of the four *rotuli* the first probably belongs to 1212 or earlier, the second two to the Easter term of 14 John, probably 1213, and the last mainly to the Michaelmas term of 1213. It presents long lists of debtors, county by county, and records the terminal payments, usually varying between £1 and 10 m., which each was making. Where a payment is described, it is usually as 'de fine pro Judeis'. There was a close connexion between the document and the seizure of the Jews. One entry appears as 'de fine suo de Bristold'[9] and occasionally Jews appear accounting 'de tallagio Bristold'. On the last *rotulus* the total receipts from the Yorkshire *debita* came to over £110 and those of Lincolnshire to over £50. If, as seems likely,[10] these terminal payments were being made four times annually, then the *debita* in Yorkshire alone were

---

[1] *Pipe Roll 5 John*, p. 99; *Pipe Roll 13 John*, p. 60.

[2] After Aaron's death he agreed to pay £160 of £304 by which the monks of Bullington compounded at the Exchequer for Aaron's debts to the value of £400. The monks had to pay £5 per annum of which Philip was to pay £3. This he did by a grant of rent which he had received hitherto from the Benniworths (F. M. Stenton, *Danelaw Documents*, pp. li, 33–34).   [3] *Pipe Roll 1 Richard I*, p. 74.

[4] *Curia Regis Rolls*, i. 392–3.   [5] P.R.O., K.R. Miscellanea, 1/8b, m. 4r.

[6] *Memorials of Bury*, ii. 23.   [7] *Chron. Melsa*, i. 375.

[8] P.R.O., Receipt Roll, 1564.   [9] Rot. 1r.

[10] See the case of Thomas of Etton, below, pp. 169–70.

producing nearly £440 per annum. After the plot of August 1212 the King promised relaxations in the collection of the *debita*.[1] Whether such relaxations occurred it is difficult to say. The receipt roll does not provide a satisfactory answer. In February 1213 the King was making inquiries into the property of the Jews in Yorkshire and Lincolnshire and the pledges due to them.[2] But if the letters of August represented little but fair words, it is nevertheless significant that in a crisis the *debita Judeorum* were a matter on which conciliatory language was politic.

At one point it is possible to see what the arid lists of the receipt roll meant in human terms. Thomas of Etton, a tenant of the Stuteville, Brus, and Fossard fees in the East Riding of Yorkshire,[3] appears on them as making terminal payments of 5 m.[4] His father had owed over £40 to two Jews of York in 1199.[5] By the later years of John's reign Thomas was in great difficulties. His terminal payments of 5 m. were for a total debt of 240 m. which he had now agreed to pay off at 20 m. a year.[6] His father had already begun the alienation of the family property in the vill of Skerne by grants in free alms to Meaux abbey and by leasing land to the monks for a term of years in return for cash.[7] Even before the King pressed his demands after 1210, Thomas had taken to the same expedient; he had leased some of his land in Skerne to the monks for a term of fifteen years in return for 60 m. 'cum multo esset debito erga Judeos obligatus'.[8] The King's new policy now involved him in much more serious measures. He at once extended this lease to twenty years and added the gift of 7 bovates and 60 acres. He agreed never to introduce any mesne right, whether permanent or temporary, between himself and the monks. He then confirmed grants by his sister and also gave them the service from a carucate of land which his brother held. The monks then bought the lordship of the half fee which Thomas held in Skerne and elsewhere of his lord, Nicholas de Stuteville, to hold all Thomas's service in free alms. Nicholas was probably a willing party to the transaction for he, too, owed

---

[1] See above, pp. 85–86.
[2] *Rot. Litt. Pat.*, p. 97.
[3] *Early Yorks. Charters*, ii. 93, 398–9; ix. 191 ff.
[4] Receipt Roll 1564, rot. 2, m. 1d; rot. 4, m. 1d.
[5] *Pipe Roll 1 John*, p. 53.
[6] *Chron. Melsa*, i. 375.
[7] Ibid. i. 318.
[8] Ibid. i. 374.

debita Judeorum;[1] the monks gave Nicholas 40 m. in cash and land in Argam in exchange. Thomas then promised that he would never sell or pledge his lands or permit any of his men to do so except to the monks, his new lords. He acquitted them of any debt they owed him for the lands and promised that they would never again be mortgaged to Jews. The monks then went with Thomas to the chirographers of the Jews at York and, 'ut versutia Judaeorum omnino devitaretur', demanded the bonds of Thomas's debts. None could be found standing against the Skerne estates, but, even so, they obtained a quittance of any demand which might be made against them for Thomas's debts. They gave Thomas a palfrey for his trouble and the sheriff of Yorkshire £10 'propter consensum suum et auxilium'.[2] It was not perhaps as easy to buy the service of a knight as it was to buy that of a villein. But it could be done. The monks estimated that these and other operations in increasing their lands in Skerne cost them 500 m. or more.[3]

The new stringency John was showing in this policy towards *debita Judeorum* after 1207 was not confined to this one sector of fiscal administration. It was injected into the whole system. On John's side it represented an effort to maintain his rights, to re-cover what was due to him and to do this as speedily and efficiently as possible. What was to him but an improvement in the machinery of the Exchequer or Chamber, however, might well appear to his barons as a fundamental alteration in their fiscal relations with the King, as a threat to their prosperity, as an assault on the assumptions which had hitherto underlain their treatment by the Ex-chequer and the King's financial agents.

In the early years of the reign the Exchequer must often have been uncertain about the exact extent of the obligations of a particular baron. The pipe rolls could provide this information, but not readily, for within each shire account a man's debts might be scattered under a dozen different headings, under old offerings, new offerings, old amercements, scutages, pleas of the forest, and so on. In addition to this, an individual's debts frequently fell on several different shire accounts. These scattered entries were not normally brought together under one single heading until a

---

[1] Nicholas was paying £7. 10*s*. per term in 1212–13 (Receipt Roll 1564, rot. 2, m. 1d; rot. 4, m. 1d). In 2–3 Henry III he owed £88 *debita* (K.R., Accounts Various, 505/13).   [2] *Chron. Melsa*, i. 375–7.   [3] Ibid. i. 320.

debtor died, when the burden had to be passed on to his heir, but even this was not always done. In a few isolated instances in the early years of the reign, block entries of this kind were made for one or two barons who were still alive and active. Robert of Tattershall's debts were so treated in 1203 and again in 1206,[1] and William de Albini's in 1205.[2] But from 1207 onwards this type of entry soon became a fairly common feature of the rolls. On the accounts for the northern shires, Roger de Montbegon's debts were arranged in this way in 1207,[3] those of Peter de Brus in 1208,[4] of Thomas of Moulton, Richard de Lucy, and Hugh de Balliol in 1209,[5] of Ruald fitz Alan in 1210,[6] and of Nicholas de Stuteville and Robert de Percy in 1213.[7] For the first time in these cases, the Barons of the Exchequer could see at a glance what a debtor's total commitments were. Rates of repayment could now be fixed for the total debt. Peter de Brus's debts were found to amount to £1,235 in 1208. He accounted for nearly £330 and was told to pay the remainder at the rate of £400 a year.[8] Thomas of Moulton's debts came to nearly £770 in 1209. At the end of the account he still owed over £600 which he was ordered to pay off within a year.[9] At the same account Hugh de Balliol was entered as owing £235 for various debts, which he now had to pay off at 80 m. a year.[10] This quiet, unobtrusive change in Exchequer procedure illustrates, perhaps better than anything else, the increasingly searching and demanding interest of the King in the individual baronial debtor.

The heavy rates of repayment fixed for Peter de Brus and Thomas of Moulton were not by any means unusual. Similar heavy rates were demanded in the case of the *debita Judeorum* of Simon of Kyme and Gilbert de Gant. Although comparable rates were occasionally demanded in the early years of the reign,[11] the King was not usually so demanding, and in many cases no rates of repayment seem to have been arranged. Hence debtors frequently

---

[1] *Pipe Roll 5 John*, p. 118; *Pipe Roll 8 John*, p. 93.
[2] *Pipe Roll 7 John*, p. 234.　　　　[3] *Pipe Roll 9 John*, pp. 81, 82.
[4] *Pipe Roll 10 John*, p. 143.
[5] *Pipe Roll 11 John*, pp. 67–68, 93–94, 175.　　[6] *Pipe Roll 12 John*, p. 154.
[7] *Pipe Roll 16 John*, p. 88. These entries refer to the previous year. No roll has survived for 15 John.　　　　　　[8] *Pipe Roll 10 John*, p. 143.
[9] *Pipe Roll 11 John*, pp. 67–68.　　　　　　[10] Ibid., p. 175.
[11] In 1202, for example, Hugh Buissel made an offer of 400 m. on which he agreed to pay 100 m. in the first year and then £100 in each of the two subsequent years (*Rot. de Ob. et Fin.*, p. 188). See below, p. 240.

made only slight reductions in their commitments; sometimes they made no attempt at all to reduce their debts. For these men the middle years of the reign brought a chill wind. In 1201 William de Mowbray had been compelled to proffer 2,000 m. to stave off claims which William de Stuteville was bringing to the Mowbray barony. William gained nothing from his proffer and, indeed, lost in that he had to surrender lands and services to de Stuteville. This perhaps was in his mind in the years which followed, for he made no payment at all until 1205,[1] and at the beginning of the account of 1209 the debt still stood at 1,740 m.[2] In that year he was suddenly required to provide pledges to cover most of the outstanding sum, he was given a rate of repayment of £100 a year and was compelled to take serious steps to comply with these instructions.[3] Peter de Brus's debts went through a similar though less dramatic change. The sum of £1,235 which he owed in 1208 went back to a proffer of £1,000 which he had made for the manor and forest of Danby in 1201, to which he had added other proffers in later years up to 1207, which, with the Danby bid, totalled nearly £2,300.[4] Of this total £200 had been pardoned. To reduce his debts to the figure of £1,235 in 1208, he had paid off approximately £850 at an average rate of roughly £120 a year. The new arrangements which he made in 1208, therefore, increased Peter's burden nearly threefold in the first year and more than threefold thereafter. By 1211 he had been pardoned £100 and paid off almost all the remaining debt.[5] Peter never entered into similar transactions with John again. He may well have realized that the King's hardening attitude was making speculation unhealthy.

Many others were not so lucky as Peter and perhaps not so acute. Some pressed on regardless of the consequences. Thomas of Moulton, for example, despite the tremendous burden of debt he was required to clear in 1209, reappeared again in 1213 with a new offer of 1,000 m. for the custody of the daughters and heiresses

[1] *Pipe Roll 7 John*, p. 46.

[2] *Pipe Roll 11 John*, pp. 130–1.

[3] William proceeded to levy an aid on his tenants (ibid.). See below, p. 172.

[4] In 1204, 200 m. and two palfreys for Carlton and Camblesforth (*Pipe Roll 6 John*, p. 188). In 1205, 25 m. and one palfrey for land in Lofthus (*Pipe Roll 7 John*, p. 60). In 1206, 1,300 m. for the custody of Roger, son and heir of William Bertram, and his barony (*Pipe Roll 8 John*, p. 208). In 1207, 400 m. for the hereditary custody of the wapentake of Langbargh (*Pipe Roll 9 John*, p. 70).

[5] *Pipe Roll 12 John*, p. 151; *Pipe Roll 13 John*, p. 46.

of Richard de Lucy, lord of Egremont.[1] In this he was supported by Simon of Kyme, who was still heavily in debt. There is something peculiarly attractive about the financial resilience of these two, a characteristic not unconnected, perhaps, in Thomas's case with the profitability of fenland agriculture. But few showed this vitality. Gilbert de Gant failed to keep the terms of repayment set for his *debita Judeorum* in 1211. The 300 m. which had been pardoned originally was reimposed in 1212.[2] Gilbert had accounted for 600 m. by 1214,[3] but new commitments had raised his total debts to nearly 1,500 m. again by the beginning of the next reign.[4] William de Mowbray's debts stood at nearly £1,200 before the account of 1209.[5] He had reduced these to £640 by the end of the Michaelmas account of 1212,[6] but he was becoming deeply committed to the Jews. The addition of *debita Judeorum* of over £400 and various other smaller sums raised the total to nearly £1,300 after the civil war.[7]

In contrast with these men, one of the King's great debtors, Nicholas de Stuteville, was not pressed for payment. In 1209 he owed approximately £6,800.[8] He made a number of proffers in later years, and when his brother William's debts were added in at the beginning of the next reign his total commitments rose to approximately £10,000.[9] Nicholas's debts originated in the proffer of 10,000 m. which he had made for the lands of his brother in 1205. He had surrendered Knaresborough and Boroughbridge as a guarantee of his proffer. These manors were worth more to the King than the cash, and the transaction seems to have been designed simply to ensure their recovery by the Crown. Nicholas accounted for just over £150 on his debts between 1209 and 1212; he may well have been somewhat irresponsible for he seems to have been beset by financial difficulties.[10] But, whether this was so or not, John clearly considered that it was better for him to travel hopefully than to arrive. He never arrived. In September 1229 Knaresborough, Boroughbridge, and Aldborough were granted to Hubert de Burgh at an annual rent of £100, along with the residue of the debt of 10,000 m. still owing from the heirs of Nicholas.[11]

---

[1] *Rot. de Ob. et Fin.*, pp. 482–3.   [2] *Pipe Roll 14 John*, p. 109.
[3] *Pipe Roll 16 John*, p. 150.
[4] Ibid., pp. 150, 153; K. R. Miscellanea, 1/8b, m. 6r.
[5] *Pipe Roll 11 John*, pp. 18, 129, 130.   [6] *Pipe Roll 14 John*, p. 36.
[7] K.R. Miscellanea, 1/8b, m. 6r.   [8] *Pipe Roll 11 John*, pp. 126, 134, 133.
[9] K.R. Accounts Various, 505/2, 505/13.
[10] See below, p. 239.   [11] *Cal. Charter Rolls*, i. 99–100, 131.

Some men could only acquit themselves by accepting John's political objectives and repaying their debts in kind. Simon of Kyme sent his son to Poitou in 1214; in return the rate of repayment of his debts was reduced from 500 m. to 200 m.[1] In the same year Robert de Vaux, whom the King had been harrying financially perhaps more severely than any other of his men, obtained a pardon on his outstanding debt of 1,000 m. by promising to provide the service of two knights and twenty sergeants for a year and one knight and twenty sergeants for a second year.[2] In 1213 John de Lacy fined 7,000 m. for his father's lands and promised payment over three years. The King said he would remit 1,000 m. if he received the faithful service he expected.[3] De Lacy accompanied the King to Poitou. In June 1214 he procured a delay in the terms of the repayment and in July recovered Castle Donington, which had been taken as a guarantee of the original agreement.[4] On 4 March 1215 he took the Cross with the King. A day later his outstanding debts, which included 4,200 m. still owed under this agreement, were pardoned.[5] Financial subjection could lead straight to political subjection. But it was political subjection of a peculiar kind, sometimes the result of a subject's folly, sometimes the expression of the King's greed, suspicion, or wrath. It lacked any kind of moral content. It was a subjection which would last only so long as the financial threat remained. John de Lacy had joined the rebels by the end of May 1215, within three months of the King's final concession of March. Others who had not been so fortunate in receiving remissions did the same once they saw that the Exchequer was losing its power to command and enforce. Those who had refused the Poitevin scutage had called John's bluff, and in the spring of 1215 it was becoming increasingly clear that they had done so successfully. Once this had happened the consequences of John's financial policy towards his barons were disastrous to himself. Fiscal ties which hitherto had acted as instruments of political discipline were now the long nursed grievances impelling men into rebellion. John had at least ensured this; in 1215 too many people had not enough to lose.

---

[1] K.R. Miscellanea, 1/8b, m.: 4r; *Rot. de Ob. et Fin.*, p. 539.
[2] *Pipe Roll 16 John*, p. 139.   [3] *Rot. de Ob. et Fin.*, pp. 494–5.
[4] *Rot. Litt. Claus.* i. 167, 169.
[5] *Rot. Litt. Pat.*, p. 129b; *Pipe Roll 16 John*, p. 93.

X

THE LAW OF THE EXCHEQUER AND THE CUSTOM OF THE REALM

F. W. MAITLAND pointed out long ago that one of the most striking features of Magna Carta was its length.[1] In 1215 the King's opponents reviewed every important feature of royal policy and attempted to set limitations to his freedom of action. They were practical in their restraints on particular lines of policy; it was a 'long and miscellaneous code of laws'.[2] They did not see themselves as attacking or suppressing some new form of government, some absolutist or authoritarian system inimical to the established social and political order. If they were in any way self-critical, they saw themselves as confirming established methods of government and the customary conduct of relations between the King and his men, against a ruler who had distorted, altered, or ignored them. At its most general, the struggle was to them one of law on the one hand, against tyranny on the other. But this was not so much asserted in the Charter as a general principle, bald and unadorned; it emerged rather as a premise, sometimes stated, sometimes assumed, sometimes well founded, sometimes false, in the numerous detailed regulations which the Charter contained. If this contrast between law and arbitrary will often appears as one of the fundamental assumptions of the leading men of the land, both clerk and lay, it was not in itself the force which impelled them into rebellion and civil war. Men thought John arbitrary, and contrasted his rule with established law, because he was mercurial, inventive, cunning, and unreliable. The *forma securitatis* of the Charter, its most radical 'constitutional' feature, sprang not so much from political theories as from the simple fact that many of the King's subjects no longer put any reliance on his good faith. John could not be trusted. If these men were to accept him as their lord once more, they were going to compel him to be a good lord. The principles of Magna Carta sprang from the particular maltreatment which each had received at his hands.

[1] Pollock and Maitland, *History of English Law* (Cambridge, 1911), i. 171.
[2] Ibid.

Such maltreatment was usually expressed initially in a financial form. For the period between May 1209 and May 1212 the loss of the chancery enrolments largely confines the historian to the resources of the pipe rolls and to information which is mainly financial in content. An emphasis on finance is thus unavoidable. But it is also justifiable, for the King's financial policy, in all its many aspects, was one of the main concerns of Magna Carta. Furthermore, John's financial relations with his men led to broad questions of right and law, to arguments about justice and custom, to a search for precedent, to a questioning of the assumptions men made about the political society of their day. What could the King do? What should he not do? What were the rights of his subjects? How might they be defended and substantiated?

The pledging of debt and the financial rights which lords claimed over their men provide typical examples of this transition from detailed financial practice to general legal principle. Under the pressure of the King's demands both for money and service the great men of the land frequently sought aid and guarantees, not only from their friends, but also from their tenants. In 1209 William de Mowbray's tenants were required to make payments on his behalf to help clear his debts;[1] in 1213 twenty knights of the Lacy fee acted as guarantors of John de Lacy's enormous fine for his father's lands;[2] in 1208 the King ordered the sheriff of Cumberland to see that the tenants of Adam son of Odard gave a reasonable aid as a contribution to the payment of their lord's relief.[3] It was clearly in the King's immediate interests to help his tenants-in-chief in passing this kind of burden on to their men. But these processes were challenged. In 1209 the Abbots of Fountains, Rievaulx, and Byland proffered £100 for the King's consideration whether they ought to aid William de Mowbray in paying his debts.[4] In 1207 a number of Norfolk men were summoned to show why they had not made aid to their lord, Robert de Mortimer, to sustain him in the King's service in Poitou. They replied that they held their tenements freely; that neither they nor their ancestors were ever liable to such aids, except for the ran-

[1] *Pipe Roll 11 John*, pp. xxiv–xxv, 21, 126.

[2] *Rot. de Ob. et Fin.*, pp. 494–5.

[3] Ibid., p. 422. For other examples see Pollock and Maitland, op. cit. i. 350; W. S. McKechnie, *Magna Carta* (Glasgow, 1914), p. 259.

[4] *Pipe Roll 11 John*, p. 139.

soming of their lord's body, the knighting of his eldest son, and the marrying of his eldest daughter; and that they would not pay the aid now required without the instructions of the court.[1] Their views were identical with the principles expressed in caps. 12 and 15 of Magna Carta.

In this case the transition from practice to the question of principle was easy and direct. The matter was put forward as a plea of service. But this kind of appeal to terms of tenure could usually only be used within narrowly drawn limits, within that field where custom was defined clearly enough to provide an adequate defence of men's claims in a court of law. Outside, there was a vast area in which all was vague and uncertain and in which the comparison of royal impositions with custom and right was a difficult and delicate undertaking. King John, by tradition and by his monarchical authority, had the power to assess individual barons with pecuniary charges, especially with amercements *pro benevolencia regis*, and with reliefs or fines on their succession to estates. Neither of these powers could be attacked as such, in the way in which the Mortimer tenants challenged their lord's demand for an aid when he was engaged in the King's service. To try to place limitations on a principle which was admitted was far more difficult than to attack the principle root and branch. Yet it was precisely this task which John's government set the barons. The sheer size of the 10,000 m. assessed on Nicholas de Stuteville as a fine for his brother's lands in 1205, or of the 7,000 m. demanded from John de Lacy for the succession to his father's lands in 1213, or of the amercement of 2,000 m. placed on Robert de Vaux for the King's benevolence in 1211, clearly raised important questions. These charges were wildly excessive, but they were not separated by a very wide gap from others imposed by both John and his predecessors; in the case of reliefs from the 1,300 m. which Eustace de Vesci had faced in 1190,[2] or the 1,000 m. which Robert de Ros had faced in the same year,[3] or the 500 m. imposed on Peter de Brus in 1198,[4] or the 600 m. imposed on Norman Darcy in 1206;[5] in the case of amercements and proffers for grace, from the 1,000 m. imposed on Thomas of Moulton in 1208;[6] or the 1,200 m. imposed on Robert de Ros in 1197,[7] or the 500 m.

---

[1] *Curia Regis Rolls*, v. 39. [2] *Pipe Roll 2 Richard I*, p. 21. [3] Ibid., p. 67.
[4] *Pipe Roll 10 Richard I*, p. 43. [5] *Pipe Roll 8 John*, p. 104.
[6] *Pipe Roll 10 John*, p. 90. [7] *Pipe Roll 9 Richard I*, p. 61.

imposed on Roger de Montbegon in the same year,[1] or the 1,000 m. imposed on William of Cornbrough in 1209.[2] In all these cases men might reasonably wonder whether limits could and should be put to the King's demands.

John and his supporters might have argued that the sums he demanded in these ways were usually less than the proffers men made for rights and privileges, that even the 10,000 m. imposed on Nicholas de Stuteville was only half the sum which Geoffrey de Mandeville offered for the hand of Isabella of Gloucester. This was true. But many of these large voluntary proffers seem to have been made on the assumption that the terms of payment would be easy, and that they could be met out of the profits of the privilege which had been purchased. They were not normally subject to the stringency applicable in the case of a fine *pro bene-volencia regis*, the demand for which might be backed by a threat of dispossession, disinheritance, or imprisonment. Further, a sharp contrast between involuntary payments imposed by the King on the one hand, and voluntary payments proffered by his men on the other, is inappropriate. Many proffers were voluntary only in the most literal sense of the word. Men naturally wished to choose to whom they should marry their sons and daughters, nephews and nieces; they were bound to be interested in the acquisition of estates contiguous to their own; they expected to enjoy the franchisal privileges normally held by men of their own rank; they sought to cut a figure in the country and advance their own and their family's interest. If there was no physical compulsion behind their proffers, there was a very strong social compulsion. When the King sold privileges he could do so on a seller's market, often dictating terms as he might when imposing an amercement. Hence arose the argument of cap. 55 of Magna Carta that fines had been made *iniuste et contra legem terre*.

These proffers also raised legal issues in quite another direction. They were often made as a result of some past action by the King. In these cases they took on some of the characteristics of an amercement, for the victims were compelled to make them if they were to maintain their position and retain their property. An over-zealous exercise of the King's rights of wardship and escheat was a frequent source of trouble here, for it could lead to the dispossession of sub-tenants. Thus in 1210 Eustace de Vesci offered 100 m. and

---

[1] *Pipe Roll 9 Richard I*, p. 114.   [2] *Pipe Roll 11 John*, p. 139.

two palfreys for land in Burton which he claimed to hold of the heir of Roger fitz Ralf, who was a minor in the custody of the Crown.[1] The estates of Henry de Puiset were taken into the hands of the King on his death in 1211;[2] in the same year Robert de Percy proffered £100 for the manor of Osmotherley which Henry had given him.[3] Though both these payments appear as proffers, in effect they amounted to reliefs assessed by the Crown on sub-tenants on the death of their lords. They take us back to the old outcry against William Rufus; it is perhaps significant that Eustace de Vesci never paid any part of this proffer.[4] Sometimes during a wardship it was not the tenants but the ward who suffered. In 1211, for example, Gilbert Hansard made a proffer of £100 for land which had apparently been seized when he had been in royal custody in the reign of Richard I.[5] Sometimes issues arose not from the exercise of the Crown's feudal rights, but from acts of arbitrary power, especially those made in past political crises, the reign of Stephen, the rebellion of 1173, or the troubled years between 1190 and 1194. In 1205 Ruald fitz Alan offered £100 and two palfreys for the land of William de Rollos.[6] This consisted of 6½ fees, being half the fee of the Constable of Richmond; Ruald obtained seisin partly because William had sided with Philip Augustus in Normandy.[7] In defending his title to these lands in 1208, however, Ruald claimed that the land was his by right and that Henry II had disseized his grandfather, Ruald, arbitrarily and unjustly.[8] The jurors in the case agreed with him and indicted Henry II in similar terms. Ruald's family had held both halves of the Constable's fee in the reign of Henry I. The Rollos tenure probably originated in a grant of the fee to this family by the Empress Matilda and a subsequent division of the fee under Henry II.[9]

Many of the possible combinations of circumstances hidden behind these proffers are well illustrated in the financial arrange-

---

[1] *Pipe Roll 12 John*, p. 40.   [2] *Rot. Litt. Claus.* i. 124.

[3] *Pipe Roll 13 John*, p. 34.

[4] Eustace was not entered as owing or rendering account for this debt in 1210, the appropriate space being left blank. This type of entry was repeated on to and including 1212. He was entered as owing it in 1214 (*Pipe Roll 16 John*, p. 90), but nothing was paid. It was not apparently included in Eustace's debts in 1219, when, of course, he was dead (*Pipe Roll 3 Henry III*, p. 187).

[5] *Pipe Roll 13 John*, p. 34.   [6] *Pipe Roll 7 John*, p. 58.

[7] *Early Yorks. Charters*, v. 98.   [8] *Curia Regis Rolls*, v. 148.

[9] *Early Yorks. Charters*, v. 89, 91–92.

ments Peter de Brus made with John in order to expand and
develop his holdings in Cleveland. In 1201 he offered the
enormous sum of £1,000 for the manor and forest of Danby, to
be held by the service of one knight and on condition that he
surrendered the three manors of Bardsey, Collingham, and Rigton
to the King.[1] This was an astonishing offer for a manor hidden
away in the middle valley of the Cleveland Esk. But there were
good reasons for John asking and Peter paying such a price.
With the neighbouring member of Glaisdale, the manor and forest
of Danby formed one of the great iron mining and smelting centres
of medieval Cleveland, in which the Brus family came to divide
control with the priory of Guisborough, of which they were
patrons.[2] In addition, the purchase of Danby was for Peter simply
the first step whereby he confirmed his position as the predomin-
ant landowner in Cleveland; the process was completed by the
purchase of the hereditary custody of the wapentake of Langbargh
for the high price of 400 m. in 1207.[3] But the factor which probably predominated in his mind was that Danby, with its castle at
Castleton, had originally been part, and probably the *caput*, of the
Brus fee. It had been lost during the minority of Peter's father,
Adam, and had passed into the hands of Adam's guardian,
William, Count of Aumale. When the Count died, the lure of
Danby had been too much for Henry II. He retained it in his own
hands and gave Adam the three manors which Peter surrendered
by the agreement of 1201. Adam, in consequence, had shifted
the *caput* of his barony to Skelton, north of the Cleveland hills.[4]
The £1,000 which his son Peter was now offering is a measure of
the indignation which the Brus must have felt at this treatment
and of the eagerness with which they preferred the lost estate to
their three new manors in lower Wharfedale, at least two days'
journey away from their main holdings in Cleveland. Peter may
well have pondered, too, on the point that while Henry II had

[1] *Rot. de Ob. et Fin.*, pp. 109–10; *Rot. Chartarum*, pp. 86b, 101.

[2] *Cartulary of Guisborough*, ii. 191, gives the division of the rights between the
monks and the Brus family. See also ibid. 195 and the final concords of 1223 covering the transaction, ibid. i. 102 ff. The mines are mentioned ibid. i. 105. In 1227–8
Peter's son recovered some of the Glaisdale property alienated at this time. See ibid.
i. 109–10. For the background and topography see J. C. Atkinson, 'Medieval Iron
working in Cleveland', *Yorks. Archaeological Journal*, viii (1884), 30 ff., especially 37.

[3] *Pipe Roll 9 John*, p. 70.

[4] See especially *Early Yorks. Charters*, ii. 11ff.; and for the earlier exchange of
these manors by Henry I, ?1103, see *Regesta Regum Anglo-Normannorum*, ii. no. 648.

considered these three manors a fair exchange for Danby, John only agreed to the reverse transaction on the proffer of £1,000.

If contemporaries showed any one attitude towards this kind of transaction or towards the enormous sums exacted by the Angevins as reliefs and amercements, it was that the King's demands should be 'reasonable'. There should be a reasonable assessment of the proper payment to demand, on the one hand, and perhaps also a reasonable effort to pay, on the other. But this word 'reasonable' scarcely cloaked the stark reality that the financial relations between the King and each of his barons were quite arbitrary. There were in fact no limiting regulations on what the King could impose as a relief or fine, or assess as an amercement, or demand for the grant or confirmation of a privilege. These actions were all aspects of feudal kingship. But they were also the product of an older polity, not wracked so tautly as was the Angevin Empire by costs of defence and an economy of rapidly increasing costs and rising prices. These feudal incidents had never been conceived as a major financial resource, as measures which could be used to finance the conquest of Normandy by Rufus, or the wars of Henry II against his sons, or the great plan for the recovery of the Angevin possessions to which John committed himself after 1204. The proper resource for these schemes lay in general taxation, especially in the feudal aid. But many forms of general taxation were subject to baronial consent, in however vague a form. Further, while taxation might raise general opposition, a heavy amercement was a narrower political risk, for it bore on one man, his friends, relations, and tenants. Each individual could live in the hope that he would not be the next to be plucked.

'Reasonable' action by the King subsumed certain conditions: that the King would maintain a traditional standard in his relations with his barons, that he would not be driven to excess by some urgent financial need, that he would not twist feudal incidents or exploit his powers to amerce so as to put them to some purpose for which they were not conceived. These conditions had ceased to exist by the middle years of John's reign. By then John was clearly using feudal incidents and his powers to amerce as instruments of political discipline, as a means to ends which were not in themselves financial. Nicholas de Stuteville's relief of 10,000 m. was imposed not so much because John wanted

10,000 m., although this was a desirable sum, but because he wanted the guarantees Nicholas surrendered, the manors of Knaresborough and Boroughbridge. John de Lacy had to face the burden of 7,000 m., not because the King considered this a fair payment for de Lacy's fiefs, but because he wanted such a hold over the young Constable that he would not dare to consider rebellion. De Lacy had to surrender his castles of Donington and Pontefract until the payment of the debt was complete and pay £40 a year to their upkeep. He also submitted a charter of fealty accepting the terms John set and agreeing that if he left the King's service he should lose all his lands. The twenty knights of his fee who guaranteed his good behaviour had to agree that in such circumstances they would side with the King. This was scarcely a normal relief at all. It was, as it described itself, a *conventio*,[1] an agreement which was primarily political in content, for as de Lacy demonstrated his dependence on the King, so John replied by progressively relaxing and pardoning the debt.[2] These arrangements could not correspond in any way with what men might consider to be a 'reasonable' relief. There is something to be said on John's side; de Lacy was suspect and was acquiring his lands at a time of crisis; but this did little more than add a dash of blatancy to the arrangements. There were other cases in which men requited their debts by actions, by a demonstration of loyalty in attending a royal campaign.[3] If the conversion of the services into cash was a marked feature of the Angevin government of England, so also was the conversion of cash into services. This was the easiest way to ensure political subservience.

There were apparent means of defence against this kind of treatment by the King, for traditionally these royal dealings with the barons were supposed to result from judgement in a court. Occasionally, as in William Marshal's bickerings with the King, this defence proved effective. In many cases, however, where financial matters were concerned, judgement in a court simply meant a judicial reinforcement of the King's will. The clearest illustration of this is to be found in John's treatment of Thomas of Moulton. When Thomas purchased the shrievalty of Lincoln-shire in 1205 with the proffer of 500 m. and five palfreys, the King addressed letters patent to all his free tenants of Lincolnshire,

---

[1] *Rot. de Ob. et Fin.*, pp. 494-5.   [2] See above, pp. 97, 174.
[3] See above, pp. 174, 150-1.

stating that he had agreed that Thomas should hold the county for seven years and that he would not be disseized of the office within this period unless he did something *quare per judicium curie nostre inde debeat dissaisiri*.[1] Thomas had guaranteed his position in the strongest possible manner. Yet all this was of no avail. He was set terms of payment for this and another proffer of the same size in March 1206, the rate fixed being not unduly heavy at £200 a year.[2] He met this in 1206,[3] but accounted for slightly less than £70 in 1207.[4] Meanwhile, he had fallen into the King's displeasure in another matter and been amerced 200 m.[5] There was nothing unusual in this, certainly nothing to explain what followed. Technically, however, by falling behind in his payments, Thomas had made himself liable to loss of office under the King's letter patent, and for some reason John proceeded to exploit this fact to the full. Thomas was deprived of the shrievalty, imprisoned at Rochester, and amerced 1,000 m. for default. The King ordered that he was to be detained until he had paid all he owed 'to the last penny'. John relaxed on this point, but not on his general demands. After the account the Michaelmas 1209 Thomas had reduced his debts to just over £600. He was ordered to pay this outstanding sum within a year on the pain of losing all he had paid hitherto.[6] Thomas had got his judgement in a court, for he was handed over to his gaoler, Reginald of Cornhill, by none other than the Barons of the Exchequer.[7] Much good had it done him.

With the court of the Exchequer at his disposal, John scarcely needed to proceed *sine judicio* in this kind of case. Further, the King's powers to amerce converted many misdemeanours into such cases, for they usually ended with the imposition of a heavy mulct. Once a misdemeanour had been converted into money, then distraint and imprisonment could be used to enforce payment.[8] Indeed, the victim of this procedure could be driven into a series of increasingly disastrous compositions. In 1210 Robert de Vaux, for reasons which are not apparent, had to proffer 750 m. for the benevolence of the King.[9] He was set terms which required completion of payment by the Michaelmas of the same

---

[1] *Rot. Litt. Pat.*, p. 57b.
[2] *Rot. Litt. Claus.* i. 67.
[3] *Pipe Roll 8 John*, pp. 103–5.
[4] *Pipe Roll 9 John*, pp. 26–27.
[5] Ibid., p. 28.
[6] *Pipe Roll 11 John*, pp. 67–68.
[7] *Rot. Litt. Pat.*, p. 85b.
[8] See Lady Stenton's comments in *Pipe Roll 13 John*, pp. xxxi–xxxiii.
[9] *Pipe Roll 12 John*, p. 139.

year, but he only managed to account for 400 m. within this time. His lands were then taken into the King's hands, he himself was imprisoned, and defaulting debtor though he was, loaded with an even greater debt. The roll of 1211 recorded that he owed 2,000 m. for the King's grace. He had to pay half this sum and provide security for the payment of the remainder before he was released from the prison to which he had been confined. The security took the form of hostages and a charter in which Robert agreed that if he failed to pay then his lands would revert to the King.[1] Even this was not the final stage of his correction. In 1214 the sum of 1,000 m. was still outstanding, and in that year Robert agreed to acquit the debt by the performance of extra military service at his own expense.[2]

Only one man felt sufficiently bitter or was sufficiently provoked to resist such treatment. This was William de Braose. In 1200–1 William proffered 5,000 m. for the lordship of Limerick, on the terms that he should pay 1,000 m. a year.[3] He never kept these terms; they were restated more precisely on the fine roll in 1204,[4] and he paid £468 on the account for 1205,[5] but nothing more had been done by the Michaelmas account of 1207. William was also burdened by another proffer of 800 m. which he made in 1205 for the three Welsh castles of Grosmont, Llantilio, and Skenfrith. Here the terms had been set at £100 per annum;[6] 350 m. was outstanding in 1209.[7] In this last year John decided to distrain on William's chattels *secundum consuetudinem regni et per legem scaccarii*, as he later put it. Under pressure William surrendered three of his castles, handed over hostages, and placed all his lands of England and Wales in pledge of his payment.

So far William's case was like that of many others. Its only exceptional feature was that he was a Marcher and John had found it necessary to organize a show of force under the sheriff of Gloucester, Gerard d'Athée, the cost of which, amounting to 1,000 m., he now charged to William. Nevertheless, all might have been well if William had submitted to the treatment. A ready payment of part of what he owed could well have led to the pardon of the rest, as it did in other instances. We cannot know what

---

[1] *Pipe Roll 13 John*, pp. xxxi, 156–7.   [2] See above, p. 174.
[3] *Rot. de Ob. et Fin.*, pp. 99, 94.   [4] *Rot. de Ob. et Fin.*, p. 232.
[5] *Pipe Roll 7 John*, p. 107.
[6] *Pipe Roll 7 John*, pp. 277, 110; *Rot. Litt. Pat.*, p. 57.
[7] *Pipe Roll 11 John*, p. 2.

made William behave differently. It may be that he imagined, rightly or wrongly, that the King was now determined to destroy him, either because of his possession of dangerous secrets or for other reasons.[1] It may be that the sight of Gerard d'Athée's men in charge of his precious castle of Radnor was too much for him. It is certain that he was not a man to take a disciplinary rein easily, especially within the Marches. When the sheriff of Hereford had been ordered to intervene in William's lands in 1199 in a matter of disseisin, he had feared to do so, and William had roundly asserted that 'neither the King, nor the justiciar, nor the sheriff ought to interfere in his liberty'.[2] As applied to the King these were strong words, and it was just such interference that John was committing when he took William's Welsh castles as pledges. At all events, William attacked the three castles he had surrendered and then extended the war to royal land.

William's tragedy was that, for all his administrative and military experience, he was politically incompetent. The Marshal, at similar crises, behaved in such a way as to retain the sympathy of his fellow barons and provide them with reasons for judging in his favour.[3] By his recalcitrance William de Braose deprived himself of any hope of real support. All his friends could do was plead ignorance and provide him with opportunities at which he or his wife could obtain terms. The King sacrificed him on the altar of his new financial policies. William and his wife were given terms which they had no hope of meeting. John was making a public example of them.

[1] See F. M. Powicke, *The Loss of Normandy*, pp. 469 ff., for the thesis that William knew too much about the fate of Arthur of Brittany. See also Kate Norgate, *John Lackland*, pp. 287–8, especially for an assessment of John's letter on the case. The most lengthy account, from which some of the detail above is drawn, is given by S. Painter, *The Reign of King John*, pp. 242–50.

[2] *Rot. Curiae Regis*, i. 426. Compare the privileges William enjoyed on his Norman lands (*Rot. Norm.*, p. 20).

[3] See, for example, his clear indication of the implications of the King's charges against him in 1205.

> . . . Seignors, esgardez mei,
> Quer, par la fei que ge vous dei,
> Ge sui a vos toz hui cest jor
> Essemplaires et mireor,
> E si atendez bien al rei:
> Ce qu'il pense faire de mei
> Fera il a chascun ou plus,
> S'il en puet venir el desus.

(*Histoire de Guillaume le Maréchal*, lines 13167–74.)

The King's account of his treatment of William contains some inaccuracies and leaves many things unsaid, but its statements on the origins and course of the quarrel must, in general, be accepted.[1] Too many important men put their seals to it for it to be a fabrication.[2] John presented William as a recalcitrant debtor who had rebelled against his king. The letter was recorded in the Black Book of the Exchequer;[3] it was very much a financial document. The Braose case underlay the King's later fiscal relations with his barons. He would have found it impossible to exact the heavy repayments he obtained from 1209 onwards if he had permitted this indiscipline right at the start. In punishing it he created a major grievance among the wide connexions of the Braose family, but his letter explaining the case is perhaps too readily taken as an *apologia*. It was not so much this as a triumphant and awful warning. Just as John had had the new Exchequer regulations of 1201 read before an assembly of barons, so now he indicated the consequences of recalcitrance. In future the shadow of William and his wife lay threateningly across every baronial account. There was no new manifestation of deliberate and contumacious default until the approach of civil war destroyed the King's power to enforce payment on his terms.

John's opponents came in the end to denounce his conduct of government as unjust and contrary to law. No book of reference was needed to substantiate this charge in the case of William and Matilda de Braose. Argue as John might that he had not overstepped the bounds of law, there was no need to quote precedents for men to believe that the King's actions were contrary to equity and reason, and, in the ultimate fate of Matilda and her eldest son, barbarous and cruel. But on more general matters, if the King was to be denounced as a tyrant, if his actions were to be shown as emanating from will, then this will had to be contrasted with some kind of legal principle, with some set of legal regulations and customs, which, it could be argued, he had

---

[1] *Foedera*, i, pt. 1, pp. 107–8. Miss Norgate has shown that John did not state the sums due absolutely accurately (op. cit., pp. 287–8). Nevertheless, the pipe rolls bear out the main charge, that William had failed to keep the terms of payment set.

[2] William of Salisbury, Geoffrey fitz Peter, Saer de Quenci, Richard de Clare, Aubrey de Vere, Henry de Bohun, and William de Ferrers, all of whom were earls, Robert fitz Walter, William Briwerre, Hugh de Neville, William de Albini, Adam de Port, Hugh de Gournay, and William de Mowbray.

[3] *Liber Niger Scaccarii*, ed. Thomas Hearne (Oxford, 1728), i. 377 ff.

broken. *Voluntas* meant little, except in contrast to *lex*. The problem was more than theoretical. The effects of John's will were material and tangible, sometimes appalling and piteous. A pragmatic, detailed system was required in defence. The best the King's opponents could do was to resuscitate the laws of St. Edward and Henry I and the coronation charter of the latter king. But, although these collections were relevant, and although men were adding sections to them in the late twelfth century to make them even more relevant,[1] they scarcely anywhere set forth clear and detailed regulations which had obviously been contravened by King John or his predecessors. Only certain sections of Henry's charter fulfilled this role in specifications on relief, marriage, and wardship, but even in these instances there was a certain imprecision in the *legitima et justa relevatio* and in the regulations on amercements in Henry's charter, which John would have been quick to exploit. Further, even if the men of this time were naïve or determined enough to believe that Henry I had in fact observed these self-imposed restrictions, nobody could argue that they had been observed by Henry II and his sons. The solid concessions of Henry I's charter had been changed into the pious and vaporous generalities of Henry II's. In 1215 Henry I's charter may have enjoyed the longevity required of custom but it lacked the usage. Its status was only established by rebellion. Similarly, the laws of Henry and St. Edward, significant as their resuscitation was, were not so much dangerous to the King in themselves, as in the principles and implications which his opponents drew from them, especially in the argument that they stood as good and ancient custom over against Angevin innovation and tyranny. Only when they began to gloss them, as they had clearly started to do in the 'unknown' charter and in the *Articuli*, could these tracts, archaic even in their own day, be set up as legal restrictions on the operations of Angevin government. Only by rebellion could this particular gloss be established as the right and proper one and forced upon the King.

Once men moved away from these ancient collections, they were left with scarcely any body of law with which they could contrast royal actions. Administration in the twelfth century was far from static. Even men who were closely in touch with its direction failed to agree on what was normal practice. There was,

[1] See J. C. Holt, 'The Barons and the Great Charter', *E.H.R.* lxix (1955), 9.

in fact, no normal, customary practice in the form of a fixed and rigid system. Instead there was a rapidly changing, organic body of precedent and expedient. Ralf de Mortimer's tenants might assert the identical doctrine of Magna Carta, that a lord was only entitled to an aid for his own ransom, his eldest son's knighting, or his eldest daughter's marriage.[1] They may, indeed, have stated the custom of the Mortimer fee in all good faith. But twelfth-century opinion and practice was in general far less definite. Glanville admitted the lord's right to take an aid to assist in the payment of his relief, or for the knighting of his eldest son and the marriage of his eldest daughter, but mentioned no aid for ransom. He also stated, somewhat tentatively, that a lord had some claim on his men when he made war.[2] Norman custom simply permitted regular aids on the three occasions named by Glanville.[3] Magna Carta itself did not settle matters immediately. The relevant clause was omitted from the 1217 reissue and within a few years the Crown was supporting tenants-in-chief in taking aids to assist in the costs of a crusade or in the payment of reliefs.[4] In all this, practice clearly varied and was subjected to interpretation by different opinions.

On the much more important problem of relief, there were again few set rules or generally accepted views prior to Magna Carta. In the last decade of the twelfth century the sum of £100 was coming to be considered as a reasonable baronial relief even by the officials of the Exchequer, but this development was to some extent offset by the emergence of the fine as an alternative or additional payment. This was an arbitrary sum and often a large one. The only rule on which almost all, including Glanville and Fitz Neal, were in agreement was that tenants by knight service of escheated honours should pay relief at £5 per fee.[5] But, if there was an apparent agreement on this, there was none on the much more intricate problem of the relationship of relief to

---

[1] See above, pp. 176–7.   [2] *Leges*, lib. ix, cap. 8; ed. Hall, pp. 111–12.

[3] See the Très Ancien Coutumier, E. J. Tardif, *Coutumiers de Normandie* (Société de l'histoire de Normandie, 1881), i. 36.

[4] In 1221 John de Lacy had the prayers of the King directed to his knights and free tenants in Oxfordshire to make aid to him to assist in the expenses he had incurred on the crusade (*Patent Rolls 1216–25*, p. 284). A year later the knights and tenants of John Biset were instructed to make him a reasonable aid to acquit his relief to the king (ibid., p. 361).

[5] See I. J. Sanders, *Feudal Military Service in England*, pp. 98–107, for the most recent review of the problem.

wardship. Glanville was quite clear that when a minor whose lands had been in custody came of age, he did not have to pay a relief to obtain the succession to his father's lands.[1] Fitz Neal, in contrast, was much less certain. He thought that a minor should succeed freely or by payment according to the King's will, but added that relief should not be taken if the inheritance in question had been in the King's hands for several years.[2] Royal practice under Henry II, Richard, and John could have left few in doubt that the King's will was the decisive factor in this matter. The fine of 1,300 m. which Eustace de Vesci offered for his inheritance in 1190 was made after his lands had been in royal custody since 1182–3.[3] William de Mowbray was charged with £100 for his inheritance in 1194 after it had been in the hands of the Crown certainly for a year and probably since 1191.[4] The enormous fine of 7,000 m. made by John de Lacy in 1213 occurred after the Lacy lands had been in custody for nearly two years.[5]

On this problem Fitz Neal and Glanville apparently differed. It is possible to combine their views, for Glanville may well have been thinking of under-tenants, while Fitz Neal was thinking of tenants-in-chief and hence had a more watchful eye on the interest of the King. But we must not expect from these two authorities the kind of logic and consistency which we expect to find in an organized system of law. Although they are of inestimable value, they are no more to be equated with the law and practice of the twelfth century than is Coke with the law of the seventeenth century or Blackstone with the law of the eighteenth. They represent not law and administrative practice, but the opinions on these topics of a royal Treasurer and a royal Justice, whether Glanville himself, or Hubert Walter or Geoffrey fitz Peter. Often they state their points as opinions or arguments.[6] What they say

---

[1] *Leges*, lib. ix. cap. 4; ed. Hall, p. 107.

[2] *Dialogus de Scaccario*, pp. 94–97.

[3] *Pipe Roll 2 Richard I*, p. 21; *Pipe Roll 29 Henry II*, p. 140.

[4] *Pipe Roll 6 Richard I*, p. 160. William's father died at Acre in 1191 (*Complete Peerage*, ix. 373). A fragmentary account was presented for the estates in 1193 (*Pipe Roll 5 Richard I*, p. 70).

[5] John's father died on 1 Oct. 1211 (*Monasticon Anglicanum*, vi, pt. 1, 315). Letters of seisin in John's favour were made out at the end of July 1213 (*Rot. Litt. Claus.* i. 147).

[6] On differences of opinion within the Glanville text see R. W. Southern, 'A note on the text of "Glanville" ', *E.H.R.* lxv (1950), 87–88. See ibid. 81 ff. for the latest views on authorship and also the important contribution of Lady Stenton in *Pleas before the King or his Justices 1198–1202* (Selden Society, lxvii), pp. 9–10.

carries great weight, but is not final. More than this, it distorts, for the very act of writing necessarily presented a system which seems more static, more rigidly bound by procedural rules, than in fact it was. These two authorities were agreed that tenants of escheats paid relief at £5 per fee. But this was not accepted as established practice under John. The King's policy was in fact quite arbitrary. In 1201, for example, he accepted £32. 10s. from Ruald fitz Alan as a relief for 6½ fees held of the honour of Richmond.[1] A year earlier Alan of Mumby had fined at over £200 for five fees held of the same honour.[2] Charges of this size were not uncommon. William of Well proffered 50 m. for one fee held of Richmond in 1207,[3] John Malebisse 300 m. for the land of his father, Richard, in 1210 when the only land he held of the Crown was one fee of the honour of Eye.[4] In this matter Magna Carta reasserted the views expressed by Glanville, Fitz Neal, and earlier twelfth-century law-books. It may perhaps have gone beyond them in extending the £5 relief to some tenants-in-chief by knight service. But there was something to be said on John's side. The £5 relief had not been applied invariably to tenants of escheated honours in the reign of Henry II.[5] The knight who paid £5 per fee was escaping lightly in a world of rising prices and increasing wealth. If John altered earlier procedure here, it was not entirely unreasonable. Change in any case could not be avoided. It was essential in any healthy system of administration. If the legal validity of John's actions is to be judged by the opinion and practice of the age of Glanville, then we may wonder how valid Glanville and Fitz Neal themselves appear if we place them alongside the *Leges Henrici Primi* or what was imagined to be early twelfth-century practice. This, of course, is just what the King's opponents did, for they were putting Henry II in the dock as well as his son. But we should be unwise to follow them for there is no stopping place short of the laws of Aethelbert.

If Glanville and Fitz Neal are not entirely adequate as witnesses in the case against John, neither is the system of assize and writ which Glanville, especially, described. The King's subjects had a traditional right to judgement, but not necessarily to judgement

---

[1] *Rot. de Ob. et Fin.*, p. 137; *Early Yorks. Charters*, v. 91.

[2] *Pipe Roll 2 John*, p. 87; *Early Yorks. Charters*, v. 269.

[3] *Rot. de Ob. et Fin.*, p. 372.

[4] *Pipe Roll 12 John*, p. 160; *Red Book of the Exchequer*, p. 491.

[5] See J. H. Round in *Magna Carta Commemoration Essays*, pp. 57–58.

by these procedures. They were the King's perquisite; he could withhold them, prevent others using them, or exercise judgement in some other way. They were, as Glanville proudly described the grand assize, *regale beneficium*.[1] Further, the immediate concern of the assizes and the function of the writ were administrative and procedural. They did not constitute immediately a body of detailed substantive regulation. The word *lex* still stood primarily for the civil law of Justinian or for the law of the Church. It was more closely approached where law could be seen more clearly as an expression of sovereign will, and where detailed regulation was aimed at preserving the rights of the King rather than those of his subjects. Men tended to talk of the *ius et consuetudo regni*, but of the *lex forestae* or the *lex scaccarii*.[2]

There were, of course, general principles, older than either Glanville or the *Leges Henrici*, which governed the practices of English kings. They should judge justly, protect their subjects lay and ecclesiastical, maintain the law, consult the more important men of the land on matters of moment. These and similar views were sometimes openly asserted, as in the coronation oath, but were always deeply ingrained in men's minds. They were as deeply ingrained in John's mind as in any other. They were axiomatic to any feudal ruler and, like other rulers, John did not normally break them or even think of breaking them. He did not do so especially because he did not need to do so; these rules were usually as vague as they were venerable; they could not have survived as rules otherwise. If the King was to judge justly, what was justice? What was the law and custom he was to maintain? Who were the magnates he was to consult? In what form was he to consult them and on what? John clearly found no difficulty in conducting even his harshest operations within these established limits. He would be the first to point to the names of those who put their seals to the letter on William de Braose. He had preserved the forms.

The obtaining of consent was never any real difficulty to the Angevin kings. Indeed, they deliberately sought it. If the grand assize was *regale beneficium*, it was also *de consilio procerum populis*

---

[1] *Leges*, book II, cap. 7; ed. Hall, p. 28.
[2] On the forest law see *Dialogus de Scaccario*, pp. 59–60. On the law of the Exchequer see the ordinance of 1201 (*Hoveden*, iv. 152) and the letter on William de Braose (*Foedera*, i, pt. 1 ,p. 107).

indultum.[1] If the royal forest was private to the King, yet the Assize of Woodstock was made apparently by the counsel of the magnates lay and ecclesiastical.[2] Although the Exchequer ordinance of 1201 was *per praeceptum regis Johannis confirmatum*,[3] yet the writ providing for the disinheritance or enserfment of laggard knights in 1205 was made with the assent of the magnates.[4] When John sought some aid or assistance for which there was no customary warrant he usually did so openly, admitting that he was doing it for special reasons and asking for compliance as an act of grace on the part of his subjects.[5] Only on one occasion during his reign was the royal will freed from some of these restraints in a time of internal peace. This was immediately after his accession, at a time when, traditionally, a kingdom lay at its ruler's pleasure. Then John could and did deny title and right, grant or withhold office and privilege, sell his benevolence, or threaten his malevolence. For a time, and to great profit, a medieval ruler could wield a new broom, but not usually in such a manner as to upset established policies and relationships, and, necessarily, for a time only. In John's case this was over within two years of his accession.

John's conduct of affairs was not in the main unlawful or contrary to custom. He was making no bid to establish an autocracy. His government was not even moving, with him unconscious of it, towards a 'new' monarchy. Occasionally, but only occasionally, he can be seen to have broken with established tenurial relations,[6] but usually such infringements were unnecessary and were avoided. If he innovated, if he stretched and buffeted custom to serve his ends, the barons did exactly the same in Magna Carta. John was rarely so bare-faced as were his opponents when in cap. 12 they associated scutage with gracious aids, or imposed cap. 61 on an unwilling king. They could find no warrant in custom for either of these measures. They were charged, and rightly charged, with trying to introduce *nova iura*. It is in fact quite impossible to define will on the one hand and custom on the other on any objective standard. Custom was what men thought it to be. The King's view of it was very different from his opponents'.

---

[1] *Leges*, book II, cap. 7; ed. Hall, p. 28.
[2] *Stubbs' Charters*, 9th edn., p. 186.   [3] *Hoveden*, iv. 152.
[4] *Stubbs' Charters*, p. 276.   [5] J. C. Holt, loc. cit., pp. 6–7.
[6] See, for example, the question of cornage tenure and overseas service, above, pp. 91–92.

It was ever changing, as it was made and as it was forgotten or abandoned. It was contrasted in men's minds with will; it became the central emotive cry of the opposition's case; but it could itself be a product of the King's will against which it was directed. Many men at the time must have known the famous words of Ulpian which opened the Institutes of Justinian. 'Justice is constant and perpetual will ensuring every man his right.'[1] Men stood their ground on custom in 1215 precisely because the Angevin system of government, especially in the administration of law, had created and developed routine. Henry II and his sons themselves accustomed their subjects to custom.

The main limitations on John's actions, as on his father's, were not so much legal as political.[2] Medieval kings were not usually permitted the luxury of wholesale illegal action; rebellion occurred first. So it was with John. Magna Carta did not so much reassert as create custom. Far from reviving the burden of the past, it imposed one on the future. Certainly all the trappings of custom were brought in; venerated practices were asserted even when John had not contravened them. But the document simply represented the sense which a section of the baronage and their advisers attached to the words 'reasonable' government, and stated what they imagined to be custom or deliberately misrepresented as custom. If the Charter is one of the first great creative statements of law in English history, it is also one of the first great essays in propaganda.

[1] 'Iustitia est constans et perpetua voluntas ius suum cuique tribuens' (*Inst.* 1. i. 1).

[2] Compare, however, the views of J. E. A. Jolliffe in *Angevin Kingship*. While giving great emphasis to royal will as a factor in government Jolliffe also presents twelfth-century custom, and even the law of the Exchequer, as established systems standing in sharp contrast to the King's will, as systems which the King ignored or broke. Thus the destruction of Baynard's Castle after Robert fitz Walter had been convicted of treason is described as a 'foray outside the law' (p. 60), debtors are harried 'beyond the Exchequer rule' (p. 76), the Exchequer ordinance of 1201 is interpreted not as a statement but as a perversion of the *lex scaccarii* (p. 83), and fines can be paid into the Chamber in a manner which 'may have violated every article of the *lex scaccarii*' (ibid.).

A disturbing amount of Jolliffe's evidence on the operations of the King's will under John is taken from the first two years of the reign. On this see above, p. 192.

XI

THE GOVERNMENT OF THE NORTH

THE government of the north was in some ways a special problem.[1] But, as such, it was neither inevitable nor continuous. Northern men and northern politics played a part in the events of Stephen's reign and again in the rebellion of 1173–4, but the north was not pre-eminent in these earlier periods as it was in 1215, nor did it re-emerge as such in the rebellious movements of 1258–65. When it did re-emerge later, it was in a different form; there was little in 1215 similar to the situation created by Thomas of Lancaster under Edward II or by the rival power of Percy and Neville in the fifteenth century. There was not so much a problem of the north as successive northern problems, each with distinct characteristics, but all with the same geographical background which made the country north of the Trent more difficult of access and more difficult to govern. The northern problem of John's time was a result of two factors. First, he, and to a lesser extent his two predecessors, integrated the north much more closely than ever before in the administration of the whole realm. Secondly, he did this on an insecure political basis; his royal authority, as represented by his officers and supporters, was too isolated.

There is no evidence that King John deliberately exploited the north more than any other part of the country. Indeed, the whole tenor of his policy was to bring all areas equally under his personal supervision and to ensure the execution of his policies everywhere throughout the land. Local conditions, however, necessarily affected the incidence of his measures. It is probable, for example, that most of the northern counties were especially hard hit by the forest law, which the Angevins enforced over vast regions, including the whole of Nottinghamshire north of the Trent, most of Derbyshire east of the Derwent and Wye, most of Cumberland

[1] See especially G. Lapsley, 'The Problem of the North', *American Historical Review*, v (1900), 440–66, reprinted in *Crown, Community and Parliament*, ed. Helen M. Cam and G. Barraclough (Oxford, 1951), pp. 375 ff.; and Rachel Reid, *The King's Council of the North* (London, 1921), pp. 1–4.

north of the Lakes, a large tract of Northumberland, and a wide
belt of land in Yorkshire running from the Ouse, Wharfe, and
Nidd to the Cleveland Esk and the coast. Only in Lincolnshire
was the forest relatively insignificant.[1] The forest was an important
issue in the politics of the northern counties,[2] in the actions of the
northern rebels[3] and in the documents, like the 'unknown'
charter, most closely associated with them.[4] Magna Carta, in
contrast, shelved the problem. It is tempting, and perhaps not
entirely unrealistic, to see in this the waning influence of the
Northerners and the comparative lack of interest in the forest of
the new leaders of the movement from the eastern and home
counties, for there were no important forests at all in Norfolk,
Suffolk, Hertfordshire, Cambridgeshire, or Bedfordshire;[5] Essex,
the only eastern county heavily afforested, had been partially deforested in 1204.[6] Similar hypotheses are possible on other points.
It seems likely, for example, that John's policy towards *debita
Judeorum* had particularly harsh effects in the north. York and
Lincoln were two of the most prominent centres of anti-Jewish
agitation; Lincoln had been the base for Aaron's operations. In
many parts of the north the indebted landowner's problems were
complicated by the baleful attentions of the Cistercian monastic
houses, ever on the watch to expand and round off their estates.[7]
Certainly, for many northern men, the King's actions in this
matter after 1207 were very serious.

These are speculations, difficult, perhaps impossible, to verify
in the present state of the evidence. However, even if we allow
that the burden on the north was little different from that imposed

[1] See Map 2. This map is based, for Cumberland, on F. H. M. Parker, 'Inglewood
Forest', *Transactions of the Cumberland and Westmorland Antiquarian and Archaeological
Society*, N.S. v (1905), 35–61; for Lancashire on W. Farrer in *V.C.H. Lancs.* ii. 437 ff.;
and for other areas on Miss Margaret L. Bazeley, 'The Extent of the English Forests
in the Thirteenth Century', *T.R.H.S.* iv. 4 (1921), 140–72, and on the unpublished
research of W. H. Liddell of the University of Nottingham, to whom I am indebted
for the bounds of the forest in Yorkshire, Nottinghamshire, and Derbyshire and
for lists of townships and vills. For Lincolnshire see W. Dugdale, *The History of
Imbanking and Draining* (London, 1772), pp. 194–5.

Areas are shown to have been afforested by Henry II where they are so described
in the thirteenth-century perambulations. Normally, the earliest surviving perambulations following the Charter of the Forest have been used. Certain areas placed
outside the forest on these occasions were later re-afforested.

[2] See above, pp. 85–86, 157 ff.   [3] See above, pp. 120–1.
[4] See above, pp. 113–14, 119.
[5] See Miss Margaret L. Bazeley, loc. cit., pp. 140 ff.
[6] See above, p. 149.   [7] See above, pp. 164, 170.

on other parts of the country, this in itself is an important point, for the burden was heavier than anything which the north had normally had to bear hitherto. In reducing the northern counties to the same level of exploitation as the rest of the country, John was in effect producing an administrative revolution. This is most obviously apparent in his remarkable personal interest in this region. Henry II only visited the north on eleven occasions during his reign.[1] Richard came once to Nottingham and Southwell in 1194 to suppress his brother's rebellion. He inspected Sherwood and found it very pleasant, but never went any farther.[2] John, in contrast, visited some or all of the northern counties at least once in every year of his reign, except 1199, 1202, 1203, and 1214, which were largely spent abroad. Clipstone was one of his favourite hunting lodges. His progresses must have become a regular feature of the year, almost an established circuit; they were often conducted in winter. John knew the north better than any king since the ancient rulers of Northumbria.

If this is a tribute to his energy, it is also a measure of the disastrous effects it had on local men. These were most obvious perhaps in 1201, at a time when John was still selling privileges and forcing confirmations on his subjects following his accession. He moved north to Lincoln in January and then on through Yorkshire, Durham, and Northumberland to Alnwick, which he reached on 12 February. From there he turned west to Carlisle, travelling through Rothbury and Hexham, and then south through Westmorland and Yorkshire, reaching Nottingham on 10 March. The profits of these two months were remarkable, leaving a trail of northern cases in the *coram rege* roll,[3] long lists of proffers on the fine roll,[4] and inflated lists of *nova oblata* on the pipe roll.[5] On the Yorkshire account these totalled over 9,000 m.,[6] on the Lincolnshire account nearly 2,000 m.,[7] and on the Northumberland account more than 850 m.[8] Towns and abbeys paid for the confirmation of their privileges or for the acquisition of new ones. Enormous proffers were taken from the nobility, especially in Yorkshire, where William de Stuteville bought the shrievalty of

---

[1] R. W. Eyton, *The Court, Household, and Itinerary of Henry II, passim.*
[2] L. Landon, *The Itinerary of Richard I* (Pipe Roll Society), pp. 85–87; *Hoveden*, iii. 240.
[3] *Curia Regis Rolls*, i. 374–98.
[4] *Rot. de Ob. et Fin.*, pp. 101–26.
[5] *Pipe Roll 3 John*, pp. xiii–xvii.
[6] Ibid., pp. 157–60.
[7] Ibid., pp. 18–20.
[8] Ibid., pp. 247–50.

the county and where Peter de Brus made his bid for Danby.[1] In Cumberland the King held inquiries into demesne lands which had been alienated and ordered resumptions.[2] He also seems to have reviewed some of the tenures peculiar to the north and found them unsatisfactory, for drengs in Westmorland, cornage tenants both in Westmorland and Cumberland, and thegns in Lancaster were later required to fine *ne transfretent*.[3] Throughout the north offences against the forest law were used to levy heavy payments.[4] At York the King got a poor welcome, and the citizens had to proffer £100 for his benevolence because they had not met him or lodged his crossbowmen, and to be quit of a demand for hostages which he had made as a result.[5] The men of Newcastle, too, made a proffer *pro bono adventu Regis*.[6] The exactions which accompanied this royal progress were emphasized by contemporaries. Wendover mentioned John's extortion of large sums from the northern provinces.[7] Howden dealt at length with some of the incidents which occurred on the journey.[8] With intentional or unintentional irony he prefaced his story with a reference to an earthquake which occurred in Yorkshire a few days before the King arrived. He summed up as follows: 'He perambulated the land and ransomed the men of the realm, by forcing them to pay ransom, asserting that they had wasted his forest. When he came to Hexham, he heard that there was buried treasure at Corbridge. He had men dig there, but nothing was found *praeter lapides signatos aere et ferre et plumbo*.' Even the Romans were required to contribute to John's treasure.

Journeys like this were not just an expression of the King's personal foibles. They marked the final integration of the north in the English realm. In the case of the three border counties the work which John was completing was of recent origin. Although the Border had been secured by Rufus as far back as 1092, it had been lost under Stephen and it was not until 1157 that Henry II was able to wrest the border counties from Scottish control. Administratively, these areas were isolated beyond the great franchises of Chester and Durham. The typical unit of Norman and Angevin administration, the hundred or wapentake, did not

[1] See above, pp. 148, 180.
[2] *Pipe Roll 3 John*, p. 254; *Curia Regis Rolls*, i. 387–9.
[3] *Rot. de Ob. et Fin.*, pp. 161, 162, 166, 167.   [4] See above, pp. 160–3.
[5] *Rot. de Ob. et Fin.*, p. 119; *Pipe Roll 3 John*, p. 159.
[6] *Pipe Roll 3 John*, p. 247.
[7] *Chron. Maj.* ii. 475.   [8] *Hoveden*, iv. 156–7.

exist here. The four northern counties, like those of Lothian, were divided into wards. Where the ward was not the operative administrative unit, it was the ancient *scir*, as in the dependent liberties of Durham, or the barony, especially when well franchised, as was Redesdale, or Copeland and Allerdale, which coincided with two of the Cumberland wards.[1] The absence of the normal hundredal organization had important consequences. There was no frankpledge system,[2] no view of frankpledge, and no sheriff's tourn. The barons of these border counties thus came to exercise wide powers. When the powers they claimed were clearly revealed for the first time by the *quo warranto* proceedings of Edward I, they included, as of course, the right to a gallows, the trial of the assize of bread and ale, infangthief, the goods of condemned fugitives, and the return of writs save for the pleas of the Crown. Thus within the barony many aspects of normal hundredal administration were in baronial hands. Farther south this was also the case in the Durham lordships of Brancepeth and Barnard Castle, in the Yorkshire honours of Richmond, Knaresborough, Hallamshire, and Tickhill, and in Hornby and Clitheroe, both dependencies of the honour of Lancaster. It has been argued with some justification that all these privileges were of ancient origin; they were certainly already established at the end of the twelfth century.[3]

Certain rights, however, were retained in the King's hands to form a framework on which regular royal administration could be erected. Without a specific grant or an acknowledged prescriptive title, a baron could not hold the pleas of the Crown or the pleas of the forest. These were only abandoned with great care and reluctance. Not even Robert de Vieuxpont obtained them from John when he acquired Westmorland in 1203 and, in fact, only the bishop of Durham, the lords of Redesdale, and possibly also the lords of Copeland, Allerdale, and Tynedale, seem to have enjoyed them.[4]

---

[1] See Rachel Reid, 'Baronage and Thanage', *E.H.R.* xxxv. 191 ff.; J. E. A. Jolliffe, 'Northumbrian Institutions', ibid. xli. 32 ff. On the wards see especially *Place Names of Cumberland*, iii, pp. xiv–xv, xxxiv ff.

[2] W. A. Morris, *The Frankpledge System*, pp. 48 ff.

[3] See J. Hodgson, *History of Northumberland*, pt. ii, vol. i, pp. 1–5; Rachel Reid, loc. cit., especially pp. 191–4; J. E. A. Jolliffe, loc. cit.

[4] For Redesdale and Tynedale see *Book of Fees*, pp. 201, 204; *Placita de Quo Warranto*, pp. 593, 600, 605. For Copeland and Allerdale see Rachel Reid, loc. cit., pp. 194, 197, and *Placita de Quo Warranto*, pp. 113–14.

The retention of the pleas of the Crown and the maintenance of the royal forest gave royal administration in these northern counties a reasonable chance of success. So also did the existence in many areas of small independent thegnage and drengage tenures which could be subjected easily to royal officials. Nevertheless, in the twelfth century, royal control was usually somewhat tenuous, and even the organization of local administration around the sheriff frequently appeared weak and unsatisfactory. Much depended on the extent of the royal demesne. In Westmorland there was none, for the county was divided into the two great lordships of Appleby and Kendal. In the normal course of events, Westmorland was not a shire, had no sheriff, and no account for it was presented at the Exchequer. It was only when the lordship of Appleby escheated to the Crown, as it did after the advancement of Ranulf le Meschin to the earldom of Chester in 1120, and again after the Scottish invasion of 1173–4, that a royal sheriff of Westmorland appears, or that an account for the farm of the shire appears on the pipe rolls.[1] With both lordships in private hands there might be some pleas of the Crown or of the forest to record, but these normally appeared on the rolls of neighbouring counties[2] and, in comparison with similar entries for other northern counties, were at best embryonic. Cumberland presented a more hopeful picture. Here William Rufus had retained Carlisle and a group of manors around and including Penrith as demesne lands. The bailiwick also came to include the important lead mining centre of Alston in Tynedale and a subsidiary mining area stretching south of Stainmore into upper Swaledale.[3] The farm of the mines and the demesne, along with the administration of the royal forest of Inglewood, kept royal agents busy and made royal authority felt. But it was only gradually that Cumberland was established as a normal county. Up to the year 1176–7 the area always appears on the rolls under the heading of Carlisle. Until this period, we may suspect, the sheriff could do little of effect outside the King's demesne. Only, in fact, in Northumberland did the Border counties present typical shrieval organization and here the Crown had adequate demesne estates, especially in the old centre of the

---

[1] For the earliest surviving account see *Pipe Roll 31 Henry I*, pp. 142–3.

[2] The pleas of the Crown usually appear on the Yorkshire account and the pleas of the forest on the Cumberland account.

[3] For evidence on the association of the Swaledale mines with the shrievalty of Cumberland see below, p. 249.

Northumbrian earldom at Bamburgh and in William Rufus's acquisition of Newcastle.

This scheme of government, by itself, was incapable of coping with the unexpected. In a crisis Border government tended to dissolve and reform along different lines, especially around the great castleries of Carlisle, Bamburgh, and Newcastle, and around escheats and custodies temporarily in the hands of the Crown. This kind of transformation is seen at its clearest during and after the war of 1173–4. The farms of the sheriffs of Northumberland and Carlisle were either spent immediately on military charges or could not be collected because of the war.[1] Robert de Stuteville, sheriff of Yorkshire, was given an overriding financial authority in the conduct of operations, and collected debts, or spent money on the fortification of castles, as far north as Northumberland.[2] When the war was over, order was restored not so much through the normal vicecomital offices as through the special position allotted to the Justiciar, Ranulf Glanville. He was placed in charge of the escheated barony of Appleby and appeared on the pipe rolls as sheriff of Westmorland. In reality he and his bailiffs enjoyed an almost independent military command. Despite attempts to restock manors and to reach an agreed farm with the Exchequer, the revenues were directed into military expenditure especially on the Westmorland castles of Appleby and Brough, but also as far north as Roxburgh.[3] By 1180 the attempt to keep a normal sheriff's account for Westmorland had ceased, and all the revenues were going into Glanville's hands without Exchequer supervision. There was no renewal of Exchequer control until the reign of Richard and that was but slight. Similar methods of control were used again in John's reign, even though the shrievalties of Cumberland and Northumberland had become more securely established by then. His administration was based on the great custodies rather than on the shrievalties, especially on the custodies of Durham, Knaresborough, and, for a time, of the archbishopric of York and the honour of Pontefract. It was from these accounts that the King's northern revenues were largely drawn and on the super-shrieval authority of royal castellans and custodians, coupled with decentralized treasures in the greater

---

[1] *Pipe Roll 20 Henry II*, pp. 105, 107.
[2] *Pipe Roll 21 Henry II*, pp. 164–5, 183.
[3] *Pipe Roll 23 Henry II*, p. 123; *Pipe Roll 24 Henry II*, p. 74–75.

northern castles, that the civil war at the end of the reign was largely fought.

It was not until the middle years of the reign of Henry II that the north began to feel the full weight of royal government. By then it bore on a group of families already in established and privileged positions, who were mentally maladjusted to it because of the earlier administrative history of the north, who saw little reason why they should accept it now, and who resisted it at every step, ultimately, at the end of John's reign, by civil war. The change was quite sudden. The only pipe roll of Henry I shows that his local justiciars were at work in the northern counties.[1] The rolls of the early years of Henry II illustrate further judicial activity, the assessment of aids and the occasional tallaging of the demesne. But the record is far from impressive.[2] Not even the judicial proceedings following the Assize of Clarendon affected the tenor of northern life to any marked degree. The great change came after the war of 1173–4. It was partly a result of the judicial activity which followed the Assize of Northampton, and partly also of the seizure of the Westmorland lands of Hugh de Morville and of others throughout the north who had sided with the Scots, or at least been lukewarm in their support for Henry. These years saw the final emergence of Cumberland as a shire and of the special command of Glanville in Westmorland. Judicial inquiries and forest eyres succeeded each other, scarcely a year passing without some new entry appearing on the rolls of either one or all the northern shires. By 1180 judicial and administrative activity was geared to a tempo which accelerated with few breaks until it rushed headlong to disaster in the severe judicial eyres, tallages, forest eyres, fiscal measures, and regular personal visitations to which the north was being subjected in the time of John.

The amercements levied in these eyres from the middle 1170's onwards are themselves significant. There were frequent impositions for criminals escaped or cases not presented; heavy payments for offences against the forest law; amercements for default or failure to appear before the justices in the shire court, £100, for example on Richard Cumin in 1176 when he was in the shire when

[1] *Pipe Roll 31 Henry I*, pp. 142, 143.
[2] For the view that northern assessments to taxation were in many cases low see F. W. Maitland, *Domesday Book and Beyond*, pp. 7, 20, 461–2, 474–5.

the summons came;[1] amercements for interference in the new royal judicial processes, £5, for example, on the knights of Copeland in 1185 for judging a plea which did not pertain to them.[2] All these were signs that the days of happy semi-independence were numbered.

There were other equally disturbing signs of change. The northern border which Rufus had won had been secured by Henry I and a number of prominent nobles working hand in hand. Walter Espec, Robert de Brus, Eustace fitz John were the great men who had built the north. This situation remained little changed in the next generation. Whatever the administrative measures, the machinery of enforcement was largely in the hands of men who represented and understood local traditions, interests, and practices. William de Vesci was sheriff of Northumberland for thirteen years prior to 1170, Roger de Stuteville sheriff for the next fifteen years, and his nephew, William de Stuteville, sheriff for the early part of Richard's reign and again in 1199. Carlisle or Cumberland was again in local hands, alternating from 1174 to the end of Henry's reign between the Vaux lords of Gilsland and the Morvilles of Burgh by Sands. In Yorkshire the Stutevilles again appeared, represented this time by Robert, Roger's elder brother and William's father, who held the shrievalty from 1170 to 1175, a period of office sandwiched between tenures of the shrievalty by Ranulf Glanville. William de Stuteville married Bertha, a niece of Ranulf Glanville. Robert de Stuteville was William de Vesci's father-in-law; his daughter, Heloise, married Hugh de Morville of Burgh;[3] Hugh de Morville's mother took Robert de Vaux as her second husband.[4] Northern administration was a family affair.

This happy situation was rudely disturbed in 1185. In that year Roger de Stuteville was retired from his Northumbrian shrievalty under the burden of a number of amercements imposed for an unspecified transgression of assize, for taking the King's venison, and for accepting bribes.[5] In the same year Robert de Vaux suffered a similar fate in Cumberland, his amercement of 100 m. being imposed for several disseisins he had committed, for

---

[1] *Pipe Roll 22 Henry II*, p. 138.   [2] *Pipe Roll 31 Henry II*, p. 186.
[3] *Early Yorks. Charters*, ix. 1, 8.
[4] *Trans. Cumberland and Westmorland Ant. and Arch. Soc.*, N.S. ix. 261–4.
[5] *Pipe Roll 31 Henry II*, p. 153.

permitting the King's prisoners to escape from his custody, and for maintaining the circulation of old currency after the recoinage of 1180.[1] Behind the peccadilloes of both these sheriffs there lay a much more serious offence. The rolls of 1185 and the next year show that they were retaining part of the profits of the Alston lead mines, the finances of which were by now in a state of tangled confusion.[2] Robert and Roger had done very well for themselves until found out.

The removal of these men was a symptom of the new confidence and energy with which Henry II was acting in the government of the north. He and his successor, Richard, were gradually introducing new men of their own into administrative positions. Hugh Bardolf appeared as sheriff of Westmorland in 1192, of Yorkshire from 1191 to 1194, and of Northumberland in 1194 and 1198. Robert of Tattershall was sheriff of Cumberland in 1197. Gilbert fitz Reinfrey, a future sheriff of Yorkshire and Lancaster, was a rising star after his marriage to the heiress of the Kendal barony at the end of Henry's reign. In Northumberland Robert fitz Roger, another future sheriff, was already an important castellan and had succeeded to his father's estates in Warkworth and elsewhere. These changes presaged the much greater changes which John was later to bring about. They were made at a peculiarly propitious time. In the last years of Henry's reign and the early years of Richard's the baronies of Vesci, Mowbray, Ros, Muschamp, and Gaugy were all at various times in royal custody. Three of the young wards were Eustace de Vesci, William de Mowbray, and Robert de Ros. They were but the second generation of northern lords to experience effective royal administration.

The changes wrought by Henry II and his sons had little immediate effect on the political security of the north. Scottish claims to Carlisle and Northumberland were still nursed after the surrender of these provinces in 1157. In 1173–4 they were the chief reason for William the Lion's participation in the attack on Henry II, and they were revived again at Richard's accession. Richard released William the Lion from the terms of the disastrous treaty of 1174 in return for a payment of 10,000 m.[3] In 1194 he also considered granting Northumberland, less the castles, to the King of Scotland for a further 15,000 m., but ultimately accepted

---

[1] Ibid., p. 187.   [2] Ibid., pp. 183, 188; *Pipe Roll 32 Henry II*, pp. 99–100.
[3] A. L. Poole, *From Domesday Book to Magna Carta*, p. 279.

a proffer from Hugh de Puiset, Bishop of Durham, who had
bought the earldom for life in 1189.[1] Scottish claims must have
been made again, however, after the Bishop's death in 1195,
when Richard and William discussed plans to marry William's
daughter to Otto of Brunswick and endow the young couple with
the Northumbrian earldom.[2] Only four years had passed since these
discussions when John came to the throne. William immediately
pressed his claims to the border shires, and John had to see to
their immediate defence.[3] It was not until November 1200 that
William was persuaded to come south to do homage,[4] and thereafter he continued to argue his case.[5] These and other issues led to
fruitless negotiations which lasted on to the campaign of 1209
and the treaties of 1209 and 1212, which, in their turn, did nothing
to solve the problem.[6] As early as 1209 William was probably in
touch with John's opponents in England[7] and in 1212 gave
asylum to his son-in-law, Eustace de Vesci. Alexander II's intervention in 1215 was a natural continuation of earlier policy.

The Scots were not the sole source of trouble. The ambitious,
if often ineffective, policies of Hugh de Puiset, John's own conflict with Richard's Chancellor, Longchamp, and his subsequent
abortive rebellion in 1194, had all disturbed the northern scene.
Geoffrey, Archbishop of York, was also a perpetual source of
danger, quarrelling now with de Puiset, now with the Yorkshire
sheriffs, ever ready to attack the judicial and fiscal superiority of
the Crown. He survived into the reign of John, his ultimate act of
resistance being directed against the Thirteenth of 1207.[8] Settled
conditions could not be expected in the north. The line between
stable government and administrative chaos, even civil war, was

---

[1] Kate Norgate, *Richard the Lion Heart*, p. 292; G. V. Scammell, *Hugh du Puiset*,
pp. 49–50, 59.				[2] *Hoveden*, iii. 308.				[3] Ibid. iv. 91.
	[4] Ibid. iv. 141.						[5] Ibid. iv. 163–4.
	[6] For the construction of the castle of Tweedmouth and the disputes it produced
see *The Chronicle of John of Fordun*, ed. W. F. Skene, ii. 272–3. For negotiations in
1205 see *Rot. Litt. Claus.* i. 43b; *Curia Regis Rolls*, iv. 15; *Rot. Litt. Pat.*, p. 56;
in 1207 ibid., pp. 69b, 76; *Rot. Litt. Claus.* i. 86, 90b; and in 1208 *Curia Regis Rolls*,
v. 189.
	[7] In discussing the reasons for the Scottish campaign of 1209 the Margam annalist
states that it was rumoured that William was in league with John's enemies (*Annales
Monastici*, i. 29). According to Wendover, John complained that William was
receiving his public enemies and fugitives from England, and giving them aid and
favour (*Chron. Maj.* ii. 525). William certainly seems to have given asylum to the
bishops of Rochester and Salisbury (*Chron. Melrose*, p. 54).
	[8] J. E. A. Jolliffe, *Angevin Kingship*, pp. 110–18.

difficult to define. On Richard's death, special provision had to be made for the garrisoning of the Lancashire and Yorkshire castles.[1] William de Stuteville was placed in charge of the defence of the Border and the administration of the Border shires.[2] John took steps to placate Geoffrey of York and made important concessions to some of the group of great lords, mostly northern men, who had refused to acknowledge him until he had restored what they alleged to be their rights.[3]

These measures only ensured peace and quiet for a time. William de Albini was apparently a party to a new bid for the restoration of rights made by some of the earls in 1201.[4] The pipe rolls bear witness to the continued retention by the King of hostages and various prisoners.[5] In the winter of 1204–5 came the first real warning of what was to come. Normandy was now lost. An attempt to take an expedition across the Channel in 1204 had failed.[6] At the Exchequer account John was using the scutage of $2\frac{1}{2}$ m., which had been granted as an aid, as an excuse to levy heavy fines *pro servicio*.[7] The early months of 1205 saw severe frosts, famine, and soaring corn prices[8] at a time when John was initiating a reform of the coinage.[9] In March and April there was a serious threat of invasion from France.[10] In June he also had to accept the unpalatable advice against attempting a continental campaign.[11]

During these months the north was on the verge of open war. In letters of 14 December 1204 John ordered the seizure of the estates of Ranulf, Earl of Chester, and Roger de Montbegon.[12] Letters of the 20th announced a safe-conduct for these two men

---

[1] *Pipe Roll 1 John*, pp. xiv–xv, 38, 71. [2] *Hoveden*, iv. 91–2.

[3] *Hoveden*, iv. 88. Howden names Earl David, Richard of Clare, Ranulf of Chester, William de Ferrers, Waleran of Warwick, Roger de Lacy, and William de Mowbray. For the grievances of these men see S. Painter, *The Reign of King John*, pp. 13–16. He fails to note that Roger de Lacy was pursuing claims to twenty fees which Guy de Laval held of the honour of Pontefract (*Early Yorks. Charters*, iii. 198–200).

[4] *Hoveden*, iv. 161.

[5] *Pipe Roll 3 John*, p. xix; *Pipe Roll 4 John*, pp. xv–xvi; *Pipe Roll 5 John*, pp. xvi–xvii; *Pipe Roll 6 John*, pp. 133, 159, 193.

[6] *Histoire de Guillaume le Maréchal*, lines 12921–6. See also John's letters to Ireland, of Feb. 1204 (*Rot. Chartarum*, pp. 133b–134).

[7] See above, pp. 89–90.

[8] *Coggeshall*, p. 151; *Chron. Maj.* ii. 490; *Annales Monastici*, ii. 256; iv. 393; *Chron. Melrose*, p. 52. [9] *Pipe Roll 7 John*, pp. xxvii–xxxii.

[10] *Rot. Litt. Pat.*, p. 55; *Gerv. Cant.* ii. 96–98.

[11] *Coggeshall*, pp. 152–4; *Gerv. Cant.* ii. 98; *Chron. Maj.* ii. 490.

[12] *Rot. Litt. Claus.* i. 16.

to come and make security in accordance with the advice of the Archbishop of Canterbury, the Justiciar, and other faithful men.[1] The Earl of Chester was in close touch with some of the supporters of Philip Augustus in Normandy; in Wales he was supporting the rising of Gwenwynwyn, and he still had unsatisfied claims to the honour of Richmond and lands of the honour of Roumare.[2] In his case the crisis passed quickly; he had recovered some of his lands before the end of January 1205, when his other claims were under discussion.[3] When Roger de Montbegon was restored is uncertain, but it was before 11 March 1205; by then some of his chattels had been sold.[4] In making his peace he had to proffer hostages for his faithful service and continued tenure of Hornby castle.[5] Other men were also in difficulties with the King. At the end of March 1205 the land of Robert de Ros was seized[6] and was not restored until 9 May,[7] probably on condition that he surrendered hostages;[8] in September Hugh Malebisse was disseised for no apparent reason and had to pay 200 m. and two palfreys for the recovery of his land;[9] Adam of Staveley and Roger de Bosco also suffered disseisin sometime during the year.[10]

John's reply to this threat was characteristic and little different from his reaction to the more serious crisis which occurred in 1212. His first measures were concerned with the security of the northern castles. Indeed, he was already preparing for the movement when it came. As early as August 1204 measures had been taken for the repair of York and Tickhill.[11] In November payments were made to Roger de Lacy for fortifying Carlisle,[12] and in March 1205 a reinforcement of crossbowmen was sent to him.[13] At the following Michaelmas allowances were made on the accounts of Yorkshire, Northumberland, the Stuteville estates, Nottinghamshire, and Derbyshire for the payment of similar troops.[14] The King accompanied this display of force with concessions. In late February and early March he journeyed north as far as York. There on 6 March he took steps to ensure the loyalty of Earl Ranulf by granting him all the Yorkshire lands of the honour of

---

[1] *Rot. Litt. Pat.*, p. 48b.
[2] S. Painter, op. cit., pp. 25 ff.
[3] *Rot. Litt. Claus.* i. 18b.
[4] Ibid. i. 22.
[5] *Rot. de Ob. et Fin.*, p. 275.
[6] *Rot. Litt. Claus.* i. 24b.
[7] Ibid. i. 31.
[8] *Rot. Litt. Pat.*, p. 59b; *Rot. Litt. Claus.* i. 99.
[9] *Rot. Litt. Claus.* i. 49; *Rot. de Ob. et Fin.*, p. 334; *Pipe Roll 8 John*, p. 208.
[10] *Rot. de Ob. et Fin.*, p. 332.
[11] *Rot. Litt. Claus.* i. 4b.
[12] Ibid. i. 15.
[13] Ibid. i. 21b.
[14] *Pipe Roll 7 John*, pp. 41, 14, 39, 221.

Richmond, except the fees of the Constable and of Henry fitz Hervey.[1] Later, on 1 April, for no stated reason, John pardoned the scutage due from the barons of Northumberland. It is highly probable that this order was also applied to the barons of Yorkshire and Lincolnshire.[2] John may have gone much further in his promises than in his actions. At Oxford, probably in March, at a time when the threat from France was increasing, he apparently swore that he would maintain the *iura regni* with the counsel of the magnates.[3]

This movement foreshadowed later events. In the persons of Robert de Ros and Roger de Montbegon it included two members of the Twenty-Five of 1215. Further, it showed that the problem of scutage, or at least of one particular scutage, was already looming large for northern men. After these years the north was never quiet. In 1207-8 it was the scene of widespread resistance to the assessment of the Thirteenth, coming not only from Geoffrey of York, but also from a number of laymen. Ruald fitz Alan was prominent among these and was deprived of Richmond for a time because of his resistance to assessment.[4] In Lincolnshire, a county in which several influential men were, like Ruald, tenants of the Richmond honour, there was a threat of general resistance. The King sent letters to the abbots and priors of the county ordering them to surrender goods which had been placed in their hands by owners trying to evade assessment.[5] By 1209, when John was also being troubled by Irish and Marcher affairs, rebellion in the north was already being planned in secret. It must have suffered many setbacks. Apart from John's increasingly tight financial control of the northern baronage, 1209 was not a suitable year for a northern rebellion, for it saw the King's successful demonstration against the Scots followed by his demand for a renewal of fealty throughout England. Our knowledge of the plot is derived solely from a transcript of a letter from Philip Augustus to John de Lacy.[6] John de Lacy was still a youth of seventeen, who can scarcely have had much backing and whose subsequent actions at

---

[1] *Rot. Litt. Pat.*, p. 51; *Early Yorks. Charters*, iv. 79.
[2] See above, p. 90.   [3] *Gerv. Cant.* ii. 97-98.
[4] *Rot. Litt. Pat.*, p. 72b; *Rot. de Ob. et Fin.*, p. 372. See also *Pipe Roll 9 John*, pp. xvii–xxi.   [5] *Rot. Litt. Pat.*, p. 71.
[6] The letter appears as a cancelled entry. The hand is distinct from the other entries on the same folio and the entry is the only one on the right-hand side of the folio. It is clearly a later insertion (Vatican Library, MS. Ottobon, 2796, f. 74v). See S. Painter, *The Reign of King John*, pp. 253 ff., which first brought the letter to the attention of English readers.

the end of John's reign do not reflect great political constancy.[1]
Nevertheless, this is the first indication of that pent-up wrath and
hostility to John which finally burst out in the conspiracy of 1212.

Only one area was comparable to the north as a potential threat
to the English Crown. This was the Welsh March, where rebellious elements could bubble to the surface and prove just as
dangerous as in the north. John had learned this lesson from the
adventures of Fulk fitz Warin[2] and later from the resistance of
William de Braose. By 1215 these dangers were largely passed.
The King had secured the support of William Marshal and Ranulf
of Chester, and the Welsh March was largely loyal.[3] Such support
as there was for the baronial rebels came largely from the Welsh
themselves and only served to drive the Marchers further into
their alliance with the King. Herein lay the great difference
between Wales and the north. To the Marchers the Welsh were
still a race to be conquered, from whom rebellion, inspired by
sub-tribal loyalties, might still be dangerous and was always to be
expected. To the Northerners, in contrast, the Scottish kings and
the Norman or Normanized aristocracy of the Lowlands were
natural allies in time of need. Socially, the Border did not exist.
In England the liberty of Tynedale and the earldom of Huntingdon were fiefs belonging to the Scottish royal house. In Scotland
the great Norman families of northern England had helped the
Scottish kings to produce a tenurial revolution in the course of
the twelfth century. Their work had been to their own profit.
The Morvilles had served as constables and had acquired Lauder-
dale and Cunningham.[4] The Brus were established in Annandale,[5]
the Unfravilles in Stirlingshire,[6] and the Balliols in Lothian.[7] The

---

[1] Professor Painter states that it 'seems rather unlikely' that John de Lacy was
a minor at this time (op. cit., p. 255). The only suggestion that he was not a minor
lies in Philip's letter, or rather in its implications. The accepted view that he was,
is based on the fact that his estates remained in royal hands for nearly two years after
his father's death (*Complete Peerage*, vii. 676). This is not conclusive but it gains
strength from the fact that John received a regular allowance for part of this period
(*Pipe Roll 14 John*, p. 4).

I am unable to follow Painter's tentative reconstruction of this affair. There is
no evidence to connect anyone else with John de Lacy's plans. His father, Roger,
was still alive and loyal, actively at work in the King's interest.

[2] S. Painter, op. cit., pp. 48 ff.   [3] Ibid., pp. 290, 357–8.
[4] A. C. Lawrie, *Early Scottish Charters*, pp. 273–4.
[5] Ibid., pp. 48–49, 162, 308.
[6] *Liber S. Marie de Calchou* (Bannatyne Club, 1846), pp. 68, 261–3.
[7] Ibid., pp. 43–44, 222; A. C. Lawrie, op. cit., pp. 207, 443–4.

Vieuxponts,[1] Bolebecs,[2] and Bertrams of Mitford[3] all held
Scottish lands by the end of the twelfth century.[4] By this time
most of these families had divided into English and Scottish lines,[5]
but the bond was being renewed continually. Robert, brother of
William de Mowbray, acquired Scottish estates by marriage.[6]
Robert de Ros married an illegitimate daughter of William the
Lion and obtained Scottish lands in marriage.[7] Eustace de Vesci
did the same and received with his bride the barony of Sprouston
in Roxburghshire.[8] During his exile in 1212–13 he could have
spent some of his time quite peacefully within a day's ride of his
Northumbrian castle of Alnwick and only a few miles distant
from the castle of his friend, Robert de Ros, at Wark.

The Border country was a social unit on its own. The Border
itself was not finally confirmed as a frontier until 1249 and even
then an area remained debatable between the two countries.[9]
John himself contributed to this vagueness. He sent mercenaries
north of the Border in 1212 to suppress MacWilliam's rising
against King William.[10] His diplomacy ranged as far afield as the
Orkneys and Hebrides.[11] He intervened frequently in Scottish
affairs, confirming Earl David's charter to the burgesses of
Dundee,[12] trying to prevent Scottish criminals finding sanctuary
in England[13] and recruiting his mercenaries in Galloway.[14] The
emergence of two clearly separate realms did not suit a King
who was trying to re-establish that paternal relationship with the
northern kingdom which his father had achieved in 1174.

---

[1] *Liber S. Marie de Dryburgh* (Bannatyne Club, 1847), pp. 53, 54; *Liber Cartarum
Sancte Crucis* (Bannatyne Club, 1840), pp. 212–13, 34–35; A. C. Lawrie, op. cit.,
p. 410.   [2] *Liber S. Marie de Calchou*, pp. 219–22.

[3] *Liber S. Marie de Dryburgh*, pp. 106, 181.

[4] Only occasionally, as in the case of the fitz Alans of Oswestry, founders of the
house of Stewart, or the Ridels, who came from the earldom of Huntingdon, were
these men drawn from outside northern England. For recent reviews of the evidence
see R. L. G. Ritchie, *The Normans in Scotland*, pp. 142–59, 273–94; G. W. S. Barrow,
'The Beginnings of Feudalism in Scotland', *B.I.H.R.* xxix (1956), 1–31.

[5] Hugh de Balliol still held land north of the Border (*Liber S. Marie de Calchou*,
pp. 43–44, 222).   [6] *Coucher Book of Furness*, vol. ii, pt. ii, p. 291.

[7] *Monasticon Anglicanum*, v. 280.

[8] Cronicia Monasterii de Alnewyke, B.L., Harl. MS. 692, f. 207; *Liber S. Marie de
Calchou*, pp. 24, 172–3.

[9] See Rachel Reid in *E.H.R.* xxxii (1917), 479–82.

[10] A. L. Poole, *From Domesday Book to Magna Carta*, pp. 282–3.

[11] *Rot. Litt. Pat.*, p. 59; *Rot. Chartarum*, pp. 100, 191.

[12] *Rot. Chartarum*, p. 28b.   [13] *Rot. Litt. Pat.*, p. 41b.

[14] *Rot. Litt. Claus.* i. 131b.

The existence of these ties between the northern aristocracy and the Scottish kingdom did not mean that their alliance was inevitable. Twice in the twelfth century, in 1138 and 1174, the great men of the northern counties had fought on their own to defeat Scottish invasions. Only a very grave crisis and serious discontent could lead these men *en masse* into the Scottish camp. Such action would place their estates farther south in jeopardy; before 1204 it would also involve the sacrifice of such Norman possessions as they had. The proximity of Scotland was important not so much because the Northerners might seek political support there, as because the Border had created a tradition and practice of independent political and military action. The battles of the Standard and Alnwick were victories of the northern baronage. The military role expected of these men was witnessed by the peculiarities of northern tenures, especially cornage, and by the large number of castles which dotted the Border counties. They were quick to defend their privileges by an appeal to the strategic requirements of the English realm. When it was alleged in 1220 that Harbottle castle was adulterine and to the damage of the royal castle of Bamburgh, its owner, Richard de Unfraville, retorted that it was situated in the march of Scotland towards the Great Waste and was to the great benefit of the kingdom, both in peace and in war; it was nine leagues from Bamburgh and had been constructed on the order of Henry II and with the aid of the whole shire of Northumberland and the whole bishopric of Durham.[1]

This capacity for independence, although most obvious in the Border shires, was not wholly absent farther south. Many factors, besides the tenurial bonds which stretched from the Border south into Lincolnshire,[2] influenced all the northern counties together. Scottish invasions did not stop at the Tees. In the 1150's Scottish power at Shap was within a day's ride of Lancaster and at the Rerecross on Stainmore within two days' ride of York. The victory of 1138 had been won not on the Border but at Northallerton; the banners over the battlefield were those of St. Peter of York, St. John of Beverley, and St. Wilfrid of Ripon.[3] The

---

[1] *Royal Letters of Henry III*, pp. 140–1.   [2] See above, p. 15.

[3] A. L. Poole, op. cit., p. 271. Compare Henry I's arrangements with St. Mary's, York, where the banners which accompanied the military levies of Yorkshire are given as those of St. Mary, St. Peter of York, and St. John of Beverley (*Cal. Patent Rolls 1258–66*, p. 636).

English forces were blessed by Thurstan, Archbishop of York, who had done much to organize resistance against the Scottish invaders.

Frequently internal stresses, too, seemed to emphasize that political problems and issues were common to several or all the northern counties. There were the interests of the Earls of Chester from the reign of Stephen onwards in their lands in Lincolnshire and in the Roumare estates and the earldom of the county;[1] Earl Ranulf, under John, was simply completing the work of his father and grandfather. John's own power, as Count of Mortain, had stretched almost continuously from Furness to the Trent and included the honours of Lancaster and Tickhill and the shires of Nottingham and Derby.[2] His fall in 1194 involved men drawn from many different parts of the north: Roger de Montbegon from Lancashire, Richard Malebisse from Yorkshire, and Gerard de Camville from Lincolnshire. Gerard's tenure of Lincoln had been one of the issues between John and Longchamp in 1191. He, in his turn, was a tenant of Hugh de Puiset, Bishop of Durham, and Hugh had been as thoroughly involved as John in the quarrel with Longchamp.[3] Hugh also quarrelled with Geoffrey of York. His power in the north was almost as extensive as John's, for he had bought the earldom of Northumberland from Richard and his influence thus extended from the Border to the manors of Northallerton and Howden in Yorkshire, and south to the fees and tenures of the bishopric in Lincolnshire.

These crises of the early 1190's affected the whole north. It is the less surprising to find bold assertions of privilege being made outside as well as within the Border counties. In 1219 the county court of Yorkshire roundly asserted that distraint for the King's debts was not to be made by any petty sergeant.[4] When carucage was assessed in 1220 it was from Yorkshire that the cry came that such a levy could not be made without seeking the assent of the barons *viva voce* or by letter. The final word of the baronial stewards was that their lords would be glad to grant an aid if the King were to ask for it when he visited York.[5]

[1] H. A. Cronne, 'Ranulf de Gernons, Earl of Chester', *T.R.H.S.*, 4th series, xx (1937), 103 ff.

[2] See the map in Miss Kate Norgate, *John Lackland*, facing p. 27.

[3] G. V. Scammell, op. cit., pp. 49 ff.

[4] *Rolls of the Justices in Eyre for Yorkshire, 1218–19* (Selden Society), no. 550.

[5] *Royal Letters of Henry III*, pp. 151–2.

King John must have been well aware of the problems of northern government as a result of his wide interest in the north in the 1190's. He was sufficiently acute to base his rising against Richard on this area rather than on his lands in Wales and the south-west. Indeed, the King who patrolled the north so vigorously was the same person who, as prince, had earlier raised rebellion in these same counties. Others could do what he had tried to do; the experience of the Prince encouraged vigilance in the King. But direct personal supervision and control were no solution by themselves. Indeed, John's personal attentions created as well as solved problems. For effective government John required local support and a local following. To devise new measures, to issue orders, to administer, was not enough. All this work could be deprived of its force or turned into a *casus belli* if local administration was not reinforced by men of substance in the shires. At best, if possible, administrators could be drawn from the more powerful and influential men. But such support was not easily sought, and the necessary administrative ability was not always found. Loyal assistance had to be paid for in kind and was always expensive. In some of the northern counties the tenurial structure and the political divisions were such that risks followed inevitably on such a harsh régime as John's. Necessarily, government office was the perquisite of a minority, and the minority proved insufficiently large and influential.

In many parts of the country John was secure in the loyalty of a very small group of influential men. William Marshal brought most of the Marchers with him into the royal camp. The Earls of Chester, Derby, and Warwick together ensured that there was little sign of rebellion in Cheshire, western Derbyshire, Staffordshire, and Warwickshire. In the south and south-west William of Salisbury, Peter des Roches, Bishop of Winchester, William Briwerre, and the Earls of Arundel and Surrey could together do much to ensure the loyalty of Somerset, Dorset, Wiltshire, Hampshire, Surrey, and Sussex.[1] These counties also bordered on or included that great belt of demesne lands, forests, and royal castles which stretched from Corfe northwards to Marlborough and Ludgershall and then east to the Thames at Wallingford and Windsor; this was the territorial foundation of Angevin power since the days of Matilda and the young Henry of Anjou. Throughout the

[1] S. Painter, op. cit., pp. 357-9, 290.

whole of this southern and south-western area friendship with these men, many of whom owed their position to the service they had given, was vital to the preservation of John's crown. They carried the shires with them just as Bishop Giles of Hereford carried Herefordshire with him.[1]

These methods would not work satisfactorily in the north. John used them continuously and skilfully, from his initial paci-fication of Geoffrey of York and Roger de Lacy, through his arrangements with Earl Ranulf of Chester in 1205, down to his hasty bids to buy and retain loyalty in the years of crisis after 1212. It was the only possible policy to follow unless the King were to turn to general appeasement by abandoning much of his internal policy. But the northern counties were not the proper field for it. Apart from Durham, Chester, and, to a lesser extent, Derbyshire, it was difficult to ensure the loyalty of a county by establishing sound relations with one man, or even with a small group of men. In some counties it was plainly impossible. In Lincolnshire the appeasement of Ranulf of Chester necessarily involved the aliena-tion of Gilbert de Gant, for both had claims to the earldom of Lincoln. Even if both could have been won over together, there would still have been several other important Lincolnshire barons capable of organizing rebellion. Similarly, in Yorkshire, rebellion would not have been prevented if John de Lacy had succeeded to the favour which his father had enjoyed, or Nicholas de Stuteville to the offices and influence of his brother, William. Throughout most of the north feudal and territorial influence were too evenly scattered, too equally divided among the Norman aristocracy, for John to succeed through the influence of a few. Land and power were not yet so concentrated that royal government was primarily a matter of personal relations with a Thomas of Lancaster or a Henry Percy. John needed, not the support of a few, but general support; for this he was not prepared to bid.

This situation was produced partly by the size of some of the northern counties, especially Yorkshire and Lincolnshire, and partly by the history of the northern frontier and its hinterland. This frontier had not been established at a single point in time but over a period. In the Conqueror's time Yorkshire and Lancashire had been frontier provinces, and this had left its mark in the creation of relatively compact, homogeneous baronies typical of

[1] See above, pp. 35–36.

Marcher lands: Richmond, covering Swaledale and Wensleydale; Pontefract, with its members at Ferrybridge and Knottingley, covering the lower Aire; and the great lordship of Roger the Poitevin lying north of the Mersey.[1] The pattern was repeated by the Conqueror's sons as they secured the land farther north. Rufus had enfeoffed Ivo Taillebois of the whole of Ewecross wapentake, the later lordship of Burton in Lonsdale, and of the later barony of Kendal along with the south-western portion of Cumberland which came to be described as the barony of Copeland.[2] He created the lordship of Northallerton for the bishops of Durham and established the Balliols in Teesdale and at Bywell-on-Tyne.[3] He was probably responsible, too, for the grant of Skipton to Robert de Romilly.[4] Many of the Northumbrian baronies were also the work of these years and the early years of Henry I.[5] Under Henry there was little change in policy. Ranulf le Meschin then held the new Cumbrian gains of the Norman house in a block of land stretching from Stainmore west to the sea and from Carlisle south to the Derwent. Even when these lands were surrendered on his accession to the earldom of Chester in 1120, they fell into a small number of compact and distinct estates: Liddel and Burgh by Sands, sub-tenures of Ranulf's own creation, Appleby, Allerdale below Derwent, Wigton, Creystoke, Kirklinton, and Gilsland.[6] Henry's attitude was conditioned not only by frontier requirements but also by the need to assert control over the northern counties during and after the uncertain years up to 1106. He imported his *novi homines* into the north, and rewarded those who were supporting him against Robert Curthose and were now to enjoy the spoils of land and office. The year of Tinchebrai probably saw the creation of the compact Cleveland

---

[1] Rachel Reid, *E.H.R.* xxxv. 197–9; James Tait, *Medieval Manchester and the Beginnings of Lancashire*, pp. 155 ff. For the castlery of Richmond see F. M. Stenton in *Royal Commission on Historical Monuments, Westmorland*, p. liii. For early references to the castlery of Pontefract see *Early Yorkshire Charters*, iii. 123–5, 185. See also F. M. Stenton, *The First Age of English Feudalism*, pp. 192–6.

[2] James Tait, op. cit., pp. 158 ff.

[3] For Northallerton see *Early Yorks. Charters*, ii. 266. For the Balliol baronies see R. Surtees, *History of Durham*, iv. 50, and R. L. G. Ritchie, *The Normans in Scotland*, p. 148, n. 2.

[4] *Early Yorks. Charters*, vii. 1–4.

[5] J. Hodgson, *History of Northumberland*, pt. i, vol. i, pp. 204–5.

[6] *Place Names of Cumberland*, iii, pp. xxxiv, xxxv. For a reference to Ranulf's *potestas* of Carlisle see *Register of the Priory of Wetherhal*, p. 2, quoted by F. M. Stenton, loc. cit., p. liv.

barony for the Brus family and their establishment at Hartlepool.[1]
At about the same time William de Warenne was rewarded for
his services with the grant of the manor of Wakefield.[2] Henry also
established a Bedfordshire knight, Walter Espec, at Helmsley and
Kirkham in Yorkshire, and in Northumberland at the crucial
strategic centre of Wark-on-Tweed.[3] He also granted, by marriage
with the Vesci heiress, the great Northumbrian barony of Alnwick
and the lordship of Malton in Yorkshire to Eustace fitz John, who
already farmed the manor of Knaresborough.[4] These moves
represented the first serious attempt to discipline the north and
bring it under direct royal government; fitz John and Walter
Espec became Henry's justiciars in the northern counties. But it
was only done by giving these administrators territorial power to
advance their influence, by perpetuating, in fact, the established
tenurial pattern of the northern counties.

The Angevins never completely abandoned the administrative
methods to which the Normans had committed them. They tended
always to try to ensure control of the north by establishing new
balances of power, even though from the late 1170's onwards they
were also attempting to reduce the northern lords to a disciplined
subjection to sheriff and castellan. The special circumstances of
the north could not be wiped out. Richard revived the Northumbrian earldom for the bishop of Durham, and John came to combine the shrievalty of the county with the custody of the bishopric.
John was largely repeating the tactics of his Norman predecessors
when he established Robert de Vieuxpont in Westmorland and
accepted William de Fors as lord of Cockermouth, Skipton, and
Holderness. But such policies became increasingly difficult to
apply. Each territorial disturbance and revolution, Rufus's campaign, Tinchebrai, Stephen's reign, left men securely established
in land and privilege. It became increasingly difficult for the King
to interfere, for him to govern by readjusting the territorial
balance in winning over certain lords or in thrusting his own men
into northern lordships. Great administrators were not necessarily
followed by equally loyal and able sons and grandsons. The
descendants of Walter Espec, Eustace fitz John, and Robert de
Brus were the rebels of 1215. By John's time, the King no longer

---

[1] *Early Yorks. Charters*, ii. 11.   [2] Ibid. viii. 178.
[3] *Cartulary of Rievaulx*, pp. xlii, xlvi; *Early Yorks. Charters*, x. 143–4.
[4] Dugdale, *Baronage*, i. 90–91.

had the clean sheet which had faced Rufus or even Henry I after Tinchebrai. He had to choose such administrators as he could find from an already powerful and established aristocracy, or he had to thrust in *novi homines* of his own and risk the possible consequence of rebellion from those already established. The choice was not mutually exclusive; in fact, most kings followed both methods. John, increasingly, chose the latter.

XII

THE KING'S FRIENDS

MEDIEVAL government was concerned before all else with managing men. The question—what is being administered? was closely related to other equally important questions. Who is conducting the administration? Who is profiting from office? Who is enjoying the King's favour, and with what justification? Governmental office at the more important levels tended inevitably to become the perquisite of a small group. There were those 'in' and those 'out'. But so long as this small group was chosen reasonably, so long as the monopoly of office did not seem too impenetrable or unbreakable, so long as those 'out' did not come to answer the questions set out above with excessive rancour and indignation, then the government would work and the King's choice of officials pass with little challenge.

Ultimately, King John did not accept these limitations on his freedom of action, for in this, as in other matters, his hand was forced by the loss of Normandy, Anjou and the Touraine. He had to provide for loyal and efficient friends and agents who had lost both estate and office on the continent. This helped to create the situation existing in 1215 in which the opposition attacked not only the actions of the King's officials but also their selection. It was now laid down that they were to know the law of the land and the more notorious of the foreigners were to be dismissed from office.[1] Wendover later wrote, somewhat loosely, of John's evil advisers,[2] and there was much gossip about the foreigners,[3] some of it perhaps the result of notoriety reflected from the downfall of Faulkes de Breauté in 1224. But the complaints of the opposition were real enough. They were best stated by a contemporary in the blunt words of the *Histoire des ducs de Normandie*— 'Molt mal homme ot el roi Jehan'.[4] This comes, it should be

[1] Magna Carta, caps. 45, 50.
[2] *Chron. Maj.* ii. 533. This is a rather curious list probably based, in part, on knowledge of those who later supported the King during the civil war.
[3] See especially *Chronicles of Stephen, Henry II and Richard I*, ii. 517–18.
[4] *Histoire des ducs de Normandie*, p. 105.

remembered, from a member of the King's camp; presumably the King's opponents dwelt on the 'evil' character of his officers even more emphatically. Jealousy cannot be excluded from these criticisms. Nevertheless, the views of the opposition deserve attention. From tenant-in-chief down to knight, these men, even when excluded from shrieval and other high office, were still very much part of the government of the land, as holders of franchises, as members of the shire court, as men who might at any time be required to journey on the King's business, attend his court, and serve on commissions or assizes or as simple jurors. Thus the differences between those 'in' and those 'out' were never so wide as to parallel the apparent mutual exclusiveness of 'court' and 'country' at later times. By its very nature, medieval government always left the door ajar so that those 'out' could see those 'in' enjoying the warmth and pleasures of the royal favour. One of the features of the situation in 1215 was that those 'out' considered the chances of being invited in so small that they combined and organized to burst wide the door, ransack the house, and eject the occupants, including the owner.

At the beginning of the reign, these days were still far off. John's initial problem was a comparatively simple one of combining his own personal supporters and his brother's old administrators in one single body capable of governing the country efficiently without his own immediate direction, for prolonged periods of royal absenteeism seemed certain. This compromise was achieved quite easily and with far less disturbance than that occasioned in 1189–90 by Richard's accession. Among the northern sheriffs in these early years, Richard's old agents were represented by the new Justiciar, Geoffrey fitz Peter, in Yorkshire, and by William Briwerre, one of the Barons of the Exchequer, in Nottinghamshire and Derbyshire. Gerard de Camville, in contrast, who was now installed in Lincolnshire, had been one of John's men since 1191, and had supported his rebellion in 1193–4.[1] Hugh Bardolf, in Westmorland, and William de Stuteville, in Cumberland and Northumberland, had been close to John at times, although they were also employed regularly by King Richard in the later years of his reign. Thus the new reign produced no clean sweep. John's initial concern in the north was not one of ejecting old officials, or even old enemies like Roger de Lacy, but of providing for the

[1] Miss Kate Norgate, *John Lackland*, pp. 31, 35.

defence of the north against Scottish threats by giving William de Stuteville control of the Border, and securing the internal peace of the northern counties by restoring his own half-brother, Geoffrey, Archbishop of York, to the recently sequestrated temporalities of his see.[1] Such changes as he made in the early years of his reign did little to alter this scheme. These northern officials might move from one county to another, as William de Stuteville did to Yorkshire in 1201. Obvious alternatives might be brought in. Thus Robert fitz Roger, who had experience as a sheriff in Norfolk and Suffolk, was placed in charge of Northumberland in 1200. But there was no crucial change in policy until the closing months of the Norman campaigns.

These dispositions probably seemed quite reasonable to the local baronage; all these officials had long experience. If it was argued that such men as Geoffrey fitz Peter and Gerard de Camville owed such territorial influence as they possessed to fortunate marriages bestowed upon them by royal favour, it was clear that this was not abnormal and that, in any case, John was not personally responsible for their rise. Further, as time passed, the financial exigencies of the Norman campaigns led to the steady sale of offices.[2] This enabled local men to buy their way into the administrative hierarchy and enjoy a share of the profits so obtained, or at least protect their own pockets by preventing exploitation by outsiders.

Several influences combined to alter this relatively stable situation. One was the death of some of John's most influential men; of William de Stuteville and Hugh Bardolf in 1203, of Roger de Lacy in 1211 and of Robert fitz Roger in 1212. Replacements for these had to be found. This was a constant problem facing any ruler. In addition, the wars in Normandy and the Loire basin provided circumstances in which men could show their loyalty and efficiency, win the King's favour, and thereby acquire landed estates and office. A prominent example is provided by Roger de Lacy, Constable of Chester. He had played an important part in supporting Longchamp in 1191 and had done it ruthlessly, hanging the knights who had betrayed Nottingham castle to John, despite the latter's intercession.[3] In 1199 he was among those who, according to Howden, only gave their allegiance to the new King

---

[1] See above, p. 205. [2] See above, pp. 148-9, 154-5.
[3] Miss Kate Norgate, op. cit., pp. 34-35.

on the condition that he would satisfy their claims to lost rights and dignities.[1] In 1205 he was made sheriff of Yorkshire and Cumberland, and although he lost these offices in 1209, he remained an important and trusted personage whose chief duties now lay in the Welsh Marches. This alteration in his relations with John may reflect Roger's reaction to the fact that in 1199 the Prince became the King. But it cannot be dissociated, either, from the noble service which Roger gave John in Normandy, especially in leading the defence of Château Gaillard in 1203–4. By then John considered Roger's good will valuable enough to contribute £1,000 towards his ransom, first as a loan, then as a gift.[2]

Roger's advancement probably gave little cause for resentment. At least, it left little room for criticism for, apart from his fame after Château Gaillard, he was among the greatest of the northern aristocracy, lord in all of over a hundred fees. But men of far humbler origins could tread the same road with equal and perhaps even greater success. Their advancement, unlike Roger's, could lead to discontent in that it offended social assumptions which the baronage scarcely questioned.

Robert de Vieuxpont was the most prominent early example of these new men breaking into the society and administration of the northern counties. He had some initial advantages. He was a younger son of a junior branch of a family which held ten fees in Normandy along with Hardingstone in Northamptonshire and Alston in Tynedale; his mother came from one of the best known northern families, for she was the sister and heiress of Hugh de Morville, lord of Westmorland.[3] Robert first appears as a royal sergeant going about King Richard's business in Normandy in 1194–5. By 1197 he had been made custodian of the honours of Peverel, Higham Ferrers, and Tickhill, and he held the last two of these until the end of the reign.[4] He lost them on John's accession but he was not in disfavour. In 1203 he appears in Normandy as *bailli* of the Roumois and he quickly acquired grants of land in the duchy including the estates of the senior branch of his own

---

[1] See above, p. 205.   [2] *Rot. Lib.*, p. 103; *Rot. Litt. Claus.* i. 4b.

[3] F. M. Powicke, *The Loss of Normandy*, pp. 519–60. On the Morville connexion see *Transactions of the Cumberland and Westmorland Ant. and Arch. Soc.*, N.S. xi, pedigree facing p. 320, and ibid., N.S. xvii, p. 234. On the probable seniority of Ivo de Vieuxpont see above, p. 67, n. 7.

[4] *Rolls of the Justices in Eyre for Yorkshire, 1218–19*, p. xxiv; *Pipe Roll 10 Richard I*, pp. 103, 118.

family, the head of which had sided with Philip Augustus.[1] At the same time he must have been pressing his interest in the Westmorland inheritance of his mother. In February 1202 he was made sheriff of Westmorland and custodian of the castles of Appleby and Brough,[2] and in 1203, somewhat hesitantly, as we shall see, he was given Westmorland as an hereditary lordship.[3] In this year he was also made custodian of Bowes Castle.[4] In the next his activities spread even wider for he was then acting as custodian of Windsor, Sarum, and Tickhill,[5] and in October was given the shrievalty of Nottinghamshire and Derbyshire.[6] In 1205 he once more accounted for the honour of Peverel.[7] By 1207 he had added the custody of the bishopric of Durham and the archbishopric of York to his miscellaneous interests and duties. By this time he was probably the greatest pluralist in the country, as well gorged with offices as the King's favoured clerks were with benefices. He had moved a long way from the household sergeant of 1194.

Robert was not alone in his advancement. His rise was accompanied by the equally rapid promotion of Brian de Lisle. This man first appears as a royal knight active in serving King John's interests in Normandy in the early years of the reign.[8] Unlike Robert's, his origins were, and still are, obscure.[9] Between 1203 and 1205 his service to the King was humdrum enough and his reward equally insignificant. He was then suddenly promoted, first as one of the custodians of the lands of William de Stuteville and then as sole custodian of the crucial residue of these lands retained in the King's hands, Knaresborough and Boroughbridge.

---

[1] *Rot. Scacc. Norm.* ii. ccliv, 549 ff.; *Rot. Norm.*, pp. 91, 106, 115.

[2] *Rot. Litt. Pat.*, pp. 25b, 27.

[3] The grant conveyed the castles of Appleby and Brough along with the bailiwick and returns of the shire and the service of all the tenants within it who did not hold by knight service. The pleas of the Crown and certain forest rights were excepted. The lordship was to be held by the service of four knights. There are transcripts of the charter in the Bodleian Library, Dodsworth MS. 70, f. 25, in *Cal. Patent Rolls, Richard II, 1396–9*, pp. 344–5, and in *Register of Wetherhal*, ed. J. E. Prescott, p. 394.

[4] *Rot. Lib.*, p. 63.

[5] *Rot. Lib.*, pp. 98, 100; *Rot. Litt. Claus.* i. 6; *Pipe Roll 6 John*, p. 166.

[6] *Rot. Litt. Pat.*, p. 46b.

[7] *Pipe Roll 7 John*, p. 223.

[8] *Rot. Litt. Claus.* i. 13b; *Rot. Norm.*, p. 87.

[9] He was the son of a Robert fitz Brian de Lisle who was involved in pleas in Hampshire and Sussex in 1203 and 1204 (*Curia Regis Rolls*, ii. 177; iii. 120). This Robert should not be confused with the man of the same name who was a tenant of the Bishop of Ely in 1212 (*Complete Peerage*, viii. 69–70). There is no obvious connexion between either Brian or his father and the main branches of the Lisle family.

He held these throughout the reign, and under his administration Knaresborough castle became one of the chief military and financial centres of the north. To this central responsibility Brian added others. In 1208-9 he became custodian of Bolsover castle, the wapentake of the High Peak, Laxton, and North Wheatley, and succeeded Robert de Vieuxpont in charge of the archbishopric of York and the honour of Peverel. He was also chief forester of Nottinghamshire and Derbyshire as the deputy of Hugh de Neville.[1] In 1212 he had expanded his interests further and now appeared as custodian of the bishopric of Lincoln and as one of the custodians of the ports of Lincolnshire and Yorkshire.[2] Brian went on to play an important role in the civil war in Yorkshire and to become a well-known justice and justice of the forest in the next reign.

The careers of Robert de Vieuxpont and Brian de Lisle were not isolated. We may assume that they were able and loyal enough to achieve promotion in the administrative hierarchy in almost any circumstances. However, the extent and rapidity of their advancement was partly due to the hectic situation created by the collapse of Angevin power in Normandy and in the Loire valley. Between 1203 and 1206, the years in which Brian and Robert were establishing themselves, there were rapid changes and switches in the personnel of local administration. Only five counties retained the same sheriff through these four years,[3] and further changes occurred in 1207 and 1208 with the arrival of yet more displaced soldiers and officials, both English and Poitevin, from southern France. These were the years of the arrival of Engelard de Cigogné in Gloucestershire, of Gerard d'Athée first in Nottinghamshire and then in Herefordshire, and of Philip Mark, first acting under Gerard's wing and then on his own, as sheriff of Nottinghamshire. But these foreigners were not alone. With them, for example came Philip of Oldcotes, a minor tenant of the honours of Peverel and Tickhill.[4] Philip had aided John's plots in the previous reign. Under the new régime he quickly acquired interests in Northumberland[5] and, in France, was given joint

[1] *Rot. Litt. Pat.*, pp. 72b, 80b, 87, 88b; *Pipe Roll 10 John*, pp. 50–51; *Pipe Roll 11 John*, p. 112.

[2] *Pipe Roll 13 John*, pp. 186–7; *Pipe Roll 14 John*, pp. 2–3.

[3] Kent, Gloucester, Northumberland, Devon, and Oxfordshire.

[4] *Pipe Roll 2 John*, p. 14; *Pipe Roll 3 John*, p. 99.

[5] *Pipe Roll 2 John*, p. 20.

charge of the important castle of Chinon, where he was captured in 1206.[1] After he had settled his ransom, part of which at least was paid by the King,[2] he was made custodian of the bishopric of Durham, along with Aymer, Archdeacon of Durham, in April 1209.[3] In August 1212 these two, along with William de Warenne, were made sheriffs of Northumberland. Philip of Oldcotes was the most active figure in this combination. During the civil war he played a role analogous to that of Brian de Lisle farther south. By the opening of the next reign he was considered suitable for the seneschalship of Poitou, scarcely the most cushioned of thirteenth-century appointments.

Philip was associated in the defence of Chinon with Hubert de Burgh, another close associate of John's who was now rapidly rising as a power in the land. He had small hereditary possessions in Norfolk and Suffolk.[4] In 1201 he was warden of the Welsh Marshes,[5] a year later he was given the custody of the castles of Launceston and Wallingford along with the county of Berkshire,[6] and in 1203 and 1204 he appears as Constable of Chinon.[7] Like Philip of Oldcotes, he was captured there and after his release came home to take over the shrievalty of Lincolnshire. He retained this office until 1213, although it is probable that as his other interests and duties multiplied, more and more of his shrieval duties fell on his deputy, Robert Aguillon. Hubert was on the way to the highest secular office in the land and the earldom of Kent. For the time being he might escape the charges which were being brought against the foreigners. But he was, like them, a *parvenu*; he faced similar charges in the end.

The administration which John had established in the northern counties by 1209 was very different from that which had existed earlier. Of the sheriffs of the early years, only one remained, Robert fitz Roger in Northumberland. There had been not so much a change as a revolution in personnel. Of the new sheriffs, Roger de Lacy, Gilbert fitz Reinfrey of Kendal, and Hugh de Neville, the Chief Forester, would have fitted easily into the established pattern of local administration. But Philip Mark, Robert de Vieuxpont, Hubert de Burgh, Philip of Oldcotes, and

---

[1] *Rot. Norm.*, p. 85; *Rot. Litt. Pat.*, p. 40b.
[3] *Rot. Litt. Pat.*, p. 91.
[5] *Hoveden*, iv. 163.
[7] Ibid., p. 40b; *Rot. Norm.*, p. 85.

[2] *Rot. Litt. Claus.* i. 82b.
[4] *Close Rolls 1231–4*, p. 443.
[6] *Rot. Litt. Pat.*, pp. 9, 11.

Brian de Lisle were a marked intrusion, a dangerous and unpleasant novelty to the established landed interests in the counties,
dangerous because they could survive only if they were efficient,
and unpleasant because their rapid advancement was an offence
to established families of good position with traditions of service
to the Angevin and Norman kings.[1]

Novi homines, of course, were always appearing on the political
scene. The most respected of the English baronage at this time,
William Marshal, was himself one. Yet the Marshal's line of
advancement had been different in that he typified the social con-
ventions of the time. He was almost too good to be true. Further,
there was a large number of John's new officials. While it was
usual for a few *parvenus* to attain high office, a press of them was
intolerable. New men, too, were associated with new and unpopular measures. The administrative changes of the middle years
of the reign coincided with renewed efforts to raise the annual
yield of the counties;[2] in the years 1209–10, when Gilbert fitz
Reinfrey took over the shrievalty, Yorkshire yielded profits of
over £700. There was another disturbing feature. The threatened monopoly was of the most dangerous kind, that exercised
by a co-ordinated group. John's new men were not isolated
individuals, but a clique, that of the *familia regis* and the royal
household.[3] Hubert de Burgh had been in John's household when
he was Count of Mortain; he is described as his Chamberlain in
1198,[4] and he continued to hold this office after his master's
succession.[5] Brian de Lisle ended the reign as the King's Seneschal.[6]
Philip of Oldcotes on occasions bore a sword ceremonially before

---

[1] It may be convenient here to list the northern shrievalties between 1204 and
1213. They were as follows:

Nottinghamshire and Derbyshire: 1204–8, Robert de Vieuxpont; 1208–9, Gerard
d'Athée; 1209–24, Philip Mark.
Lincolnshire: 1199–1205, Gerard de Camville; 1205–8, Thomas of Moulton;
1208–13, Hubert de Burgh.
Yorkshire: 1204–9, Roger de Lacy; 1209–13, Gilbert fitz Reinfrey.
Northumberland: 1200–12, Robert fitz Roger; 1212–20, Philip of Oldcotes, in
the first year with William de Warenne and Aymer, Archdeacon of Durham.
Cumberland: 1204–9, Roger de Lacy; 1209–13, Hugh de Neville.
Lancaster: 1200–4, Richard de Vernon; 1204–15, Gilbert fitz Reinfrey.

[2] See above, pp. 152–6.
[3] See J. E. A. Jolliffe, *Angevin Kingship*, pp. 146–7 and 166 ff., especially 178.
[4] *Cal. Docs., France*, i, nos. 565, 873; *Ancient Charters prior to A.D. 1200* (Pipe
Roll Society), p. 110.   [5] *Rot. Litt. Claus*. i. 33.
[6] *Rot. Litt. Pat.*, p. 164.

King John.[1] Gilbert fitz Reinfrey, Roger de Lacy, Robert de Vieuxpont, Robert fitz Roger, Hugh de Neville were all deep in the King's counsels and might be involved at different times in military or administrative duties unconnected with their shrievalties. In dealing with these men, the baronage and gentry were faced not simply with local officials, but with men of wide experience and great skill, who had direct, continuous and confidential access to the King. It would be difficult to create that happy understanding between sheriff and local landowner which could make medieval government both profitable to the one and genial to the other.

These changes were accompanied by a hardening of the King's relations with his tenants-in-chief. As the reign proceeded, it became increasingly difficult for established men to acquire a favoured position among the King's familiars. The path followed earlier by Roger de Lacy, for example, became more and more difficult to find and in the end was entirely lost. An important stage in this was reached with the settlement between John and Ranulf of Chester, which followed the latter's threatened defection and the death of Earl Robert of Leicester in 1205.[2] Henceforth Ranulf and his brother-in-law William de Ferrers, Earl of Derby, along with William de Warenne, provided the main support for the King and his officials in the northern counties. Little was done to reinforce them from the northern aristocracy. John de Lacy in 1213 and John fitz Robert in 1212 succeeded to their fathers' lands, but not to the positions of trust which Roger de Lacy and Robert fitz Roger had held. John was now trying to strengthen his hold on the north by the introduction of men like Peter de Maulay and William de Fors. Such measures could only widen the gap between the local aristocracy on the one hand, and the King's officials and friends on the other. The King might acquire support which was not of his own creating, as he did apparently from Hugh de Balliol after 1212; some individuals, most obviously Robert de Ros, might vainly try to bridge the gap; but the monopoly of office and of the royal favour had come to be more limited and exclusive, and the King's government, as a result, more and more open to attack.

If the King was not disposed to break this monopoly, neither were those who enjoyed his favour, especially those who owed

---

[1] *Memorials of Bury*, ii. 95–96.   [2] See above, pp. 204–6.

their advancement entirely to him. They might enjoy great offices, they might be loaded with wardships, custodies, and money fees, but it was rare for them to be granted hereditary lordships of any great importance. Most of these men could be deprived of the offices, revenues, and custodies they enjoyed at a nod. Sometimes, when they fastened on to something more solid and permanent, special arrangements might be made. Robert de Vieuxpont, for example, acquired Westmorland as a lordship by degrees and subject to conditions. Although he ceased to account at the Exchequer for his custody of the county after Michaelmas 1202, it was not until 28 October 1203 that he was granted the hereditary lordship.[1] Letters patent ordering the tenants of the lordship to do homage to Robert were not made out until March 1205.[2] Meanwhile Robert had to undertake that he would not use or show to anyone the charter recording the grant of 1203 as long as the King lived, unless with the King's consent.[3] John was clearly unwilling to cut the traces. Robert, and still more Philip Mark or Brian de Lisle or Philip of Oldcotes, had little alternative to loyalty. If John was committed to them, they were equally committed to him.

Their relations with the King, however, were not completely subservient. They must have been ambitious, they were making careers, they wanted rewards, they expected to profit from office. There was still the conflict between the sheriff and the King's financial officers in the Chamber or across the green cloth of the Exchequer. Moreover, John sometimes made experiments which failed and which required alteration. Robert de Vieuxpont, for example, was overburdened. By 1207 his offices included the custodies of Nottinghamshire and Derbyshire, the honours of Peverel and Tickhill, the archbishopric of York and the bishopric of Durham. Robert quickly ran into difficulties in presenting a proper reckoning. In February 1208 he agreed to render £100 as annual 'profit' on the two shires, but the King had to grant him delay in presenting his accounts.[4] In the following December Robert offered 4,000 m. for the King's benevolence on the understanding that he should surrender Whinfell forest, which was part of his Westmorland lordship, and the Nottinghamshire barony of Doun Bardolf of which he had had custody since 1205. He also

---

[1] See above, p. 221.
[2] *Rot. Litt. Pat.*, p. 51b.
[3] *H.M.C. Wells MSS.* ii. 549.
[4] *Rot. Litt. Claus.* i. 104b, 111b.

had to present a reasonable account of his custody of Nottingham-shire, Derbyshire, the archbishopric of York and the bishopric of Durham. Regulations were laid down for future accounts and it is probable that Robert had to surrender his nephew as a pledge of his good behaviour.[1] He paid 1,000 m. of his proffer into the Chamber. The remaining 3,000 m. were pardoned,[2] but Robert's wings were clipped. He lost control of Peverel, Tickhill, and the two shires after Michaelmas 1208, and Durham and York had been removed from his charge by the following spring.[3] Hence-forth his activities in the north were more strictly confined to the Border.[4]

Differences of this kind were always liable to arise. Brian de Lisle's relations with the King passed at times through periods of unease. In 1207 he had to proffer £100 for the King's benevo-lence.[5] In 1209 he was suddenly and unaccountably deprived of his offices.[6] Whatever was the trouble he must have come to heel quickly, for he accounted at the Exchequer for most of them at the end of the year and continued to enjoy them later.[7] In 1212 Hugh de Neville, also, was in difficulties. He proffered 6,000 m. for the benevolence of the King. Among other things, he had allowed two prisoners to escape, a delinquency to which John was usually very sensitive. In return for his proffer he was ac-quitted of all his accounts for the forest up to All Saints Day 1212; he was given severe terms, but then pardoned 1,000 m.[8] The real significance of these cases, as of Robert de Vieuxpont's, lay in the ease with which John was able to impose and maintain discipline. In the last resort these men would meekly accept his control because he had made them what they were. In the civil war there were defections among them, especially when Prince Louis's fortunes stood high in the summer of 1216. But on the whole they

---

[1] *Pipe Roll 10 John*, p. 45; *Rot. Chartarum*, p. 184. Robert's nephew was in the custody of William de Beauchamp in Mar. 1209 (*Rot. Litt. Pat.*, p. 89b).

[2] *Pipe Roll 10 John*, p. 45.

[3] The two shires were transferred to Gerard d'Athée and Philip Mark, Peverel and the archbishopric of York to Brian de Lisle, Durham to Aymer, Archdeacon of Durham, and Philip of Oldcotes, Tickhill to John of Bassingborn.

[4] He was, however, sheriff of Devonshire from 1209 to 1215 and of Wiltshire from 1210 to 1212.   [5] *Pipe Roll 9 John*, p. 28.

[6] *Rot. Litt. Pat.*, p. 89.   [7] *Pipe Roll 11 John*, pp. 14–15, 112.

[8] *Pipe Roll 14 John*, pp. 157–8. See also *Patent Rolls 1225–32*, p. 247, where there is also a reference to a fine of 1,000 m. which Hugh made because he had permitted the enclosure of the park of Taunton without the King's permission.

remained a co-ordinated if somewhat quarrelsome group in support of John until the end. That John expected this, that he was
entirely dependent on this, is demonstrated by the ferocity with
which he punished the few renegades when they came within his
grasp. Among his northern sheriffs there was only one, Gilbert
fitz Reinfrey. When Gilbert made his peace with his angry master
in January 1216, he had to face far harsher terms than those imposed on ordinary rebels. These involved a fine of 12,000 m.[1]
After John's death he wrote plaintively to the Justiciar complaining that he was unable to meet the severe terms of payment of
2,000 m. a year which had been imposed, even if he were to sell
his land or mortgage it for the remainder of his life. The most he
could offer was 300 m. a year.[2] On Gilbert's death, his son,
William of Lancaster, was so impoverished that he could not make
the outlay to go south to do homage to the young King Henry.[3]
John clearly intended Gilbert and his family to regret what he
had done.

There were, therefore, few weaknesses in the administrative team
which John had created. The most obvious ones in 1215 were
those which he had been forced to create himself, after the plot of
1212, or following the settlement at Runnymede, by the rejection
of his own men in favour of others who would not arouse so
much local opposition. In the event, during the civil war, Robert
de Vieuxpont, Philip of Oldcotes, Brian de Lisle, and Philip
Mark, supported by other household men who were just beginning to acquire local office, like Geoffrey de Neville, Hubert de
Burgh's successor as Chamberlain, together constituted such
royal government as still existed. They had few, if any, interests
outside the north; they had long experience of northern conditions; they had local financial resources in the castle treasures of
Nottingham and Knaresborough; they could, if necessary, carry
on by themselves, with little supervision or direction. John might
be thankful for the support of an earl of Chester or Derby, but
it was the men of his own making who really ensured his political
survival and the acceptance of his son after his death.

To an increasingly disaffected baronage, John's agents and
supporters were one of the main targets for attack. They were
responsible, in the first place, for applying and abetting harsh

[1] See above, p. 137.
[2] P.R.O., Ancient Correspondence, i, no. 92.   [3] Ibid., no. 135.

policies. If in addition to this, if they were to profit from their offices they were likely to incur charges of extortion. In 1213 the King tried to meet the rising storm of protest by removing three of his northern sheriffs and ordering investigations into the activities of two of them.[1] It is difficult to grasp the exact nature of these complaints or the details of shrieval misbehaviour. There is nothing in the north equivalent to the storm aroused by Gerard d'Athée and Engelard de Cigogné in the west. As in their more notorious case, such evidence as the post-war judicial proceedings revealed pointed more to administrative irregularities than to maltreatment of the men in their charge. The former rather than the latter was still the chief concern of royal justices.[2] The clearest evidence of these northern eyres lies against Gilbert fitz Reinfrey in Yorkshire, one of the men, significantly enough, who were investigated in 1213. In 1219 he was found to have committed numerous misdemeanours. He had made hardly any attachments of those who had been appealed as breakers of the peace.[3] As this suggests, he had certainly been accepting bribes.[4] He had also been peculiarly interested in the chattels of condemned felons. In over fifty cases these had come into his own hands and remained there without any further account.[5] There could be little wonder that although Gilbert's proffer of 12,000 m. in 1216 was taken as cancelling his private debts at the Exchequer, King John stipulated that he was still accountable for the offices he had held.[6]

Peccadilloes such as Gilbert's were probably quite common. The eyre of 1218–19 also revealed that Brian de Lisle had retained escheated chattels.[7] Several of the old King's officials failed to come before the justices to answer for their custodies.[8] One, Robert Aguillon, who had been deputy to Hubert de Burgh in

---

[1] See above, pp. 85–86.

[2] For the evidence against Gerard d'Athée see *The Pleas of the Crown for the county of Gloucester, A.D. 1221*, ed. F. W. Maitland, pp. xiv, xvii, and *The Rolls of the Justices in Eyre for the counties of Gloucestershire, Warwickshire and Staffordshire, 1221–2* (Selden Society), pp. lxiii–lxv. For further discussion see C. J. Turner, 'The Minority of Henry III', *T.R.H.S.*, N.S. xviii. 250–4.

[3] *Rolls of the Justices in Eyre for Yorkshire, 1218–19*, nos. 637, 835.

[4] Ibid., no. 944.   [5] Ibid., *passim.*

[6] *Rot. de Ob. et Fin.*, p. 570.

[7] *Rolls of the Justices in Eyre for Yorkshire, 1218–19*, nos. 754, 762, 766, 796, 829.

[8] Ibid., nos. 429, 1096. Gilbert fitz Reinfrey, Peter fitz Herbert, the sheriff of Yorkshire in 1214–15, William fitz Ralf, the custodian of Pickering in 1214, and the Constable of Chester, were all named. The last was probably John de Lacy who was baronial sheriff of Yorkshire for a time during the civil war.

Lincolnshire in 1213, was put in mercy for his default.[1] But there were more serious malpractices where local interests were affected, and in these cases memories were long. As late as 1263 it was recorded that Philip of Oldcotes, as sheriff of Northumberland, had prevented Nicholas of Byker, chief royal sergeant between Tyne and Coquet, from exercising his hereditary right to appoint and dismiss all bailiffs in this area.[2] In Nottinghamshire at about the same time it was reported that Philip Mark, now dead for nearly thirty years, had accepted an annual fee of £5 from the burgesses of Nottingham in return for his good will and the maintenance of their liberties.[3] In the later years of John's reign and on into the minority of Henry, Philip's conduct of his shrievalty included robbery, false arrest, unjust disseisin, and persistent attacks on local landed interests, both secular and ecclesiastical. Ralf of Greasley, Roger de Montbegon, Robert de Neville, the Earl of Derby, Matilda de Caux, the monks of the house of Grosmont near Whitby all clashed with Philip on different issues. The civil war, Magna Carta, the death of some of the Poitevins, and the exile of others seem to have made no difference at all to the energy with which he pursued his interest and advancement. He was as zealous, thrustful, and dangerous under Henry as he was under John. For fifteen years, on to 1224, when he finally lost his shrievalty, he envenomed the local politics of Nottinghamshire and Derbyshire.[4]

The increasing unpopularity of Philip and his colleagues was not all of their own doing. The King and his financial agents in the Chamber and Exchequer drove them on. Further, as the King accumulated escheats and custodies, these men were placed in positions in which they enjoyed more immediate control than that which a sheriff normally had. By the later years of the reign vast estates of this type were in the Crown's hands. To the usual northern custodies of Peverel and Tickhill were now added the archbishopric of York, the bishoprics of Durham and Lincoln, the abbey of Whitby, and, among secular estates, Knaresborough, Boroughbridge, and, in 1211–13, the estates of Roger de Lacy. Apart from Peverel and Tickhill none of these lands were farmed.

---

[1] *Rolls of the Justices in Eyre for Lincolnshire 1218–19 and Worcestershire 1221*, no. 204.
[2] *Cal. Inq.*, P.M. i, no. 465.
[3] *Cal. Inq.*, *Misc.* i, no. 256.
[4] J. C. Holt, 'Philip Mark and the Shrievalty of Nottinghamshire and Derbyshire', *Transactions of the Thoroton Society*, lvi (1952), 18 ff.

They were in the charge of custodians who were held to account
for their total yield and they were exploited directly and severely.
The first account for the lands of William de Stuteville, for
example, contained large sales of corn and stock.[1] In later years
the tenants of Knaresborough suffered from the enforcement of
the forest law,[2] and the steadily falling revenues which Brian de
Lisle returned may reflect a deliberate policy of 'wasting'.[3]
Similar policies were followed when Roger de Lacy's lands came
into royal custody in 1211. They were immediately tallaged to the
tune of £330, and sales of corn and stock yielded nearly £200.[4]
But all this seems comparatively mild by the side of the treatment
meted out to the men of Durham. Here were wider fields and
greater possibilities. The first years of the royal custody saw a
detailed inquiry into the knight services of the bishopric.[5] In 1211
the custodians accounted for over £200 for the tallage of manors,
and nearly £360 for pleas and perquisites. In the same account
fines for marriages and to hold assarts came to nearly £200, and
735 m. was received from the knights of St. Cuthbert for a confirmation of their privileges.[6] By Michaelmas 1211 the custody of
the bishopric over a period of three years and two and a half
months had yielded nearly £16,800 and even this figure excluded
vast amounts of corn which had been put to the King's immediate
use.[7] Among the tenants of the bishopric we may note Eustace
de Vesci, Richard de Percy, Peter de Brus, and Roger Bertram.[8]
By 1215 they had old scores to settle with the custodian, Philip
of Oldcotes. Indeed the King's administration of many northern
escheats had been such that, when the time came, the tenants of
these lands were predisposed to rebellion.[9]

In causing the quarrel, the position of these men was just as
important as the measures they had to enforce. Office was more
than an administrative post; it was also an estate, and this estate
was coming to be confined to a small group. Men outside this
favoured clique might be used on diplomatic errands, as justices,

---

[1] *Pipe Roll 5 John*, pp. 222–3.

[2] *Pipe Roll 8 John*, p. 218; *Pipe Roll 9 John*, p. 125.

[3] In 1206 the gross revenues of the estate amounted to nearly £540 (*Pipe Roll
8 John*, pp. 217–18). In the next two years they fell to £340–£350 (*Pipe Roll 9 John*,
pp. 125–6; *Pipe Roll 10 John*, p. 50), and in 1209 and 1210 they stood at under £220
and £260 respectively (*Pipe Roll 11 John*, p. 14; *Pipe Roll 12 John*, p. 135).

[4] *Pipe Roll 14 John*, pp. 3–4.   [5] *Book of Fees*, pp. 23–31.

[6] *Rot. Chartarum*, p. 182.   [7] *Pipe Roll 13 John*, pp. 35 ff.

[8] *Book of Fees*, pp. 24, 25, 26, 28.   [9] See above, pp. 47–49.

or as assessors of taxes. Occasionally they held custodies. Peter de Brus farmed the wapentake of Langbargh; he had had to pay heavily for its custody.[1] Robert de Vaux farmed Pickering and several other Yorkshire manors,[2] only to lose them before he was imprisoned in 1211. Thomas of Moulton's brief flight as sheriff of Lincolnshire ended equally disastrously. Apart from these far from happy instances, it was not until 1213 that there was any hope that the administrative monopoly would be broken, and the breach only occurred then as an enforced and temporary concession. To many great northern families this monopoly must have seemed not just an insult but a denial of the natural order. Nicholas de Stuteville could look back on the service which his brother William and father Robert had given the Angevins, John de Lacy and John fitz Robert more immediately on the intimacy between their fathers and King John. More distantly, Eustace de Vesci's father had been one of the great northern sheriffs of Henry II's reign. Eustace's descent went back in two generations as John de Lacy's did in four, to Eustace fitz John. Robert de Ros's great grandmother was a sister and co-heiress of Walter Espec. Through her he inherited Espec's great castle of Wark. Robert and Eustace might well feel that they had claims on office superior to those of a Robert de Vieuxpont or a Philip of Oldcotes. A king could ignore such claims perhaps, in his own excessive confidence of desperation, but only at his peril.

There was a more material side of the problem. As an estate, office yielded profits and benefits to the holder. Just how much it yielded is now, as it certainly was then, a well-kept secret. The records of Exchequer and Chamber cannot reveal facts which of their very nature were withheld. But we can, like John, have very strong suspicions. When Roger de Lacy offered 200 m. a year as a fine for the 'profits' of Yorkshire, he was offering between 20 and 25 per cent. of what the 'profits' were shown to be as soon as he left office.[3] The King's officials often presented accounts for what were then very large sums of money. When they fell into the King's displeasure they were peculiarly able to pay the pecuniary impositions which resulted; indeed, the amercement imposed on Robert de Vieuxpont in 1208 looks very much like a composition for his accounts; that imposed on Hugh de Neville in 1212

---

[1] See above, pp. 172, 180.　　　　　　[2] *Pipe Roll 13 John*, pp. 44–45.
[3] See above, p. 154.

certainly was.[1] They were also peculiarly able to exploit the financial difficulties of others who did not enjoy the opportunities which office gave. When pressed, they were able to offer large sums to stave off investigations into their activities. In 1208, when retiring from the shrievalty of Herefordshire, Walter de Clifford offered 1,000 m. to avoid any inquiries into his exactions in the county.[2] When Roger de Lacy died in 1211 his steward, Robert Walensis, who had acted as Roger's deputy as sheriff of Yorkshire, offered 1,000 m. that he should not be troubled to render account for his stewardship. Knights could not normally dispose of such large sums. Six other men of Roger's made smaller proffers of the same kind.[3] In Yorkshire, in Roger's time, there seems to have been a hierarchy of administrative and financial malpractice. Whatever its extent, those excluded from such positions of trust and opportunity no doubt exaggerated it.

But if the financial benefits enjoyed by the King's agents were in the last resort unknown, there were other fields in which their advantage could be appraised more exactly. With office and the King's favour went the prizes of medieval politics, the wealthy heiress, the profitable wardship, the well-endowed widow, and the custody of abbeys and bishoprics. These gilded fortunes, like Roger de Lacy's, which were already golden, or gave substance to the position of a Philip Mark or a Brian de Lisle. To follow the King's men through the records of the Chancery is to follow a trail of fortunate marriages, of grants made or proffers accepted in their favour. Robert de Vieuxpont married Idonea, heiress of John de Busli, an important tenant of the honour of Tickhill. Through her he pressed claims to the honour itself.[4] In the early years of the reign he was making an enviable collection of wardships, the most important being the barony of Doun Bardolf which consisted of twenty-five fees in Nottinghamshire,

---

[1] See above, pp. 226–7. [2] *Pipe Roll 10 John*, p. 191.
[3] *Pipe Roll 13 John*, pp. 33–34. Lady Stenton takes a different view of these proffers in that she does not relate them to Roger's tenure of the shrievalty of Yorkshire (ibid., p. xxxiii).
[4] *Rolls of the Justices in Eyre for Yorkshire, 1218–19*, p. xxiv. Lady Stenton here follows Dugdale in stating that John de Busli was lord of Tickhill, but this was not the case. John represented a junior branch of the Buslis of Tickhill which held six fees of the honour and had a claim to the whole of it after the extinction of direct descendants in the elder line. Robert and Idonea tried to recover it from the holder, the Countess of Eu, at the beginning of the reign of Henry III. See J. Hunter, *South Yorkshire*, i. 225–8, 261–2, and *Rotuli de Dominabus*, ed. J. H. Round, p. 12 n.

Derbyshire, and Lincolnshire.[1] In 1209 he offered 500 m. and five palfreys for the custody of the land and heirs of William fitz Ranulf and the marriage of the heirs and widow.[2] In this instance some of the scheming behind the transaction can be appreciated. It gave Robert temporary control of the Greystoke fee in Yorkshire and Cumberland.[3] The sum was nicely calculated to his own long-term advantage for the Cumberland estates alone were valued at £50 per annum in 1219. He ended by marrying his daughter to the heir.[4]

All this was typical enough. If the barony of Doun Bardolf was not being used to bolster the fortunes of Robert de Vieuxpont, then it was being used to reinforce the hand of Philip Mark, along with the lands of other Nottinghamshire wards, including Andrew Luterel and the heir of Robert of Muskham.[5] If the Fossard inheritance, admittedly somewhat depleted now, was not being passed by marriage to one *curialis*, Robert of Thornham, then it was to another, Peter de Maulay. Such ventures were outside the range of most local men; the Fossard lands yielded over £400 in the hands of royal custodians in 1212,[6] and Peter proffered 7,000 m. for the hand of the heiress, Isabel of Thornham.[7] The King's friends, in contrast, basked in the sunny atmosphere of his beneficence. Roger de Lacy was able to recover twenty fees which Guy de Laval, a Norman, had held of his honour of Pontefract;[8] he also obtained custody of the lands and heirs of Richard de Muntfichet.[9] William Briwerre held the wardships of Roger

---

[1] *Rot. Litt. Claus.* i. 20b. Robert's other custodies included the heirs and widow of Hugh son of Gernagon, who held one fee of Gilbert de Gant in Hunmanby, Yorks., and 3½ fees of the honour of Richmond (*Rot. Lib.*, p. 66; *Rot. Chartarum*, p. 120b; *Early Yorks. Charters*, ii. 430; v. 40–43, 57). This was obtained in 1203; in 1205 the widow, Matilda, daughter of Torphin, assigned her dower in Carthorpe, Yorks., to Robert. In 1204 Robert obtained the custody of the heirs of Richard of Sherrington, who had held two fees in chief of the Crown (*Rot. Chartarum*, p. 120b; *Pipe Roll 2 Richard I*, p. 143; *Pipe Roll 4 John*, p. 28; *Red Book of the Exchequer*, pp. 71, 314), and the marriage of Helen, widow of Hugh of Hastings, daughter and heiress of Alan son of Torphin, who held land of the Crown in Yorkshire and estates in Westmorland (*Rot. de Ob. et Fin.*, p. 215; *Early Yorks. Charters*, i. 113–14; 301–4, 312; *V.C.H. North Riding*, ii. 421). In 1205 Robert acquired the custody of the widow and heirs of William de London of Tynelawe, who held by sergeanty of the honour of Tickhill (*Rot. Chartarum*, p. 156b; *Book of Fees*, pp. 33, 352).

[2] *Pipe Roll 11 John*, p. 96.   [3] *Early Yorks. Charters*, ii. 507.

[4] *Book of Fees*, p. 265.

[5] *Rot. Litt. Claus.* i. 120; *Book of Fees*, pp. 287, 358.

[6] *Pipe Roll 14 John*, pp. 5–6.   [7] *Pipe Roll 16 John*, p. 94.

[8] *Pipe Roll 4 John*, p. 65. Roger de Lacy had made claim to these lands as early as 1199 (*Early Yorks. Charters*, iii. 198–200; *Rot. Litt. Pat.*, p. 26; *Rot. de Ob. et Fin.*, p. 26).   [9] *Pipe Roll 5 John*, p. 132.

Bertram of Mitford, William de Percy, and Joanna, daughter of
Hugh de Morville, of Burgh by Sands.[1] He married a nephew to
Joanna de Morville and a daughter to William de Percy. Gilbert
fitz Reinfrey obtained the custody of Oliver de Aincurt for a time
and of the heir of Theobald Walter,[2] Robert fitz Roger that of the
Crammaville barony of Whalton in Northumberland,[3] Philip of
Oldcotes that of the land of Sewal fitz Henry in Northumberland
and Andrew de Fougères in Yorkshire,[4] and Brian de Lisle
acquired revenues in Nottinghamshire and estates held of the
honour of Leicester.[5] This was the time and the way to make
fortunes. The King not only permitted but encouraged it. The
greater the reward, the better the service. It is well to remember
the words with which he was said to have addressed the Marshal:

> 'Ge ne voil mie deservir
> Q'os ne m'aiez de quei servir,
> Quer bien sai, comme puis avreiz
> Que mielz e mielz me servirez.'[6]

These phrases embody one of the great informing principles of
John's government of England.

The King's friends may have argued that these prizes were open
to men outside their own circle, if they could pay, and that their
own service and loyalty might reasonably be taken as decreasing
or cancelling the cost. There was point in this, for reward for
service was a mark of good lordship. Moreover, the stream of
royal favour was often tapped by those willing to gamble and
take a risk, and many men were only too ready for this. But it
required the co-operation of the King; only if he was willing
would such proffers be accepted. Favours were his to bestow, or
withhold, or sell. When he was faced with the enormous problem
of administering monastic lands during the Interdict, he gave to
certain lords custody of the abbeys and benefices of their fee and
advowson.[7] In the northern counties grants of this kind were

---

[1] *Rot. Chartarum*, p. 48b; *Rot. Litt. Claus.* i. 10b, 11.

[2] *Rot. de Ob. et Fin.*, p. 215; *Rot. Litt. Pat.*, pp. 59b, 110b.

[3] P.R.O., Cartae Antiquae Rolls, 25/36; *Rot. Litt. Claus.* i. 35b; *Book of Fees*, p. 200.

[4] *Book of Fees*, pp. 204, 248, 265; *Early Yorks. Charters*, ii. 14.

[5] *Roll. Litt. Claus.* i. 105b; *Book of Fees*, pp. 20, 151.

[6] *Histoire de Guillaume le Maréchal*, lines 12963–6.

[7] C. R. Cheney, 'King John and the Papal Interdict', *Bulletin of the John Rylands
Library*, xxxi (1948), 303–5; 'King John's reaction to the Interdict in England',
T.R.H.S. 4th series, xxxi (1949), 129 ff.

made to Roger de Lacy,[1] Robert fitz Roger,[2] Gilbert fitz Reinfrey,[3] Hugh de Neville,[4] Ranulf of Chester[5] and William de Warenne.[6] Only one man not fully within the court and official circle received the same privilege. He, characteristically enough, was Robert de Ros.[7] We may well speculate on the feelings of William de Mowbray, whose family had founded Newburgh and Byland, and of Peter de Brus whose ancestor had founded Guisborough, or of Richard de Percy who could see the family house of Whitby under the control of Gilbert fitz Reinfrey, in whose hands it was returning a gross yield of over £200 a year.[8]

This kind of bias in royal action was not exceptional. It might appear in simple proffers for land and privilege. In 1211 Robert de Ros concluded a long struggle for the possession of the manor of Market Weighton with a proffer to the King. He inherited a Trussebut claim to this estate, a claim which was strong enough for the heirs general of the Trussebuts to attempt recovery in the royal court in 1204.[9] The sitting tenant, Henry de Puiset, son of the great Bishop Hugh of Durham,[10] proved too influential, and the way for Robert was only opened by Henry's death in 1211. He now got half the manor on the proffer of 500 m.[11] The other half went to one of the King's familiars, Peter fitz Herbert, who may also have had a claim, but, if so, a very tenuous one which he never seems to have pursued at law.[12] He too offered 500 m. Then his offer, but not Robert de Ros's, was pardoned.[13] This was blatant, even as it is recorded in the bare phrases of the rolls.

Litigation was another wide sphere of private action in which royal influence could be brought to bear. The courts were the king's, the justice dispensed there was his; prior to 1215 and even afterwards he could influence the course of justice within

---

[1] *Rot. Litt. Claus.* i. 112. [2] Ibid. i. 109b. [3] Ibid. i. 111b.
[4] Ibid. i. 111. [5] Ibid. i. 113.
[6] Ibid. i. 112b; *Curia Regis Rolls*, v. 174. [7] Ibid. i. 111b.
[8] *Pipe Roll 14 John*, p. 5. It is relevant to note that Whitby had been under the patronage of the Crown since the later years of Henry II (Susan Wood, *English Monasteries and their Patrons*, Oxford, 1955, p. 99, n. 6).
[9] *Rolls of the Justices in Eyre for Yorkshire 1218–19*, no. 1151; *Curia Regis Rolls*, iii. 113, 148; *Early Yorks. Charters*, x. 14–16.
[10] Hugh apparently bought the manor for Henry in 1176 (*Gesta Henrici*, i. 160–1; *Pipe Roll 22 Henry II*, p. 100). [11] *Pipe Roll 13 John*, p. 29.
[12] In 1133 Henry I granted the church of Market Weighton to the see of York as a prebend for William fitz Herbert, younger son of Herbert the Chamberlain, from whom Peter fitz Herbert was descended (*Early Yorks. Charters*, i. 120–1).
[13] *Pipe Roll 13 John*, pp. 29–30.

wide limits. We may doubt whether William de Stuteville would have won his famous action against William de Mowbray without King John's support, or whether he would even have begun it without the King's encouragement.[1] Intervention by the King played an equally important part in the litigation between William, Earl of Salisbury, and Henry de Bohun, over the honour of Trowbridge, and, with a less clear political slant, in the disputes between Geoffrey de Say, father and son, and Geoffrey fitz Peter and his sons over the Mandeville inheritance.[2] These cases must have acquired some notoriety. Less obvious to contemporaries, but perhaps more infuriating in the long run, was the differential treatment meted out at the Exchequer. During the last Norman campaigns, and again in the last years of the reign, service to the King was frequently rewarded by the remission of debts. These benefits naturally went to the King's friends first, and secondly to those who seemed to be, or might become, his friends. Their proffers were frequently pardoned, their misdemeanours and the resulting amercements forgiven. Only when a William de Braose proved refractory, or a Gilbert fitz Reinfrey deserted the fold, were these men harried. John might discipline them strictly at times. But, while he deprived Robert de Vieuxpont of his shrievalties and custodies, he left him with his lordship of Westmorland, and while he demanded 4,000 m. from Robert for his benevolence, he pardoned three-quarters of this sum. This was very different treatment from that meted out to Thomas of Moulton and Robert de Vaux. There was no similar pardon for them.

This personal bias in the operations of government must have been as obvious then as it is now. John's letters, indeed, asserted as a principle that it was right to treat his supporters better than his enemies.[3] Those excluded from favour, however, or those who received the worst of John's attentions, did not always need to look to the Exchequer, the King's court, the stream of royal grants, or even the royal dinner table, to appreciate this point. It was impressed upon them sometimes in a much more telling way. The financial advantages of the official and the royal familiar were such that he could buy land, snap up mortgages, and sometimes, we may suspect, play the part of the local usurer. What

---

[1] See above, p. 172.   [2] S. Painter, *The Reign of King John*, pp. 262–3.
[3] *Rot. Litt. Claus*. i. 87.

these men got from the royal favour and what others lost could be measured by the fact that they were buyers and creditors while others were sellers and debtors, that they were able to buy and lend because of their favoured position, while others were sometimes compelled to sell or borrow because of some special act of harshness by the King, or because they had gambled on obtaining the royal favour and had lost. When the King had finished with a man, he was ready for plucking by the King's friends.

Operations of this kind may often lie hidden. We can never know how many simply bore fruit in a perfectly normal grant or charter of enfeoffment. Even so, it was clearly a popular and profitable activity in which many of John's agents engaged. Philip Mark first acquired property in Eaton as security for a loan of 100 m. which he had made to a certain Peter Marshal. He held the property with the consent of the chief lord of the fee, the Bishop of Coventry. When the mesne lord, Robert de Neville, challenged his title, he obtained his consent too, at the cost of a further 20 m.[1] Gilbert fitz Reinfrey was engaged in similar transactions. In 1211 he paid 100 m. to Thomas of Middleton to assist him in paying his debts to the Jews. In return, Thomas gave Gilbert his land in Middleton and Kneeton, Yorkshire, for his homage and fealty and the yearly render of 1 lb. of cumin.[2] In 1208 the forest justices imposed an amercement of £100 on Ranulf de Sules, one of Gilbert's Westmorland tenants, for having venison in his possession.[3] He did not pay, and his land in Newby was taken into the King's hands. Gilbert then acquired it with a proffer of 5 palfreys.[4] The manor was still in his hands ten years later.[5]

In Westmorland, Robert de Vieuxpont's acquisition of the honour was the signal for a territorial revolution in which he set about accumulating demesne estates. His energies are witnessed in a series of charters in which tenants of the honour made lands over to him.[6] He bought the vill of Langton from Ada, daughter of John Taillebois, at the cost of 20 m.,[7] and the wood of Sandford and land in the same village from Robert of Sandford at the cost of 10 m. and a horse.[8] Walter de Morville surrendered land in

[1] J. C. Holt, 'Philip Mark and the Shrievalty of Nottinghamshire and Derbyshire', loc. cit., p. 20.   [2] *Pipe Roll 13 John*, p. 49.
[3] *Pipe Roll 10 John*, p. 55.   [4] *Pipe Roll 11 John*, p. 16.
[5] *Book of Fees*, p. 265.
[6] Bodleian Library, Dodsworth MS. 70, ff. 1–63.
[7] Ibid., f. 26v.   [8] Ibid., ff. 22v–23.

Brampton on Troutbeck[1] and Adam, son of Waldein, the advowson of the church of Kirby Thore, with its chapels of Sowerby and Milburn.[2] Two of his greatest successes came early. His purchase in 1203 of the marriage of Matilda, daughter and heiress of Torphin and widow of Hugh son of Gernagon, soon had results. Matilda had already assigned her dower lands in Carthorpe, Yorkshire, to Robert in 1205,[3] and in 1206 she sold all her inheritance in Westmorland to him for 300 m.[4] This included a purparty of the manors of Waitby and Warcop. By this time Robert had also absorbed the Stuteville lands in Westmorland. Some time in 1201 or 1202 Nicholas de Stuteville granted him the whole vill and grange of Milburn.[5] Later he leased to him the whole Stuteville fee in the county in return for a gift of 300 m. This lease was to run for 100 years and the service Robert had to perform, apart from the forensic services, was the almost nominal one of an annual rent of 1 m.[6] Nicholas later transferred all these lands to Robert in fee simple, adding the render of a hawk to the services.[7] These arrangements clearly reflect the rising fortunes of de Vieuxpont on the one hand, and, on the other, the financial difficulties into which Nicholas de Stuteville was plunged by the threat embodied in the proffer of 10,000 m. he had made to the King for his brother's lands in 1205. It was in this same year that he leased his Westmorland estates to Robert. From this point Robert worked steadily to found that territorial power on which, later, the fortunes of the Cliffords were built. In 1220 he had apparently seized the Stuteville estates in Cumberland, including Liddel castle, at a time when Nicholas's grandson, Eustace, was in the custody of Roger de Quenci.[8] In 1223 he was a defendant against John of Newbiggin in an action of novel disseisin over land in Newbiggin, Appleby, and Kirby Thore.[9] A year later William of Lancaster complained that Robert was distraining him for suit of shire and hundred and various other services, contrary to the privileges which the lords of Kendal enjoyed by charters of King Richard and King John. Robert's case was that if the lords of Kendal had these privileges by charter, neither William nor his father, Gilbert fitz Reinfrey, had ever used them, and he went on

---

[1] Ibid., f. 21. [2] Ibid., f. 18. [3] *Rot. Chartarum*, p. 152.
[4] Dodsworth MS. 70, f. 25. See also ibid., ff. 20v–21, for a confirmation of Matilda's sale by her husband, Philip de Burgh.
[5] Dodsworth MS. 70, f. 63. [6] Ibid. [7] Ibid., ff. 25v–26.
[8] *Patent Rolls 1216–25*, p. 243. [9] Ibid., p. 410.

to demand a verdict in the matter from a jury drawn from the neighbouring counties of Yorkshire, Lancashire, and Cumberland. William, in contrast, argued that if the privileges had not been used, it was because Robert had prevented it.[1] This was very much a battle of rival potentates.

Under this kind of pressure families might lose position and status completely, to the resultant profit of the King's men. The history of the Buissel owners of the Lancashire barony of Penwortham was especially significant. The last members of this family to enjoy these lands were incorrigibly litigious. From 1189 to the early years of John's reign the title to these estates was disputed, first between Hugh Buissel and his uncle Geoffrey, and then between Hugh and Geoffrey's son, Robert. Hugh was recognized as the lawful heir in 1193.[2] In 1200 Robert backed his claim to the land with an offering of 100 m., stating that his father had been disseized by an illegal process, and in the subsequent action Hugh defaulted.[3] The King took the lordship into his own hand and in 1202 Hugh offered 400 m. for its recovery and for the King to warrant his default. He agreed to pay 100 m. of this within a year and £100 in each of two subsequent years.[4] This was a crucial error. He could not pay. Imminent disaster united the litigants for a time, for they tried to account for the proffer jointly. But it was useless. At Michaelmas 1205 they still owed over half the original sum.[5] Before the end of the year Hugh surrendered the whole lordship to Roger de Lacy. Roger agreed to pay 310 m. as Hugh's outstanding debt at the Exchequer.[6] As a matter of record, apparently without any payment by Roger, these new arrangements were entered on the fine roll.[7] Penwortham was now a Lacy possession. The Buissels can scarcely have been comforted by the knowledge that it was almost all their own work.

Transactions such as these, the harshness and corruption of some administrators, the harshness of the policies which they had in any case to enforce, the quasi-monopoly of office and of the King's favour, form an ever-present background to the rebellion and civil war at the end of the reign. One of the first actions of

---

[1] *Curia Regis Rolls*, xi. 547–9.   [2] *V.C.H. Lancs.* i. 335–6.
[3] *Rot. de Ob. et Fin.*, p. 49; *Curia Regis Rolls*, i. 262.
[4] *Pipe Roll 3 John*, p. 276; *Rot. de Ob. et Fin.*, p. 188.
[5] *Pipe Roll 7 John*, p. 179.
[6] W. Farrer, *Lancashire Pipe Rolls and Early Charters*, pp. 379–80.
[7] *Rot. de Ob. et Fin.*, p. 341.

the rebels was to choose their own sheriffs. The war was not just a war against John, but also a series of bitter local conflicts between the rebels and the King's agents and friends. These conflicts were not just secondary effects of the main campaigns conducted by the chief protagonists. They were logical extensions of the rival interests of the curialist and non-curialist groups, and they were often carried on quite independently of what was happening elsewhere. Both sides had a vital stake in them, the officials attempting to widen their power and influence even at the expense of each other and the royal interest, the rebels revelling in the opportunity for self-advancement of which John had long starved them and which the war now presented.

All this received encouragement from the King. In circumstances of war he had few men on whom he could rely. He could scarcely afford to lose any of them. Accordingly, he multiplied the positions in their charge and loaded them with grants transferring rebel estates. Ranulf of Chester got control of the honour of Lancaster both within and without the Lyme, and of Staffordshire and Shropshire along with Bridgenorth castle.[1] Before the war was over he was Earl of Lincoln, and seems to have been reviving the old claims of his family north of the Mersey by claiming the earldom of Lancaster.[2] Thomas of Moulton's lands were granted to Ranulf of Chester,[3] most of Robert de Ros's to William de Fors,[4] Simon of Kyme's to the Chamberlain, Geoffrey de Neville, now sheriff of Yorkshire,[5] Robert de Vaux's to Robert de Vieuxpont,[6] Gilbert de Gant's to Gerard de Rhodes,[7] Maurice de Gant's to an important curialist, Philip de Albini,[8] the baronies of Morpeth and Mitford to Philip of Oldcotes.[9] The list of such writs could be expanded to wearisome lengths. No doubt John's orders often did no more than give the recipient an empty title, impossible or difficult to enforce in the face of rebel intransigence. Even so, they were important. If they failed to achieve any real alteration in the territorial balance of power, they nevertheless added to the fury of many a local conflict. They provided prizes

---

[1] Ibid. i. 284; *Rot. Litt. Pat.*, pp. 164–164b, 175b.
[2] For a reference to Ranulf as Earl of Chester and Lancaster see P.R.O., L.T.R. Memoranda Roll, 2 Henry III, m. 7d.   [3] *Rot. Litt. Pat.*, p. 164b.
[4] *Rot. Litt. Claus.* i. 246b.   [5] Ibid. i. 247, 247b, 248.
[6] Ibid. i. 246b.   [7] Ibid. i. 249.
[8] *Rot. Litt. Pat.*, p. 164b.
[9] *Rot. Litt. Claus.* i. 246b.

for which the King's men could fight and put the rebel barons to defend their homes and patrimony.

The result was a shabby, ugly struggle. Once the King's men were loosed, their master's control weakened. Once the master was dead, they could scarcely be brought to order. To make them release their gains became a matter of high policy, one of the prime topics discussed in the epistolary interchanges between the governors of the realm, the Marshal and Hubert de Burgh, Peter des Roches and the Legate. When discussion led to decision and decision to instructions, writ after writ might cross the realm before the order was in fact executed. Some cases achieved notoriety because of the intransigence of the men concerned. In Lincolnshire William de Fors refused to surrender his wartime acquisition of Castle Bytham, holding on to it and surrounding lands despite various actions brought by its rightful owner, the old rebel, William de Coleville.[1] Ultimately, in 1221, de Fors rebelled in the hope of defending this and other gains. Robert de Gaugy, similarly, disobeyed repeated mandates ordering him to surrender Newark castle to the Bishop of Lincoln, and was only ejected eventually by military force and the personal intervention of the Marshal.[2]

Such recalcitrance sprang from an indiscipline which had spread generally. In Yorkshire William de Fors was apparently preventing royal officials from executing their duties.[3] The Earl of Chester had seized fees of the honour of Richmond retained by the Crown[4] and his bailiffs were refusing entry to the sheriff.[5] North of the Tees, the government faced similar trouble. Here Hugh de Balliol was interfering without warrant in the royal mines of Tynedale.[6] Philip of Oldcotes, also, was proving loath to release his custody of Norham, Durham, and the appurtenances of the bishopric of Durham to the new bishop, Richard Marsh.[7] The border-line between this kind of disobedience and open and violent aggrandisement was easily crossed. Throughout the north

[1] *Rolls of the Justices in Eyre for Lincolnshire and Worcestershire*, pp. liv–lvi.

[2] S. Painter, *William Marshal*, pp. 247–8.

[3] *Rolls of the Justices in Eyre for Yorkshire, 1218–19*, no. 1105.

[4] P.R.O., L.T.R. Memoranda Roll, 2 Henry III, m. 3.

[5] *Rolls of the Justices in Eyre for Yorkshire, 1218–19*, no. 1145.

[6] So Robert de Vieuxpont complained to Hubert de Burgh (P.R.O., Ancient Correspondence, i. 209).

[7] See letters coming from June to Oct. 1217 (*Patent Rolls 1216–25*, pp. 76, 81, 86, 98). See also *Rot. Litt. Claus.* i. 327.

the loyalists had used the war as an opportunity for robbery and the expansion of their estates. Hugh de Balliol was clinging on to the lands of Robert de Mesnil in spite of the fact that their custody belonged to the Archbishop of Canterbury.[1] Nicolaa de la Haye was accused of seizing chattels of William of Huntingfield worth over £270.[2] William Talbot and Robert de Burgate had plundered Doncaster,[3] and Geoffrey de Neville, William de Fors, Philip of Oldcotes, and Philip de Albini were all found to have seized goods of merchants trading in the north.[4] Scarborough seems to have been a centre for organized piracy by the King's agents.[5]

These activities were far from indiscriminate. The rebels were bound to be the main target, for they could not hope for protection from any but themselves and their friends. In Lincolnshire, after the war, William de Fors was found to have committed disseisins against several men, including Gilbert de Gant.[6] In Nottinghamshire Roger de Montbegon had great difficulty in recovering his manors of North Wheatley and Clayworth from the hands of the sheriff, Philip Mark.[7] Philip was also in conflict with Ralf of Greasley over the estates of Robert of Muskham. For three years, too, he denied Matilda de Caux full possession of the forestership of Sherwood.[8] In Yorkshire it was found that Brian de Lisle had exacted money from Robert de Percy's land in Carnaby after the war had ended,[9] and Robert failed to recover his pre-war seisin in Osmotherley which he held of the Bishop of Durham.[10] In Northumberland Richard de Unfraville complained that Philip of Oldcotes was building a castle at Nafferton to the damage of his own castle at Prudhoe.[11] His arguments had little immediate effect. The destruction of Nafferton was not ordered until 1221; by then Philip was dead.

[1] *Rot. Litt. Claus.* i. 346, 361b. Hugh surrendered these lands in Apr. 1219 (P.R.O., K.R. Memoranda Roll, 3 Henry III, m. 4).

[2] *Rolls of the Justices in Eyre for Lincolnshire and Worcestershire*, no. 495.

[3] *Rolls of the Justices in Eyre for Yorkshire, 1218–19*, no. 1135.

[4] *Rot. Litt. Pat.*, p. 198; *Patent Rolls 1216–25*, pp. 2, 8, 9, 102.

[5] *Patent Rolls 1232–47*, p. 168.

[6] *Rolls of the Justices in Eyre for Lincolnshire and Worcestershire*, pp. li–liv.

[7] *Royal Letters of Henry III*, i. 101–4.

[8] J. C. Holt, 'Philip Mark and the Shrievalty of Nottinghamshire and Derbyshire', loc. cit., pp. 19–21.

[9] *Rolls of the Justices in Eyre for Yorkshire, 1218–19*, no. 999.

[10] Ibid., no. 1125.

[11] *Rot. Litt. Claus.* i. 379b.

Sometimes a highly complicated situation might arise. In 1216 Roger Bertram's castle at Mitford fell to King John and, with his barony, went to swell the power of Philip of Oldcotes. In September 1217 Philip and Richard Marsh, the new Bishop of Durham, were ordered to give Roger full seisin of his lands as soon as he had guaranteed faithful service.[1] They were summoned to appear before the Council at London on 31 October,[2] and a week later, when Roger had provided his guarantees, Philip was ordered to restore the castle.[3] He disobeyed. In April 1218 the sheriffs of Nottinghamshire and Yorkshire and the Bishop of Durham were ordered to seize his lands if he continued further in his disobedience.[4] But this had no effect and in 1219 the affair rapidly became a *cause majeure*. New orders for the transfer of the castle were issued and messengers hastened to and from Northumberland.[5] In April, Philip was given special safe-conducts to appear before the Council at Reading,[6] for by now he was alleging that he was surrounded by treacherous enemies waiting to pounce in his absence.[7] He was probably right. Whether he attended this meeting or not is uncertain. At the end of the year, however, or early in 1220, he sent to Hubert de Burgh a letter which was quite remarkable for its specious excuses. He could not, he alleged, surrender Mitford, because Hugh de Balliol and his men, who were in the castle, were preventing him from doing so. Hugh, he said, would not consider its surrender until he had gained his rights in the manor of Mere in Wiltshire, and would rebel if the transfer were effected without this. He went on to assert that any agreement he had accepted on the surrender of the castle was dependent on the satisfaction of Balliol's claims and also on the payment of his own outlay on the upkeep of the castle. He concluded by asking for the somewhat dubious mediation of Philip Mark.[8]

This caused concern. Hubert de Burgh forwarded the letter to Pandulf, Bishop of Norwich, who reflected with pompous phrases on the peace of the realm and requested a meeting of the Council.[9] By 6 February 1220 a decision had been reached. Letters

---

[1] *Rot. Litt. Claus.* i. 321; *Patent Rolls 1216–25*, p. 90.
[2] *Rot. Litt. Claus.* i. 336b.　　　　　　　　　　　[3] Ibid. i. 342.
[4] Ibid. i. 357b.
[5] Ibid. i. 389b, 391b, 394; *Patent Rolls 1216–25*, p. 192.
[6] *Patent Rolls 1216–25*, pp. 190, 192.　　　　　　　[7] Ibid.
[8] *Royal Letters of Henry III*, i. 11–13.　　　　[9] *Foedera*, i, pt. I, p. 158.

of this date which carried the whole weight of legatine and con-
ciliar authority were sent to Philip; they left him no room for
manœuvre. He was to surrender Mitford in fifteen days on the
pain of excommunication for contempt and disobedience; his claim
to expenses was irrelevant; the tenure of Mere was not part of any
agreement to surrender; if Hugh de Balliol had complaints they
would receive justice in the King's court.[1] The right and wrongs
of the case cannot now be settled. Hugh de Balliol was certainly
being excluded from Mere. Letters of seisin specifically forbidding
interference by William of Salisbury were first drawn up in
November 1217. They were still being repeated in October 1219.[2]
But if William of Salisbury was the culprit here, it is worth
noting that he also was in a like situation. In June 1218 Philip of
Oldcotes was ordered to give him custody of the lands of Eustace
de Vesci.[3] These instructions were being repeated in April 1219,[4]
and although William obtained possession in 1219 or 1220 he still
had claims to the revenues of these lands since the date of the
initial instructions. Clearly, Roger Bertram was the chief sufferer
in a situation in which several of the old King's friends were at
fault.

The letters of February had their effect. Some time in 1220
Philip surrendered Mitford into the King's hands. Measures were
taken to remove him from the Northumbrian scene. In June
Hugh de Bolebec was made sheriff of Northumberland.[5] Philip
was given advancement and appointed Seneschal of Poitou in
September.[6] By a fortunate chance his comments on the situation
survive in a letter addressed to Pandulf. In burning and insolent
phrases he declared that he did not consider himself bound by the
arrangements whereby the legate was restoring Mitford to Roger
Bertram. He was no longer of a mind to give good service. Some
other man should be sent to Poitou because no trust could be
placed in him either in going there or executing his duties once he
had arrived. His lands and castles were surrounded by his enemies;
he could not leave them *inconsula et immunita*.[7] Despite all this he
went, turbulent and truculent to the end, submitting a long
petition in which he requested letters of protection for his men,
lands, wards, and possessions, and various stays of execution

---

[1] *Patent Rolls 1216–25*, pp. 225–6.   [2] *Rot. Litt. Claus.* i. 340, 400b, 407.
[3] Ibid. i. 364b.   [4] *Patent Rolls 1216–25*, p. 192.   [5] Ibid., p. 236.
[6] Ibid., p. 249.   [7] P.R.O., Ancient Correspondence, vol. ii, no. 15.

against writs and actions levied against him. He even asked for a suitable provision to the value of £300 from the next escheats in exchange for the Vesci estates he had lost.[1] Within the year he was dead. But Roger Bertram did not profit from all this immediately. In August 1220 Hugh de Bolebec, the new sheriff, was asked to give him Mitford as soon as William Bertram, his son, was placed as hostage in the hands of the Bishop of Durham.[2] But Hugh refused to act on the evidence of letters patent alone, a course in which he was supported by the Archbishop of York and the Bishop of Durham. The Archbishop reported that by this action he had incurred the wrath of Roger and all his relations, friends, and supporters. That they were wrathful and nothing more says much for their self-restraint. It was only apparently when the Bishop of Durham agreed to make out letters witnessing the surrender that Roger finally recovered his home.[3] Success in the end came only through one of John's men.

In this kind of conflict the rebels were at an obvious disadvantage. They sometimes had to face other disabilities. Many of them were burdened with ransoms at a time when money cannot have been easy to raise. Those who were captured early in the war were relatively lucky. Their ransoms were heavy; that of William de Albini was placed at 6,000 m.,[4] and William's family, like that of Thomas of Moulton, spent the war years searching for means of payment. John sometimes exacted harsh terms; William de Albini was required to pay 2,000 m. by July 1216;[5] but the Exchequer could be expected to relent a little, particularly when John was dead and the war was over. Its handling of ransoms, and even John's harshest exactions of this kind, pale beside the persecutions which his men inflicted on those who came into their hands. Here the victory of Lincoln provided a golden opportunity, for by then John was dead, and there was no question of ransoms being due to any but the captors.[6] They exploited their luck to the full. Nicholas de Stuteville was captured at this battle and had to

---

[1] P.R.O., Ancient Petitions, file 340, no. 16038.
[2] *Patent Rolls 1216–25*, pp. 246–7.
[3] *Royal Letters of Henry III*, i. 153–4.
[4] *Rot. de Ob. et Fin.*, p. 599; *Pipe Roll 3 Henry III*, p. 126.
[5] *Rot. de Ob. et Fin.*, p. 599.
[6] There was possibly some attempt by the Exchequer to collect ransoms due to William Marshal after his death, but it was laid down that only the captors had any right in this matter (*Rot. Litt. Claus*. i. 600b; Pipe Roll 7 Henry III, rot. 11, m. 2d).

provide a ransom of 1,000 m. He was to pay it at four terms, 250 m. at mid Lent, 1218, and the same sum at Whitsun, on 1 August, and 10 November. The gages were his manors of Kirby Moorside and Liddell. If he failed to keep the first term then he was to surrender 50 librates of land from these manors. If he failed to keep the second term he was to surrender another 50 librates, and so on for the remaining two terms. If the two manors could not yield an income of £200 then the deficit was to be made up from his other lands.[1] These refinements of financial torture might have been envied by King John in his heyday. But they were not the work of one of his familiars, of a Robert de Vieuxpont or a Philip of Oldcotes. Their author and Nicholas's captor was that paragon of feudal virtue, William Marshal. We may suspect that William's urgent, almost helmetless rush into the fray at Lincoln was inspired by other things besides a quixotic gallantry and a desire to taste once more the joys of his youth. There was clearly good business to be done that day in the narrow streets beneath the castle.

Others suffered a fate similar to Nicholas de Stuteville. William de Mowbray was also captured, and ransomed himself to Hubert de Burgh by surrendering his manor of Banstead, in Surrey.[2] Another captive, Maurice de Gant, had to ransom himself to the Earl of Chester for 1,500 m. When payment failed the Earl seized Maurice's security, the manors of Leeds and Bingley.[3] As late as 1218, Philip de Albini, to whom Maurice's fees had been granted during the war, was collecting scutage on his Yorkshire estates.[4] Several less important men were in similar difficulties. Eustace de Mortain's estates were handed over to William de Cantilupe when he failed to keep the terms on which he had been freed.[5] A ransom of £200 due from Henry Bek to Geoffrey de Neville ended in the transfer of some of Henry's lands, first to his lord, the Bishop of Durham, and then to de Neville.[6] Alan of Bolsover's surrender of certain Nottinghamshire and Lincolnshire estates to Philip of Oldcotes may well have arisen from a ransom,[7] and

---

[1] *Pipe Roll 5 Henry III*, p. 135.

[2] *The Coucher Book of Furness*, vol. ii, pt. 2, p. 291; *Book of Fees*, p. 686; *Cal. Charter Rolls*, i. 83.

[3] *Rolls of the Justices in Eyre for Yorkshire*, no. 1133. Bingley was later granted by the Earl to William de Cantilupe for the service of two knights (*Cal. Charter Rolls*, i. 115).   [4] *Rot. Litt. Claus.* i. 377.   [5] Ibid. i. 355b.

[6] *Rolls of the Justices in Eyre for Lincolnshire and Worcestershire*, no. 898.

[7] *Rot. Litt. Claus.* i. 400, 400b; *H.M.C., 11th Report*, pt. 7, p. 91.

John of Beverley's lands were taken into the hands of the Archbishop of York until he satisfied the Archbishop in the matter of
300 m. he had paid to Philip Mark as the ransom of John and his
father.[1] Through war, family fortunes were being won or restored,
depleted or lost. War, even civil war, was a business, an occasion
for trafficking in prisoners, ransoms, and estates. The rebels were
only saved from complete destruction, perhaps, by the fact that
there was no openly avowed policy of disinheritance as there
was towards a later generation after Evesham in 1265. Disin-
herited, nevertheless, some of them were, at least of part of their
estates.

Sometimes the end came not in sudden dispossession but in
the long-drawn agony of debt and dependence, a culmination at
once of John's financial measures and of failure in war, for no
doubt many of these commitments would have been ignored if
the rebels had won. Frequently churchmen gave a helping hand.
The Mandeville brothers, Geoffrey and William, were in debt to
Stephen Langton for over 7,000 m. Their sister Maud, who survived them, later resigned the two manors of Saffron Walden and
Debden to Archbishop Edmund until the debt was paid by an
annual reduction of £120.[2] At Lincoln in 1227, Bishop Hugh of
Wells agreed to lend Roesia, relict of Simon of Kyme and her son,
Philip, 200 m. in return for a ten-year lease of two of the Kyme
manors in Lindsey. Such transactions were delicate and difficult
to maintain. In this case Roesia and Philip submitted themselves,
their chattels, estates, and their Christianity to the Bishop and
the Chapter, denying any right to appeal against ecclesiastical
censure and admitting that the Bishop and Chapter could alter
the agreement to their greater security.[3] There was an element
of compulsion in these arrangements, and on many occasions the
kindly assistance of a churchman hid more material and grasping
intentions. At Carlisle the new Bishop, Walter Mauclerc, continued his dead master's fiscal persecution of Robert de Vaux.
In 1228 Robert assigned all his land in Cumberland to the Bishop
for sixteen years at a rent of 80 m. Robert had already received
500 m. of this, 200 m. into his own hand and 300 m. which had
been paid on his behalf to his Jewish creditors; as a result, he was
to receive no rent until the seventh year of the lease.[4] By then a

---

[1] *Rot. Litt. Claus.* i. 346. [2] *Cal. Charter Rolls*, i. 196.
[3] Ibid. i. 62–63. [4] Ibid. i. 76.

new agreement was necessary. In 1234 Robert fined for himself, his heirs, and all his tenants of Gilsland in the sum of 700 m. because he had disseized the Bishop of the manor of Gilsland which he had conveyed to the Bishop at farm, and for seizing his chattels and for other wrongs. This cancelled out the rent due until the sixteenth and final year of the lease.[1]

Sympathy for the rebels would be out of place, for they too were capable of robbery and murder.[2] Even after the war, Robert de Percy gaily slew one of Robert de Vieuxpont's men and then asked that the jury dealing with the matter should not be drawn from Richmondshire where he admitted he had committed many evils during the fighting.[3] Like the loyalists the northern rebels had committed numerous disseisins. In Lincolnshire Gilbert de Gant had thrust himself into estates belonging to the honour of Richmond,[4] and in Yorkshire the first two eyres after the war uncovered several cases of this kind against both him and Richard de Percy. Robert de Ros was found to have committed twelve disseisins in Yorkshire alone, activities which now cost him amercements totalling 350 m.[5] Some of the loyalists, too, experienced difficulties in recovering their rights and exercising their offices. Letters of August 1218 suggest that William Briwerre was meeting opposition in securing his custody of the land and heir of Alan de Arches of which he had been disseised during the war.[6] Robert de Vieuxpont, now the custodian of Carlisle, was driven to complain to Hubert de Burgh of the interference of Ruald Fitz Alan, Constable of Richmond, in the mines of Swaledale, which Robert claimed to be appurtenant to the bailiwick of Carlisle.[7] The blame for the situation during and after the war lay with both sides. Richard de Unfraville's complaints against Philip of Oldcotes' castle of Nafferton might be acceptable as an expression of injured innocence were it not clear that Richard

[1] Ibid. i. 189.

[2] See the cases of Geoffrey de Lascelles and Alan of Haisthorpe, both probably Brus tenants (*Rolls of the Justices in Eyre for Yorkshire*, nos. 1022, 972), and also the case between William Fairfax and William Malesoures (ibid., no. 1147).

[3] Ibid., nos. 1079, 1140.

[4] *Rolls of the Justices in Eyre for Lincolnshire and Worcestershire*, no. 47, and p. lxi.

[5] P.R.O., K.R. Miscellanea, 1/8b, m. 7d.

[6] *Rot. Litt. Claus.* i. 367b.

[7] P.R.O., Ancient Correspondence, i. 210. Compare *Patent Rolls 1216–25*, p. 366, which suggests that the mines of both Tynedale and Swaledale were appurtenant to the bailiwick of Carlisle.

also was improving his castle of Harbottle against royal orders.[1] Whenever possible, the rebels clearly gave as good as they got. That they appear more sinned against than sinning is because they lost.

[1] *Rot. Litt. Claus.* i. 436b–437. For Richard's reply to these allegations see above, p. 210. Work was also going on after the war on Gilbert de Gant's castle of Folkingham (*Royal Letters of Henry III*, i. 64).

EPILOGUE

D URING the civil war Runnymede and Magna Carta must
have been distant memories to men who saw, on their
own doorstep, the golden prospect of castles to be taken,
land to be seized, manors to be plundered, merchants to be robbed,
and towns to be burned. The scene of John de Lacy's surrender
to the King, with the accompanying disavowal of Magna Carta,
is significant of the wider importance of the rebellion and of what
the Charter was to become with the passage of time. But it represents general baronial aims, open and avowed, and these were
often only distantly and tortuously related to the passions which
inspired individuals in the heat of rebellion. That John de Lacy
disavowed the Charter does not mean that he had rebelled just
for it and nothing else. It was not for the Charter that Robert de
Percy committed murder or Robert de Ros left a trail of disseisin
through the county of York. Sometimes quarrels and conflicts
of interest were in the nature of things. In a civil war Gilbert de
Gant and Ranulf of Chester were likely enemies; so were Richard
and William de Percy. But the rival claims which pitted these men
against each other were not important or even common springs
of action. There were none similar to sharpen the quarrel between
Philip of Oldcotes and Roger Bertram. Here all that mattered was
that Philip was a favoured royal agent who was attempting to
retain what he had gained during the war for as long as possible.

Once John had gone and the war had ended, the lines of
political division altered. The Charter was quickly reissued, in
a more limited form. Very soon ex-rebels and the native loyalists
were working easily together; Brian de Lisle, Hugh de Balliol,
Robert de Vieuxpont, by the side of Thomas of Moulton, Robert
de Percy, or Robert de Ros. Loyalist and rebel now found a
common interest and a common bond in unseating John's
foreigners, in breaking the grip which Robert de Gaugy, William
de Fors, and Faulkes de Breauté still had on the administration.
The letters of November 1218 concerning grants by the young
King Henry were witnessed, among others, by the Earls of Aumale, Clare, Hereford, Essex, and Oxford, by Robert fitz Walter,
Robert de Ros, Geoffrey de Say, William of Huntingfield, and

William de Albini, by ten, in fact, of the Twenty-Five of 1215.[1]
The writ of 1224 assessing an aid for the Bedford expedition
against Faulkes's men was witnessed, among others, by Gilbert
de Clare, William de Mandeville, Hugh Bigod, John de Lacy,
William de Albini, Thomas of Moulton, John fitz Robert, Richard
de Muntfichet, Peter de Brus, and Richard de Percy.[2] In 1225 the
reissue of Magna Carta was attested by ten of the Twenty-Five of
1215. The waters John had parted had closed once more.

There was therefore a certain artificiality in the war-time
divisions. The problems of defending the Angevin empire may have
made some major crisis in royal power inevitable; John's administration of the northern counties may have made it certain that they
would be a centre of disturbance; but, within the north, we can
only explain why one man was for the King and another against
him by looking at their relations with John and at their place
in the administration and in the royal favour. Can we imagine
that the Earl of Chester would have shown himself so loyal but
for the arrangements John made with him in 1204–5? His record
before 1204 suggests not. If Nicholas de Stuteville and John de
Lacy had been permitted an easy succession to their predecessors'
estates and to some of their official positions, would they have
rebelled? Can we suppose that even Eustace de Vesci would have
opposed the King if, for example, he had been enjoying a lucrative
tenure of the shrievalty of Yorkshire? William Marshal, who
certainly did not disapprove of the principles of Magna Carta,
and Ranulf of Chester, who granted a charter of liberties to the
men of his palatinate, both seem to have placed the King's favour
and their loyalty to him before any attraction they may have felt
to the rebel barons' programme. In some families, such as the
Mowbrays, traditions of rebellion were perhaps deeply ingrained;
but it seems likely that at any time before 1212 John could have
won over almost any one of the great northern magnates who
rebelled in 1215 by making the appropriate moves. John had no
pathological mistrust of the baronage; some barons he did trust;
for the rest he simply had no use. He committed himself to some
at the cost of the increasing alienation of others. In some ways
this was unavoidable. Such were the immense burdens which
John placed on the barons that widespread unrest, perhaps even
rebellion, was bound to follow. There was bound to be a sharp

[1] *Patent Rolls 1216–25*, p. 177.　　　　　　　[2] Ibid., p. 465.

division between those 'out' and those 'in'. But the choice of those who were to enforce his policies and enjoy his favours lay largely with him. He chose decisively and with few half measures.

To a large extent men still accepted this exercise of royal patronage and personal influence. Magna Carta scarcely touched it, and the ancient law and custom, on which the barons fought, was here on the King's side rather than their own. But law and tradition were not their sole resource. They also had a common background in the imaginary world of Arthur's court and the Grail, of Tristan and Alexander, of Charlemagne and Roland. This was a world of chivalry, as yet raw and undeveloped, a world in which kings and lords could be benevolent and kindly, hot tempered and vengeful in turn, a world in which honour and treachery were engaged in a battle both material and supernatural. It was a world in which there were general rules of conduct which men might equate with law. But before all else, it was a world in which kingship was personal and in which the personal relations between the King and his men were of paramount concern and interest. This reflected actual circumstances. The personal nature of kingship was recognized even by those who took the greatest pride in the working of the machinery of government. 'To some', wrote Fitz Neal, 'the King does full justice for nothing, in consideration of their past services or out of mere goodness of heart; but to others (and it is only human nature) he will not give way either for love or for money.'[1] To many John must have seemed an enemy, not because he broke what they took to be law, but because, in their eyes, he had long ceased to exercise a tolerable and honourable lordship judged by the standards of current literary images. If contemporaries could compare his rule with Arthur's, they might well wonder how the Arthur of romance would have dealt with his namesake of Brittany, or with Matilda de Braose.

No reflection on John's character and achievement can safely ignore the complete rift in the English aristocracy which followed on his methods of administration, especially his choice of the personnel of government. That the great men of the land were divided stands in his favour. The struggle was not one of King against barons, but, in addition, of some barons against others. But we may be in danger of making too much of the support

[1] *Dialogus de Scaccario*, p. 120. I have followed Mr. Charles Johnson's translation.

which John got from his men, from William Marshal, and Ranulf of Chester, or from Philip Mark and Faulkes de Breauté. He held their loyalty to the end, certainly, but the methods he used were those whereby the loyalty of most men could be guaranteed. Chancery clerks might indulge in rhapsody on William Marshal, 'who, in the hour of need, proved himself like gold in the furnace',[1] but, this case apart, there is little evidence that the tie between the King and his men was based on anything but the continued expectation and provision of material reward in return for material service. This was not loyalty, but government by *quid pro quo*. As a governmental technique it was, and is, common enough and in any case should not be underrated. John was a past-master in its manipulation. To this ability he added an energy in government, a cunning in politics, a brilliance in conception, a determination in execution which, at their best, rivalled his father's powers. We should not forget that he was the favourite son of a man who did not suffer fools gladly, nor his own fondness for seeking precedents in his father's reign.

But the obvious comparison lies not perhaps with his father, but with his grandson, Edward I. If John brought Magna Carta on his head, Edward brought the Confirmation of the Charters and the *Articuli super Cartas* on his. Both enjoyed to the full an instinct in exploiting law and custom, such as they were in their day, to the interest of themselves and their office. In this, indeed, they both excelled. Both could impress themselves on contemporaries in the assertion of their authority, for John, like Edward, could surround himself with terrible and authoritative majesty. But there was one important difference. With John, there is no trace of the *mystique* of monarchy, no ability to lead and inspire by character and personality. At a lower level, he could not act as the figurehead of mediocrity, or appear to the respectable as the essence of respectability, or convince the less intelligent and persuade the indecisive by pious words and airy platitudes. There was little of the sanctimonious in him. In this he lacked a quality which his grandson had in as full a measure as any medieval English king. It was a highly valuable quality, one which could help to obfuscate political issues, confuse political opponents, and influence men's minds and actions. John could try to do all

---

[1] 'tamquam auram in fornace sic se in necessitate probavit' (*Patent Rolls 1216–25*, p. 10).

this by cunning and cultivated intelligence; no man was readier to turn the tables in argument or borrow the language of his opponents. But this was not the same. It was sometimes too rational, too obvious, sometimes too much of a conjuring trick; John was not too cruel as a medieval king, but too supple, too clever. There was nothing in his character to cushion him from the logic of his actions, nothing to blur the hardening lines of political division, nothing around which a neutral body of opinion could form. Few men have ensured so effectively that those who were not for him would be against him.

NOTES FOR FURTHER READING

Much the best study of the regions of England is Cyril Fox, *The Personality of Britain* (Cardiff, 1933); and the most considered and useful short discussion of the North is John Le Patourel, 'Is Northern History a Subject?', *Northern History*, xii (1976), 1–15, reprinted in his *Feudal Empires, Norman and Plantagenet* (London, 1984). Helen M. Jewell adds further comment in 'North and South: The Antiquity of the Great Divide', *Northern History*, xxvii (1991), 1–25.

The various contributions of Professor G. W. S. Barrow are fundamental to an understanding of northern history. The most useful for the present purposes are his 'Northern English Society in the early Middle Ages', *Northern History*, iv (1969), 1–28, two chapters, 'The Anglo-Scottish Border' and 'Pre-Feudal Scotland: Shires and Thane', in his *Kingdom of the Scots* (London, 1973), and 'The Pattern of Lordship and Feudal Settlement in Cumbria', *Journal of Medieval History*, i (1975), 117–38. His Ford Lectures of 1977, *The Anglo-Norman Era in Scottish History*, (Oxford, 1980), is the major study of the settlement of the Normans in the Borders and, in the case of certain families, further south. Also valuable is his 'Frontier and Settlement: Which Influenced Which? England and Scotland, 1100–1300', in *Medieval Frontier Societies*, ed. Robert Bartlett and Angus Mackay (Oxford, 1989), pp. 3–21. Among other local studies R. B. Smith, *Blackburnshire: A study in Early Lancashire History* (Leicester, 1961) is particularly useful. Alongside this work there is William E. Kapelle, *The Norman Conquest of the North: The Region and its Transformation, 1000–1135* (London, 1979), which is original and thought-provoking in its approach. More generally, there is now R. R. Davies, *Domination and Conquest: The Experience of Ireland, Scotland and Wales 1100–1300* (Cambridge, 1990).

There is very little which straddles these social and institutional studies and the political history of the reign of King John. Edward Miller's 'The Background of Magna Carta', *Past and Present*, xxiii (1962), 72–83, a review article based on the first edition of this book, is invaluable in trying to bridge this gap. For an earlier period, and more exlusively political in approach, there is also Judith Green, 'Aristocratic Loyalties on the Northern Frontier of England, *c.*1100–1174', in *England in the Twelfth Century*, ed. D. Williams (Woodbridge, 1990), pp. 83–100. This draws on R. C. Johnston's splendid edition, *Jordan Fantosme's Chronicle* (Oxford, 1981), the prime source for the war in the North of 1173–4, as does Matthew Strickland, 'Securing the North: Invasion and the Strategy of Defence in Twelfth-Century Anglo-Scottish Warfare', *Anglo-Norman Studies*, xii (1989), 177–98.

There have been some notable family histories and territorial studies: W. E. Wightman, *The Lacy Family in England and Normandy 1066–1194* (Oxford, 1966), Barbara English, *The Lords of Holderness 1086–1260* (Oxford, 1979), and Kathleen Major, *The D'Oyrys of South Lincolnshire, Norfolk and Holderness 1130–1275* (Lincoln, 1984); the last is particularly valuable in that it gives serious attention to a family of the second rank which came to be involved in the rebellion of 1215 and was enmeshed, in the Fenland, with the more consistently rebellious families of Kyme and Moulton. Among biographical studies, K. J. Stringer, *Earl David of Huntingdon* (Edinburgh, 1985) is an outstanding contribution. R. V. Turner, 'William de Forz, Count of Aumale: An Early Thirteenth-century English Baron', *Proceeding of the American Philosophical Society*, cxv (1971), 221–49, seeks to revive the reputation of that somewhat slippery customer. B. E. Harris, 'Ranulph III, Earl of Chester', *Journal of the Chester Archaeological Society*, lviii (1975), 99–114, is a very useful, brief comment; there is a lengthier account in J. W. Alexander, *Ranulf of Chester: A Relic of the Conquest* (Athens, Ga., 1983). For further studies of individual Northerners there are M. J. Vine, 'Two Yorkshire Rebels: Peter de Brus and Richard de Percy' *Yorkshire Archeological Journal*, xlvii (1975), 69–79; and Brian Golding, 'Symon of Kyme: The Making of a Rebel', *Nottingham Medieval Studies*, xxvii (1983), 23–36, which analyses the discontents of one of the more prominent Lincolnshire rebels.

There have been numerous contributions to the study of government, finance, and taxation. On the management of the royal demesne see P. D. A. Harvey, 'The Pipe Rolls and the

258 *Notes for Further Reading*

Adoption of Demesne Farming in England', *Economic History Review*, 2nd. ser. xxvii (1974), 345–59, and B. E. Harris, 'King John and Sheriffs' Farms', *E.H.R.* lxxix (1964), 532–42. D. A. Carpenter, 'The Decline of the Curial Sheriff in England 1194–1258', *E.H.R.* xci (1976), 1–32, should also be consulted. P. D. A. Harvey, 'The English Inflation of 1180–1220', *Past and Present*, lxi (1973), 3–30, is an important and provocative paper, which emphasizes the effects of an average annual rate of inflation of less than 3 per cent. C. R. Young, *The Royal Forests of Medieval England* (Leicester, 1979) sets the northern forests in a more general context. David Crook, 'The Struggle over Forest Boundaries in Nottinghamshire 1218–1227', *Transactions of the Thoroton Society*, lxxxiii (1979), 35–45, is a scholarly study of more than local importance. R. B. Dobson's *The Jews of Medieval York and the Massacre of March 1190* (Borthwick Papers, no. 45, York, 1974) is a valuable addition to the study of the Jews. See also Gavin I. Langmuir, 'The Jews and the Archives of Angevin England: Reflections on Medieval Anti-Semitism', *Traditio*, xix (1963), 183–244, which reviews H. G. Richardson, *The English Jewry under the Angevin Kings* (London, 1960). The whole question of the financial effects of Angevin policy on the fortunes of the aristocracy is examined systematically by T. K. Keefe, *Feudal Assessments and the Political Community under Henry II and his Sons* (Berkeley, Calif., 1983). See also Brian Feeney, 'The Effects of King John's Scutages on East Anglian Subjects', *Reading Medieval Studies*, xi, *East Anglian and other Studies presented to Barbara Dodwell* (1985), 51–73.

There have been important additions to the study of the events and documents of 1215. Particularly important are C. R. Cheney, 'The Twenty Five Barons of Magna Carta', *Bulletin of the John Rylands Library*, i (1968), 280–307, and V. H. Galbraith, 'A draft of Magna Carta (1215)', *Proceedings of the British Academy*, liii (1967), 345–60. These and other works are discussed in J. C. Holt, *Magna Carta*, 2nd edn. (Cambridge, 1992). For the minority of Henry III see the full-scale study by D. A. Carpenter, *The Minority of Henry III* (London, 1990).

On the problem of local communities and their political activities see the valuable paper by J. R. Madicott, 'Magna Carta and the Local Community 1215–1259', *Past and Present*, cii, (1984), 25–65. Susan Reynolds, *Kingdoms and Communities in Western Europe 900–1300* (Oxford, 1984) is an illuminating study of the whole question.

INDEX

—— Forest Boundaries.

- - - - County Boundaries.

▨ Forest areas defined by the perambulations following the Charter of the Forest of 1217 and 1225.

▭ Areas excluded from the forest by these perambulations or, where noted, by earlier deforestation.

• Vills and townships amerced for forest offences 1154–1215, which lay outside the forest areas defined by these perambulations.

+ Vills and townships similarly amerced in areas which purchased deforestation before 1215.

□ Vills and townships amerced for forest offences 1154–1215 in areas for which no perambulation has been found.

✕ Northumbrian vills and townships which compounded for deforestation in 1282.

   1. Burgh by Sands, afforested by Henry II.
   2. Allerdale forest.
   3. Allerdale barony, put in regard by Henry II.
   4. Between Pallet and Uldale, afforested by Henry II.
   5. Inglewood.
   6. Inglewood, east of Eden, afforested by Henry II.
   7. Milburn, alienated to William de Stuteville 1201.
   8. Lonsdale.
   9. Amounderness.
10. West Derby.
11. Farndale.
12. Pickering.
13. Ryedale, deforested in 1204.
14. Hertfordlythe, deforested in 1204.
15. Knaresborough.
16. Galtres.
17. Wharfedale, deforested in 1204.
18. Ainsty wapentake, deforested in 1190.
19. Between Ouse and Derwent, afforested by Henry II, deforested in 1234.
20. The Peak.
21. Between Derwent and Erewash, afforested by Henry II.
22. Hatfield.
23. Sherwood.
24. Le Clay.
25. Kesteven, deforested in 1230.

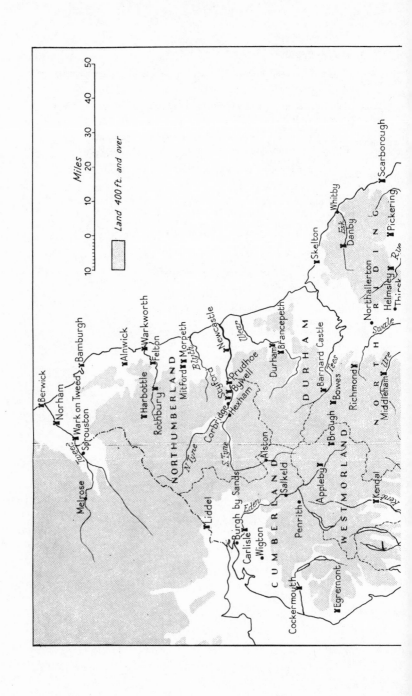

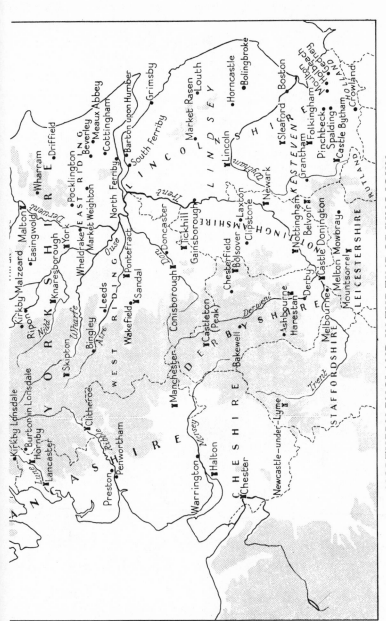

NORTHERN ENGLAND IN THE TIME OF KING JOHN

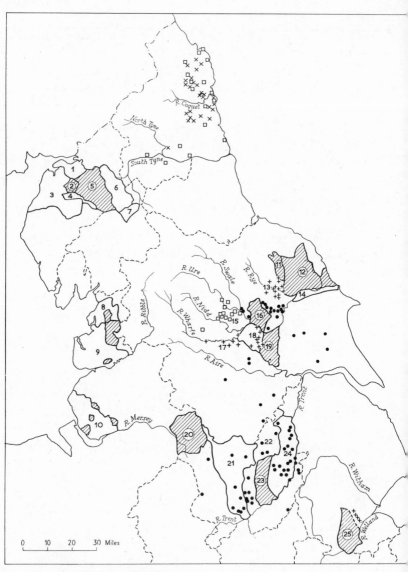

NORTHERN ROYAL FORESTS IN THE TIME OF KING JOHN